**EVERYTHING YOU EVER WANTED TO KNOW
ABOUT CLEANING!
LEARN THE SECRETS PROFESSIONALS USE.
FIND OUT . . .**

- How to oust odors from plastic containers. It's ingenious and downright yummy.
- What pumpkin pie spice can do for your microwave. You'll love it!
- What simple cleaning tip can make your CDs last forever—and what you should never, ever do.
- Why no-wax floors may need waxing, and the right product for the project.
- How plumber's Teflon tape can save time . . . and make deep-down bathroom clean-up a breeze.
- What clever storage trick will keep silver jewelry bright. It takes only a second too!
- How hair spray can stop the blues—especially when a ballpoint pen leaks on an item you cherish.

**PLUS—THE PRODUCTS THAT WORK BEST, FROM
DUSTERS TO DETERGENTS
(AND WHICH DON'T, SUCH AS THAT OLD-TIME
FAVORITE . . . VINEGAR!)
AND MORE!**

Other Books by Don Aslett

THE CLEANING ENCYCLOPEDIA

AMERICA'S #1 CLEANING EXPERT

DON ASLETT

ILLUSTRATED BY KERRY OTTESON

A DELL BOOK

Published by
Dell Publishing
a division of
Random House, Inc.
1540 Broadway
New York, New York 10036

Excerpt from *Clutter's Last Stand,* copyright © 1984 by Don Aslett. Reprinted by permission of Writer's Digest Books.

ISBN: 0-440-23501-4

Printed in the United States of America

Published simultaneously in Canada

April 1999

10 9 8 7 6 5 4 3

OPM

ACKNOWLEDGMENTS

An encyclopedia never has one author; it is a composite of the knowledge and experience of many, many individuals as well as companies and organizations. It also means a lot of seeking out and boiling down and reconciling of both written and oral information. This book tapped all of the above, including many of my professional cleaner colleagues, in addition to my own more than thirty-five years of professional cleaning experience. Thanks to all the contributors who teamed up on this, the big cleaning book of all time, dedicated to making the world a cleaner place.

CONTENTS

Author's Note / *ix*

Introduction / *xi*

Before You Start to Clean / *1*
Why Clean? 3
Who Cleans? 4
How to Clean Anything (or First Things First!) 5
Prevention of Cleaning 6
Design Dirt Out 6
Clean Green 8

The A to ZZZ of Cleaning / *11*

Index / *387*

About the Author / *399*

AUTHOR'S NOTE

As I was attempting to solve a serious stain problem on a national broadcast, an expert carpet cleaner in the Chicago area called in with a classic comment: "In stain removal, there are no heroes." No one could have said it better, and the same is true of cleaning instructions. We all want a complete and easy answer to the problem at hand. But as we approach the twenty-first century there are at least 10,000 different types of objects and surfaces in the average home, including designs and materials that no one knows how to clean. The directions in this book are ones I and hundreds of other experts use as our general guide to alienating dirt from that particular article. But we run into some stumpers and you will too, even following the directions in this book perfectly. The age of something, the length of time the stain or soil has been on or in it, what you or someone else has done previously in an attempt to clean it, and what else has happened to it since— all conspire to foil even the most professional approach. Some stains and soils are permanent, and there's nothing you or anyone can do about it. In the following pages I've done my best to guide you in the right direction. But there are so many variables and unknowns over which I have no control that I can't be held responsible for any damage which may result from any particular application of the procedures outlined in these pages. So be content with the 98 percent of your efforts that work and count it experience when the occasional something doesn't come clean easily or at all.

INTRODUCTION

One time-management expert says we spend four years of our life cleaning; others claim we spend as much as a decade at the process of purifying our homes, ourselves, and our surroundings. I can't tell you which is right, but I do know that even one year is too much. How will we ever get to the things we really care about in life with one hand on the garbage can and the other in the toilet?

My whole mission for more than thirty-five years now has been to reduce, if not eliminate, cleaning and make what cleaning is necessary fun, fast, and easy. I've written a dozen books on the subject to date, and I'm told they've cut millions of hours of housework out of the world, kept countless marriages together, and saved thousands of tons of raw material (in household furnishings that don't have to be replaced before their time). One thing I've discovered in the process is that not only do we not have days or hours to clean anymore—maybe only minutes—we also have a lot more kinds of things to clean. And even if Mother knew how to clean all of them, she probably didn't have time to teach us. So we need something to tell us how to do it and what to use, or just to reassure us that we in our own infinite wisdom are doing it the fastest and best possible way. In other words, a complete A to Z cleaning reference book, based not on old wives' tales or clever hints and tips but on the techniques and tools of the professionals. Who better to do it than the World's No. 1 Cleaning Expert? The book you hold in your hands is a catalog of cures for over 500 different items. I hope you find it not only useful but enjoyable.

DON ASLETT

BEFORE YOU START TO CLEAN

Why Clean?

You can sum it all up under five big strong "S's": *Sanitation . . . Safety. . . . Scenery and Serenity . . . and Savings.*

Sanitation

Staying alive and healthy is one very good reason to clean. Germs (bacteria, fungus, viruses, etc.) and bugs thrive in unclean conditions. And dust can cause breathing problems for those of us with asthma or allergies. Cleaning beats aspirin in fighting the common cold and all kinds of debilitating and dangerous diseases. And it'll do more to discourage unwanted little intruders than the best mousetrap or roach killer. We spend a lot of money on perfumes and deodorizers to get rid of unpleasant household odors, but cleaning doesn't allow them to exist—it eliminates the bacteria and molds that create them.

Safety

Keeping things neat and orderly around your home and workplace—in other words, keeping it clean—will do more to prevent accidents and injuries than any other single thing. Many auto accidents also are caused by stuff hanging all over the car, rolling around on the floor, or from dirty windows that interfere with vision. Dirt and clutter kills . . . literally. (And if your home is clean and inviting, you'll spend more time there where it's safer!)

Scenery and Serenity

We'll do anything (legal or not), spend any amount of time or money to make ourselves feel good. And what ultimately makes you feel better than "clean"— clean sheets, a clean shirt, sparkling windows, a newly vacuumed rug or freshly waxed floor? Keeping clean not only keeps you in a position to function well physically, it keeps you mentally and emotionally healthy too. Keeping the home, yourself, and the world clean generates peace in all three places. (Believe it, cleaning cuts family fights!) Dirt and disarray rob you of space, freedom, health, respect, position, and production. Sloppy surroundings carry over into your thoughts and emotions and affect the way you feel, love and perform at work and at home. *We clean to feel good about ourselves and our surroundings!*

3

Saving Money

Cleaning saves so much money you'd flinch if I showed you all you've wasted so far. Dirty things depreciate (wear out) faster. Neglected surfaces have to be repainted, repapered, and replaced more often. An unkempt carpet, for example, will only last half as long as it should. Leaving things messy eventually takes more cleaning chemicals and cleaning effort. Stains and soils cling harder the longer they're left, and if you let them go you triple the cost of removal. Dust and dirt wear down and grind up floors, plug up coils and vents, and waste electrical energy. And people are much more likely to abuse a cluttered or unclean place.

Cleaning reduces expenses enormously! And it costs almost nothing to be neat, orderly, and clean.

Who Cleans?

A lot of research recently has gone into revealing something we already know—we're still laboring under the erroneous assumption that the female is supposed to clean up after everyone.

So about 90 percent of all messes are still made by men and children, and 90 percent get cleaned up by women. And women still go out of their way, often, to be gracious and kind and let those who make a mess leave it. When a guest or relative says "Oh, let me help clean," they say "Oh, no, you just sit down and enjoy yourself, I'll do it." And they do it. And keep on doing it.

Yet as the fast food folks have shown us, it's amazing how little cleaning is necessary (just whisking up a few last crumbs) when people clean up after themselves. It will be the beginning of a new life for you when the people who are doing most of the messing up start cleaning up. Bad habits die hard, but put mess makers to work! Anyone old enough to mess up is old enough to clean up!

It's never too soon to start teaching that if you got it out or dropped it there, then you pick it up and put it back. We, and we alone, are responsible for the mess we make in the process of living. When you think about it, what's more degrading or disrespectful than asking someone else to clean up after you? A terrible thing happens when we give our children, employees, students, and fellow citizens the impression that they are not responsible for their mess, that someone else will retrieve what they leave or toss or dirty up. This slowly and surely teaches them that they aren't responsible for their

▶ **Executive stress:** A career woman on a cruise asked my daughter Elizabeth what she did for a living. Liz said, "I run a family and stay home with my children." The lady said, "Man, I tried that; it was too hard, so I went back to work."

own actions. Then when people mess up in other, bigger ways (morally, emotionally, or economically), we as leaders or parents fret and wring our hands and ask "What did we do wrong?" "Why this? Why us?" Well, because we took care of their messes from the time they were two years old to the time they graduated college, and they don't believe or even know their messes are their own problem. We shape our society inside our own homes. Cleaning, a basic human responsibility, is an *individual* responsibility.

Living as if no one were coming behind us to clean up our mess would revolutionize our homes and our country, especially as every day there is more stuff—more packaging, more wrappers, bottles, papers, discards—to be dealt with. Mother Nature can't absorb any more trash and litter, and states, towns, and cities can't tax us enough to do all our cleaning for us. Who cleans? *We all do*, and if you and I can help get that idea across (rather than bear it all alone), it will solve more cleaning problems than all the chemicals and equipment ever invented to do it.

▶ A half-dozen places to turn for help with housework:
• Family (kids and your other half too)
• Guests
• Volunteers
• People you can trade labor with
• Professional cleaners
• The government: If you're aged or disabled, you may qualify for assistance. Check with your county or state.

How to Clean Anything (or First Things First!)

Trying to wash a dish before scraping off the bones, crusts, and baked potato skins would seem pretty silly, as would mopping a floor before we sweep it to remove all the grass, grit, and gravel. All cleaning should be done with this same logic of first removing the bulk of the mess—all the loose dirt and dust you can by sweeping, vacuuming, scraping, and so on. Doing so will expose the surface you're trying to clean to the action of the cleaning chemical and get rid of a lot of stuff that would just muddy up your cleaning water. Now leave the solution on long enough to do its work. Most of the soil or dirt on something can be removed by the solution itself, instead of a lot of hard scrubbing. Then you want to remove the softened and dissolved soil and the now-dirty solution.

A quick review now:
1. *Eliminate.* Remove all loose dust, dirt, and debris from the surface with a vacuum, brush, scraper, broom, dustcloth, or lambswool duster—whatever seems best for the object at hand.

2. *Saturate.* Wet the item or area well with the cleaning solution.
3. *Dissolve.* Leave the solution on until all the soil that remains is soft and easily removable. Allowing the solution to dissolve and emulsify the dirt is a lot easier than strenuous and possibly harmful scrubbing.
4. *Remove.* Now, with a sponge, squeegee, cleaning cloth, wet/dry vac, or whatever, you can swiftly wipe away all that stuff that was once dried, stuck, or cooked on.

Prevention of Cleaning

The first principle of efficient cleaning is not to have to do it in the first place. Stopping the cause is the smartest thing to do. See "Airborne Grease and Soil," "Heat Types and Cleaning," "Water," "Junk and Clutter," "Mats, Walkoff," "Sealing," and "Soil Retardants," the next section, and many of the other entries that follow.

Design Dirt Out

Now that's an idea you've had many times as you've tried to clean or fix something and found it nearly impossible because of the way it was built. Too rough, too delicate, inaccessible, unwashable, unreachable, and you say "Who invented this?" Well, here's your chance to fix it. Do you realize at least half of the high-maintenance items in your home, the things you really hate to clean, are things that are replaced every five or ten years? When you repaint, recarpet, or get a new fixture or faucet, simply ask "How will this be to clean?" And you'll find yourself switching from that show-every-little-thing style to a maintenance-free model that's a lot simpler to care for.

You've probably thought of most of the ideas that follow but just haven't had a chance to put them in practice.

Make it out of low-maintenance material: It'll be much less of a headache if it's smooth or stainproof, for example. Before you buy it, find out if it will absorb, stain, soil, shrink, rot, rust, fade, scratch, crack, peel, splinter, deteriorate, dent, or wear off.

Simplify: When simple clean lines or construction (such as on a faucet) will do the same job, why put up with something that has all kinds of hard-to-clean corners and crevices? Every surface needs maintenance—so *the less surface the better*. A louvered door, for example, has much more surface than a simple, smooth door. Eliminate ledges and edges wherever possible. Likewise, the more kinds of surfaces and materials you have in something, the more tools and supplies and time you'll need to clean it. Keep your decor simple and you'll keep your cleaning simple.

Choose the right color: Camouflage is a great ally in cleaning. Match the color of your furniture and decorating schemes to the number of kids you have, the color of your pets, and even the shade of your local soil; it will lighten your cleaning load. Who wants to spend a lifetime picking lint off the carpet or dog hair off the couch? Let it blend in between cleanings. Restaurant carpets often appear clean because they're done in patterns that combine food-spill colors like gravy brown, butter yellow, carrot orange, and smashed-pea green. Solid white, light blue, and yellow carpets show dirt like a billboard, but reddish-browns and tweeds in sculpted patterns, especially, can hide it for a month.

Suspend it: Up off the floor! Anything on the floor is in the way when cleaning, it takes time to get around, and it may get grazed or broken in the process. When anything can be hung or mounted up off the floor, do it. Consider how much cleaning time and clutter is saved by those appliances—toasters to can openers—that mount under cupboards instead of sitting on counters! Likewise you will bless lamps, coat racks, or waste containers suspended from the wall or ceiling every time you clean. At home my wife and I have a table with suspended chairs that seats eight; it has nothing but a single center support. That means thirty-five fewer legs on the floor to vacuum and sweep around, catch mop strings or spaghetti, move out of the way, and rearrange. Get enough things out of the way and it'll save you weeks of time over a lifetime.

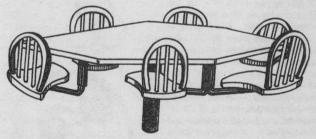

This suspended table and chairs has 27 fewer legs to clean under and around!

Build it in: It'll save space and leave only the front to clean. Built-ins are out of harm's way too, meaning airborne dirt, dust, and passing teens have trouble getting to them. The furniture stores may not display built-ins, so be sure to ask if they have a model that can be built in. It's worth a little extra cost and effort to get rid of cleaning under, behind, on top, and the sides—forever!

▶ **Remember:** The first principle of cleaning is not to have to do it!

▶ **Design:** Keep thinking: Design, design, design. When building, remodeling, or buying a house, new furnishings, fixtures, rugs or drapes, think How will I clean these? The design and material will make all the difference in the ease of cleaning.

Make sure it's reachable: Something might look nice or even cost less, but it if needs to be serviced or cleaned and you can't get to it without calling the fire department, you have a problem. If it's too high, too low, or too far only adds agony to the aggravation of cleaning. If you have to use an extension ladder to get to something, the time and cost of cleaning it triples.

Designing work out of your home is unquestionably the shortest path to household freedom. You don't have to be a pro to make these changes either. Just bear in mind the principles of cleaning efficiency and watch for a chance to put them in action. If you'd like a little more inspiration here, check out the book my daughter and I wrote on the subject—*Make Your House Do the Housework*.

Clean Green

"Clean up the earth now" is the rallying cry as we head toward the twenty-first century. Who's going to do it? Point the finger in the right direction—at ourselves, not the government, big factories, organizations, the media, and the like. For some strange reason we always think "they" are doing all of the environmental destruction, leaving all the litter around, creating all the waste and pollution. Not so. If things are going to change, we are going to have to do it—you and me together. Here are some simple things we can all do that will have worldwide consequences.

• Think reusable. Use cleaning cloths instead of paper towels, and so on.
• Use concentrated cleaners. Cleaning chemicals that you mix in your own spray bottles with water are a reality professional cleaners have been taking advantage of for years. They save a lot of packaging and

bottle-lugging, and save money too! An increasing number of supermarket cleaners are also available now in less packaging-intensive forms. Use them!

- Recycle the cleaning product containers that can be recycled.
- Dispose of leftover or outdated cleaning products safely. Check with your local Environmental Protection Agency if in doubt as to how.
- Simplify your cleaning equipment. A few basic tools and cleaners are all you really need. (See pp. 58 and 75.)
- Take care of everything you have. Get good-quality tools and equipment to begin with and keep them clean, maintained, and repaired. And keep your home furnishings and surfaces clean so dirt and grit won't degrade and damage them. This will double the life of most things and drastically reduce both the need for new purchases and the solid waste problem. We forget that much of what we throw away became "tossable" through *neglect*.
- Don't use more of any cleaning solution or preparation (laundry detergent, dish detergent, etc.) than you need. It doesn't just waste water and chemicals, it won't do as good a job. Cleaning chemicals are designed to work at a certain ratio of dilution. If you add more to the water than the label says, it won't just leave dulling detergent residue and call for extra rinsing. It'll actually lessen the solution's dirt-dissolving power.
- Use energy efficiently when you're cleaning. (See "Energy Saving While Cleaning.")
- Don't procrastinate. Waiting to clean almost doubles the energy and cleaning supplies needed to accomplish the job, plus it gives us a bad attitude. Cleaning when it's first needed is easier on us and the environment too.
- Clean up after ourselves. Right! If from today on we would all take just five minutes at work and five minutes at home and even two minutes in our classroom or motel and pick up just after *ourselves*, we wouldn't have to devote hired labor, chemicals, or energy to making it right later.
- Do all you can to *prevent* housework. This will save not only equipment and supplies but human and electrical and other kinds of energy.

▶ **Think maintenance-free:** Several years ago the Bell System asked me to help design its new headquarters in Atlanta to minimize cleaning and maintenance. Midway through the project someone humorously suggested that if we situated the salad bar right beneath all the indoor plants and greenery, any leaves that fell would land in the salad, so they'd never need to be cleaned up! This got a few laughs from the committee, but the concept of arranging your place to cut the expense and effort of cleaning is an entirely serious and practical idea.

THE A TO ZZZ OF CLEANING

Abrasive Cleaners

Abrasives, small particles of grit that help cleaning chemicals do their job, are found in many types of cleaning products. Everything from polishing compound to toothpaste, from metal polish to scouring powder, contains abrasives, added by the manufacturer to help scour away stubborn soil that detergent action alone won't remove. Abrasives perform an important job in cleaning but can also cause problems when used unwisely or when too harsh an abrasive is used for the task at hand. The old-style scouring cleansers, for example, contained silicates (sand), which did untold damage to household surfaces before manufacturers started using milder abrasives. (See "Cleansers.") Tooth polishes with overly strong abrasives (such as some of those that promise to whiten smoke-stained teeth) can cause premature wearing away of tooth enamel. Most colored nylon scrub pads are also impregnated with abrasives, the hardest of which can scratch even glass. Scotch-Brite and many other brands of scrub pads are color coded—white, tan, and yellow ones generally contain little or no abrasive; blue and red are slightly abrasive; green is medium; and the dark colors such as brown and black are the most ferocious. Steel wool is also very aggressive, especially in the coarser grades, and will dull or scratch most household surfaces. (See "Steel Wool"; "Sandpaper.")

Whenever you use an abrasive cleaner, test it in an out-of-the-way place first to make sure it won't injure the surface you're working on. And apply only as much pressure as needed to get the job done. Pushing down hard and grinding away furiously can leave deep scratches that a gentler approach would avoid. Even tiny hairline scratches may not show at first, but over time they will dull and mar a finish. A good rule of thumb is: Use abrasives only where gentler methods fail. Abrasive cleaners get to be a vicious cycle, because once a surface is scratched and abraded, soil clings more tightly to the porous surface and then you *have* to use abrasives to get it off.

Absorbents

Absorbents are powdery or granular materials used to soak up fresh stains, especially grease and oil. If left on long enough (several hours to overnight), absorbents can often completely remove an oil stain without your having to resort to harsher methods.

Commercially prepared absorbents are available, but most don't work any better than some common household products. You can use cat litter, for example, for things like oil drips in the garage or vomit on the carpet, and cornmeal on light-colored fabrics. Fuller's earth (available at pharmacies) works better on dark-colored fabrics. Cornstarch and talcum powder can be used too but are sometimes hard to remove from fabric.

After the absorbent has done its work, simply brush or vacuum it away. If the stain isn't quite gone, try a second application. Absorbents can also be mixed with water, detergents, and solvents to make poultices for drawing stains out of stone, concrete, brick, wood, and other porous surfaces. See also "Oil Stains"; "Poultice."

Acetic Acid

Acetic acid is often used in stain removal to neutralize alkaline stains or provide a mild bleaching action. Acetic acid is available at pharmacies and photo stores in a 10 percent solution; white vinegar, a 5 percent solution of acetic acid, can also be used in spot removal. Acetic acid is especially helpful because it's safe for silk and wool, which do not tolerate alkaline spotters well. It can be used on cotton and linen if diluted with equal parts water, but test the fabric for damage first. It should not be used on acetate at all. See also "Vinegar."

Acetone. See "Solvents."

Acid Cleaners. See "Cleaners, Acid."

Acoustical Tile

We all have it somewhere, sometime. Most likely on the ceiling. Acoustical tile is generally white originally, and it's usually tacked or glued to the ceiling. The acoustic ceilings found in commercial buildings are often the soft absorbent type made of compressed fiber; there are also acoustic ceilings made of Styrofoam-like material applied in sheet form (though it often still looks as if it were separate tiles). The spray-on type of acoustic ceiling known affectionately as "cottage cheese" is also popular. Acous-

Absorbent compounds can pull certain types of stains right out of porous materials.

tical tile's amazing ability to absorb sound unfortunately extends to other things. It can and will collect everything that goes up, including cigarette smoke, airborne dirt and grease, flung baby food, fly footprints, whatever. And the fiber type stains easily if anything above it leaks.

How do you clean it?

1. *The dry method.* This won't clean stained or tobacco-yellowed or greasy tile but it works wonders for plain old dirt accumulations. For this you need a professional tool called a dry sponge. (See "Dry Sponges.") Holding it in your hand or clamped into a holder on a pole (also available at a janitorial supply store), make swipes across the tile. Keep going until the sponge gets dirty and seems not to be removing any more dirt, then switch to a cleaner part of the sponge. When it's black on all surfaces simply throw it away. You can't dry sponge the cottage cheese type of ceiling, however.

2. *Bleaching or chemical cleaning.* In this process a chemical (basically a bleach) is sprayed on the ceiling. The bleach will strip the color out of anything, including bad smoke stains, so the ceiling will be white again. You can hire someone to do this for you for about 25 cents a square foot. You can also buy the chemical at a local janitorial supply store and do it yourself using a spray bottle or garden sprayer. Be sure to

▶ "If everyone would sweep the street in front of their own house, the whole world would be clean."
—*Goethe*

▶ **Clean smarter, not harder.**

This is the first rule of the professional. Clean with your head whenever possible—there are *always* easier ways to do things. Many are contained in these pages, but you may invent your own. Clean smarter, not harder.

follow the instructions carefully and cover everything in the room up first, including yourself—the chemicals are toxic and can damage other surfaces. And close the door and turn off the heat or air conditioning, so the mist won't float around and bleach everything else in the house.

Bleaching will work on cottage cheese ceilings and any type of absorbent tile. If the tile isn't absorbent, this method can still be used, but it may be more trouble than it's worth—you will have to wipe the chemical off by hand.

3. *Touchup.* Acoustical tile is often stained from an exploding bottle of pop, a water leak, a hanging lamp installation, and the like. A little white liquid shoe polish, daubed on and feathered out, generally will cover things like this. If the mark shows through, swab a coat of shellac on it to seal it off, then apply the polish again after the shellac dries. Acoustical tile dealers also sell touchup cans of spray paint to match ceiling tile colors.

4. *Wet-wash.* This process is almost impossible on the fiber type of tile because it will suck in both the water and the dirt. I have managed to degrease kitchen ceilings, however,

by quickly sponging the surface—putting degreaser solution on and wiping it off fast. The ceiling never comes perfect but is usually an improvement. And if you decide to paint the tile, you have to clean it this way first. The Styrofoam type of acoustic ceiling can be washed fairly successfully—just don't press too hard or you'll leave fingerprints!

5. *Paint.* If the tile is too good to rip off but gets dirty easily and you don't really care about the sound absorption aspect (you didn't install it for that reason in the first place, the baby is grown up now, or you also have carpet), paint it with a semigloss latex enamel. First wash as described above, then apply at least two good coats, and you'll be able to clean it easily. If you must have the "matte" look, use a flat white latex paint, but don't plan on it being very washable. Cottage cheese ceilings can be painted too.

Aerosol Cleaners. See
"Cleaners, Aerosol."

Afghans

These inhabitants of couch backs, laps, bed bottoms, car seats, and cedar chests are usually handmade.

Whether knitted, crocheted, or woven, afghans can easily stretch out of shape (when wet, especially), so treat them as gently as possible. A wool afghan should be washed by hand with Ivory Snow or Woolite, in cool or lukewarm water. Avoid drying with heat, or you may end up with a potholder. Air-dry it instead, using the air setting in your dryer. Don't

hang it to dry or your afghan will stretch for sure.

Afghans made of acrylic yarn are easier to care for: Using a gentle cycle, machine-wash with warm water; machine-dry on low heat. As with all handmade knits, check to see that all knots are tight before the first wash so that they won't unravel.

For older or doubtful drapables, the dry cleaner would appreciate the business as much as you'll appreciate the nice results.

Agitate (as used in cleaning).
See "Chemistry of Cleaning."

Airborne Grease and Soil

All of those tiny floating oily particles and other emissions from our cooking, cars, factories, aerosols, and other chemicals have to go somewhere. They don't all go up into the sky and away forever—they settle on the surfaces of our home. Then they collect and hold the 5,000 different ingredients in household dust. (See "Dust and Dust Control.") That awful stuff on top of your refrigerator or on the range hood is a good, if slightly exaggerated, example of the result. Any exposed surface soon has a sticky coating of soil. If it weren't for airborne grease, cleaning would be a snap because most dirt would just be lying around loose and could be vacuumed or dusted up.

For airborne soil, you need something that will dissolve the grease. A high-pH cleaner (one with a pH of 12 to 13—see "Chemistry of Cleaning") generally works best. Leaving the solution in contact with the soil long enough for it to work is the other secret of success.

The kitchen is usually the worst because the extra heavy concentration of airborne grease here makes a thick, sticky coating that must be emulsified (see "Emulsify") for removal. In the kitchen, a degreaser may be necessary. A spray bottle is a good way to apply it, followed by a cleaning cloth. If the deposit is thick, gently scraping off as much as you can before using a degreaser will speed things up.

To Cut Down on Airborne Soil

1. Use that kitchen exhaust fan! Most people use it only when the stove is going full bore. I know it's noisy, but use it.
2. Whenever possible, use covers on your pans when cooking, and use a screen guard when you're frying.
3. Try to use all steam or oily vapor-producing appliances under the hood. This will contain a lot of the fallout. If you ever get a chance, next time you build or remodel, design the kitchen so the hood will cover more than just the range. Ideally it should cover the counters too.
4. Design your kitchen with a minimum of surfaces to collect grease. Arrange to have the refrigerator, for example, slide completely in under a cabinet. Hang cabinets all the way up to the ceiling, and so on.
5. Clean high, flat surfaces more than once a year. You will be doing

it more often, but it'll go a lot faster.
6. Change your furnace filters at least monthly during periods of heavy kitchen use. Filters eliminate a lot of soil *if* they're maintained.
7. Consider an electronic air cleaner (see "Air Cleaners, Electrostatic.") They're an effective way to combat the aerial attack.
8. Make use of the bathroom exhaust fans too. The steam from showers also bonds dirt together and deposits it throughout the house.

Air Cleaners, Electrostatic

Have you ever stopped to think how much of the dirt in the average home is an airborne invasion? Dust, for example, is always suspended in the air and constantly raining down on every surface. And cooking vapors float out from the stove to deposit a greasy film on everything. Central heating system filters can't stop this. But there is a machine that will just sit quietly in the basement (or wherever your furnace is) and remove about 95 percent of the pollen, dust, mold spores, cigarette smoke and other minute debris from the air. When the air in the house is clean, life is a lot easier for anyone with allergies, and your walls, drapes, upholstered furniture, and carpet will stay a lot cleaner.

I'm talking about a precipitron or electrostatic precipitator. This is an electronic air filter that can be mounted in your central heating/cooling system. It has an electrode where the air comes in that puts a (positive) electric charge on all the dust and other particles in the air. Then the air is circulated past some large collector plates that have the opposite (negative) electric charge, so they attract the charged dirt particles to the plates and hold them there.

These devices are pretty amazing because they can even remove odors—right after you cook cabbage or fish or someone lights up a cigar the smell is gone, really gone. This is possible because most household odors are just fine particles in the air, and they too can be charged and collected. Electrostatic air cleaners cost $400 to $500, but they do an amazing amount of cleaning for the money.

Call your local air conditioning or heating and plumbing supplier for more information. People who have these swear by them.

Air Conditioners and Heat Pumps

Any maintenance beyond routine cleaning requires a trained serviceperson, but routine cleaning is an important job you can do yourself. Dust and dirt make your heating and cooling system less efficient, and waste energy.

A central air conditioner generally consists of two main components: the condenser, which usually sits outside, and the evaporator coil, which is mounted in the air-handling section of your furnace. A heat pump is just a sort of reversible condenser, and should be cleaned just like an air-conditioning condenser.

Keep the outside condenser unit free of leaves, grass, weeds, and anything else that could obstruct the air flow. At least once a year, turn off the power to the unit and remove the protective grille that covers the thin metal fins on the condenser coil. Carefully clean the fins with a soft brush to remove dirt and debris, being careful not to bend them. If some are bent, get a special fin comb from an appliance parts store and straighten them. A garden hose can be used to flush out the coil; just be sure to spray from the inside out, to avoid jamming debris tighter into the coil.

To reach the evaporator coil, you'll have to remove the access panel on the plenum (air duct junction box) on top of your furnace or on the front of the furnace itself. Be sure to turn off the power to the furnace before opening it up. You may have to loosen the screws holding the coil and slide it out a little to gain access to it; be careful not to bend the connective tubing. Use a stiff brush to comb the underside of the coil and remove any dust and dirt, being careful not to bend the fins here either. Clean the condensation tray under the coil with ½ cup chlorine bleach in a quart of water to kill mold and mildew. If the weep hole that lets water drain out of the pan is plugged, open it with a stiff wire.

To get maximum efficiency out of your system, you'll also need to clean or replace the filters, and clean and lubricate the blower and motor. (See "Filters, Heating and Cooling System"; "Furnaces.") If the condenser is running and the air distribution system is moving air and you still don't have adequate cooling, have the system checked by a technician. It may need a Freon charge or adjustment.

Room air conditioners have the condenser, evaporator, blower, and controls all in one unit, which usually sits in a window. Removing the front panel will usually give you access to the filter, coils, and drain pan. These parts should be cleaned at the beginning of the cooling season and once a month while the unit is operating. (See "Filters, Heating and Cooling System.") Consult the owner's manual for specific instructions for your model. If you can't remove an air conditioner from the window during the winter, get a cover for it to keep it clean and stop cold air from leaking in through it.

Alcohol

As well as being a potent antiseptic and a solvent used to thin shellac, alcohol has a multitude of uses in cleaning. (And I don't mean for making yourself oblivious to the fact that you're doing it!) Because it's a solvent that will mix with water, alcohol is added to such products as glass cleaners to help them cut greasy soil, to keep them from freezing in cold weather, and to make them dry faster. It's a good grease cutter and does a great job of cleaning the tar and nicotine film off windows in smoking areas—just mix it 1:4 with your window cleaning solution and squeegee away. Alcohol will also dissolve the film of body oils and makeup on metal jewelry and leave it bright and shiny.

(Don't use it on lacquered metal jewelry, though.)

Alcohol has long been a part of the professional cleaner's spot removal kit. It's effective on grass stains, indelible pencil, some inks, and a number of dye stains. Pretest first in an inconspicuous spot, to be sure alcohol's powerful solvent action won't cause the fabric dye to run. Use either denatured or isopropyl alcohol for cleaning and stain removal. You don't want rubbing alcohol—which may contain dyes, perfumes, and excess water.

CAUTIONS: Never use alcohol on wool, and always dilute 1:1 with water for use on silk or acetates. Remember, it's poisonous and flammable, so use it only in a well-ventilated area and keep it out of reach of children. See also "Solvents."

Alkaline Cleaners. See "Cleaners, Alkaline."

All-Purpose Cleaners. See "Cleaners, All-Purpose."

All-Purpose Spotter. See "Spot Removers."

Alpaca

These yarns and fibers are obtained from the alpaca, a domesticated South American animal that looks like a llama but is a closer relative of the camel. The term is also used to refer to the fine, silky fibers obtained from llamas, and even for synthetic and synthetic/wool blends that have the luxurious feel of true alpaca. Alpaca is used primarily in tailored suits and coats and for sportswear. Classified as a woolen, it should be cared for like wool, carefully following any care label directions. (See "Wool" under "Fabrics.")

Aluminum

Aluminum is sensitive to salt and alkalies: Aluminum outdoor trim will corrode in salt air, and salty foods left sitting in aluminum cookware will pit the surface. Alkaline foods and dishwasher detergents may also leave a dark film on aluminum cookware. (See "Cookware.") Strong alkalies such as ammonia, washing soda, and heavily ammoniated glass cleaners shouldn't be used on aluminum, as they can also discolor or pit the metal, but you can use solvents such as lacquer thinner on it. For general cleaning of aluminum, use all-purpose cleaner and wipe or wash with uniform pressure, following the grain of the metal if there is one. Be sure to rinse. If you have to scrub aluminum, use a white nylon-backed sponge or fine steel wool if necessary.

Don't expect to keep the bright shine of mirror-finish aluminum without a lot of effort. The easy way out is to scour aluminum like this in straight lines with a wet steel wool soap pad and learn to love the smooth satin finish this will put on it.

Aluminum exposed to the elements and airborne pollutants will eventually oxidize and start looking dull, and you'll always get those annoying black smears of oxide on your clothing, hands, cleaning rags, and anything else that touches it. If you try to clean oxidized aluminum, you're going to have to look at that blackened cloth for satisfaction, because you sure aren't going to see much difference in the aluminum. If you do have to clean aluminum storm windows and trim, use all-purpose cleaner solution applied with a spray bottle or a sponge and a white nylon-backed scrub sponge where necessary.

Anodized (colored) aluminum has a coating on it to prevent oxidation and deterioration of the metal. See also "Metal Polishes"; "Tarnish, Metal." Aggressive alkaline or acid cleaners should never be used on it. Never clean anodized aluminum while it's hot (even from the sun), since any chemical reactions that occur will be highly accelerated and the result may be a patchy light and dark mottled surface. Be careful too about using strong cleaners on window glass and other places where they may come in contact with anodized aluminum. You can use a white nylon-backed scrub sponge (gently!) on anodized aluminum, but avoid abrasives and hard rubbing and scrubbing, since it could damage the finish.

For aluminum car wheels, use fine steel wool and scrub lightly and evenly. If irregular pressure is applied, you may end up with dark spots. A product called Aluminum Brightener can be used to renew aluminum vehicle trim. You spray it on and wait a few minutes, then wipe it off with a soft dry clean cloth.

For aluminum cookware, see "Cookware."

Ammonia

Guess what? Ammonia is actually an alkaline *gas*—a compound of nitrogen and hydrogen. A solution of ammonia and water is properly called ammonium hydroxide, but when we cleaners refer to this staple of the grime-fighter's arsenal, we just say ammonia. Even a mild solution of ammonia is quite alkaline (see "pH in Cleaning"), so it works well on most acid soils and is a decent grease-cutter. Since it dries clear and streak-free, it makes an inexpensive and fairly effective cleaner for glass, no-wax floors, and shiny appliances. It works well on light accumulations of grease but is not as effective as a butyl degreaser (see "Butyl Cellosolve") on tough jobs, such as range hood filters. (A pan of ammonia left in the oven overnight will make oven cleaning easier, however.)

Ammonia is available in clear, sudsy (detergent added), or perfumed formulas (lemon or pine-scented) from supermarkets. Clear is best for streak-free cleaning of windows and appliances, but sudsy and scented are okay for general use. For spot removal, either clear or the chemically pure 10 percent solution available at drugstores is what you want. Ammonia's mild bleaching action makes it useful for removing a wide variety of stains. See "Spot and Stain Removal." For general cleaning, ammonia is usually used at a rate of about ½ cup per gallon of water, but you can go stronger, all the way up to full strength, if you can stand the smell.

Do be careful when you're using ammonia: Store it out of reach of children, as it's poisonous if swallowed. Don't inhale ammonia vapors or get ammonia on your skin or in your eyes. Don't mix ammonia with chlorine bleach; doing so creates toxic fumes. Don't use ammonia on waxed floors (unless you're trying to strip them), varnished surfaces, mirrors, marble, soft plastics, or leather. Don't soak aluminum pans in ammonia, it will darken them. Don't use strong solutions on paint. Dilute with equal parts water for use on silk or wool. Ammonia can alter the color of some dyes, so always pretest on fabrics. If a dye change occurs, rinse with water, apply vinegar, then rinse with water again.

Ammoniated Cleaners.

See "Cleaners, Ammoniated."

Amyl Acetate

Alias banana oil, amyl acetate is a solvent that safely removes nail polish, lacquer, and airplane glue from acetates and other fabrics that would be damaged by acetone. You can find it at pharmacies—ask for the chemically pure kind. Because it can damage furniture finishes and plastics, be sure to protect your work surface when you use it, and since it's flammable, keep it well away from sparks or flame.

Angora

Also called mohair, angora refers to soft, silky yarns and fabrics made from the fine hair of the Angora goat.

The term may also refer to articles made from Angora rabbit hair, even though the rabbit hair is not considered a true woolen. Angora is used alone and in blends to make fancy dress goods such as hats, suits, sweaters, and mittens, and for upholstery fabrics. Care for all types of angora the same way you do wool, always following label directions and being very gentle. (See "Wool" under "Fabrics.")

Antiques

Antiques are made of all kinds of materials, from wood, cloth, and china to much more exotic things. But in general we can be sure they are old, weak, and worn as well as often delicate and worth a lot less if you clean them wrong. If you do anything at all to an antique, it should always be with the gentlest possible procedure and cleaning product. Confine yourself to the three D's approach:
1. Dust.

2. Dry sponge. (See "Dry Sponges.")
3. Damp wipe: Use a soft cloth dipped in a neutral cleaner (see "Cleaners, Neutral") and wrung almost dry, and wipe it quickly over the surface. Follow immediately with a soft dry cloth.

For anything beyond this, call an antiques dealer specializing in that particular item. Cleaning cautiously here will save many dollars and a lot of grief.

Antiredeposition Agent.
See "Detergent."

Appliances, Small

A few general rules for cleaning small appliances.
• Some need to be cleaned after every use. (You know which ones they are.)
• Wait until they are cool before attempting to clean them.
• Unplug any appliance before cleaning.

▶ **Appliances: Color me clean!** All of us who bought those dark, stylish decorator appliances have been driven crazy trying to keep them clean. Almond and off-white are the most sensible color choices when it comes to cleaning. (Love those orange-peel textured, no-fingerprint models.) Black is the worst; it highlights every little drip and speck of dirt.

To clean black-front appliances, use a glass cleaner, such as Windex. Use a soft cloth instead of paper toweling to avoid worsening the lint problem. Always spray the cleaner onto the cloth; spraying directly onto the appliance surface will cause streaks. Following this procedure with a quick once-over using a Masslinn dust cloth (see "Dustcloths"), should pick up any lint or small particles left behind by the cleaning cloth.

If you have to scrub, use a white nylon-backed sponge—the green nylon type will scratch. You can remove old hard deposits carefully with a single-edge razor blade. (See "Razor Blades.")

- Never immerse an appliance in water unless specified by the manufacturer.
- Don't attempt to take an appliance apart and clean anything inside unless the manufacturer tells you to.
- Wash immersible parts in warm, sudsy water.
- No abrasives—they'll mar the surface and make it more dirt-prone.
- Use an all-purpose or glass cleaner and cleaning cloth: Spray, wipe, and polish dry. Don't forget to wipe the cord.
- Watch out for sharp edges.
- Keep drips and sprays out of the motor area.
- Carefully dry any disassembled parts before reassembling. Repairpeople say water dripping into the housing and rusting gears is a common cause of problems.
- Pull out countertop appliances weekly to clean behind them and at the same time give them a once-over to keep them shiny and inviting to use.
- Appliance covers keep that airborne greasy goo from settling on appliances. (But don't forget to toss the covers in the washer once in a while too!)

Aprons, Cleaning

Using an official cleaning apron with pockets and places for brushes, spray bottles, and the like can make sense when you're doing long and steady cleaning, especially as a professional, but not for everyday cleanups. It's like a carpenter's apron, a real lifesaver when you're doing a whole siege of nailing and installing, but for quick jobs, it's cumbersome, gets in your way, and spills when you're crawling or leaning over. Seventy percent of good home cleaning is done in short spurts of time, and finding and wearing a bulky bottleflopping, shin-poking, damp-clothdripping apron is one of the surest ways to slow yourself down and irritate yourself.

An apron is good for housecleaning day or when you're doing maid work (dusting, furniture polishing, spot cleaning, etc.) on the move in a number of rooms at a time—it keeps all the tools you need at your fingertips and saves a lot of steps. If you're just doing something like cleaning the bathroom, a caddy (see "Caddy, Cleaning") would make more sense.

If you do use an apron, you want one that clings close to your body, so it won't hang loose and get in your way. You can buy a pro cleaning apron at a janitorial supply store, or make your own to fit your needs.

Aquariums

Most of us overdo aquarium cleaning, when we do get around to it. If you're in the habit of tearing your fish tank down periodically to give it a thorough cleaning, you're not only making it hard on yourself, you're endangering your fish. Transferring fish too often can shock them, and cleaning the inside of the tank damages the delicate ecological balance of their watery world. In an aquarium with an undergravel filter (which I do wholeheartedly recommend), all the fish droppings and uneaten foods are pulled down into the gravel. There they de-compose, giving off ammonia and other byproducts that are poisonous to the fish. Fortunately, friendly bacteria develop in the gravel that feed on the ammonia and help keep it to a level the fish can tolerate. It takes four to six weeks for these bacteria colonies to develop, so when you take the tank apart to clean up the gravel, you're destroying what it has taken nature weeks to accomplish. You should stock a freshly set up aquarium with just a few hardy fish until these helpful little ammonia scavengers have a chance to get established, and then just leave them alone.

In an aquarium without an under-gravel filter, you will want to vacuum the gravel with a "gravel vac" such as a Hydro Clean and replace a portion of the tank's water once a month. The gravel vac siphons out some of the tank's water as you use it to clean the sediment and debris out of the gravel, so you get these two jobs done at once. You want to remove about one-third of the water in this manner and replace it with fresh water to keep ammonia levels down. (Be sure to dechlorinate the new water and adjust its temperature before adding it.)

Clean or replace the glass wool, charcoal, or whatever in the tank filters as the instructions specify, or at *least* once a month.

That's all the tank cleaning the fish require, but there are a few other things you'll want to do for yourself. Algae growth doesn't harm the fish, but it does give the glass and fittings of the aquarium a dirty look and make it hard to watch the underwater show. An algae-eating fish can be a real asset here, but don't put one in until the tank has been established for a month or two and there's something there for it to eat. Any algae that the fish misses can be scrubbed from the tank walls with one of the long-handled brushes or sponge pads designed just for this purpose, or you can reach right down inside the tank with a white nylon-backed scrub sponge or a paint scraper if that doesn't bother you. Magnetic devices are also available that enable you to guide a scraper inside the tank with a magnet outside. When algae builds up on aquarium fittings and decorations, you can take them out and scrub them in a bucket containing about 3 tablespoons chlorine bleach per gallon of water. Be sure you air-dry the items completely afterward and let the chlorine dissipate before putting them back in the tank, though; chlo-

A gravel vac.

rine is extremely toxic to fish. Locating aquariums out of direct sunlight will help reduce algae.

Clean the outside of the tank with a spray-on glass cleaner such as Sparkle that does **NOT** contain ammonia. And spray the cleaning cloth, not the glass. Spraying toward the tank can get cleaning chemicals into the water, and that won't do anything for the fish. Cleaner-polishes such as Outright Aquarium polish not only clean clear plastic safely but leave an invisible coating on there that helps hide tiny scratches and repel dust as well as fingerprints, noseprints, and other smudges. Hard-water scale or "water lines" can be scraped off with a single-edge razor blade, scrubbed off with a green nylon-backed scrub pad, or wiped off with aquarium cleaner, but using soft water in your tank to begin with is easier. There are water-softening tablets available that can be put right in the tank filter.

Don't use soap or detergent of any kind to clean anything in or from a fish tank. Use some plain table salt if you must use anything and rinse even that off very well. In general, scrub only with a plastic or nylon scrubber that has never seen soap, and plain water.

Coral can be dropped into a container with a couple of denture-cleaning tablets (an easy way to get into those innumerable tiny crevices). Be sure to rinse well afterward as denture tablets contain bleach.

Since the tank light is probably dirty and spotty, unplug it and work it over with a damp white nylon-backed scrub sponge as needed and finish up with some Sparkle to rebrighten it.

Art Objects

By "art" I mean anything with real artistic, cash, or sentimental value, and the best advice I can give about it is: Don't clean it. Many irreplaceable art objects have been ruined or diminished in value by uninformed attempts at cleaning or spot removal.

Protection is the order of the day. Valuable pieces deserve careful climate and dust control to prevent damage. Prints, drawings, lithographs, etchings, watercolors, pastels, and the like should be framed and covered with clear glass to prevent staining and damage. If it's a valuable work, ask for conservation framing, in which acid-free backing, mat, and tape are used to prevent staining of the paper. Oil paintings are not covered with glass, but they're pretty impervious to stains anyway. Be sure to hang art where it won't be exposed to the fading and drying effect of direct sunlight.

Three-dimensional objects such as pottery, sculpture, and basketry can be displayed in dustproof glass cases. Some wood and stone sculptures can be preserved with a thin coating of carnauba wax (see "Wax"), and silver or brass can be lacquered, but jobs

---

▶ Feeding those little rascals is one of the great pleasures of aquarium ownership, but don't overdo it. It's not good for Mr. and Mrs. Guppy, and it's the biggest reason tank cleaning time rolls around again so soon.

like this should be left to a pro. Bronze sculptures should be left to form their own protective patina. For advice on handling various art media or to locate a professional in the cleaning and restoration of art objects, contact a local museum or art gallery.

Once it's properly protected and displayed, about the only care you'll want to render your artwork is regular dusting with a feather duster. Wood frames can be wiped with a damp cloth and even waxed, if desired, and glass can be kept clean with a Windex-type glass cleaner. Just be sure not to spray the glass itself, lest a dribble of liquid find its way inside. Spray the cleaning cloth instead and use it to polish the glass. When handling art objects, it's a good idea to wear white cotton gloves, as the acid from your hands can damage them. If your valuable art pieces need care beyond these simple measures, seek out the services of a professional.

► **Oil Paintings:** Do get a gradual coating of airborne oil and dirt, plus an occasional caress from a too-close admirer. Cleaning fine art or any expensive or valuable painting should be left to the pros, but if you just want to brighten up the landscape Aunt Tillie did, you can run over the surface lightly with a dry sponge. (See "Dry Sponges.")

Ashtrays

Dump them first, of course. Janitors are trained to pick ashtrays up by placing their palms over the top and grasping the edges with their fingers. This way if there's still a glowing butt in the tray they'll feel the heat, and it might save burning down the place. To be safe, always empty ashtrays into a metal trash can and not one filled with paper and other combustible trash. We pro cleaners often just wipe the inside of ashtrays with a plain damp cloth. If they have lots of sticky tar, burned-on stuff, and parked pieces of candy in them, however, after dumping, we spray a couple of squirts of all-purpose cleaner in them and leave them to soak for five minutes while we do something else. You should do the same. Then when you come back the crud will be dissolved and loosened so you can wipe them out well with a paper towel, then polish with a dry cloth. Glass, chrome, and shiny ashtrays can be polished with glass cleaner.

If ashtrays have had heavy use, their smell alone is a killer, so they need to be washed, not just emptied. Run them through the dishwasher or soak, then scrub them in a sinkful of soapy water.

Asphalt Tile

Almost all resilient floor tile manufactured today is vinyl, but a fair amount of asphalt tile is still found in older homes and commercial buildings. The name here is a little misleading, since only the very darkest shades contain any asphalt. The lighter shades use light-colored resins and plasticizers to bind together the asbestos, limestone, and other mineral fillers tile is made from. Asphalt tile is essentially the same as vinyl asbestos, except that the binder in the latter is vinyl instead of resinous. (See "Vinyl Tile.")

The big drawback to asphalt is its sensitivity to oils, solvents, and strong alkaline cleaners. These break down the binders and cause the tile to get brittle, crack, and decompose. A sure sign of this is color bleeding. For this reason, asphalt tile should always be sealed with an acrylic sealer. Then on top of the sealer use a water-based floor finish (or "wax") to protect the floor and give it a good gloss. Damp-mop as needed with a neutral cleaner solution. As necessary scrub and wax, and strip off built-up wax. Don't use hot water or harsh alkaline strippers, as these will deteriorate the tile. Old, faded tile can often be rejuvenated with the asphalt tile restorer still carried by some janitorial supply stores. See also "Vinyl Asbestos Tile"; "Floors, Resilient."

Attics

Attics have two big negatives: (1) all that junk deposited up there; (2) their unfinished construction—which means splintery rafters, shedding insulation, grimy raw wood floors, decades of accumulated dust, inaccessible cubbyholes, and littered rafter spaces (those openings full of plaster bits, shriveled spiders, dead mice, and lost golf balls, where the flooring ends and the roof begins). If you're not careful, you can easily bump your head on that low slanted ceiling or (in old, old buildings) fall right through the attic floor.

At least five years of your life is spent cleaning. Learning how to clean faster will give you back a lot of precious minutes, hours, and days—give you more time for life AFTER housework, the things that light up your life.

On top of that, it's hot up there and there isn't much light or room to work (but at least, no visitors). Wait for a cool spell, and then dejunk it of the stuff you'll never use, don't really want, and that doesn't have redeeming sentimental value. Then, with 60 percent of the stuff gone, I would take a shop vac to all the dust, cobwebs, rodent fallout, and loose insulation bits. If you insist on using an attic for storage, first exterminate to get rid of pests. Otherwise, they'll chew everything, boxed or not. Then get a hold of a bunch of sturdy cardboard boxes or secondhand suitcases or Kmart–quality trunks and package and *seal up* anything that goes up there, and be sure to identify the contents! At the very least, put everything you've got stored in the attic under old bed sheets or into heavy-duty plastic bags tied shut. When you need something, take it downstairs and leave the (by then dirty and dusty) bag behind up there. Label your bags too unless you don't mind spending an afternoon opening and closing bags and cussing.

The floor of an attic can be made a lot easier to clean by covering it with inexpensive sheet vinyl or giving it a couple of coats of deck paint. This will also brighten up the attic and give it a more finished appearance. Parti-cle board is a low-budget way to finish the walls and roof, and an attic fan will make things more bearable not only up there but in the whole house.

▶ **Attitude** is everything in cleaning. A good upbeat one will do more to make cleaning fast and fun than a carload of professional tools and chemicals.

B

Bowl Patrol: The name of the cleaning team that tends the outhouses on the slopes of the famous Sun Valley resort.

Baby Clothes

For starters, don't expect baby clothes to be spotless. The darling white pinafore will be the first thing to have beets burped on it.

Spray those treasured garments the minute they come out of the box with a soil retardant such as Scotchgard fabric protector so spills can be wiped off before they soak in. Then bib, bib, bib—it's a great way to prevent damage! Don't feed snookums in fancy, hard-to-clean stuff with lace, embroidery, or appliqués on it, hand knits or crocheted things.

Baby clothes should be washed separately with one of the special baby soaps or detergents, such as Ivory Snow or Dreft, that will leave them with a soft finish and no irritating detergent residue. Flame-resis-

29

tant sleepwear, however, should *not* be washed in any soap product—check the care label. You can keep better track of wee washcloths and minisocks and the like if you put such things together in a mesh bag. Baby wash loads should always be well rinsed (yes, that means a second rinse). Speaking of rinsing, be sure to rinse off any clinging blobs that came from either end of the baby and pretreat stains before washing. Take extra care in pretreating the stains according to what caused them.

Potty stains: Presoak serious ones in a warm enzyme detergent (such as Biz) solution. Elastic around the tummy and legs will help keep diaper mess in the diaper.

Breast milk: Pretreat or presoak with an enzyme detergent before laundering. Because of the fat in breast milk, dry-cleaning fluid (see "Dry-Cleaning Fluid") may be necessary to remove such stains completely.

Formula: When it's fresh, formula will wash right out. After it dries, it's sometimes impossible to remove. Formula stains are protein based and are best removed with enzyme detergent. Soak in a warm enzyme detergent solution first (at least thirty minutes—see label directions), then launder as usual.

Fruit and fruit juice stains: Rinse with cool water immediately, treat with a pretreat, and wash in cold water. Heat in any form sets fruit stains, so if that doesn't do it, soak in digestant (see "Digestant") and relaunder. Don't put in the dryer or iron until the stain is gone.

Vomit and spitups: These should be rinsed off immediately because the stomach acids that come back up with the strained carrots can bleach as well as stain.

Lipstick from smoochy relatives: Carefully scrape off any you can without smearing it around and pretreat before washing. Dry-cleaning fluid may be called for.

When they emerge from the washer, tumble those tot togas dry, but don't overdo it or you'll speed up the outgrowing process.

Backpacks and Stuff Sacks

Backpacks, bike bags, stuff sacks, and similar items of camping gear are usually made of nylon, either coated (waterproof) or uncoated. If you have a dirty pack of uncoated nylon, you can machine-wash it with no problem. Just be sure to zip up the zippers and secure straps and buckles to avoid damaging them in the washer. Pretreat any stains, take external frame packs off the frame, and remove the interior stiffeners from internal frame packs before washing. If the seams have cut edges that aren't heat-seared to prevent unraveling, you won't want to use much agitation. Front-loading washers in laundries employ much gentler agitation than top-loading automatics, and should be used for large or delicate items. For instructions for washing nylon, see "Nylon" under "Fabrics"; see also "Sleeping Bags."

Coated nylon shouldn't be machine-washed—the coatings used to waterproof it tend to deteriorate with repeated washings and will eventually start to crack and peel away from the fabric. (You'll know it's coated nylon if one side has a smooth, flexible coating that obscures the texture of the fabric.) Wash coated fabric items by hand with laundry detergent, soaking as needed to loosen stubborn soil. Rinse the item and let it drip dry, stuffing it with paper (not newspaper!) to hold it in shape if necessary. Don't dry with heat or attempt to iron coated nylon. For care of Gore-Tex and similar waterproof/breathable fabrics, see "Gore-Tex." If you've used soil retardant or water-repellent treatments on uncoated nylon, it must be reapplied after washing.

Bacteria/Enzyme Digester

Digesters are the most effective way to deal with urine, vomit, fecal matter, and other organic stains and spills in porous surfaces such as carpeting, upholstery fabrics or clothing and concrete. The digester contains a culture of dormant friendly bacteria activated by mixing with warm water. The living bacteria produce an enzyme that actually digests (eats) the organic matter. As long as the food source exists, the bacteria keep reproducing and digesting until the contaminant is all gone, then they die for lack of nourishment.

Digesters are the best way to deal with odors caused by organic decay, because they eliminate the source of the odor. One good brand of bacteria/enzyme digester is Outright Pet Stain Eliminator from Brampton Labs (also marketed simply as Out!). Bacteria/enzyme drain openers also are available; although they take more time to work than strong acid or caustic drain cleaners, they're much safer for both humans and plumbing fixtures. Bacteria/enzyme products work best within certain temperature ranges and usually can't be mixed with other cleaners, so follow directions exactly for best results.

Baking Soda

Baking soda (sodium bicarbonate) is a less alkaline relative of washing soda. It's used in some powdered cleaners and presoak products to provide a little alkalinity but isn't a major ingredient in prepared cleaners. Around the house, it's a handy deodorizer. Leave an open box in the fridge or freezer, or sprinkle a little in dishwashers, drains, garbage disposers, and cat litter boxes to keep unpleasant odors under control. Baking soda is also a mild abrasive that can be used to scour such things as fiberglass and Formica—just use a light touch and don't bear down too hard on it. It's also a mild bleach, so a poultice of baking soda mixed with water will often pull stubborn stains from countertops, fine china, and similar surfaces. Although a baking soda and water solution is often recommended as a general-purpose cleaner, it doesn't have as much cleaning power as a detergent.

Bamboo. See "Rattan and Bamboo."

Barbecue Grills. See "Grills, Barbecue."

Baseball Caps. See "Hats and Caps."

Baseball Gloves

For the most part age and dirt just give baseball gloves personality, but if for some reason yours needs to be in World Series shape, rub a soft cloth into a can of saddle soap and give the mitt a generous lather of it (see "Leather"; "Saddle Soap"), working it in especially well to the soiled areas. Then wipe it clean with a damp cloth and after it's good and dry, oil with neat's foot oil. (See "Neat's Foot Oil"). If you give it just one more inning of cleaning, it will look like new!

Basements

Basements are crammed with semi-active stuff, and they're fed faster than they assimilate, so they're always a cleaning problem. Always dejunk them first. If there's a workshop somewhere down under all that, replace things where they belong and convert that clutter perch back to a workbench today. Get all that stuff off the stairs and out from under the stairs too.

1. Make sure you have closable cupboards or containers for what you do keep—it will amaze you how much less litter a basement invites if the stuff stored there is relatively hidden. What you keep sealed up in trunks, sturdy boxes, or old suitcases won't get spread around. Closed cabinets or enclosed "fruit rooms" are also better than dusty, cobwebby shelves full of home-canned stuff.

2. Keep at least a few key cleaning tools in the basement. Half of the dread of doing this particular job is rounding up the tools and chemicals and lugging them down there—and then back up.

3. If the basement is unfinished, with lots of exposed construction, seal all the concrete. It will stop dust from bleeding off the floor. If you put two coats of finish on a concrete basement floor, it will shine, can be swept swiftly with a dust mop, and won't absorb spills, stains, and animal accidents! Caulk and seal cracks in floors and walls to keep out moisture and control pests. As for that unfinished overhead, full of exposed wooden joists and rafters, ducts, pipes, cobwebs (and odd stuff

---

▶ **Baseboards** get beaten to a pulp. They get gouged and chipped and painted and repainted, and the more often we paint them the rattier they look. Why? Baseboards collect many coats of wax, and few people remove it prior to painting. The wax keeps the new paint from adhering properly—one touch and it flakes right off. So first wash and scrub the baseboard with a white nylon-backed pad and wax remover or ammonia solution, until you're sure it's bare. Then hit it lightly with medium sandpaper. The paint will stick like glue and it'll be easy cleaning for years. See also "Woodwork."

such as old pool sticks and broken fishing rods we stuck up there to get out of the way), a Sheetrock ceiling is one solution.

4. If you do have raw unfinished concrete walls and floors down there, clean them as described in "Concrete."

5. The dampness (and mildew) situation can be improved by any or all of the following: (a) Install a dehumidifier, or if it's really wet down there, a sump pump; (b) Coat the walls, whether masonry or block, with a water seal such as those by Thompson or Thoroseal; (c) Install a raised floor over the floor proper, made of plywood over a 2 by 4 grid; (d) (The ultimate) Water-seal the exterior foundation walls, then dig a French drain system around them that connects to a dry well some distance away!

Baskets

A tiskit a taskit . . . never soak your basket—whether it's painted, varnished, or in the raw. Getting a basket soaking wet can cause it to mildew or warp out of shape. Baskets are made of a great variety of plant materials, from willow and wicker to ash and oak and hemp, and some of these do benefit from an occasional short sprinkle or shower in the tub. But if you don't know what a basket is made of and no instructions came with it, the safest approach is as follows: A good vacuuming with an upholstery brush should take care of everyday cleaning, and if a basket seems to need more than that, just use a damp cloth. You may want to use a little oil soap, such as Murphy's, following the directions on the bottle. Oil soap solution can even be used on painted and varnished baskets. But get the moisture on and off *fast*—wipe with a damp cloth and then blot with a terry cleaning cloth. Then be sure to let it air-dry completely (but not in the sun, which might shrink it) before storing or reusing.

Mildew on baskets can be removed with a hot chlorine bleach solution (1:5 chlorine bleach/water). Marks or stains on unpainted, unfinished baskets can be removed with fine sandpaper, though this may temporarily leave a lighter spot on a basket with that aged appearance so popular with basket lovers. A little mineral oil (or lemon oil, if you never keep food in that basket) rubbed lightly over a basket after cleaning will give it back the "decorator" look.

Bathrooms

Q: How do you tell a dirty bathroom?
A: By the way it smells.

A big part of bathroom cleaning is killing germs, because even when a bathroom looks okay, bacteria can cause offensive odors. For this reason, maids and housekeepers, the professionals who clean rest rooms every day, have learned to spray-clean with a disinfectant cleaner. Everything in the average bathroom except the mirror can be cleaned this way in just three or four minutes a day. First, swab the inside of the toilet bowl with your bowl swab and a squirt of quaternary disinfectant solution. (See "Disinfectants.") Then lightly spray all the fixtures and vanity top with a mist of disinfectant cleaner, and polish dry with a cleaning cloth. Stubborn soap scum or soil can be loosened with a white nylon-backed scrub pad. The mirror is the next thing to clean, using a Windex-type spray glass cleaner. The cloth you've been using to polish everything else dry will be just damp enough by now to do a quick but effective wipe-up of the floor, and you're done! That's all there is to daily cleaning that will keep a bathroom fresh-smelling and clean all the time. Add to this a once-a-week deep cleaning of the toilet, tub, and shower, and that's all most bathrooms will need. See also "Bathtubs"; "Cleaners, Disinfectant"; "Disinfectants"; "Hard-Water Deposits"; "Shower and Tub Enclosures"; "Toilet Bowl Swab"; "Toilets."

Bathtubs

How you clean them depends on what they're made of. Enameled steel or cast iron tubs are very durable and resistant to most cleaning chemicals. (See "Enameled Metals.") You can use heavy-duty cleaners and degreasers to remove bathtub ring, and even a little scrubbing with mild cleansers from time to time won't do any harm. Be careful of harsh powdered cleansers and colored nylon scrub pads, though, and don't use heavy pressure with even a mild cleanser, or it will eventually dull the surface. (See "Abrasive Cleaners.") Keep strong acids such as bowl cleaner and hydrofluoric rust remover out of enameled tubs

too; if you need to remove a rust stain, use oxalic acid. (See "Oxalic Acid"; "Rust.")

Fiberglass tubs must be treated more tenderly. (See "Fiberglass.") Shy away from any kind of abrasive cleanser (even the gentle liquid type), colored nylon scrub pads, steel wool, or anything that can scratch and dull the surface. Scrub only with a white nylon-backed sponge, and if absolutely necessary, a mild cleanser such as the new-formula Comet, which is approved by many fiberglass manufacturers for use on their products. For general cleaning, you can just use a neutral cleaner, not a specialized fiberglass cleaner. If you have a heavy soap scum or hard water buildup, remove as per directions in "Shower and Tub Enclosures," and consider waxing afterward as suggested to prevent further buildup. Fiberglas De Scal-It (available at spa supply stores) works well on hard water deposits on fiberglass, and you can also use mild phosphoric acid. (See "Phosphoric Acid.") Don't use any strong acids or alkalis or solvents, such as toilet bowl cleaner, oven cleaner, acetone, or lacquer thinner, though.

The secret of efficient tub cleaning, like all cleaning, is keeping after it. A tub that's been neglected for a month or more will be a challenge even for a pro. A mild phosphoric acid solution is the best keep-up cleaner for tubs. Use a white nylon-backed sponge to apply it (you don't want to be breathing in spray mists in such close quarters) to the tub and all its hardware and let it sit on there for three or four minutes. Make sure you get the corners and all those places that accumulate hard-water deposits. Then scrub lightly with the nylon side of the sponge and rinse. Proceed top to bottom: tub edges, sides, and then the bottom, working your way from the high water end down toward the drain. Buff dry with a cleaning cloth, and do the hardware last. See also "Grout."

Bathtub Rings

Rings are the high-water mark—a combination of body oil, dirt, soap, and hard-water deposit that clings to the side of the tub instead of washing down the drain with all the rest. Wiping the ring zone right after every bath with a white nylon-backed sponge, or even a washcloth, while the water is draining out, is by far the easiest and best way to banish bathtub ring. If you let it accumulate and harden, you'll have to scrub harder or use chemicals. Cleaning the bathroom fixtures regularly with mild phosphoric acid solution (see "Phosphoric Acid") will also keep rings under control.

If you haven't kept your ring guard up and there's a buildup as black as a skid mark on there, spray it down with heavy-duty cleaner solution, give it a chance to penetrate and loosen the soil, then hit it with a white nylon-backed scrub pad. Finally rinse and buff to a shine with a dry cloth. If your tub is old and worn or you or a previous owner were in the habit of using powdered abrasive cleansers on it, then the tub ring will cling and be extra hard to remove.

Beams, Exposed

These decorative timbers lend atmosphere to a home and some hard-to-reach surfaces for dirt collection. Airborne dust and grease stick to beams, spiders frolic there, and forgotten thumbtacks and Scotch tape linger on many beams.

Smart folks make sure their exposed beams are sealed or painted to make dusting easier and so nothing can penetrate the wood and stain it. Settled dust and dead bugs are the worst cleaning problems with beams—an extension section on your canister or shop vac hose capped with an angled dust tool head can pull all this off instead of dropping it down all over everything. Or you can use a lambswool duster with an extension handle to remove cobwebs, lint, and the like. This leaves beams in good shape and saves you a lot of trips up and down a ladder (and maybe the big one to the hospital).

Accumulations of airborne grease on rough-hewn beams can be a real problem. Since most beams are stained with wood stain, they're sealed to at least a degree against moisture. Even so, you'll have to use a scrub brush and a solution of degreaser whipped into a foam so you don't saturate the beam. Spread the foam on the surface to emulsify the grease in an arm's length area at a time—then soak up the now-dirty foam with a terry cleaning cloth. This is a slow process. Use rubber gloves and safety glasses to keep any chemical splashes from your eyes, especially if you have to work over your head.

Beds

There's nothing like crawling between clean sheets! Strip that bed and launder bedding (sheets and pillowcases) weekly. That's a great time to quickly dust the head and footboards too. A bedspread is a good idea too. It will keep your bed looking good and lengthen the time between blanket washings.

A quilted or plastic mattress pad/cover will protect the mattress from accidents and can be laundered just like bedding. Pretreat spots and presoak heavily soiled or stained pads. (See "Spot and Stain Removal.")

Turn mattresses once a month to prevent sagging, and vacuum to pick up the dust mites and other unmentionables. (Remember, we shed our skin entirely, flake by flake, in the course of two years!) Treat spots and stains with upholstery cleaner.

Making beds and stripping and replacing sheets are jobs easily done by men or women, adults, teenagers, or children. No one should make another person's bed! It takes just a minute in the morning and starts you off on a neat and orderly day. Besides, it's a lot nicer to climb into a made bed at night.

Baths before bed keeps the kids' sheets cleaner longer.

Changing the Sheets

When you change the sheets, do it as hotel professionals do—with a minimum of effort. They walk around the bed only *once*.

Stand beside the bed and spread both top and bottom sheets across the mattress. Make sure they're smooth and straight. Next comes the blanket, then turn a few inches of the top sheet back and fold it over the blanket. Now, with everything shipshape, begin your circuit of the bed.

Starting at the headboard, tuck the bottom sheet firmly beneath the mattress. (Hospital corners are snazzy if you know how, but not necessary. They'll keep your sheets in place even during nightmares.) Along the sides and bottom, you're tucking at least two layers—if there's a blanket, three. Keep tucking—tight! smooth!—straightaway up the other side and you're home free. Now whip on that bedspread, making sure the overhang is equal on all sides and that there's enough at the head of the bed to cover the pillow plus a little slack. Why the slack? So you can tuck it under the edge of the pillow. If the bed is against the wall, make sure the long side of the spread away from the wall reaches the floor. This gives a professional, finished look to a room.

Making the Bed

The day-to-day of bed-making is relatively simple. First, make sure that the top and bottom sheet are still firmly tucked beneath the mattress—this is where fitted sheets are timesavers. Hospital corners will keep nonfitted sheets tucked tightly. Pull up the blanket, make sure it's straight and smooth, and fold the top few inches of the top sheet over the blanket. Then repeat the tucking routine and continue with bedspread and pillows as before.

No fair taking the ostrich approach—leaving the top sheet and maybe even the blanket bunched up at the bottom of the bed and covering it up with the bedspread. This only creates a nasty lump that's magnified by the spread. Besides, a minute in the morning will save you from crawling into a damp, wrinkled minefield at night.

And don't let your sheets hang out—tuck those babies in when they come loose. They look tacky peeking out from under the spread!

For those of you convinced it doesn't make any sense to make a bed when you're just going to sleep in it again, there is a respectable way out. Minimize the number of blankets and covers you use—a couple of thick ones are better than four thin ones that you'll spend half the morning smoothing and straightening out. Or buy a comforter that can serve as a bedspread too. Electric blankets also resolve this problem nicely and make for less weight on the users.

As for decrumbing a bed, the traditional approach is to beat the bed with flat palms to loosen debris and then, when no one is looking, whisk it on the floor, but crumbs aren't the only thing we come across here. If bed-changing is delayed long enough, everything from dirty underwear to

---

▶ **Once awake, make!** Beds—only one rule for kings, counts, or cronies. If you sleep in it, you make it, now! Before bathroom or breakfast. If you keep this rule, the divorce rate will go down at least 17 percent nationally.

---

dead ticks get trapped down there. Either change the sheet more often or brush it all out into a trash can held at the edge of the bed.

Cleaning under the bed is usually a matter of fishing out lost socks and puzzle pieces and flushing out dust bunnies. On hard floors this is best done with a dust mop; a canister vac is fine for carpet.

Any good pack rat, of course, can cram in so much underbed storage there's no room for dust—built-in underbed storage is a better idea if you must have it. (See "Design Dirt Out" on p. 6.)

Bedspreads

The best way to keep a bedspread clean is as my grandmother did: Never let Grandpa sit on it, and fold and remove it faithfully from the bed every night.

Bedspreads are made from such a variety of materials, there's no general way to clean them. If you intend to wash a spread at home, first test an inconspicuous area to see if the colors will run. If so, take it to a dry cleaner. Many spreads are machine-washable—check the label. See "Quilts and Comforters" for hand-washing procedure. If you also have a matching set of curtains, it's best to clean them at the same time (in case there's a color change—at least they'll still match). See also "Blankets."

A Few Specifics

Cotton: If it says washable, do not dry-clean. Most cotton dye colors are solvent-soluble, meaning they will run if dry cleaned.

Knitted/crocheted: Be sure to block (see "Blocking") these if you wash them—dry-cleaning is probably worth the cost.

Satin: The distinctive weave of this fabric is what gives it its shiny surface. Be careful not to deluster it with too alkaline a detergent. Make sure the detergent you use does not contain a builder (check the label), or use Ivory Snow.

Polyester: Tough stuff—no special precautions are needed.

Nylon: You can't do much wrong with nylon either. Just don't overdry.

Rayon (cellulose acetate): Loses its strength when wet and can shrink. It's best to dry-clean. However, if you do wash, use a gentle cycle and dry at a low temperature.

Silk: Is apt to have colors that run. Dry-clean in most cases.

Velvet and velour: Although these are generally made of acrylic these days, it's best to take them to a dry cleaner, because you could easily crush the pile or leave handprints in it.

Before You Start to Clean.
See p. 1.

Biodegradable

The word *biodegradable* simply means the ability to be broken down into harmless substances through natural processes such as the action of bacteria. Long-lasting residues from cleaning products affect the world we all live in, and we need to be mindful of what we inflict on the

▶ **Behind things:** What you can't see won't hurt you may be true in things such as TV and boy/girl watching, but not in cleaning. If it's left behind or under long enough it becomes attached, smelly, a breeding ground for bugs, and a lump creator and conscience pricker. This isn't an everyday or even every week or month job, but you need to clean behind often enough to show it who's boss.

environment. While most soaps and detergents manufactured now are readily decomposed by bacteria and fungi in the soil and water, many of the solvents and specialty chemicals we use are not. It makes sense to use the least offensive cleaner that will do the job, and take care in the disposing of solvents, strong acids, and other harsh chemicals. Call your local sanitation department or state environmental protection agency when in doubt as to how to dispose of a particular chemical.

To minimize the number of empty cleaning product containers that must be discarded, use concentrated cleaners (see "Cleaners, Concentrated") and reusable spray bottles. You also can choose to patronize manufacturers who make an effort to package their products in biodegradable containers.

Black Marks

On floors it's heels and dragged objects that leave those highly visible, hard-to-remove marks; on walls it's usually bumps and scrapes from furniture or carried things. One thing you can be sure of, black marks aren't just lying there, they're usually etched on by force. First, the no-nos for getting them off. Because they are lodged on, we too often try to rasp them off with steel wool and other sandpaper-style warfare, which leaves a white or light or dull area that's generally uglier and more obvious than the original mark. Hard scrubbing and harsh cleansers will take off a lot more than you intended (usually part of the surface). Always think chemical removal first. On walls, doors, and the like, some all-purpose cleaner solution dabbed gently on the mark might release it. If that doesn't work, gently scrub the mark with a fingertip covered with a dry-cleaning fluid or a paint thiner–dampened white terry towel. If you see results (your towel darkening), then continue. If the mark still isn't gone, use a white nylon-backed scrub sponge to apply more pressure, which will generally get rid of it. Always rinse and buff the area dry after cleaning, so loose bits of that black stuff won't be left behind to make a new mark. Whatever you do, don't grind away at it with dry powdered cleansers or dry anything. Be sure to check, lots of bad black marks are actual *surface damage* that can't be removed with mere cleaning.

Black marks on a waxed floor are a breeze to get up, because the mark is on the wax, not the floor. Enamel paint will also usually confine black marks to the surface (they penetrate flat paint). Wax not only protects the surface of the floor itself from black marks, it helps keep them from being deposited on the floor. An outbreak of black marks usually indicates that the wax on a floor is getting thin. A thick, smooth, hard wax finish doesn't mark easily, so the pros know it's time to rewax when black marks start showing up.

Remove black marks from a floor with all-purpose cleaner solution and a white nylon-backed sponge, moving to a green nylon pad only if necessary. If a white or lighter spot is left on the floor by your removal efforts, you can reduce the contrast by first rinsing the area with a 50:50 vinegar/water solution, then lightly rewaxing the spot after it dries with a clean cloth dampened with wax. Feather (see "Feathering") the edges to help blend the spot with the surrounding area.

When removing black marks from a painted floor, take special care not to abrade the surface. A light coat of wax on a painted floor will help with the black mark problem and heighten the shine.

Blankets

Follow directions on blanket care labels when available. Some wool blankets must be dry-cleaned. If yours can be washed by hand, see the procedure under "Quilts and Blankets." Most blankets can be machine-washed as follows: First, repair any loose binding. Then shake out the blanket and pretreat any spots; fill the washer with warm water and dissolve the detergent in it; loosely arrange one blanket only in the machine and turn on the short (under five minutes) or gentle cycle; cold rinse;

tumble-dry on warm. The air-dry setting may also be used to reduce shrinkage.

Much of a blanket's warmth is provided by its loft (nap or fluffiness), which traps air that serves as insulation. Machine-drying will fluff up a blanket, while line-drying may make it stiff and require brushing up the nap. Straighten and smooth out the blanket over the clothesline while damp, turning it over once on the line to complete drying.

You can help reduce pilling by rotating blankets when you make the bed so that the same part isn't always snuggled against you.

Bleach

A whole battery of bleaches are available for household use. Listed from strongest to weakest, they are:

Chlorine bleach: Liquid sodium hypochlorite bleach, such as Clorox or Purex. A potent bleach and powerful oxidizer, useful in the laundry to whiten and remove spots from whites and colorfast fabrics. Can weaken and cause permanent color loss in fabrics and damage metals and other household surfaces if mixed too strong. Never use on silk, wool, spandex, fiberglass, or on permanent press or flame-retardant fabrics treated with resins. Always pretest for color change before using on any dyed fabric. Avoid breathing fumes or getting it on skin or in your eyes. Don't use straight—dilute according to label directions. Always rinse immediately after use. For removing mildew stains in showers, using chlorine bleach, see "Mildew."

▶ Try to make a cleaner meaner? Be careful! Never mix chlorine bleach with other cleaners. Doing so can create a toxic gas. This mistake has done in any number of hopeful homemakers.

Color remover: Designed to prepare fabrics for redyeing, color removers can also be effective stain removers. Very useful in removing unwanted dyes from whites that have been washed with colored items by mistake ("pink loads"). Rit Color Remover is a common one, available at drug and grocery stores. Poisonous: Always use strictly according to label directions.

Hydrogen peroxide: A mild bleach that is effective yet safe for most fabrics and surfaces. Get the 3 percent solution sold as an antiseptic, not the stronger solution used for bleaching hair. Don't buy too much, as it loses strength when stored for long periods.

Oxygen bleaches: Oxygen or "all-fabric" bleaches, such as Clorox II and Snowy, can be used to brighten and remove stains from all colorfast fabrics. They can be used in the washing machine or mixed with water to form a paste for spot bleaching.

Ammonia, lemon juice, white vinegar, and good old sunlight: Mild bleaches that are useful in many stain-removal procedures.

Blenders

Always clean and dry the cutting assembly and container immediately after use. Follow the directions included with your blender; some parts are dishwasher safe (top rack), others are not. Don't take a chance!

A shortcut here is to fill the container halfway with water and add a drop of dish detergent; run on low speed for thirty seconds to several minutes, depending on the mess. A bottle brush comes in handy to clean the blade area and any stubborn clingons. Rinse thoroughly and dry. Or you may want to take the unit apart and wash the pieces separately. Just be careful not to use abrasive scouring pads or cleansers, which can damage plastic and metal parts. The cutting assembly should be washed in hot sudsy water (don't soak!), rinsed thoroughly, and dried. You can finish up by spin-drying it at high speed for ten to fifteen seconds on the machine.

Cleaning the base: Never immerse it—unplug and wipe with an all-purpose cleaner, being careful not to get the inside wet. To clean around buttons and knobs, use a cotton swab dipped in cleaner.

Blinds

No wonder we hate to clean blinds. Hanging right against the least insulated place in the house (the windows) as they do, all those separate little surfaces are the perfect settling place for airborne dirt and grease. Dusting or vacuuming them in place is possible and should be done at least once a month. Then the dust that collects here won't have a chance to be cemented on by cooking vapors and shower steam. For dusting, use a lambswool duster or Masslinn or other dust-collecting cloth (see "Dusting"), and for vacuuming, a dust or upholstery brush. Close the blinds all the way up flat and dust the front, then reverse them, close them in the opposite direction, and dust the other side.

For real degriming and defingerprinting, however, when blinds finally need to be washed, forget trying to do it in place. It won't do a thorough job, it stresses the blinds, and it takes forever. And don't try to wash them in the sink or bathtub either. It's too slow and messy. After thirty years of experimenting with methods, I've found the fastest and best way to do it is as follows:

1. Take the blind down and find a slanted surface, outside if possible, and lay an old blanket, quilt, rug, or dropcloth on it.
2. Let the blind out all the way and make sure all the louvers are flat.
3. Lay the blind on the padding, and mix up a bucket of all-purpose cleaner or ammonia solution.
4. Scrub with a soft brush parallel to the slats, and be sure to get back under the ribbons. Then turn the blind over and do the other side. Use a little powdered (bleaching) cleanser on the ribbons if they aren't coming clean. The cushioning cloth will be soapy by now and help clean the blind, plus protect it from being scratched or dented.
5. Hold the blind up or hang it on a ladder or clothesline and rinse it with a hose.
6. Shake it to get all the water off you can, then let it air-dry the rest of the way and rehang.

If you have dark-colored blinds and

Tricket with sponges

Tricket with squeegees

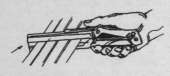

The neatest way to wash vertical blinds—or louvered windows—is with a little tongslike device called a Tricket, available at janitorial supply stores.

live in a hard-water area, rinsing with a hose will leave spots. You'll have to either use softened water to rinse or blot your blinds dry.

Cloth-covered blinds: Try to get by with just vacuuming or dusting them. Don't use any kind of treated dust cloth on them, though. If you must do more than that, wipe them occasionally with a cloth dampened with carpet shampoo solution.

Vertical blinds: The neatest way to clean these is with a little tongslike device called a Tricket (see illustration). This makes short work of cleaning blinds because you can

wash, then squeegee dry, both sides at once.

If you'd like your blinds to look like new—cords, slats, ladders, and all—without all this effort, look in the Yellow Pages under "Blinds Cleaning" for someone who does ultrasonic cleaning. It's expensive but effective, a chance to start all over with a clean slat!

Mini blinds: Can be cleaned by all of the methods described above; they just need to be handled a little more gently because they're more fragile and breakable.

For woven wood blinds, see "Shades and Roll-up Blinds."

Blocking

Blocking literally means "to make something square." You block freshly washed lace or doilies or the like while they're still wet so they will dry straight or in the exact shape you want. Things being blocked are often starched first (see "Starch"; "Doilies") and then rolled in a towel to remove excess water. Then you smooth them out by hand and use rustproof (stainless-steel) straight pins to pin them to a stiff piece of cardboard (free of dye or coloring) or a clean towel or sheet spread out on the carpet or bed. A piece of the wallboard known as Celotex works even better.

The term *blocking* is also used for the process of returning something, such as a hat or piece of needlework, to its proper/original shape. This is usually done by relaxing the fibers with steam and then pressing or stretching the item back into shape.

Blot

Blot is a word we often see in instructions for removing stains and cleaning up liquid messes. In stain removal, *blot* means something very specific. Put a clean absorbent pad of cloth on the stained side of the fabric if possible. Then, using another clean cloth pad or sponge, blot the stain-removing agent through the fabric from the back side and into the absorbent pad.

Liquid spills on absorbent surfaces should always be blotted first to remove all the liquid possible before applying any kind of cleaning chemical. The reason we blot (gently) instead of rubbing or scrubbing (vigorously) is to avoid spreading the mess around and to avoid doing damage to delicate fibers. When instructions say blot, *believe it*—the process may take a little longer, but it keeps small stains from becoming big ones.

Bluing

Bluing is a blue dye or pigment added to wash or rinse water by our mothers and grandmothers to give a bluish tint to white fabrics (and offset the tendency of white fabrics to yellow with repeated use and laundering). Blue-white, in case you're wondering, is generally considered more appealing and clean-looking than yellow-white. (See "Yellowing.") Textile and laundry detergent manufacturers now incorporate fluorescent dyes and optical brighteners into their products to achieve the same result.

Bone/Ivory

Plastic has replaced bone in most uses—I'll bet most of the stuff you think is bone is plastic made to imitate it.

If you do have real bone, bear in mind that it may have a hard reputation, but it's actually fairly soft, so go easy on it. Use a mild soap such as Ivory Snow to clean your ivory and bone. Mix up a solution and apply it with a soft cloth and blot and polish dry with another soft cloth. If you have to scrub, do it gently with the grain, using a soft-bristled brush (stiff bristles can scratch) or a white nylon-backed scrub sponge. Don't use baking soda, strong alkaline cleaners (including ammonia), or acids on bone—they can damage it. Never soak or boil bone-handled utensils or put them in a dishwasher, as the heat and moisture can melt or dissolve the glue holding on the handle.

If you wipe off the handle of your bone hunting knife right after you're finished with it, it may never need cleaning!

Bone Scrapers. See "Scrapers."

Bonnet System of Carpet Cleaning. See "Carpet Cleaning—Surface."

Books

Books shouldn't be a problem, since almost everyone we know has an opinion on what to do with dirty books! Admittedly many books these days are almost disposables, with paper covers and weak bindings and flimsy pages. But we all have our own nice little library and what should we do for it, besides keep it away from bathtubs and eating areas? Dust it, for starters. Books seem to have a special attraction for dust. Accumulated dust not only makes it all too clear how long it's been since we cracked any of those impressive volumes, it speeds the deterioration of books and bindings. To dust, use a good dust cloth, such as the New Pig Dust Cloth (see "Dustcloths")—here you don't want any kind of treated cloth—or a vacuum with a dust brush attachment. You can vacuum the books as they stand, right on the shelf, and use a crevice tool (see "Vacuums") for tight spots. If you use a cloth, make your strokes from the spine outward or away from the spine, so you aren't shoving dust into the binding. To get a particular book out to give it a more thorough going over, slide it out, don't tuck your finger into the top of the binding and pull; doing so weakens the binding.

To dust the shelf itself without removing everything, grab three or four books at once and tip them forward and with the other hand whisk over the shelf underneath. Let them fall back in place and do three more. Lining up your books flush with the very edge of the shelf will eliminate that tiny ledge that collects dust so efficiently.

For cleaning stains on cloth covers, wipe a mild liquid carpet cleaner over the stain and a little beyond to avoid a ring. (Experiment first on an unobstrusive spot on the cover.) Rinse with a lightly dampened cloth. Grease stains on pages can usually be removed with K2r. The page the baby rumpled can be restored to at least a semblance of its former self by ironing, preferably with a steam iron. Put a piece of paper down over the page first for protection.

For mildewed book covers, try wiping with a cloth dampened in disinfectant cleaner; if mildew has affected the whole book, dispose of it or put it in quarantine, or it could damage your entire collection. To prevent mildew in the first place, get your books out of those boxes in the dark, damp basement or garage and store them in dry, cool places.

Leather bindings should be conditioned from time to time with saddle soap or a mixture of half lanolin (soften it in a double boiler) and half neat's-foot oil. Apply it sparingly with a small piece of soft clean cloth, being very careful to stay away from the endleaves and the pages.

Boots. See "Shoes/Boots."

Borax

Borax is a naturally-occurring mildly alkaline salt (sodium borate) used in laundry products as a preservative, and as a mild deodorizer. The white crystals of borax are used in small amounts in some laundry detergents, or can be added to a washload to boost cleaning power. Borax helps keep the dishwasher alkaline enough to clean well and aids in loosening soils and stains. Borax is also incorporated into many diaper presoak products because it helps neutralize the ammonia odor of urine.

Bottles/Vases

Don't laugh! Do you know how many people get fingers stuck trying to clean inside bottles? Dishwasher-safe bottles can go in the dishwasher, and all bottles, even quality decorator ones, can be cleaned in a sinkful of hot water and dish detergent if you're careful. You can push your scrub sponge or dishcloth inside wide-mouth jars or bottles to loosen clinging dirt, even shake it around in there.

For skinny-necked bottles or vases with dirty insides or bottoms, you have a few choices:

1. Fill the bottle one-third full of soapy water, add a handful of un-cooked rice, and shake like crazy. The rice acts as tiny scrub brushes (sand will work too, if you happen to have a beach handy). In sturdy and expendable bottles you can even use small steel shot.
2. Reach in there with a bottle brush—there are at least a thousand styles! If you have lots of certain kinds of bottles to clean, a quality bottle brush is a lifesaver. If you can't find the perfect one, drop down to a janitorial supply store and ask to look through a brush supply catalog. It'll be worth a special order. Buy two or three while you're at it because they wear out and get borrowed!
3. Mineral film or buildup on bottles can be removed with phosphoric acid cleaner. (See "Phosphoric Acid.") Glued-on grease or grime

can be coaxed off with acetone or lacquer thinner.
4. Extra-cruddy containers can be filled to the top with ammonia wa-ter or heavy-duty cleaner solution and left to soak overnight. If you have a really stubborn stain or deposit on or in there, as long as this isn't a bottle or vase with delicate painted or metallic overlay decoration (just glass!), you can soak it in a solution of automatic dishwasher detergent and water, using 1 tablespoon detergent for every cup of water. (If it looks like it might not be worth it, you have an entirely respectable way out— recycle!)

Always rinse bottles well after cleaning.

Bowl Caddy. See "Toilet Bowl Caddy."

Brass

Brass is an alloy of copper and zinc that polishes to a high shine, so it's easy to see why it's been used for so many decorative items over the ages. It tends to tarnish quickly when exposed to air, and is often given a clear coating of lacquer to prevent this. Lacquered brass should be gently washed with a mild detergent solu-tion, to avoid damaging the lacquer coating. Never use metal polishes or steel wool on it. When the lacquer gets chipped or scratched, the metal underneath will tarnish. Eventually the lacquer will have to be stripped off and the piece relacquered. Tung oil (see "Tung Oil") will also protect brass from tarnishing, and it doesn't turn dark and is easier to remove than lacquer. Car wax helps too, but doesn't last as long as tung oil.

Unlacquered brass can be left "antique," with its distinctive greenish-brown patina of tarnish intact, or it can be polished to a high shine. To polish solid brass, use a cream brass polish or one of the convenient polish-in-a-rope products such as Met-Pol or Nevr-Dull. These polishes coat the brass with a thin film of oil to help retard future tarnishing. For *plated* brass, avoid the more abrasive cream polishes as they will eventually wear through the plating and expose the metal underneath. See also "Metal Polishes"; "Tarnish, Metal."

Brick

Outside brick can accumulate moss, mildew, and white mineral deposits, especially in damp climates. Mineral deposits alone can be cleaned off with a rented pressure washer or phosphoric acid. (See "Phosphoric Acid.") But inside brick, especially hearths and fireplaces, really gets bad.

Remember, brick is porous, and what's on it is also often in it—penetrated and stained into the masonry—so don't jump off the brick wall you're trying to brighten if it doesn't come clean instantly or at all. Remember, those stains built up on the brick for years—they aren't going to pop right off. If takes time, patience, even ingenuity. First, vacuum the brick to remove any bug carcasses, soot, sand, dust, then dry-sponge it. (See "Dry Sponges.") This will remove surface grime that would otherwise sink in when you start ap-

plying any solution. The cleaner the brick is before you actually begin to wash it, the better. Once you have the loose stuff off, thoroughly protect the surrounding floors and walls. You're going to have an Amazon River of dirty runoff water, so if it's a wall you're cleaning, for instance, roll terry-cloth towels into tubes and lay them against the bottom of the wall to catch the water. Then mix a solution of degreaser or strong alkaline cleaner and apply it with a stiff brush or a sprayer such as a weed sprayer. Let the solution sit on there for ten or fifteen minutes. If it soaks all the way into the surface during that time, rewet it, because chemical penetration is the only way to attack dirt deep in the pores of masonry. Then scrub in all four directions: north/south, east/west. You'll see the grime coming off, and when it looks clean flood the area with clear water. If all the dirt isn't off repeat the process; if it doesn't come off in two attempts it probably won't.

If you have a mark or stain that won't budge, let it dry, then use some solvent (dry-cleaning fluid or paint thinner) on it. Just be sure to give it a chance to penetrate the stone. If that doesn't work, try a poultice. (See "Poultice.") A wire brush or sandpaper will remove some tough stains too. You can also try using chlorine bleach in your cleaning solution—this may lighten the stain by oxidizing it. Be careful about adding bleach with other chemicals; read the labels of both products first to be sure you won't end up with a dangerous chemical reaction. Phosphoric acid or a shower wall cleaner such as

Tilex or any good tub and tile cleaner may also work well for this. Don't use these products with bleach, and be sure to use a stiff-bristle brush when you use them. Sandblasting brick is a last-ditch measure best employed by a professional. Bear in mind that sandblasting will leave a rough and even more porous surface, and if it is not done carefully, it can eat away the mortar badly.

Once it's cleaned, you may want to seal your brick with masonry sealer. (See "Sealing.") It forms an impenetrable barrier that keeps dirt out and makes the surface much easier to clean.

If you have brick that's all stained or whitened and soiled, you can also paint it with semigloss or eggshell enamel. Painted brick looks great and lasts well, and can just be washed to clean it.

Brocade

Brocade is a rich fabric with elaborate raised woven designs of figures and flowers and the like, and sometimes metallic threads, usually on a satin or twill background. Brocade used to be exclusively silk, but it is now made in a wide range of natural and synthetic fibers, in many weights, for apparel and furnishings. Some durable brocades are washable, but most should be dry-cleaned by a knowledgeable professional. Always iron brocade on the wrong side, on a padded surface such as a terry towel.

Cleaning brocade upholstery is also best left to a pro. If you do decide to tackle it yourself, be sure to test the shampoo you intend to use a day ahead, so your test patch has a chance to dry. A foam-type shampoo is best, applied very gently by wiping and dabbing; vigorous scrubbing can loosen and distort the weave. Then dry gently by blotting with clean terry towels.

Bronze

When copper is alloyed with metals other than zinc (see "Brass"), it is called *bronze*. Bronze is usually a mixture of copper with tin or manganese, used for artwork and other decorative items. Bronze is more resistant to corrosion than brass, and it too forms a protective greenish-brown patina on the surface, which is often left on artwork and hand-rubbed to heighten the effect. If a bright finish is desired, bronze can be polished with brass polish and lacquered as described for brass. See also "Metal Polishes"; "Tarnish, Metal."

Brooms

Brooms have a long and honorable history of helping us to clean, but there are now better ways of accomplishing much of what they used to do. Large expanses of smooth flooring, for example, can be "swept" much faster and more effectively with a treated dust mop. Brooms are still great for fast spot cleanup and for small areas of hard flooring—and for large rough-surfaced areas such as sidewalks and unsealed garage floors. Brooms are also a good quick way to clean the edges of carpeted floors and stairs.

When you do use a broom, be sure

Push broom with handle brace

Angle broom

to use the right kind. For concrete and other textured surfaces or floors with a lot of heavy debris, you want hard stiff bristles of plastic, nylon, or bassine. These coarse bristles can handle leaves, gravel, sand, sawdust, and snow as well as ordinary old dirt. If you have walkways, driveways, or rough cement floors to keep clean, you should own an 18- or 24-inch push broom with synthetic bristles and a brace to keep the handle from breaking.

For smooth indoor flooring you want bristles that will leave behind as little fine dust as possible. This is where the old straw or corn brooms fall short. They not only shed all over, they won't get all the fine stuff. Far better are the modern angle brooms. They not only have split-tip nylon bristles that will last a long time and pick up much more effectively but the angled head reaches into corners better. And when we hold them in our natural (angled) sweeping posi-

tion, the whole head—not just part of it—is in contact with the floor. Just be sure to store plastic bristle brooms hanging up, not standing on the bristles, or you'll give them a permanent wave.

Horsehair brooms are still around,

▶ **Brushes:** Toothbrushes to tank brushes, 99 percent of brushes aren't cleaned properly (or at all) when we're finished with them. A lot of crud is scrubbed loose during cleaning. If we leave it all on there, it simply sets up as it dries or nestles down at the roots of the bristles. Take a minute to rinse your brushes vigorously before you put them away and work them over occasionally with a stiff comb or hair pick to remove all the lint at the base of the bristles. Always hang brushes face-down so any clinging moisture will run off the tips instead of into the base. See also "Hairbrushes."

and their fine bristles do a good job, but their expense and the coddling they require has pretty much made them a specialty item.

Brooms are inexpensive, so keep one in every often-swept location: garage, porch, basement, upstairs.

Buckets

Bigger buckets don't mean better work, but better buckets do. For starters, quit using old ice cream pails and blacktop or roof paint containers—the former were designed for a frozen solid load; full of liquid, they'll cave in and spill. And the latter will rust and be impossible to carry full. I know those 5-gallon plastic pickle buckets are free, but they are too big for household use. A 10-quart bucket is the best all-around size for household use. A bigger bucket is okay if filled only two-thirds full, but we can never resist filling it and then we get bulged-out eyes trying to carry or dump it. Plastic gives a good (nonrusting, nonscratching, undentable) bucket for a low price, so why not buy a good sturdy one, such as the Rubbermaid Roughneck? Professionals prefer square or rectangular to round because square is more stable and fits on ladder platforms and the like better. There are even diamond-shaped buckets now, designed to overcome the old problem of how to fit a sponge mop or window-washing wand into a normal-size bucket. They're also easier to pour neatly and more comfortable to carry. Your local janitorial supply store will have a nice selection of all kinds. If a bucket has

Square buckets are harder to tip than round ones!

A diamond-shaped bucket designed to accommodate sponge mops and window-washing equipment.

a handhold on the bottom for dumping and a padded grip on the handle, so much the better. I like bright colors because they serve as a safety cone so buckets get tipped over less. The only place I use the old metal galvanized buckets now is on exterior work. They don't deform under heavy loads and the handles won't pull out.

As for two-compartment buckets, these could put you in a rubber room. Ever tried to empty one side without spilling the other? They're great for carrying garden vegetables and fencing tools, but forget about using them to clean with.

Buff

To buff means to polish or shine by rubbing. We do a lot of buffing in the course of cleaning. When we polish our shoes or brass buttons, we do the real shining up right at the end as we buff with a brush or a soft cloth. We take our car in to have the paint buffed or polished with an abrasive polishing compound and a buffing wheel. Even the final licks we give to glass, mirrors, and chrome as we dry them could be called buffing. Custodians and homemakers alike have used floor polishers for years to buff and shine various types of floor polishes. In fact, most professionals still call their floor polishing machines buffers. For years floors were waxed with natural carnauba waxes, which were buffed with lambswool or fine steel wool pads or with polishing brushes. Today most floor finishes are synthetic polymers and are buffed with spun nylon or polyester pads or grit-impregnated brushes. *Spray buffing* usually means misting the floor with a liquid cleaner/polisher and then buffing it dry. A fairly new concept of floor maintenance involves the high-speed buffing of thermoplastic finishes. (See "Burnish.")

Builder (in Soaps and Detergents)

A builder is a chemical that boosts the cleaning power of soaps and detergents. Builders do this by softening hard water, by supplying additional alkalinity and helping to keep alkalinity constant, by emulsifying oily soils, and by keeping soil from redepositing during the cleaning process. Until recently, the complex phosphates were the builders of choice, and they are still much used. However, concern over eutrophication (oxygen depletion caused by runaway algae growth) of lakes and rivers accelerated by phosphates has brought them under scrutiny, and some areas of the country have banned phosphates entirely. Manufacturers are searching for ways to increase the cleaning power of detergents without relying so heavily on phosphates and have voluntarily reduced the amount they now use in many laundry products. See "Detergent"; "Soap"; "Phosphates"; "Emulsify"; "Water Conditioning."

Burlap Wall Coverings.
See "Wall Coverings, Woven."

Burnish

To burnish is to make smooth or shiny by rubbing, especially with a tool. No manicure is complete, for example, without burnishing the fingernails to bring out their luster. When we hear the term in cleaning it usually has to do with the high-speed floor finishes often used in commercial buildings. Here it means to renew the finish, using a high-speed floor polisher and a synthetic buffing pad. (See "Buff.") Most high-speed floor finishes are thermoplastic. That is, the heat of friction produced by the burnishing pad softens the finish, allowing the pad to spread and smooth it, thus healing scratches and scars to produce a glistening, seamless surface. This is how supermarkets get those super-shiny wet-look floors.

Butcher Block. See "Chopping Boards or Blocks."

Butyl Cellosolve

Butyl cellosolve is an ingredient (glycol ether) commonly used in heavy-duty cleaners and degreasers. Butyl has the uncommon ability to mix readily with either water or solvents and to dissolve grease into a water

solution. Because of these special properties, butyl has long been used in commercial cleaning products, but it has come under fire recently as a possible health hazard. We now know that butyl is absorbed by the skin, and although no health risks have been established for certain, some experts feel it may prove to be injurious. Other chemicals from the same family will do the same job as butyl, but manufacturers have been slow to introduce them because of higher costs and limited acceptance by cleaning professionals. In light of the concerns over butyl, the intelligent course would be to limit exposure to it until more is known and to follow all manufacturer's safety precautions when using it.

C

Cow trails—those embarrassingly obvious traffic patterns—will quickly de-class a carpet. Cow trails can be prevented by keeping cows out of your house, and using professional door mats both inside and outside every door. (See "Mats, Walkoff.") Regular surface cleaning of your carpets (see "Carpet Cleaning—Surface") will also help.

Cabinets, Kitchen

We don't clean our kitchen cabinets enough or right because we're afraid of ruining them. You won't! Most cabinets are factory manufactured and finished, and even the wooden ones have enough varnish or other protective coating on them so that you can use a cleaning solution on them. The oil slick that builds up on cabinets (especially around the handles) is a combination of kitchen grease, food smears, skin oil, and hand lotion transferred to the door. Regular all-purpose or light cleaners just won't cut it, which is why you often have icky cabinets.

If your cabinets are plastic laminate (Formica) or other plastic, metal, painted metal, or glass, you can wash them all over with a strong alkaline cleaner, such as Soilmaster from a janitorial supply store, or a heavy-duty cleaner from the supermarket, such as Formula 409. Mix according to directions and apply the solution with a sponge. Let it sit a minute or two (most people massage the dirt instead of emulsifying it) then take a white nylon-backed sponge and scrub a little anywhere it seems necessary.

Remove the grimy suds from the sponge by squeezing it into the sink or a slop bucket, *never* back into your cleaning solution. Then rinse with a damp cloth and wipe dry with a terry cleaning cloth, which will remove any last traces of scum and leave the cupboards clean and glowing.

Never use acids or powdered cleansers on cabinets. A good overall washing of your cabinets once a year should be enough. Keeping a spray bottle of all-purpose cleaner handy the rest of the time and spot-clean after heavy kitchen use.

On *wooden* cabinets, you want to take a gentler approach. To get off the tough stuff, wash around all the handles and any other grease zones first with that gentle degreaser we all have handy—hand dishwashing detergent—then wash the entire cabinet, including the handle areas you just did, with oil soap (see "Oil Soaps") solution. Just wipe lightly with the solution, don't saturate, and buff dry immediately with a terry cleaning cloth. Always wipe dry with the grain or pattern, if there is one. Seldom do you need to add any polish because the surface has its own sheen, which will shine forth if it's clean. If your cabinets are dull from wear or age, a light, light spray of furniture polish once a year or so will fill in the pores and bring some life back.

You can clean the insides every two years because they don't get dirty. Make sure they have a good coating of protective finish and you won't need sticky paper! If you do use shelf paper, use the nonattached type that you can just pull out and replace.

Caddy, Cleaning

Also called a maid basket, a cleaning caddy is the best way to organize your supplies. These inexpensive plastic tool-carrying trays or open toolboxes are often used by gardeners and repairpeople. They keep everything you need for a particular job right at your fingertips and they're quick to grab in an emergency. They enable you to work like light infantry—travel fast, move in quick, and get out.

Take your caddy into the target area with you and work right from it. Using a caddy helps you clean without backtracking and constant trips back and forth. Just be sure to always move it with you so you don't end up running back to it (rather than the sink) for supplies! Always return each bottle or piece of equipment to the caddy the minute you're done with it. When you set things down outside

A cleaning caddy or maid basket is the best way to organize and transport your supplies.

the caddy—on a counter, table, or the floor—you have wasted motion retrieving it, trouble finding it again, and possible damage to the surface you set it on.

Keep a caddy in all the areas you clean frequently, filled with what you need to clean that area.

Calcium Carbonate

Calcium carbonate is the principal ingredient in hard-water mineral scale (lime scale). Calcium salts are dissolved out of rocks by the groundwater, then deposited on the surfaces over which the water passes. Those dramatic rock icicles (stalagmites and stalactites) in limestone caves are mostly calcium carbonate, leached out of the limestone rock. Lime scale forms very hard, crusty deposits on the inside of pipes and on plumbing fixtures, shower walls, windows sprayed by sprinklers, and the like. Acid delimers are usually called for to dissolve and remove lime scale. See "Hard-Water Deposits"; "pH in Cleaning"; "Cleaners, Acid"; "Delimer (Descaler)."

Calphalon Cookware. See "Cookware."

Camcorders. See "Videocassette Recorders and Camcorders."

Camel Hair

The fine, woollike underhair of the Bactrian camel of Asia is used to make yarns and garments. True camel hair is scarce and expensive, so consider yourself lucky to have something made of it. The fabric has a soft, silky, luxurious feeling and is most often used for suits, coats, sweaters, and sportswear. Camel hair is sometimes blended with wool for blankets and Oriental rugs. Care is the same as for woolens, following label directions. (See "Wool" under "Fabrics.")

Cameras

Camera technicians say there's one thing you can do for the *inside* of your camera—get a can of compressed air and blow the dust out of it regularly. This will prolong the life of the inner workings and help avoid scratches on your film. You'll have to remove the lens, or open the back—or both—to do this; your owner's manual will guide you here. CAUTION: Don't direct a strong blast of cleaning air directly at the mirror in your SLR or at the cloth shutter. Other than this simple blowout, leave the inside alone! Don't try to clean, oil, or fix the innards of your camera yourself; take it to an expert if it needs attention. And take it *immediately* if you've done something like drop it into a sand dune or swamp.

The outside of the camera body should be kept clean too. Lenses should be cleaned with a liquid lens cleaner and special lens tissue, not with facial tissue or paper towels. Blow the dust off the lens surface with compressed air before doing any cleaning, to avoid scratching the lens. A soft dry toothbrush is great for brushing dust and dirt out of all the little crevices and hard-to-reach places. You can damp-wipe soil off the exterior of the camera, but wring the cleaning cloth out as dry as possible and work carefully, making sure no water seeps into the cracks. Vacuum or blow out the inside of the leather case from time to time—dust and grit can accumulate here too. Store camera equipment in a cool, dry place— put a desiccant pack (moisture-absorbing chemical such as silica gel) into the case in humid climates. Clean dirty battery contacts by rubbing them with a pencil eraser. Don't leave batteries in an unused camera for long periods—they can leak and gum up the works.

Can Openers

The blade of a can opener can be one of the ickiest places in the house (rivaling the rim of the toilet in a frat house!). With all the punctures your can opener makes—from pumpkin pie filling and pet food to sardines and tomato paste—it's no wonder that little blade gets coated and cruddy in a hurry.

For sanitation's sake, clean the blade whenever it's dirty, at least twice a month in normal use. Given the myriad of openers on the market, the most all-around cleaning instructions I can give are: Unplug electrics!; be careful around that sharp blade; use a toothbrush and dish detergent solution to loosen stubborn deposits; let the solution soak on there for a while if necessary; rinse in hot water; clean the whole opener (if it's a manual) or any removable parts of an electric in the dishwasher if possible (follow manufacturer's in-

structions); dry well before replacing. Wipe electric opener housings with a damp cloth, polish dry. Note: Abrasives will scratch plastic and chrome surfaces.

Candlesticks

I could tell you in detail how to clean every single part of Candlestick Park (San Francisco's famous baseball stadium, especially after the quake), but plain old candlesticks have to rest upon your own good sense.

Try to remove wax drippings while they're still fresh and easy to remove. Be careful how you do it on shiny-finish candlesticks. If you scrape with anything, make sure it's soft plastic. To remove old stuck-on wax, hold or soak the afflicted part in hot water and lightly scrub and rinse in hotter water. Burned-down candle ends can be removed from metal holders by softening the wax in hot water first. Wooden and other watershy candlesticks can be placed in the freezer for an hour or so—the wax stubs may shrink just enough to pop right out. Otherwise, it's back to prying gently with the head of a small screwdriver. Then to keep your candlesticks festive, use the following guidelines.

Silver: Clean with a soft cloth (not a paper towel) and silver polish.

Wood: Use furniture polish. If it's trimmed with brass, be careful not to get polish on the brass.

Brass: First you need to determine if it is lacquered; generally the more expensive items are. Usually older candlesticks and any brass from India is not.

If you're unsure, wait awhile to see if it tarnishes. If so, it's unlacquered, and should be polished with a brass or metal polish such as Brasso or dip-cleaned in one of the commercial acid dip cleaners. If you're tired of polishing, you can have lacquer coating added to your uncoated brass at a lamp store (one that actually makes the lamps).

If the candlestick is lacquered, DO NOT USE METAL POLISH or it will remove the lacquer coating. To clean it, just use a soft damp cloth. If lacquer is missing or blackened in spots, remove all lacquer with metal polish and a very fine steel wool pad (grade 000). Have the candlestick recoated if desired.

To preserve and enhance the brownish patina that develops on bronze, brown boot polish is an age-old formula. If you don't want to preserve it, use regular metal polish or Ajax Liquid Cleanser.

Pewter: No longer considered just the poor man's silver, pewter is now almost more desirable because it looks good tarnished (all you have to do to clean it is wipe it with a soft cloth), yet it can be polished (with metal polish) to a brilliant sheen.

Glass/crystal: Use a glass cleaner containing ammonia, and buff with a soft cloth.

Tin: Treat the same as tarnished pewter, but be careful, because it bends easily.

Ceramic: Wipe with a cloth dipped in all-purpose cleaner solution, then wipe dry.

Cane, as Used in Woven Furniture

The woven cane we see in chair and seat backs, and wrapped around the joints on rattan chairs, is made from strips cut from the tough outer stalk of the rattan plant. Woven cane holds up fairly well in humid climates but tends to dry out and get brittle in dryer areas. To keep it moist and supple, it should be misted with water or wiped down with a damp cloth occasionally. If the piece is unfinished rattan, the whole thing will benefit from a misting. (See "Rattan and Bamboo.") Soiled cane can be wiped with a cloth dampened in neutral cleaner solution (see "Cleaners, Neutral") and scrubbed with a soft brush if needed. Sagging cane seats can be tightened by soaking them with hot water and drying in the sun. If the cane is attached to lacquered or varnished wood, however, be careful not

to soak the finished wood parts. Varnished or painted cane seats shouldn't be soaked—just damp-wiped.

Moisture is often good for cane, but be careful about getting look-alike types of woven seat materials wet. Some seats are made from fiber rush, which is actually just kraft paper twisted into tight cords to look like natural rush. It will unravel if soaked with water, but if it's been sealed with paint or varnish it can be damp-wiped. Twisted cords of sea grass or Hong Kong grass are also used to weave seats, and likewise tend to unravel when wet. Sea grasses should be treated like fiber rush. For care of rattan and bamboo furniture, see "Rattan and Bamboo." For woven furniture, see "Wicker."

Canvas

This coarse, heavy cotton material is used for beach hats, tents, and chair seats, and it serves well whether crisp and new or covered with who-knows-what. Canvas is a tough fabric made for hard use, not to keep sparkling clean. (Which is fortunate, since it doesn't always yield up its dirt easily.) Water won't harm canvas unless it's been molded with a water-soluble stiffener such as sizing or starch. Certain hats and decorative wall hangings are made like this; if they get wet, they will lose their shape. On something like this test a very small portion before proceeding so you can see the result of the moisture. Many of the smaller canvas creations such as tote bags can be cleaned in the washing machine. Be sure to pretreat any spots first, and

reapply soil retardant such as Scotch-gard after washing. The biggest problem with canvas is mildewing when put away damp—be sure it's dry!

To clean large expanses of canvas such as *tents,* mix up a warm solution of all-purpose cleaner. Dip a scrub brush with short, stiff bristles into it and work over the surface. If the canvas has been treated for water repellency, the dirt you're loosening now should come off easily. If the canvas is untreated, removing the dirt and stains will take more wetting and brushing.

If you find yourself with a mildewed canvas tent, set it up and scrub the exterior with a disinfectant cleaner solution. This should kill the mildew and resolve the problem except in the most extreme cases. Don't scrub the inside of the tent because this will affect its water repellency (leading to a wet bed in the forest).

Canvas can be rinsed with a hose and allowed to dry in the sun or on a line.

Caps. See "Hats and Caps."

Carbon Tet

Carbon tetrachloride is a colorless, nonflammable solvent formerly used extensively in dry-cleaning and spot removal. It is not used anymore because it's highly poisonous and has an unpleasant aroma reminiscent of chloroform. If you still have an old bottle of carbon tet kicking around, get rid of it (check with your local EPA for the safest way to do so) and get a can of Energine or Carbona or one of the newer, safer dry-cleaning solvents.

Care Symbols, International

Like the silhouette of a leaping deer that warns us of what might bolt across the road in front of us, symbols are an attempt to get the message across faster and more memorably than words. Symbols can break the language barrier too. The International Care Symbols (see illustration p. 204) were developed to perform these worthy services for the often confusing business of caring for the fabrics and garments we buy.

If you don't often see them on those little care tags attached to your clothes, it's because American law requires manufacturers to give care instructions in words, and they may or may not include the symbols as well.

The care symbols are used widely abroad, including by many of the countries we import textile products from, so they're worth knowing. There are some variations from country to country, but the five basic symbols and what they mean are shown on page 204. A slash through a symbol means NEVER do this, and red/amber/or green dots on a care label (just as in stoplights) mean No, stop!/Proceed with caution/Go!

Carpet

Carpet has been available over the years in a variety of natural and synthetic fibers. While a certain amount of wool, Acrilan, and polypropylene is

► Pro cleaners stranded on a desert island (or in an ordinary dirty house) would have plenty of the universal solvent, water. What would they want beyond that?

My TEN Favorite Cleaning Tools

It was a tough choice, but here are the ten cleaning tools I wouldn't be without. The following assumes you use good professional cleaning chemicals as I've described throughout this book and good safety equipment when you need it. You'll find all of these described under individual entries.

Bucket
Cleaning caddy
Cleaning cloth
Extension handle
Lambswool duster
Professional trigger-spray bottle
Scrubbee Doo, long-handled floor scrubber
Squeegee
Utility brush
White nylon-backed scrub sponge

still used, nylon has emerged as the fiber of choice. It resists abrasion and crushing well, is mothproof and mildew resistant, keeps its appearance over a long life span, and is easily cleaned. Nylon fiber has gone through several stages of improvement, with each generation of fiber having a distinct advantage over the previous one. Among the latest improvements is stain-resist nylon, in which the dye sites used to color the fiber are sealed against further color intrusion, making the fiber much more resistant to staining after installation. The stain-resist fibers even repel red

Kool-Aid and other stubborn food and cosmetics stains, which were all but impossible to remove from earlier nylons. The smart choice in carpeting today is one of the stain-resist nylons in a medium shade, with texture, sculpting, a tweedy design, or slight variations in hue that hides soiling and wear patterns.

Carpet Care Basics

Most carpeting uglies out before it wears out—it ends up being replaced because of unsightly "cow trails" and stains. Much of this damage could be prevented with an effective carpet maintenance program.

Vacuuming is the key to carpet maintenance. Carpeting can hide a lot of dry soil, and if not removed regularly by vacuuming these little particles of grit will grind and abrade the carpet in traffic areas, and cut and crush the fibers, leading to prematurely worn areas in otherwise good carpet. Regular vacuuming will do more to extend the life of carpeting than anything else. See "Vacuums," "Vacuum Care," and "Vacuuming" for advice on choosing the right machine and getting the most out of it.

Spots and spills happen all the time, and most are not too hard to remove if you get to them right away. Left to set and oxidize, many harmless spots can develop into permanent stains. Quick attention is the secret. For information on removing spots and spills, see "Spot and Stain Removal."

Airborne oily soils, such as environmental pollutants and cooking grease, bond tightly to carpet fibers and cannot be removed by vacuuming. These in turn attract and hold dry soils, and eventually demand some kind of deep cleaning.

Carpet Maintenance Program

A typical carpet maintenance program would go something like this:

Vacuum: Every day or every other day in traffic areas, with special attention in high-soil locations such as entrances, hallways, and major walkways; once a week in nontraffic areas; once or twice a month for corners and edges.

Spot clean: The minute it happens, to keep innocent spots from developing into nasty stains—especially true for pet indiscretions.

Surface clean: Once a month or so as needed to remove surface soil and keep dirty traffic patterns from appearing. (See "Carpet Cleaning—Surface.")

Deep clean: Once a year or so, to clean carpeting all the way down to the roots and remove detergent residues left by surface cleaning. Deep cleaning is usually called for when surface cleaning no longer makes the carpet look good or when the carpet seems to resoil quickly afterward. (See "Carpet Cleaning—Deep.")

Apply soil retardant: After deep cleaning, to keep soil, spots, and spills from penetrating the fibers and to make cleaning easier.

Since carpeting hides soil so well, it's easy to ignore problems until it's too late. Take the time to care for the carpeting in your home the way they do in commercial buildings, and it will look a lot better and last a lot longer.

Carpet Cleaning—Deep

Whether you surface-clean your carpet or not (see "Carpet Cleaning—Surface"), the time eventually comes when it needs deep cleaning. This can be done with a variety of methods, including rotary shampooing, hot water extraction (so-called steam cleaning), and dry (absorbent compound) cleaning. Each has its pros and cons.

Shampooing: Long one of the most common ways of deep cleaning carpet. A rotary floor polisher with a dispensing tank feeds shampoo solution onto a nylon brush that scrubs the carpet clean. The dirt-laden foam is then vacuumed up wet or allowed to dry to a powder and vacuumed out. Probably the best of all the methods at dislodging stubborn soil, shampooing has several drawbacks: There's a very good chance of overwetting the carpet, this method doesn't really provide a good way of removing the dislodged soil, the carpet takes a long time to dry, and a lot of detergent residue is left in the carpet.

Hot water extraction: Often improperly called steam cleaning, this method sprays a jet of hot cleaning solution into the carpeting under high pressure and immediately sucks it back out with a powerful vacuum. The most effective extraction units are the truck-mounted type, which generate higher water temperature and pressure and stronger suction than the portable units. Extraction does an excellent job of removing loose soil (even from deep in the carpet) but isn't as good at actually dislodging stubborn soil as is shampooing. The

absence of any kind of mechanical agitation and the short time the solution is on the fibers ("dwell time") are the limitations here. One way of overcoming the dwell-time drawback is by prespraying heavily soiled areas ten minutes ahead of the extractor so the chemical can be working on the soil for a while before the vacuum removes it.

Absorbent compound cleaning: Usually involves an absorbent powder that is impregnated with solvents and detergents. The compound is spread on the carpet, brushed or agitated either by hand or with a machine, and then left to dry. The solvents and detergents soften and emulsify the soil, which is then absorbed by the compound. After it dries, the dirt-laden compound is vacuumed up. Absorbents have the advantage of no water being used, quick drying time, and no waiting to put the carpet back in service. This process is generally more time-consuming and expensive than wet cleaning, and it is sometimes hard to get all the compound back out of the carpet. Absorbent cleaning is best used on carpets where using water or having the carpet out of service would be a problem.

Combination systems: Probably the best deep cleaning is done using a combination of shampooing and extraction. Some professional carpet cleaners, for example, shampoo traffic and heavily soiled areas first and then extract the entire carpet. Some extractors have built-in agitation heads that brush the pile in between the injection of the water and vacuurning it back out. Such methods take advantage of the best features of both systems.

Do it yourself or hire a professional?: By the time you rent the equipment and buy the cleaning solution, haul it all home and spend a whole weekend cleaning your carpets, you'll probably wish you had hired a pro. Not only do pros have better, higher-powered equipment, they also have the technical knowledge needed to prevent damage to carpet and furnishings and to do the job right. Having the necessary chemicals and expertise to pretreat troublesome spots and spills before you start, for example, can mean the difference between spots that come out and those that become permanent stains.

Carpet Cleaning— Surface

Why do the carpets we see in certain banks, offices, and other business buildings look crisp and new, showroom sharp, almost all the time?

Not just because they're vacuumed regularly and shampooed occasionally, important as those practices might be. The pro cleaners who clean these places perform an extra little step called surface cleaning, and it can keep your carpets looking newly installed month after month, all year round. And prevent those tacky, ugly cow trails (all-too-obvious dirty traffic patterns) from developing. Surface cleaning will delay the need to shampoo and lengthen the life of carpeting too.

You can surface-clean your carpets several ways:

1. With the inexpensive **do-it-yourself extractors** now available to homeowners from Bissel and other manufacturers. These units don't have the high-injection pressure and powerful suction required to truly deep-clean carpeting but are handy for picking up liquid spills and keeping traffic lanes touched up. Investing in one of these home carpet cleaners or a bonnet outfit, as described below, will pay big dividends in terms of the appearance of your soft floors.

2. With a **dry carpet cleaner** such as the Host, Capture, Sears, or Amway dry-cleaning systems. You apply the powder by hand or a special machine designed to scrub it in and then vacuum it up afterward.

3. By the **bonnet system**, whereby a yarn pad or disc called a *spin bonnet* is wetted with a special cleaning solution and attached to a floor machine that massages it into the carpet. You can also bonnet by hand with a moplike cotton applicator or simply a towel wet with the solution. Hand bonneting is okay for small areas but a lot of work for large ones. This method, like all surface cleaning, does not deep clean, and a certain amount of soil and detergent residue is left in the carpet. To minimize detergent residue buildup you should use a bonnet cleaning solution that contains mostly solvents and dries to a vacuumable powder. Argosheen or CMA's Carpet Pre-treat

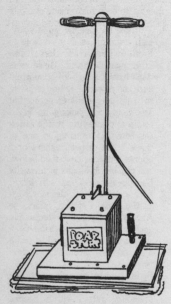

A floor machine of the type used for bonneting.

61 are both good ones. You also need a 12-to-15-inch regular-speed rotary floor polisher and at least one yarn spin bonnet, all of which can be found at a janitorial supply store. Small floor polishers can also often be found second-hand or at auctions for a reasonable price.

4. **Orbital cleaning:** Done with heavy towels and a special machine that vibrates them on the carpet. Orbital machines are quite expensive and don't cover the

ground as quickly as the rotary floor polisher used for bonneting.

Surface cleaning should be done about once a month. If you use an extractor or one of the dry-cleaning systems, follow the manufacturer's instructions. If you decide to use a mop or the orbital equipment, just substitute the word *mop* or *towel* for *bonnet*:

• Mix enough cleaning solution to cover the area you want to clean, and put it in a garden sprayer or spray bottle.
• Wet the spin bonnet and wring it out as dry as possible.
• Spray the cleaning solution onto an approximately 10-foot by 10-foot area of carpeting.
• Run the bonnet over the wetted area with the machine, using even, overlapping strokes.
• Turn the bonnet over when it's dirty. When both sides are soiled, replace it with a clean bonnet, or rinse it out and reuse it.
• Launder soiled bonnets while still wet, before accumulated soil can harden.
• After the surface is dry run over the whole carpet quickly with a vacuum to restore the nap.

Carpet Shampooing. See "Carpet Cleaning—Deep."

Carpet Sweepers

Carpet sweepers are the nonelectric, light hand units such as the Hoky that have one or two brushes powered by the simple turning of the wheels when you push them along. They're fine for surface litter and quick cleanup—for spilled popcorn or corn-flake pickup, living room straightening, fast cosmetic surgery before company comes, and the like. A couple of quick passes and it's up and off the carpet. But since they have neither suction nor a beater bar (see "Vacuums"), carpet sweepers won't pick up fine dust or anything that's down inside the carpet. Constant cleaning with carpet sweepers will leave your carpet impacted with dust and dirt. They make things look good for a while, but you can't use them for the deep cleaning that all carpet needs to have done regularly.

Convenience is their single greatest asset—the fact that they aren't heavy and cumbersome to haul out and you don't have to plug them in often means things get cleaned up faster. Restaurants use them (and you can too) where they need to clean quietly, and they're great for RVs and wilderness retreats with no electricity.

A lot of people now use cordless vacs where they used to use carpet sweepers.

Cart, Cleaning

You've all seen and maybe long envied those well-equipped maid or janitor carts at the motel or the hospital. I've seen you eyeing them as they're wheeled by, checking out what's on there and thinking, Boy wouldn't that make my cleaning a cinch. Well, it won't—unless you live in a giant uncarpeted place with no stairs. It's not easy to roll one from bedroom to basement without a service elevator. And most homes don't have enough

large stretches of continuous uniform flooring to even make using one possible. Forget the cart concept and get yourself a cleaning caddy. (see "Caddy, Cleaning.")

Cashmere

Originally, cashmere meant yarns spun from the fine, downy undercoat of the cashmere goat (from the Kashmir province of India and vicinity). These days, the term refers to any number of soft woolen materials containing camel hair and other fibers. Care for sweaters and other articles made of cashmerelike woolens as you would any fine woolen. Always follow care label directions, and be very gentle. (See "Wool" under "Fabrics.")

Cast Iron

Cast iron is a brittle alloy of iron that is cast in molds to form cookware and plumbing fixtures, among other things. It withstands and conducts heat well without warping, but has to be cast quite thick and heavy so it won't break easily. (You know about the heavy part if you've ever packed a dutch oven anywhere.) Cast-iron sinks, bathtubs, lavatories, and the like coated with porcelain are among the most durable of plumbing fixtures. These should be cleaned as described under "Porcelain."

About the only uncoated cast iron we ordinarily deal with is in cookware. Cast-iron skillets, griddles, and dutch ovens will rust if not protected, and should be seasoned with oil or fat according to the manufacturer's directions. After that, don't scour or wash them with detergent as this will remove the seasoning. Mild soap can be used, but most folks prefer to just wipe their cast iron out with hot water, scrubbing any stubborn soil away with a plastic scrub pad. Boiling a little water in the pot with a lid on will loosen hardened food. Wipe dry and apply a light coating of vegetable oil to keep it seasoned and protected. If a cast-iron pot gets rusty or has burned-on food that won't come off, it can be scoured (with a pumice stick or steel wool) and then reseasoned. Don't store food in cast-iron utensils, and avoid using them for acid foods such as tomatoes and vinegar.

Cast iron is also used for such things as burner grates on gas stoves, wood-burning stove parts, and fireplace grates and grilles. These items may be either coated with enamel or other vitreous material (see "Enameled Metals") or left raw, but in either case they don't require any special seasoning or care. Decorative cast iron should be vacuumed or dusted with a Masslinn cloth (see "Dustcloths.") Don't use moisture on it unless absolutely necessary. If the surface rusts after washing, work it over with an oil-based furniture polish on a soft cloth, then buff with a dry cloth. If it looks streaky, reapply oil until a uniform surface is achieved. This will give it a nice patina and prevent future rusting. Old cast-iron banks and toys can be brightened up by applying a light coat of paste wax and then buffing.

Caustic

Anything corrosive, or capable of destroying or eating away organic material or living tissue by chemical action, is caustic. In the cleaning industry, and especially in soap and detergent formulation, caustic always refers to a strong alkali, such as lye. Caustic soda (sodium hydroxide) and caustic potash (potassium hydroxide) are the alkalies most often combined with animal or vegetable fat in the manufacture of soap. Our ancestors obtained lye for soap-making by leaching it out of wood ashes with water. Strong caustics, such as those in oven and drain cleaners, must be used with great care because of the severe skin burns they can cause. See "Lye."

CDs. See "Compact Discs."

Ceilings

Fortunately ceilings don't get the same abuse the walls and floors do. In the bedroom or living room, cleaning can be stretched out to once every four or five years, or about every third time you clean the walls. An occasional dusting with a long-handled lambswool duster will do it otherwise for the dust and cobwebs.

The kitchen, with all of its airborne grease and soil, is a different story, as are ceilings that suffer from heavy nicotine exposure. These may need to be washed twice a year. Badly yellowed or water-leak stained walls should simply be repainted.

Vacuum any air vents up there

first, and then clean flat painted or matte-finish ceilings with a dry sponge. (See "Dry Sponges.") You just hold the sponge folded in half in your hand and swipe it across the surface. Dry sponges made to fit on a long handle are also available.

Wash ceilings with gloss or enamel paint with an ordinary sponge and all-purpose cleaning solution. Two buckets are needed, one to hold your cleaning solution and the other to squeeze the dirty sponge into as you go along. To start, dip a sponge only half an inch into the cleaning solution, to prevent it from running down your arm while you're cleaning or down the walls as you clean the edge of the ceiling. Apply the solution to an area you can comfortably reach and go over it twice. Remember to squeeze the dirty solution into the spare bucket. Then wipe the cleaned area with a clean dry towel.

Clean the edges first and finish up in the middle of the ceiling, overlapping your strokes. For heavy accumulations of grease or nicotine, use a heavy-duty cleaner or degreaser solution. Rinsing may be necessary to eliminate streaking.

A 2- by 12-inch plank supported by a ladder on each end, or a ladder on one end and a sturdy plywood box on the other (see page 277), is the single biggest help and safety precaution in washing ceilings. You can clean almost a quarter of the room without getting down or falling off the ladder.

See also "Acoustical Tile"; "Textured Walls and Ceilings."

Ceramic Tile

When we unearth evidence of early civilizations, what is it we usually find? Ceramics! Those pieces of broken pottery are the same stuff our modern floor and wall tiles are made of—it's almost indestructible! No wonder it's so popular as a home furnishing. Usually glazed with a lustrous, glassy finish, carefree ceramic tile resists all kinds of stains and soil and wipes up easily with a damp cloth. Used for walls, floors, tub and shower enclosures, and countertops, it makes an extremely low-maintenance surface. It's just a shame that tile installation requires that pesky line of grout between the tiles—this is what creates the cleaning problems! There are things you can do to make grout less of a problem, however. (See "Grout.")

Ceramic tile floors don't need any wax or floor finish, and all you have to do is sweep and mop them regularly to keep them clean and shiny. Mop with clear water (or add just a dab of liquid dish detergent), and change the mop water as soon as it gets cloudy. Too much soap or dirty mop water will leave a dulling or sticky film. For removing mildew from tile showers, see "Mildew"; for removing hard-water deposits and soap scum from tile, see "Hard-Water Deposits"; "Soap Scum"; for maintaining unglazed quarry tile, see "Tile, Clay" and "Quarry Tiles." Don't use brown or black nylon-backed scrub pads on ceramic tile, or you could scratch that smooth shiny surface.

Ceramics. See "Clayware."

Chamois

Originally made from the hide of a goatlike alpine antelope, "chammys" now are specially tanned sheepskins. They will absorb up to seven times their weight in water and are used for lint-free drying of automobiles, windows, mirrors, even fine glassware. It sounds odd, but before you can dry anything with a chamois, you have to get it wet. It'll take a little soaking to get it saturated, but once that baby's good and damp all over, it will really absorb. Just squeeze the water out of it each time it gets full, and keep on drying. To do large areas such as automobile roofs and hoods, it works best to flop the skin out flat on the surface and just slowly drag it off. Dry chamois skins are also used to polish jewelry and to make protective bags for jewelry and optical instruments.

A dirty chamois won't do a good job and won't last as long as it should either, so it should be washed out after each use. Wash in warm soapy water (not detergent, which will rob the skin of its natural oils). The leather tears easily when wet, so don't wring it or stretch it; just squeeze the suds gently through the skin. Rinse in lukewarm water and dry in the shade. Gently flexing it as it dries will keep it from getting stiff.

Synthetic chamois (which doesn't work as well as the real thing) is also available now, and it can be cleaned, like the napped fabric it is.

Chandeliers

As dust and airborne soils quietly build up on chandeliers, they lose their brilliance, the whole reason they exist. When dirt can't be dodged any longer, there are several ways to clean chandeliers.

If grease and grime haven't encrusted the chandelier, you can *drip-clean* it. Turn off the power to the fixture, then vacuum carefully to remove loose dust and cobwebs. If bulbs and sockets point upward, place a plastic sandwich bag over each one and secure it with a rubber band.

Place a dropcloth down to protect the floor and then lay out towels or newspapers over it to catch the drips. Lighting dealers sell ready-to-use chandelier cleaner such as Sparkle Plenty, or you can mix your own. Use 1 part isopropyl alcohol to 3 parts distilled water. This is safe for metal as well as crystal, glass, or plastic parts of most chandeliers.

Spray a generous amount of the solution over the whole thing (stay away from bulbs, wires, and sockets) until water drips from each part. Make sure you get every side of every pendant. The crystals should drip dry without streaks or spots. A slight film may remain. If you can't live with that, rewet the crystals and take a clean cloth and buff them after the solution's been on a few minutes. After the crystals are clean and dry, remove bags and wipe any saucers and noncrystal parts of the light with a soft cloth dipped in the same solution. Let the whole thing dry overnight before turning on the power.

If the chandelier is really dirty and

you want first-class results, there's no escape from *hand-cleaning* each crystal. You can spray and wipe each piece in place, working your way from top to bottom, and being careful not to put pressure on the wires that attach the pendants. Don't pull on them—just hold them in place with one hand while you wipe and polish with the other.

Or you can remove all the crystals for cleaning, and then rehang them, but don't plan anything else that day. If you're insecure, make a sketch of the chandelier, or photograph it from all angles before you start dismantling. To avoid scratching the prisms, use a plastic tub for cleaning solution and another for rinse water. Carefully take down a dozen or so pendants (or one tier) and lay them in the bottom of the tub to soak in the solution described earlier, till all the dirt is dissolved. Don't let them touch each other. Then dip them into the rinse water and polish with a clean dry towel. After you clean all the prisms in the tub, replace them on the chandelier (use needlenose pliers to bend the small wires back into place) and take down the next set. Doing only a small area at a time will help you remember where each piece is supposed to go.

Chemistry of Cleaning

Whether we're cleaning walls, carpets, or windows, washing a shirt or behind Junior's ears, the basic process of cleaning is the same. To get the job done, we have to:

1. *Identify the soil.* (See "pH in Cleaning"; "Soil.") Exactly what is it we're trying to remove? We can't plan our attack until we know the enemy.
2. *Choose and apply the proper chemical.* (See "pH in Cleaning.") To loosen, dissolve, and suspend the soil in the solution.
3. *Agitate.* Some soils yield to chemical action alone, some need mechanical action of some kind—or agitation—to aid the process. Agitation can be supplied by scrub brush or cleaning cloth and elbow grease, the agitator in a washing machine, a high-pressure spray, ultrasound vibrations, and various other methods.
4. *Remove the suspended soil.* Get the dirt-laden solution off the surface before the soil can redeposit. (Wipe with a sponge, rinse, squeegee away, extract, pump out dirty water and replace as in a washing machine or dishwasher.)

Whether we're stripping old wax off the kitchen floor or washing baby blankets, all four steps need to be accomplished. Trying to speed the job up by skipping one step will only slow you down and produce disappointing results.

Chimneys

Ho, ho, ho! Who wouldn't go up on the housetop to clean one of America's 60 million fireplace chimneys? Well, most of us wouldn't—and shouldn't. If you're afraid of heights, slipping off a two-story roof wouldn't do a thing for you or the soot and creosote buildup that woodstoves and fireplaces create. But leave it on there long enough and you're risking

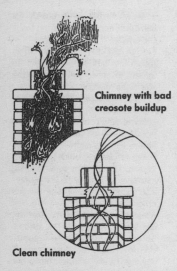

Chimney with bad creosote buildup

Clean chimney

a chimney fire (just like a blowtorch, only bigger). High-use chimneys should be cleaned once a year, say the experts; if they're used seldom, once every three to five years should be enough to keep the danger down and also allow your fireplace to operate more efficiently. Another common chimney problem, believe it or not, is blockage from animals or birds building homes there.

Cleaning chimneys isn't terribly technical. (The pioneers did it with a burlap bag filled with straw and brick tied to a rope and pulled up and down.) However, it is messy and dangerous. You have two choices:

1. Call a pro chimney sweep: There are lots of them now and they have all that's needed to clean chimneys while keeping living rooms

clean. See the Yellow Pages under "Chimney Cleaners."
2. Do it yourself: Chimney sweep kits (with directions) are available at hardware stores and home centers. You'll need to know the diameter of your chimney to get the right one.

China, Fine

Or the elegant, expensive stuff such as porcelain or bone china we may use only on special occasions, if we're lucky enough to have it.

Most fine china made in recent years is dishwasher safe, with the exception of some hand-painted china and the gold or silver decorated type. If you have china with gold or "silver" (it's actually platinum) bands or designs on it, the safest thing is to hand-wash it unless the manufacturer assures you otherwise. Ditto for antique china and older china of any kind that came to you without benefit of instructions.

When you do fine china in a dishwasher, be extra careful to place it in there so that it doesn't bump against anything or get dislodged in the washing process. Use a regular dishwasher detergent such as Cascade or Calgonite, and you could use a little less than the instructions specify.

If you want to be 100 percent sure you don't have any hard-water spotting, let the china cool to room temperature first, then hand-wipe with a soft cloth.

Many people prefer to hand-wash even china that can safely navigate an automatic dishwasher. Though the klutz factor greatly increases here, it *is* a way to spend a little more time with those lovely pieces before banishing them back to the china closet. When you wash by hand, use a plastic dishpan or rubber mat in the bottom of the sink, and watch that faucet head! Use a mild hand dishwashing detergent and don't soak patterned china in it long. Never rub or scrub hard or use any kind of abrasive pad or scrubber. And don't pour scalding hot water over china that isn't dishwasher safe. You can air-dry or wipe, though wiping is the best way to end up with a shiny, unspotted surface.

Then be sure to handle those nice clean dishes by the edges, to avoid fingerprinting, and be gentle when you stack them. Keeping and using the separators that came with them will do a lot to reduce tiny scratches. (Paper plates make a good substitute if you didn't save the separators.)

Chopping Boards or Blocks

A surface we cut food on needs to be not merely clean but sanitary, which a wooden board can rarely manage. Wood is porous, and when used in a chopping board or butcher block it can't be sealed or varnished, so meat juices and germs sink right in. And all those little cuts and chinks in the surface give them a great place to collect and sour or grow.

So if you can't switch to a nice nylon board that's a breeze to wash and disinfect, do as follows:

• Wipe a wooden board well with clean dishwater after every use, then rinse and wipe dry. Make sure it has a chance to get good and dry.

This alone will help reduce the germ count.

• After you cut meat and poultry on it, or at least every once in a while, wet it down well with disinfectant cleaner or 1:10 chlorine bleach/water solution, leave the solution on there for ten minutes, then rinse well and dry.

• To deodorize, apply a baking soda and water solution or fresh lemon juice, let it sit there for about fifteen minutes, then rinse and dry.

• Wooden blocks also need oiling from time to time to keep them from getting brittle. When the block is clean and dry, coat it well with oil—mineral oil is best because it won't get rancid, but any vegetable (cooking or salad) oil is okay too. Rub it in well and leave it on there for an hour or even overnight, then wipe away the excess.

"Butcher block" that's not used for food preparation (if it doesn't already have a varnish or urethane coating on it) should be oiled occasionally with a product designed for oil-finished furniture, such as Danish oil.

Chrome

The word *chrome* is short for "chromium-plated," chromium being a bright metal that is alloyed and plated onto steel, brass, and other metals. Its brilliant silver finish is resistant to most chemicals and to tarnishing. We may not be able to surround ourselves with the gleam of gold, but we can have shiny chrome faucets, dinette sets, light fixtures, and trim on our cars. The price we pay for all this splendor is that the mirrorlike surface of chrome shows (if not magnifies) every fingerprint and water spot and keeps us constantly polishing. Bear in mind that the gleaming surface is just a thin plating that can be easily worn away by abrasive cleaners or metal polishes (See "Abrasive Cleaners.") And even tiny scratches will show up on that sparkling finish, so be ever so gentle with your cherished chrome. Wash it with glass cleaner or neutral cleaner, scrub it with a white nylon-backed pad or plastic Chore Boy only, and polish it with a soft towel. Use silver or chrome polish only if absolutely necessary to remove stains. (Simply keeping it *clean* is the best polish you can use on chrome indoors.) Keep chrome trim on automobiles well waxed to help keep rust spots from developing. See also "Metal Polishes"; "Tarnish, Metal."

Cigarette Smoke. See "Smoke, Cigarette."

Citric Acid

This acid is what gives fruit juice drinks their bite. Obtained from citrus fruits, especially lemons, citric acid also has a mild bleaching action useful for removing certain kinds of stains. You can get chemically pure citric acid from pharmacies as either a liquid or a powder, or simply squeeze some juice from a fresh lemon. Lemon juice has long been used by homemakers to deal with coffee, tea, liquor, and other tannin stains. Mixed into a paste with salt, lemon juice will often remove even tough stains such as wine and rust

from fabrics that can't tolerate harsher chemicals. See also "Cleaners, Acid."

Citrus Cleaners. See "Cleaners, Citrus."

Clayware

Stoneware and other pottery items are usually made of a coarser clay than porcelain, fired at a lower temperature. Their strength and the hardness of the finish depend on the type of clay, glaze, and firing used. Stoneware and glazed ceramic pieces can generally be cleaned following the directions for porcelain, but be sure to check the manufacturer's instructions if available. Raw, unglazed ceramic items such as earthenware pots and planters, quarry tile, and some art objects will stain easily unless sealed—see "Sealing"—with Duncan mat spray, available at craft, ceramic, or hardware stores. Reapply after each cleaning.

Earthenware, whether decorative or food service, often cracks if subjected to quick changes in temperature. High heat and harsh detergents can also cause fine cracks in the glazing or decorations. Hand-washing in hand dish detergent (in a sink with a rubber mat in the bottom) is the safest approach. Don't use abrasives or harsh scrubbers on earthenware—they can mar the finish.

Terra cotta is a form of earthenware so porous it will absorb detergent in a dishwasher; always handwash it and never soak it, even in the sink, or it will absorb too much water.

Cleaners, Abrasive. See "Abrasive Cleaners."

Cleaners, Acid

Because the majority of soils are mildly acid, most soaps and detergents are alkaline. (See "pH in Cleaning"; "Cleaners, Alkaline.") Certain alkaline soils and food stains respond best to acid cleaners, however. Such soils include lime scale (see "Hard-Water Deposits"), rust, tannin (coffee and tea), most alcoholic beverages, mustard, and other alkaline foods. Here are the most common acids used in cleaning products:

Acid	Typical Uses	Characteristics/Cautions
Acetic (vinegar)	Mild deliming; acid spotter; rinsing agent for alkaline cleaners	Clear white distilled vinegar is best for cleaning; can weaken cotton and linen.
Citric (lemon juice)	Used as an acid spotter and as a mild bleach in stain removal	Can tarnish metals if left in contact with them.
Phosphoric	Bowl cleaners, tub and tile cleaners, delimers. (Also an ingredient in soft drinks.)	Mild but effective; safe on metals at 9 percent concentration or less.
Hydrochloric (Muriatic)	Bowl cleaners, cleaning mortar spills off new brick, and etching floors before sealing them. (Your stomach uses it to digest food too.)	Bleaches nylon, eats cotton and rayon, dissolves the binders in cement and mortar; very corrosive to metals at 8 percent or greater concentration. Poisonous. Strong concentrations will damage skin and mucous membranes.
Sulfuric	Drain cleaners	A powerful oxidizer—attacks nylon, vinyl, and most organic substances. Not as corrosive to metals as hydrochloric, but burns skin more readily. Oxidation reaction in drainpipes can produce noxious fumes and enough heat to sometimes crack iron pipes.

Acid	Typical Uses	Characteristics/Cautions
Hydrofluoric	Commercial rust removers	Etches glass and porcelain, causes severe skin burns.
Oxalic	Bleaching agent—removes rust stains, but not as quickly as hydrofluoric	Extremely poisonous if ingested; not corrosive to metals.

► When using strong acid cleaners, always wear rubber gloves, goggles, and other protective clothing as needed. Make sure you have good ventilation. Protect surrounding surfaces from contact with the acid, and always rinse well after using.

Cleaners, Aerosol

All kinds of cleaners come in handy push-button cans, with the prime advantage being convenience. You pay for that ease of use by the smaller quantity of anything you get in an aerosol can. In certain situations (applying insect repellants, some kinds of lubricants, paints, furniture polish, spray starch, and so on), aerosols are an advantage. Aerosols can apply a product with pinpoint accuracy, or very lightly and evenly over a surface. And they can reach some otherwise very hard-to-reach places. But for everyday use, cleaners mixed from concentrates in good-quality trigger-spray bottles are cheaper, last longer, and produce less superfine mist to be inhaled. You won't have to worry about propellants or be left with dangerous pressurized empty containers to add to our garbage problems either. See also "Fluorocarbons."

Environmentally safe, rechargeable air-pressure powered dispensers for cleaning are beginning to be avail-

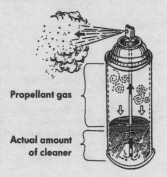

Propellant gas

Actual amount of cleaner

able to professionals, but it will be a while before they reach a price range that makes them practical for home use.

Cleaners, Alkaline

The majority of the soils we deal with every day, including fats, oils, grease, and many foods, are slightly acid. (See "pH in Cleaning.") Since acid soils are best removed by alkaline cleaners, most soaps, detergents, and cleaning products are alkaline.

Cleaner	pH	Uses/Cautions
Heavy-duty cleaners Degreasers Wax strippers Automatic dishwasher detergents Lye drain openers Oven cleaners	12–14	Very caustic; avoid silk or wool; harmful to skin; can permanently damage paint, aluminum, copper.
Laundry detergent All-purpose cleaners	8–12	Safe for most things except delicate fabrics.
Neutral cleaners Hand dishwashing detergent Woolite	7	Safe for most everything.

Cleaners, All-Purpose

Many of the household cleaners standing at attention on supermarket shelves, advertised as all-purpose cleaners, should really be classified as heavy-duty. A good many of them are highly alkaline (have a pH of 11 to 12) and some contain solvents, ammonia, and even bleach. Most of them can damage aluminum, brass, and paint if applied full strength, and some are caustic enough to call for the use of rubber gloves. A true all-purpose cleaner should be mild enough to use on any surface without damage and gentle on the skin. For general-purpose cleaning I recommend a light-duty detergent, such as the neutral all-purpose cleaner you can get at janitorial supply stores. (Buy it in concentrated form—see "Cleaners, Concentrated"—and dilute it yourself.) Or you could use hand dishwashing detergent. (see "Detergent, Dishwashing.") Only break out the heavy artillery, such as Formula 409 or Fantastik, when the going gets tough and circumstances demand a stronger product. Even stubborn spots will often respond to the milder detergent if you just do a little soaking or gentle scrubbing with a white nylon-backed scrub pad.

Cleaners, Ammoniated

Ammonia is added to a number of household and commercial cleaners to boost their alkalinity (see "pH in Cleaning") and enhance their grease-cutting ability. Because it dries clear without streaking, it's also a staple ingredient in glass cleaners and specialized cleaners for shiny surfaces. Long used to increase the emulsifying power of wax strippers, it is falling out of favor for this purpose because the aroma can overwhelm even the

---

▷ **Clean:** A condition that can solve more problems of humankind than anything except faith. Clean is convenient, kind, cuddly, contagious, and congratulated.

hardiest of cleaners. Most ammoniated cleaners are mild enough to use as general-purpose cleaners, but strong concentrations can damage some surfaces. (See precautions under "Ammonia.")

Cleaners, Citrus

With increasing pressure to limit the use of butyl cellosolve (see "Butyl Cellosolve") as the solvent in heavy-duty degreasers, manufacturers are turning more and more to citrus formulations. If a cleaner has to contain a solvent (and many of them do—see "Solvents"), a "natural" solvent distilled from orange or lemon trees seems to be somehow nicer than one made from petrochemicals. However, most citrus cleaners don't contain orange or lemon oil per se, but a terpene distilled from citrus oils called d-Limonene. Citrus terpenes differ from those distilled from pine trees only in aroma, but "turpentine" listed as an ingredient on a cleaner's label doesn't sound as good as "natural citrus solvent" or "orange oil."

When used in solvent-based cleaners such as De-Solv-it, the limonene boosts the ability of the other (petroleum) solvents to dissolve such tough stains as chewing gum and tar. In water-based cleaners, the solvent action of the limonene helps cut grease and oil, but not as effectively as butyl cellosolve. Chemical manufacturers are pushing citrus-based cleaners as an alternative to butyl. But the cleaning action of water-based "citrus" cleaners is still achieved largely with traditional surfactants, and many of these products still include small

amounts of butyl to increase their degreasing ability. And since d-Limonene smells more like lemons than oranges, citrus cleaners that smell "orange fresh" usually have a perfume added to the mix.

Cleaners, Concentrated

When you buy a gallon of cleaner in the supermarket, you're actually buying nearly a gallon of water with a couple ounces of chemical in it. Why pay for water? Why lug gallons of water home from the store? Why store gallons of water in your cramped cupboards?

Professional cleaning chemicals, which you can find at janitorial supply stores, are available as concentrates and come in larger containers. With concentrate you can mix up your own cleaning solution at home in reusable spray bottles. (See "Spray Bottles.") A gallon jug of concentrated disinfectant cleaner from the janitorial supply store, for example, costs seven or eight dollars, and would last the average household two years or more. This is not only a substantial savings in cost and bottle-lugging, but also reduces the number of plastic containers you'll be contributing to our national mountain of nonbiodegradable trash.

You can also buy premeasured concentrates—measured amounts of cleaner packaged in little plastic envelopes. All you have to do is snip one open and add it to a spray bottle filled with water as directed. There's no guesswork or room for error—the dilution is always right. That's important because too weak a solution

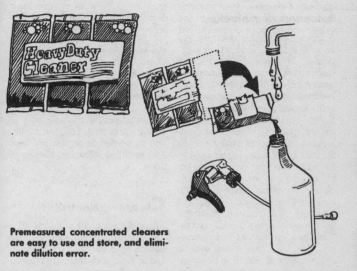

Premeasured concentrated cleaners are easy to use and store, and eliminate dilution error.

won't do the job, and too much cleaner can be just as bad. Too much chemical in the water will take extra rinsing, leave a film or streaks, and may damage or corrode some surfaces. The packets cost about a fourth as much as ready-to-use glass cleaner, take almost no room to store, and further reduce the amount of packaging to be disposed of. When manufacturers start using biodegradable plastics to package these premeasured concentrates, they'll be riding the wave of the future.

If your spray bottles are quart size be sure to choose premeasured chemicals that dilute with one quart—don't buy the gallon size unless you want to mix that much ahead in a gallon jug and store it.

When mixing up cleaners from concentrate, fill the bottle with water first before you add the concentrate. This way you won't have 4 inches of foam in the bottle, and it prevents chemical splashes too.

▶ Simplify your cleaning arsenal. With the following four cleaners mixed up inexpensively from concentrate, you can do most of the cleaning needed in the average home:

    Neutral cleaner
    Glass cleaner
    Heavy-duty cleaner
    Disinfectant cleaner

(If hard-water deposits are a big problem for you, add phosphoric acid cleaner to this list.)

Cleaners, Disinfectant

A disinfectant cleaner cleans as well as kills germs. Most disinfectant cleaners are made with quaternary disinfectants, since they combine most readily with detergents. These combination products compromise both cleaning power and germ-killing ability a little when compared to specialized cleaners or dedicated disinfectants, but they're strong enough for most of the sanitizing we need to do and are real time-savers. Don't try to make your own disinfectant cleaner by mixing disinfectant with common cleaners—most soaps and detergents will reduce or destroy a disinfectant's ability to kill germs. Some pine oil cleaners (see "Cleaners, Pine Oil") have a high enough concentration of pine oil to be classified as disinfectant cleaners. See also "Disinfectants."

Cleaners, Drain. See "Drain Cleaners."

Cleaners, Glass. See "Glass Cleaners."

Cleaners, Heavy-Duty

Heavy-duty cleaners are powerful detergent formulas designed to remove grease, oil, and stubborn soils. Most are highly alkaline, and some contain solvents, ammonia, and other ingredients to boost their cleaning power. Many household cleaners advertised as "all-purpose" should actually be classified as heavy-duty. (See "Cleaners, All-Purpose"; "pH in Cleaning.")

When using these products, a little care is in order. Heavy-duty cleaners can soften or damage paint, metals, and some plastics when used straight or left on the surface too long. Some of them also contain butyl and other ingredients that shouldn't be used with bare hands. (See "Butyl Cellosolve.") Don't automatically reach for the strongest stuff—use only as strong a product and as strong a dilution as needed to get the job done. And read and follow the label directions.

Cleaners, Neutral

Although technically a neutral pH is 7.0 (neither acid nor alkaline), most neutral cleaners have a pH between 7 and 9. Neutral cleaners are nonetheless mild enough to clean nearly every surface safely, and they're especially good for light-duty cleaning jobs such as floor mopping and wall washing where you don't want any streaks or detergent residue. To prolong the life and looks of your household furnishings, neutral cleaner is what you should always use before resorting to anything stronger.

One neutral cleaner we're all acquainted with is liquid dishwashing detergent. Although it foams too much for some jobs, it can be used for any number of everyday cleaning tasks. See "Detergent"; "Dishes, Hand-Washing."

A janitorial supply store sells large jugs (some even come with pump dispensers) of neutral all-purpose cleaner concentrate, which can be diluted with water as needed. This will take care of most of your daily cleaning needs quite inexpensively. Neutral all-purpose cleaner is also available in premeasured packets. (See "Cleaners, Concentrated.")

See also "Cleaners, Acid"; "Cleaners, Heavy-Duty."

Cleaners, Oven. See "Oven Cleaners."

Cleaners, Pine Oil

These cleaners are all-purpose cleaners formulated with pine oil, a natural resin distilled from pine trees. Pine oil won't dissolve in water but forms an emulsion in the presence of soap—which is why pine oil cleaning solutions always have that milky appearance. Don't confuse pine oil cleaners with cleaners and disinfectants that smell like pine and may even be called pine this or that. Unless pine oil is listed on the label as a major ingredient, the "pine" is probably just a perfume. Some people like pine oil cleaners because they can clean, sanitize, and deodorize all at once. To qualify as a disinfectant, however, the product must contain at least 20 percent pine oil, and even then it isn't as good a germ-killer as a quaternary or a phenolic disinfectant. See "Disinfectants"; "Cleaners, Disinfectant." Cleaners with 20 percent or more pine oil are effective cleaners, though, and a good choice for anyone who likes that pungent piney aroma.

Just don't use them straight or leave them soaking on waxed or painted surfaces—pine oil is a solvent and a relative of turpentine!

Cleaners, Toilet Bowl. See "Toilet Bowl Cleaners."

Cleaning, Deep

Deep cleaning is that thorough cleaning we do annually, semiannually, or every few years—when we move everything and clean under, behind, and everywhere. The individual entries in this book will tell you how to deep clean just about anything. Of course, if you clean as you go, which is easier on you and what you're cleaning, deep cleaning will be much less necessary (and maybe even a forgotten art).

Cleaning, Emergency. See "Emergency Cleaning."

Cleaning Solution

Yes, it could be an ingenious answer to a classic cleaning problem, but the term *cleaning solution* usually refers to a cleaning chemical (or more than one) dissolved in water or another solvent. We use a liquid *solution* to emulsify or dissolve the soil and hold it in suspension until it can be removed. (See "Chemistry of Cleaning.") We usually want warm solutions because they clean better, are more pleasant to use, and dissolve cleaners more easily. Scalding hot solutions don't usually accomplish much for large-area cleaning, because the solution becomes room temperature within seconds of application to the wall, floor, or whatever, and the whole bucketful may be cooled off by the time we reach the far corner. For laundry and dishwashing, where hot water temperatures can be maintained, a hot solution really is a lot more effective. Home cleaners often overlook the importance of keeping the solution uncontaminated with soil. (See "Walls" for a discussion of the two-bucket method, which will accomplish this.)

Cleansers

We've always known the extra "s" in there (*cleanser* versus *cleaner*) meant get-tough cleaning. The powdered scouring cleansers used to rely heavily on harsh abrasives to grind away soil. The old-type scouring cleansers contained a silicate (quartz), which is actually harder than steel or glass. No wonder they scratched and dulled countless sinks, tubs, and pots and pans! As more and more plastic and fiberglass surfaces appeared in the home, the damage from scouring powders intensified. To make cleansers safer for these softer surfaces, most manufacturers have reformulated their products. Many cleansers, especially the liquid variety, rely more on chemical cleaning power now and less on abrasive action, and the abrasives they do contain are milder. A number of cleansers also contain bleach to help in removing stains.

For stubborn spots on hard surfaces such as porcelain, vitreous china, matte-finish stainless steel, and baked enamel, any of the new, milder cleansers should be safe, as long as you keep the surface wet and scrub gently. Of the powders, new-formula Comet is the least abrasive,

Bon Ami somewhere in the middle, and Ajax the most aggressive. For more delicate surfaces such as fiberglass, cultured marble, and plastic laminate (Formica), if a mild detergent won't get results, use one of the liquid cleansers. Mr. Clean Lemon Fresh Soft Cleanser is one of the most effective and is also quite safe, while Soft Scrub is a little more abrasive. Avoid using cleansers wherever possible, especially for chrome and mirror-finish stainless-steel cookware, because over time even the tiniest scratches will accumulate to dull a shiny finish. The safest course is to use a neutral cleaner and a white nylon-backed scrub pad, which won't scratch at all.

Clocks

Battery-operated or electric clocks are well sealed and can be wiped with a cleaning cloth dampened with all-purpose cleaner. Be careful not to bend the hands if they are exposed.

Movement clocks should be professionally cleaned every five years, and ultrasound is the preferred method. Keep clocks away from heat, cold, vents, and anything that blows air (and therefore dust and airborne soil!). Leave the interior of any clock to the experts, but dust the exterior frequently and treat fine wood as you would fine wood furniture. Use glass cleaner and a soft cloth on glass and avoid touching any gold or brass. (See "Brass.") Be extra careful to avoid scratching when cleaning plastic faces. (See "Plexiglas.") Follow instruction manuals carefully for oiling and maintenance of your clock.

As for clocks such as cuckoos with intricately detailed exteriors, my best advice is to get a can of compressed air (the kind to clean computers) and blow the dust away.

Closets

Closets are kind of the home's aspirin—they relieve the pain of things we don't know what else to do with. Hence they're generally stuffed. The newer the home, the more and bigger the closets—even walk-in closets, and you guessed it, Virginia, they're still crowded! When we professionals clean a whole house, people often want the closet washed and cleaned when we do the bedroom. Because of all the stuff in the way, it usually takes longer to do that tiny little space than three whole master bedrooms. All kinds of closet-expanding therapies are now available—racks, shelves, space savers, organizers, multilevel hangers. It's easy for these to end up being junk bunkers—in other words, ways to stack unused stuff higher, tighter, and neater.

The cure? Two simple words, *dejunk* and *discipline*. Closets are an important and active part of the home, not dead-end storage, so get and keep the old retired or seldom-used or seasonal stuff out of there. Keep only what you need and use regularly, and your closet will be organized.

As for the closet itself, when you finally get to it, it may be dusty, but it's seldom dirty. A few metal marks from hangers or scrapes from suitcases maybe, but not dirt. Sealing up closets against invading dust by keeping the doors closed, weatherstripping them, and using garment bags as necessary saves a lot of clothesbrushing and makes frequent closet cleaning unnecessary. If a closet has a good coating of enamel paint inside (if it doesn't, give it one!), you should need to wash the walls and ceiling with all-purpose cleaner only once every five years or so. The floor is a different story—you might want to vacuum or wash it monthly.

Cloth, Cleaning

For that final wipe and shine in the cleaning process, a cloth is superior to anything I've found so far. Not all cloth is conducive to cleaning, however—synthetics such as polyester, nylon, and rayon were designed to *not* be absorbent (and absorbency is the whole point of a cleaning cloth).

▶ **Cleaning cloth aftercare:** If you just wad your cleaning cloths together somewhere when you're done with them, they'll smell and sour and maybe even mildew. And if you let dirt and stains dry in your cloths, you'll have stained, ratty-looking "rags." Remember, your cloths absorb cleaning chemicals. Once they've been used, even if they look clean, they're stiff, not soft and pliable, so they won't reach into all the little crevices or do their absorbing job well. So just toss them in the washer, and they'll come clean and look fresh. And to keep them ultra-absorbent, always dry them in the dryer, not on the line or on the shelf.

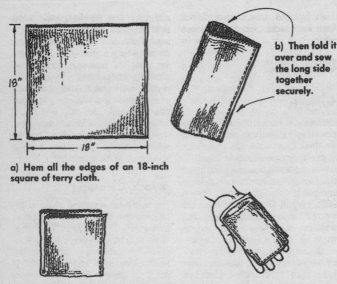

a) Hem all the edges of an 18-inch square of terry cloth.

b) Then fold it over and sew the long side together securely.

c) When it's finished fold it once, and then again, and it will just fit your hand.

The pros know that pieces of old shirts and pantsuits are a joke and never use them. Our secret weapon is cotton cloths. Cotton diapers, cotton flannel, or cotton knits make good polishing or dusting cloths. But cotton terry ("Turkish") toweling is the best by far. It absorbs quickly and well, polishes at the same time, and protects your hand while you're working with it. *Make your cleaning cloths as follows.*

Take a piece of good sturdy 100 percent cotton terry cloth and cut an 18-inch square out of it. Any color is okay, but white is preferable because you can easily see the stain and dirt

as you remove it (and it'll give you a real sense of accomplishment). You won't have to worry about dye bleeding out of a white cloth either. Hem all the edges, fold the square in half once, and sew the long side together securely, leaving the ends open to form a tube. By folding the tube in half, then in half again, you'll have the perfect size cloth to fit your hand. Flip and refold as the sides become soiled then turn it inside out for a total of sixteen cleaning surfaces! When the whole cloth is dirty, toss it in the washer and tumble dry.

When using a cloth, do fold it to the right size for the job at hand so it won't flip and drag around, knock down knickknacks, and pick up loose hair.

Clotheslines

Clotheslines were common in pre-dryer days. Wire or rope was strung up, usually in the backyard, between two trees or cross arms to air-dry the wet wash. Lines are still a good idea—they not only save electricity or gas and provide a little exercise, but they give that clothesline-fresh smell and crisp feel that's never been duplicated.

You can make your own clothesline, and for this any rope or wire will work, but the best is smooth galvanized wire about ⅛ inch in diameter, or the plastic-coated twisted clothesline wire. Both will hold clothespins perfectly. You can put a turnbuckle at one end to keep the line taut. Five

and a half feet off the ground is the right height for reaching and for keeping big blankets and long pants from dragging on the ground. Build it good and sturdy because part of the joy and pain of a kid's life is swinging on a clothesline pole, or riding a "horse" under the wire and getting scraped off!

P.S. Don't leave clothes on a line too long, or they'll end up getting dirty again (by birds, tree fallout, blowing off onto the ground, etc.).

Clothespins, Wooden

The coming generation won't even know what wooden clothespins are. If you happen to have some dirty ones, soak them in a bowl of warm water with a little bleach and detergent (more clothespins are mildewed than dirty) for ten minutes or so, then rinse. They might still be ugly, but they won't mark clothes. Then if you're into wooden clothespins (because they last longer than the plastic ones) don't leave them outside when you aren't using them!

Clutter. See "Junk and Clutter."

Coats/Jackets

One good way to help keep coats and jackets in good shape is to keep them off the floor, off the backs of chairs, and so on.

When it's time for cleaning, be sure to follow label directions to the letter. If it says dry clean only, it means it! Failure to follow directions

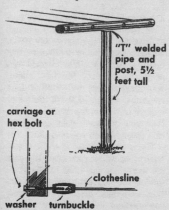

"T" welded pipe and post, 5½ feet tall

carriage or hex bolt

clothesline

washer   turnbuckle

A sturdy homemade clothesline with turnbuckles to adjust the tension.

here will not only damage the garment by shrinking linings or ruining the fill material, but it will undo water resistance and any other special properties the outerwear may have been treated for.

The water-resistant treatment on raincoats and the like needs to be reapplied after cleaning by your dry cleaner. A soil retardant such as Scotchgard will keep coats cleaner longer—it too will have to be reapplied after cleaning.

If a coat or jacket is machine washable, pretreat soiled areas with a laundry pretreatment. On children's coats this may mean spraying entire cuffs and sleeves and collars—and the flaps around the pockets.

Before placing coats in the washer, check and empty *all* the pockets! Zip up zippers, buckle buckles, clasp clasps, close Velcro closures, and so on. Leave detachable hoods attached. This protects the zipper or snaps from agitation damage as well as protecting other clothes from the zipper. Remove belts but wash them together with the coat they came from, so the color of belt and coat stays the same. Remove any removable lining and wash it separately.

Fill the washer with water and dissolve the detergent in it before adding the coat. It's important to avoid crowding a coat in the washer and to avoid underloading the washer. To balance out the load of a small coat or jacket, you should add some white nonlinting fabric, such as cotton or muslin. Muslin is inexpensive enough that you can buy several yards just to add to such loads as necessary. Hem the cut edges first, or they'll eventu-

ally unravel, leaving you with loose threads several yards long. A white cotton sheet is a good substitute for the muslin.

Follow manufacturer's directions for water temperature and drying cycle to use. Dry coats with plain white cotton fabric too to fill out the load. Underloading the dryer causes streaks. If you take a coat out of the dryer before it's dry, lay it flat to finish drying.

A Few Specifics

Wool coats: Can you wash them at home? "NO, NO, NO," says the Fabric Care Institute. They'll lose their shape (it will damage the interfacing and stiffeners) if washed in a machine, and hot water will shrink the wool. Wool coats *must* be dry-cleaned.

Fur or fur-trimmed coats or jackets: Fur and leather must be professionally cleaned. Even if the coat is otherwise washable (if it's costly enough to have fur on it, it probably isn't), anything with fur or leather permanently attached must be cleaned by a professional fur or leather cleaner. Your dry cleaner will send it to a specialist. Check to see if the fur or leather trim or collar is removable—then you can wash your coat if the care label advises you to do so.

Down or synthetic fiber-filled garments: Follow the care label. If it says it's washable, use a low temperature (under 140 degrees), medium agitation, and rinse *twice*. When drying, use medium heat, and add a clean tennis ball or a tennis shoe to help return the filling to fluffy and evenly distributed. (Otherwise it will clump up and look awful.)

Synthetics: Follow the care label. In general, synthetics require a lower water temperature and regular agitation, although this depends on the fabric. Obviously a delicate fabric will need a gentle cycle.

Vinyl-trimmed coats and jackets: Follow the care label. Assuming that the whole coat is washable (if not, it must be dry-cleaned), wash it at a low temperature with light agitation. Do not use a dryer; dry flat or hang to dry.

See also "Shearling/Fleece"; "Fur, Imitation"; "Fur, Genuine."

Cobwebs

Cobwebs, which are just spider webs, can appear overnight, so they aren't an index of inept cleaning. Wetting or scrubbing cobwebs rolls them into sticky grimy threads, which smear all over. To clean cobwebs, *lift* them away from the surface with a lambswool duster. Watch how impressively they stick to the wool! Or vacuum them up with a brush attachment. For those mile-high webs, get a lambswool duster with an extension handle.

Coffee Makers

I did meet a percolator lover once who demanded the pot never be cleaned inside—but most of us enjoy our coffee a lot more without a buildup of rancid oils. The interior of a percolator and the removable parts should be scrubbed with soapy water after every use. Remove stains with

Dip-It and hard-water deposits by adding 1 tablespoon vinegar, baking soda, or cream of tartar to a cycle with plain water. Rinse well before brewing your next batch. Tubes and spouts may require a special skinny percolator brush or pipe cleaner.

Wipe the outside of (unplugged!) electric coffee makers with a soapy sponge or cleaning cloth, and polish dry. Never immerse the electrical base in water. Most carafes, lids, and baskets are safe in the top of the dishwasher and should be cleaned after each use. Do not use abrasives on these. Soak stains in a solution of ½ vinegar and ½ water or 1 tablespoon cream of tartar per quart of water.

Automatic drip coffee makers need their insides demineralized every month or so. You can run 1 quart of white vinegar or a citric or tartaric acid solution through it or use products such as Mr. Coffee Cleaner or Dip-It 2, an odorless descaler made especially for coffee makers. Check the manufacturer's directions for any special preference here. Run at least one cycle of clear water through after this.

▶ **Collection:** There are so many kinds of collections that need to be cleaned, three encyclopedias couldn't explain how to clean them all, so you're on your own. But I can tell you how to reduce collection cleaning: Keep that collection locked up behind glass doors or in nice glass cases. This will reduce dusting as well as all the problems caused by unsolicited handling of, or drooling on, your arrowheads or butterflies.

Combs

Holding them under a tap of running water doesn't clean combs—it just washes off the loose dandruff. The hair oil, lotions, and potions stuck on a comb need a solution of soap or detergent to do it. If it's a plastic, rubber, or metal comb, you can soak it for a while in dish detergent solution (with a little ammonia added if it's really grungy). If necessary, use an old toothbrush to remove any last stubborn deposits. Then rinse and shake dry and at last, a clean comb to loan!

More delicate, exotic combs made of materials such as tortoiseshell, bone, or varnished wood shouldn't be soaked in anything—just scrubbed clean as necessary with neutral cleaner solution and a soft brush. If you ever need to sanitize a comb, soak it in disinfectant cleaner solution for 10 minutes.

Comforters. See "Quilts."

Compact Disc Players

For the most part, CD players have few upkeep requirements. But they are highly sophisticated pieces of electronic equipment. Most of us only attempt to keep the outside of the machine dusted and the environment around the player as free from dust and dirt as possible. It's a good idea to keep your CD player in a cabinet or under a cover to cut down on airborne dust, for example. Attempting to clean the machine itself without the proper knowledge can cause damage to the lense, the device that reads the disc. If and when your disc player begins reading erratically, take it to a professional for expert attention.

Compact Discs

In addition to superior sound reproduction, one of the great advantages of compact discs is the fact that the sounds they preserve don't wear out and deteriorate over time the way LP records and magnetic tapes do. The digitally produced sound is read by a laser beam from the inner part of the disc, and the outer part is encased in a tough layer of clear plastic. Since there's no mechanical action on the disc to wear it out, experts say they should last indefinitely with proper care. Dust, dirt, and fingerprints, which spell disaster for a record, can be simply wiped off the surface of a disc with a soft cloth.

▶ **Compliments for cleaning:** are hard to come by, so let me give you a few here, to award yourself or make available to tongue-tied others: *Nice job! . . . That's the best it's ever looked! . . . That's quite an improvement! . . . Terrific! . . . Good Show! . . . Who would have thought it was possible? . . . I hardly recognized it! . . . It looks like a new ————! . . . It's never looked this good. . . . It really sparkles/shines. . . . What a transformation! . . . How'd you ever get it so clean? . . . My, I can see myself in that ————. . . . Incredible! . . . Amazing! . . . Beautiful! . . . Bravo! . . . Beyond belief! . . . Who removed the window? . . . Gad, I knew it smelled clean when I drove in.*

CDs aren't indestructible, though. Always handle them by their edges, keeping fingers off the playing surface, and keep them in their protective cases when not in use. Wipe off dust with an antistatic cloth and remove any stray fingerprints with a soft, lint-free cloth dipped in alcohol. When you clean a disc, always wipe from the center toward the edge, as if you were following the spokes in a bicycle wheel. Wiping in circles may leave tiny scratches parallel to the data tracks, which can interfere with proper playback. If you use one of the disc-cleaning kits sold at audio stores, make sure it's designed to clean in a radial pattern. Never use solvents, abrasives, or harsh cleaners on compact discs—they can injure or scratch the surface.

Compound, Polishing. See "Polishing Compound."

Computers

Twenty years ago *computer* wasn't even part of our vocabulary. Now, at home and work, we have one or more of them, and with all the fingers, lint, hair, perspiration, smoke, airborne grime, and paper dust constantly on and about them, the little buggers *need cleaning*! Especially since they actually pull dust and dirt to them by static attraction. Let's leave the inside to the technician who comes to repair them, but the outside is fair game for all responsible owners.

Computer (and printer) housing and screen:

1. Can be vacuumed with a soft dust brush attachment on a canister vac, or one of the tiny minivacs (available at computer and vacuum stores) designed for keyboards.
2. If necessary, they can be wet-cleaned with the special foam or alcohol-based products available from computer stores and supply catalogs. This is safer than using even the most lightly dampened cloth with any kind of liquid cleaning solution on it. Denatured alcohol will remove spots and smudges.

The keyboard:

1. Dust and vacuum thoroughly, then remove any remaining lint or dust with a can of compressed air.
2. If wet cleaning is needed, use one of the premoistened towelettes made for just this purpose, also available from computer places. Once the dirt on there is loosened run cotton swabs along the cracks of the key line. As soon as one swab is dirty and saturated, grab another.

Complete computer cleaning kits are also available with antistatic cleaning solution and everything else you need to keep that expensive little hummer working and looking good. The best approach is to clean your computer often enough that it never needs deep cleaning.

If the area right around the computer is kept good and clean, less dirt will end up on and in the computer. So make sure that you (or the janitorial staff at the office) vacuum and dust daily—or nightly. And don't forget the chair and the computer stand!

Concentrated Cleaners.
See "Cleaners, Concentrated."

Concrete

For outdoor concrete such as steps, driveways, and sidewalks, the way maintenance men have been doing it for years works about as well as anything: Wet it down with a hose, and sprinkle on some Tide or other powdered laundry detergent. Scrub with a stiff-bristled push broom, then hose it off. For removing oil stains, see "Oil Stains." Specialty concrete cleaners are available from janitorial supply stores for removing rust and other stubborn stains.

Cleaning newly laid concrete with muriatic acid is okay the first time to remove any stray mortar drops and etch it a little so it will hold seal or paint better. But giving concrete repeated acid baths will soon begin to dissolve and erode the surface.

To make indoor concrete easier to clean, it should be sealed. (See "Sealing.") Unsealed concrete will continually wear down as it's walked on, creating a never-ending supply of gritty dust to be tracked onto other floors and spread through the house. It's also very porous, which means it absorbs stains instantly as well as being rough and hard to clean. A smooth-sealed concrete floor can just be dust-mopped and damp-mopped like any other hard floor from time to time, and spills will wipe up easily since they don't penetrate.

If you do have to clean unsealed indoor concrete, use heavy-duty cleaner and flood the floor with the solution. It'll really drink up the water, so you'll have to use plenty to be sure it gets a good wetting. Make sure heavily soiled areas are especially well covered with the solution and kept moist for a few minutes before scrubbing with a stiff-bristled broom to loosen stubborn spots. Then pick up the dirty water with a floor squeegee and dustpan, a wet dry vacuum, or even a mop. Count on the floor taking quite a while to dry. You can lighten any old, deep stains you have left with a poultice (see "Poultice") of cat litter and heavy-duty cleaner solution.

Concrete Block

Concrete block may look impervious, but it's just a hard sponge that thirstily absorbs not only dirt but stains and spills. Loose or surface dirt can be scrubbed or pressure-washed off, but any stain will sink into untreated block and generally won't come out.

The best way to spruce up ugly raw block is to paint it. Before you paint, give it a generous coat of block filler. This will help fill and level the face of the block so that when you paint it, you'll be left with a smoother, more washable surface. If you've got new or freshly cleaned concrete block that you want to leave natural, apply a masonry sealer right away (see "Sealing"), preferably in a single coat with a pressurized sprayer.

When you clean unpainted concrete block, for best results use a pressure washer. (See "Pressure

Washers.") The high water pressure will provide the agitation necessary to remove soils from the pores. If the block is painted, be careful; you can strip the paint off if you get too close. Most pressure washers have a chemical metering system that you set to get just the right dilution of cleaning chemical to water. Use a heavy-duty cleaner to dissolve and remove even grease and oil. If a garden hose is all you have, scrub the wall first, using a medium- to stiff-bristled brush with a bucket of heavy-duty cleaner. Then rinse the loosened soil away with the hose. Indoors, if a lot of water can't be used, scrub the block with a brush and then dry it with terry cleaning cloths.

Painted block walls indoors can be cleaned the same as any painted wall. (See "Walls.")

Antidotes for Specific Stains

Efflorescence: That white powdery residue found on basement walls. It's caused by moisture forced through the porous concrete by hydrostatic pressure and is especially bad around any cracks in the foundation. When the moisture evaporates, white mineral deposits remain.

First try to remove it with just a scrub brush and water; then go to detergent; if that doesn't help or it recurs, use a 1:9 solution of phosphoric acid to water. Neutralize afterward using a solution of ⅛ cup baking soda per gallon of water. If that doesn't do it, try a 1:10 solution of muriatic acid and water. Soak the spot with water, then apply the acid

solution with a scrub brush. When it stops bubbling, wash the wall with 1 part ammonia to 2 parts water. Then rinse with plain water.

The best stain prevention is to eliminate moisture by correcting drainage problems around the foundation and sealing any cracks in the concrete wall. Sealing the inside of the foundation walls with a waterproof paint alone won't do the trick because the water will just push the paint off the wall.

Graffiti: Use a heavy-duty cleaner or graffiti remover from a janitorial supply store. Don't expect 100 percent removal. Most promise perfect results but may leave a slight shadow of the image. You have a much better chance of removing graffiti from sealed block than from raw, untreated block.

Asphalt:
1. Scrub with hot water and scouring powder.
2. If that doesn't work, try a poultice of lighter fluid and whiting or undiluted citrus cleaner; dab the surface with a cloth. If necessary rub or wipe.

Mildew: Another big problem in unpainted concrete block. Moisture will accumulate in blocks and make a perfect breeding ground for mold and mildew. Scrub the area down with strong disinfectant cleaner solution. Where surrounding surfaces will not be damaged, you can use a 1:5 solution of liquid chlorine bleach (Clorox) and water. The bleach will not only kill the fungus but will remove most of the existing mildew stains. Then rinse well. Where possible you can use a pressure washer to blast off stubborn mildew stains. Mold and mildew will come back if the area is not kept dry. Some mildew stains may be impossible to completely remove.

Dried paint: Scrub with commercial paint remover; then scrub any remaining stain with 1 part muriatic acid to 10 parts water. Neutralize the acid with 1 part ammonia to 2 parts water afterward.

Cooktops, Ceramic

The inventor of the flat cooktop rates right up there with the inventor of the microwave in my book—both have saved us millions of hours of cleaning time. Ceramic cooktops have no grooves or niches, no burner rings— NO DRIP PANS. The induction types don't even get hot! Several cooking systems utilize ceramic cooktops, including halogen, induction, and solid-disc elements. Each has its own peculiarities and each brand its own instructions—follow them to the letter and your cooktop will be the showpiece of your kitchen for years to come.

Most manufacturers will give you some cleaning cautions to keep your cooktop looking new, such as wiping the bottom of cookware before placing it on the cooktop to remove moisture (which dries into mineral deposits), dust, and any particles that could get between the pot or pan and the surface and scratch it. Never slide cookware or anything across the cooktop. Wipe it with a clean, damp, never-been-used paper towel before each use—dishcloths and sponges can leave a film that discolors the surface when heated up. As soon as the cooktop is cool, remove any spills and splashes. For daily care, just wash and dry with a solution of liquid dish detergent and a clean paper towel. For burned-on spills, use only the manufacturer's recommended cleaners, which may include Bon Ami, Soft Scrub, ASAP Cleaner-Conditioner, or Bar Keepers Friend. If you do any scrubbing on the top, always do so with paper towels or a nylon or plastic scrubber, and always rinse with a clean wet paper towel and dry the surface afterward. For stains, make a paste of a gentle powdered cleanser and water, apply to the stained area, cover with plastic wrap and let it sit overnight. Remove gently and rinse. Repeat as necessary.

The manufacturer may recommend using a razor blade for hardened spills—follow the directions carefully! Never use green scrub pads or pads with metal fibers such as steel wool. And keep abrasive cleaners, oven cleaner, bleach, and rust remover well away.

Cookware

A few general rules first: Not surprisingly, liquid dish detergent is the best thing to hand-wash cookware with (since it was carefully designed for this very purpose). Always allow cookware to cool before washing—putting a hot pan in cold water will warp it. Soak cooked-on food overnight in soapy water rather than trying to scrub it off, or let a solution of water and liquid dish detergent boil in the pan for a while. If that doesn't do it, always try a plastic or nylon scrub pad before resorting to metal scrubbers or steel wool. These days, most cookware can go in the dishwasher, but check the manufacturer's directions or look for "dishwasher safe" stamped on the bottom.

Aluminum: A relatively soft metal, so use wood, plastic or other non-scratching utensils on it and a plastic or white nylon-backed scrubber only. If you must use something stronger, go to a steel wool soap pad or green nylon pad (on unpolished aluminum only) and be sure to scrub with the grain. Allowing salty or alkaline food to sit in aluminum pieces will darken them and even pit the metal; aluminum is also easily discolored by heat, automatic dishwasher detergents, or strong alkaline cleaners of any kind, including ammonia and baking soda. To relighten, boil a strong vinegar solution or 2 teaspoons cream of tartar per quart of water in the pot or pan for ten to fifteen minutes. Cooking acidic food such as tomatoes or green apples or scouring with a steel wool soap pad will lighten it too.

Calphalon-type cookware: This heavy-duty cookware is made of anodized aluminum, meaning that the surface of the metal is altered by an electrolytic process, and, in the case of Calphalon, the pores are then chemically sealed. The resulting smooth yet tough dark surface will not oxidize or react chemically with foods and is stick resistant (without a coating!). It's also easy to clean.

Before you use Calphalon for the first time, wash it in hot, sudsy water to remove any oils left from manufacturing; rinse and dry. For everyday washing, use a nylon scouring pad such as Scotch-Brite and a chlorine cleanser such as Comet or Ajax as necessary—otherwise food particles or a greasy residue may remain that will cause food to stick.

For burned or dried-on food, fill the pot with sudsy water and boil over medium heat to loosen the deposit, then scrub it away and rinse. A paste of chlorine cleanser and water can be applied to stains for ten to fifteen minutes and then rubbed in a circular motion with a nylon pad. For stubborn stains or abrasions, use Dormond, the cleanser specially formulated for Calphalon, available where you purchased the cookware.

Don't wash Calphalon in the dishwasher or ever use oven cleaner on it—the harsh cleaning agents will discolor and destroy the surface."

Cast iron. See "Cast Iron."

Ceramic or glass cookware (such as Corning Ware or Pyrex): Check to see if dishwasher safe. (Depending on type of paint used on the ceramic, most are dishwasher safe.) To wash by hand, use regular hand dishwashing detergent. To remove cooked-on food, try soaking first. Get off as much as you can with a white nylon-backed scrub sponge, then soak again. Repeat the process until the cremated pot roast is gone. Patience wins here. If you must, use only a mild cleanser such as baking soda or Soft Scrub. Anything abrasive, such as steel wool or metal scrubbers, will scratch the finish.

Clayware: See "Clayware."

Copper: Keep copper out of the dishwasher and keep steel wool and scouring cleansers off it. Ordinary tarnish or blackening actually improves its cooking ability, but if you insist on shining copper, use a copper cleaner according to the directions on the package. A nonabrasive paste polish such as Wenol with no special ingredients for removing oxidation is best. Copper cookware is usually lined and the lining must be replaced if scratched or worn, so be sure to use wooden or plastic utensils to prevent damage. Unlined copper may develop spots of green "rust" called verdigris that *must* be removed, as it is poisonous. To do so, boil in a solution of ½ cup vinegar and ½ cup salt, or 1 teaspoon ammonia, per quart of water. Copper that has a protective lacquer finish should not

be used in cooking; these pieces need only be dusted or wiped with a damp cloth.

Enameled cast iron or steel: Handle with care to prevent chipping, and avoid overheating empty pans especially. Don't use steel wool or metal scrubbers of any kind—they will mark the surface. For stubborn spots, soak as described above or use a plastic scrub pad, baking soda, or mild, nonabrasive cleanser. If slight stains remain, do not bleach as it will etch the surface of the enamel.

Microwave cookware: Follow manufacturer's instructions, but in general, it should be dishwasher safe. (Inside a microwave is hotter than inside a dishwasher.) Use the top rack if it makes you feel better, but the manufacturer should specify. To hand-wash, follow directions for glass or ceramic cookware.

Nonstick cookware: The same qualities that make nonstick cookware a pleasure to cook with make it a cinch to clean after using—just let it cool, then wash or wipe with sudsy water, rinse, and dry. Hand-drying is better than air-drying in this case, because it removes any mineral deposits from the rinse water before they can build up on the surface. You can also put nonstick cookware in the dishwasher, but the key here is not to overclean—scrubbing can damage that nice slick surface! So don't let scouring powder, colored scrub sponges, steel wool, or metal scrubbers anywhere near it. And make sure you stir and cook only with plastic or wooden utensils that won't mar the finish. Once the finish is gone you're stuck with "stick" cookware again. The manufacturer's instructions for care and cleaning will tell you how to condition or season your cookware when you first get it to ensure its nonstick properties. After that, retreating with oil from time to time will help it retain its effectiveness, especially with foods containing a lot of fruit or sugar. Avoid high cooking temperatures, which can stain the finish. Nonstick finishes can develop a spotty white film of hard-water minerals that can be removed by wiping with vinegar or lemon juice (or phosphoric acid solution, if it's a heavier buildup). Rinse well and reseason afterward. To remove more serious stains from nonstick cookware, you can mix any of the following with 1 cup of water and let it simmer in the pan for ten to fifteen minutes: 1 tablespoon chlorine bleach and 1 tablespoon vinegar; 3 tablespoons oxygen bleach; 3 tablespoons automatic dishwasher detergent. Wash thoroughly, rinse and dry; then reseason.

Steel: Untreated rolled steel such as used in woks and some crêpe pans rusts easily. Wash it well before using it for the first time, because manufacturers often coat it with machine oil to prevent rusting in transit and on the shelf. Then dry and season the entire surface with unsalted salad oil. Heat the oiled pan until it starts smoking, remove it from the heat, and let it stand for a few hours before you wipe off the excess. Whenever you use a steel pan thereafter, just wipe it out with a paper towel, cloth, or sponge dampened with dishwater. Don't scrub, scour, put it in a dishwasher, or do *anything* to disturb the smooth black coating that will

▶ **Pot scrubber:** My favorite is one called Jaws. It has real scour power, but it won't scratch. Safe for Teflon, Silverstone, glass, porcelain, tile, and metals. It's made of "Honey-Combe-Fome" by a company called Swiss-Tex. If you can't find one, write to me: Don Aslett, P.O. Box 39-E, Pocatello, ID 83204.

develop on the surface and not only prevent it from rusting but improve its cooking performance. If rust develops on a steel pan, only then do you scour to remove, and reseason. Always dry steel immediately and well—the way to ensure this is to put it back on the burner, or into a warm oven, for a few minutes.

Steel, stainless (with or without aluminum or copper bottoms): Avoid using curly metal (or any metal) scrubbers or steel wool—they will scratch that gleaming surface. Use a nylon scrubber. Check the manufacturer's directions: Many do not recommend using the dishwasher. Don't leave salty or acid foods in stainless steel cookware for any length of time—it will pit the surface.

You might want to polish your stainless pots occasionally with one of the commercial polishes such as Vista. Burned-on, stuck-on messes are best soaked away in a solution of hot water and dishwasher detergent. To scour stainless, use a plastic or white nylon-backed scrub pad. If the cookware should discolor from overheating, use a stainless-steel cleaner such as Cameo or Bon Ami Polishing Compound, following directions on the container.

If the cookware has a copper bottom, use a polish or cleaner made especially for copper to keep it looking good. Copper bottoms will darken somewhat, no matter how careful you are.

Tinned steel: See "Tin."

Coolers and Jugs, Picnic

As you unpack from your trip, it's easy to rinse out the chest coolers with a hose and turn them upside down to drip dry. Now, if you brought the fish home in one of these babies, that's another story.

The plastic lining in food containers like these is similar to the lining in your refrigerator and should be cleaned the same way. Washing with warm neutral cleaner solution and rinsing will usually do the trick, and small coolers and jugs can be done right in the sink. Scrubbing with baking soda and water may be necessary for stubborn stains or odors. For lingering odors, you can also wipe down the whole inside with a 4:1 solution of water and vanilla extract, leaving the vanilla-soaked rag inside the closed container overnight, then wash as usual. The outside of coolers and jugs can just be wiped down with a damp cloth. To get pebbly plastic surfaces clean, use a scrub brush. Don't use anything sharp or abrasive on either plastic or painted metal surfaces.

Always prop the lid open until the cooler is good and dry or mold will grow inside. To discourage mold, mildew, and "plastic odor," store jugs and coolers with the lids ajar. Should you come upon a moldy cooler, wash with a solution of bleach and water (1:5) to kill the mold and bleach out the stains, then rinse well and leave open to dry.

Copper

When used outdoors for roofing and flashings and the like, copper is usually just left to develop its characteristic green tarnish, which actually protects the surface. The copper we end up cleaning is that in decorative items and cookware, even though there's something to be said for leaving cookware a little unshiny too, at least on the outside. Copper is used in pots and pans because it transmits heat quickly and evenly, and it really does a better job if left a little black and dull. The green tarnish, or verdigris, should be kept cleaned off the inside, however, as it is toxic. If you want shiny copper, use a cream copper or brass polish—either one will work. For cookware and food-service items, use one of the rinse-off copper cleaners. These remove tarnish quicker than cream polishes and don't leave as much residue, but you won't get as high a shine. If copper has been given a clear coat of lacquer to prevent tarnishing, don't use any kind of metal polish on it—or any abrasives, ammoniated cleaners, or even hot water. Just wipe with a cloth dampened in neutral cleaner solution as needed.

See also "Metal Polishes"; "Tarnish, Metal"; "Copper" under "Cookware."

Copy Machines

The areas we're concerned with are the glass we place our original on and the cover that comes down over it. Any dirt here is not only recorded for the ages, but in duplicate and more. Look the glass over carefully first—if there's a speck anywhere on it, it'll turn up on every copy you make. Dust will dust away, dirt will wipe away with glass cleaner, but if there's a copy-blemishing culprit left that won't come off unless you use your fingernail, it's the copy toner itself. Go after it with a tissue dampened with nail polish remover. The acetone-based remover will cut through the toner as well as any marker or ink marks on the glass. Always keep sharp tools and heavy objects of any kind off the glass to prevent scratches and chips that will leave a clear record of themselves on your copies.

Next, clean the platen cover, especially the underside, with a damp cloth or a mild solution of all-purpose cleaner if necessary. If the cover becomes badly stained, replace it. Marks and stains on the cover will show right through the paper and onto your copies.

Keep the outside of a copier looking nice with regular dusting and damp wiping with all-purpose or glass cleaner. Never spray cleaner on the copier, spray the cloth instead.

P.S. Don't handle the copy paper while your hands are wet or oily, or you may see some all-too-familiar whorls and swirls on all 33 copies of your next report.

Coral. See "Shell/Mother of Pearl/Coral."

Cords

Electric cords, that is! Before you give me a yawn or think this is nit-picking, I'll plug you into a shocker. The cords of lamps, mixers, toasters, and even our cleaning tools themselves, such as vacuums, are kind of like doorknobs: They do a lot of work and see a lot of action but seldom get cleaned. The doorknob spreads germs, which is bad enough, but electric cords are dragged over, under, and through all sorts of stuff in the floor, food, and foot areas and pick up even worse stuff. They get coated and crusted and if you have a run-in with them, it'll leave black lines on your pant legs or the furniture they run over or around.

Once a year is probably enough to clean cords, and it's easy. Unplug first, of course. Then generously spray all-purpose cleaner into a thick towel and pull the cord through the toweling while it's in your hand. Give the cleaner two or three minutes to work and then pull the cord through a clean, dry cloth. If the wiping towel is really black, give the cord an encore and you'll be the cleanest customer your power company has. The cord will look better, roll easier, and won't create more housework. And running it through your hands like this gives you a chance to notice cuts in the wire or worn or damaged insulation. It will help here if you quit tossing your cords into a tangled heap with whatever they're attached to. Take a minute to roll them up neatly. Remember, your spouse, kids, and guests' are watching and will follow your example.

Corian

"Say yes to abrasives!" I'll bet you never thought you'd hear that from me, but it's true—Corian, a strong, elegant molded acrylic from Du Pont, can be cleaned with abrasives with no fear of scratching or surface damage. In fact, it's recommended: "the occasional use of an abrasive cleanser or scouring pad over the surface will not only clean but help maintain the original luster and beauty of Corian," says the manufacturer itself. Countertops, sinks, showers, windowsills, or wherever it's found, Corian will safely come clean with abrasives. Even cigarette burns, knife cuts, and stubborn stains will come off this satiny smooth, nonporous surface: Use a household cleanser such as Comet or a fine sandpaper (320–400 grit) followed by a Scotch-Brite pad used in a gentle circular motion to return the surface to like-new condition. CAUTION: Keep paint remover, paint thinner, drain cleaners, nail polish, and nail polish remover well away from it, however.

For day-to-day cleaning, just use your all-purpose cleaner—most stains will wipe right off. Corian is highly resistant to most stainmakers such as coffee, grape or beet juice, ink, and food colors, and the occasional difficult stain can be removed easily with an abrasive cleanser.

Like other fixture materials, Corian can collect hard-water buildup, but you can use not only phosphoric acid cleaner but abrasives (including green nylon-backed scrub pads) to remove it.

Cork

Cork is a wood product (the bark of the cork oak) and basically is treated like any other wood. Unsealed, as in bulletin boards, it's porous and hard to clean. It will absorb stains and odors like crazy and hold on to them forever. About the only way to clean raw cork is to wipe it with an art gum eraser or a dry sponge (see "Dry Sponges") and use dry-cleaning solvent to blot out oily stains. The smart thing to do with any raw cork wall covering (unless sound absorbence was the main reason it was installed) would be to seal the surface with a good coat of varnish or shellac. Thus protected it can be gently damp-wiped, but don't flood it. For cork floors, see "Floors, Cork."

Cork Floors. See "Floors, Cork."

Corners

Corners are the most overrated problem in cleaning. Since they're not easy to get to, they're often missed—so what! People, furniture, and traffic can't get to corners either to abuse them. Just a few odds and ends and a little harmless dust gets kicked and settles there. As nobody walks on the floor right in the corner, nothing there is going to be worn or ground into the flooring as it will in the traffic patterns—it's strictly a matter of appearance.

Brooms, upright vacuums, and most other cleaning tools weren't designed for corners, so they are mostly a hand operation. Hard-floor corners are the worst—and another reason angle brooms are better. When you scrub or mop the floor, just scrub the corners by hand with a white nylon-backed scrub pad while the floor is wet. A putty knife will handle any hard buildup. Carpeted corners can be hit with the dust brush attachment on your canister vac or just wiped out with a damp cloth.

Cosmetics Cases

Yes, cosmetics cases. When was the last time you cleaned yours? Or the cosmetics themselves, for that matter? These are things we not only carry right with us everywhere, we handle them more than once a day and apply them to that pampered part of our anatomy, the face! Freshen up your makeup—it won't take more than a few minutes.

Discard any makeup over one year old—bacteria buildup can cause problems, especially with mascara and other eye makeup. Take a good hard look at your eye makeup applicators. If they are old and slimy looking, replace them with new sponge-tipped applicators or use disposable ones. Ditto for powder puffs or foundation applicators. Lipsticks you never really liked, or so old they're down to a ¼-inch stump, or almost dried up, should just be junked!

To clean the case itself and the individual makeup containers, use a soft cloth (or paper towel) lightly dampened with all-purpose cleaner solution. Wipe down the outside of the cases and compacts, and dry with another cloth. Do the same on the inside, taking care not to wipe across the surface of the makeup itself. Inside the case often has eyebrow pencil lines, lipstick or mascara smears, and the like that will come off with a little heavy-duty cleaner and scrubbing if necessary. Liquid makeup remover on a cotton ball will make quick work of marks like these, if you happen to have some. Wipe off the bottles of foundation, and don't forget to clean inside the caps and on the bottle threads. As for that powder-encrusted compact mirror, a damp tissue followed immediately by polishing with a dry one will make it possible to see your favorite features clearly.

To clean makeup and eyebrow brushes, swish them around in a bowl or pan filled with water and a few drops of shampoo. Lipstick brushes may need to be soaked for several hours in a solution of warm water and liquid dish detergent. Rinse thoroughly, reshape with your fingers, and let air-dry overnight. Be sure the metal base of the brushes gets good and dry too to prevent rust.

Counter Brush or Broom

Just as the name implies, counter brooms were made to clean and sweep the counters in factories, repair centers, workshops, stores, and the like where there is larger debris, such as paper and sawdust along with the dust, so dusting with a cloth is slow and inefficient. Don't confuse a

Counter brush or broom

counter broom with a whisk broom—counter brooms have a long handle and an 8-inch head with 3-inch-long synthetic or horsehair bristles. The bristles often have flagged tips and are soft enough to get even the finest dust and crumbs off the surface. Professional cleaners and maids keep one hanging on their cart for quick sweeping of counters, shelves, desks, ledges, large windowsills, and so on. A counter broom also is an A-1 tool for "detailing" the edges and corners of a hard floor before you dust-mop. It's great too for picking dust and dirt up into a dustpan after sweeping a floor with a dust mop or a large broom.

A counter brush is by no means a must, but it speeds some jobs up substantially, and once you buy one you'll keep it busy. Counter brushes can be found in most home centers or hardware stores from about $5 for the cheapos up to about $15 for a good horsehair or synthetic. Keep yours right at the counter, workbench, or wherever else the action is. Hang it by the hole in the handle so you can just grab and use it. (Old-timers called these *foxtail brushes*,

and some call them *shop* or *bench brushes*.)

Counters, Kitchen

Although generally plastic laminate (see "Plastic Laminates") such as Formica, kitchen counters come in all kinds of materials (ceramic tile, Corian, wood, stainless, slate, etc.), in every color and condition. The biggest mistake we make cleaning counters is using plain water when a soap or detergent solution is needed to release and lift the dirt and grease from the surface. The second biggest mistake is using a harsh cleaner or tool that damages the finish, leaving a rough surface that's harder to clean and will only get dirty faster.

The fastest counter cleaning in the best-kept homes is done as follows: Remove all litter and loose objects (lids, recipe cards, apple cores, unopened mail, old magazines, jars, bottles, marbles, rocks, shoes, and ashtrays). If you're feeling ambitious or can't avoid it any longer, go all the way and strip it of canisters, small appliances, dish drainers, knife blocks, and the like too. Brush, wipe, or "Dustbust" any crumbs or debris off before you wet the surface. Then wet a white nylon-backed scrub sponge with dishwashing detergent solution and use the sponge side to go over the counter quickly, wetting the whole surface and dislodging the easy stuff. (Don't forget the backsplash.) Let the solution sit on there a few minutes to soften hard droplets (jam, dried syrup, spilled tomato soup). Then make a trip over it with the nylon side of the sponge, scrubbing as necessary to remove any stubborn stuff. Then flip the sponge over and pick up all the moisture. Last—the secret of showcase counter cleaning—dry and polish with a dry cleaning cloth. It's fast, and any soap residue and last little traces will surrender to it.

As counters wear they get porous and absorb spills such as grape juice, but don't get excited; stains like these often work themselves out with daily cleaning. Don't use powdered cleanser on counters or ever scrub them with steel wool or colored scrub pads. A light coat of car wax or silicone sealer such as Beauty Seal will keep small appliance marks easy to get off an aged, worn counter.

Above all, ease counter cleaning by removing anything that absolutely doesn't have to be there!

Cross Stitch. See "Needlework."

Crumbs

Crumbs are a centuries-old problem still fought here in the twentieth with a damp rag to round up and pick up what we can, then we catch the rest in a cupped hand at the edge of the counter or table. Or we sic Fido on them. Nobody has perfected the technique or equipment for the chore.

One thing you can do is have a hand vac, such as a Dustbuster, handy to vacuum up crumbs as they happen. And one thing *not* to do (except in dire emergencies) is whisk crumbs off the chair, table, or counter onto the floor. Get rid of 'em while you've got 'em corraled. Why clean them up twice, or give them a chance to roll under the stove or get embedded in the rug?

Tiny tabletop carpet sweeper–type devices are available but they're temperamental. They work better on big stuff than small stuff and on tablecloths than on bare tables. Far better is something restaurant-supply stores carry called a *crumber*—a pocket-size piece of curved aluminum about 6 inches long. It works just like a squeegee for the tablecloth. It even has a pocket clip!

You never want to use a wet cloth on crumbs. Keep them dry, so they don't stick to everything. The fastest way to get crumbs off a countertop is by pulling them toward you with a dry hand. Hold a plate or bread board under the lip of the counter and sweep the crumbs right off onto it. As for those inevitable crumbs near the toaster, a large acrylic cutting board nearby is a great place not only to make sandwiches but to catch crumbs. When you're done all you have to do is pick it up and rinse it off under the faucet.

The combination of whisk broom and dustpan is handy for furniture crumbs. And you simply have to sweep—*often*—beneath just about any kitchen or dining-room table.

Crystal. See "Glassware."

Cuisinarts. See "Food Processors."

Curlers/Rollers, Hair

Who would want something snuggled up to their scalp as long and as often as curlers are, with never a thought to cleaning? To clean plastic rollers, use hair shampoo solution and a bottle brush to scrub off the grimy buildup of hair mousse and gels that accumulate. Don't forget the inside! Just about all types of rollers should occasionally be sloshed around for a minute or two in a sink of clean dishwater or shampoo solution, then rinsed. Or you can tuck them into a net bag and drop them in with the next load of laundry. The "Velcro finish" type of roller needs to be de-haired occasionally with a stiff comb—you won't believe how much comes off.

Check the instruction booklet; hot rollers may not be immersible. Just wipe with a cloth dampened in cleaning solution. They may need a vigorous toothbrushing to remove setting gels and the like.

Goody Hair Products suggests the following formula for removing buildup on curlers, combs, brushes, and other hair accessories: Mix in a bowl ½ cup white vinegar and 1 cup water, add item(s) to be cleaned, and soak for 1 hour. If necessary, carefully use a small brush or a toothbrush to loosen hairspray or gel residue. Rinse thoroughly and let air dry.

If hair oil is more the problem, soak in a solution of dish detergent plus a tablespoon or two of ammonia, then rinse well and dry.

Curtains/Drapes

How do they get dirty just hanging there? The light and view windows offer, and the convection currents they create, attract people, pets, and houseplants, a fine assortment of insects and airborne dirt—none of which fails to get something on the curtains. Dirt from outside and rain make a contribution too, when we leave the windows open, as do frost and condensation when the temperature changes.

An occasional vacuuming (don't forget the tops!) will keep the dust down and help delay the need to wash or dry-clean curtains. Those fabric-covered wooden valances (and unremovable others) can only be vacuumed, so make them a regular part of your living-room routine. Then before you spend any time and money on cleaning, carefully feel and stretch the back side of the fabric in the drapes or curtains in question to make sure they aren't sun-rotted. If they are, go shopping! (When you're looking, remember that sheers help save the drapes themselves from sun rot.)

When you take curtains or drapes down, stick up a piece of tape to help you remember where the hooks or tiebacks were so you hang them correctly when you put them back. Read the care label carefully, and if you wash, be especially wary about using bleach or overvigorous cycles on delicate and fancy styles. Be sure to remove all hooks and nonwashable trim before washing.

Curtains with chenille balls/tassels,

▶ **Could there be such a thing as too much suction?** We're all looking for the vacuum with the ultimate suction, yet you'll find a little opening (called an air bleeder) on the handle of most vacs to actually reduce suction. And guess what? By opening that valve you'll find it easier to vacuum curtains and drapes, carpet fringes, lampshades, clothes, pets, and what have you. Your vac will be able to pull out the dirt without swallowing the whole thing in a whoosh!

etc.: The same: cold water, delicate cycle wash, hang-dry.

Lace curtains: Use cold water and a delicate cycle with Woolite. Anything made from cotton should be hung to dry; polyester blends can be machine-dried on a delicate cycle. You can spot-clean this kind of lace like any other fabric.

Lined/insulated curtains: Insulated: wash in cold water, line-dry, iron on the fabric side when dry if desired. For permanent press: delicate wash and delicate dry (for a few minutes).

Ruffled curtains: People have lots of problems with these, but they're actually easy to care for as long as you don't overdry, which causes lots of wrinkles. Cotton ruffles will have to be ironed and probably starched to look as good as they should; cotton/poly blends and all-synthetic ruffles can be spun dry and hung to finish drying. Just don't tie them back until they're dry. If you want to put them in the dryer, do so only for a *few minutes* on low heat.

Sheers/delicates: Usually made from 100 percent polyester—use cold water, delicate cycle. They will be almost totally dry after the spin cycle.

Hang immediately to finish drying. Don't put these in the dryer or they will get millions of tiny wrinkles that will never come out.

Washable kitchen curtains and the like are easier to iron if they're not dried completely; take them out while they're still slightly damp. And rehang them the minute they come off the ironing board to prevent wrinkles. Likewise, if you have your curtains dry-cleaned, remove them from the hangers and rehang them as soon as you get them home.

Curtains or drapes treated with soil retardant need to be retreated after washing or dry-cleaning.

Cushions, Underneath

Pick up cushions and purge underneath at least once a month, before anything under there has a chance to sprout. You can either haul in the canister vac and remove the cushions, vacuuming under and behind them, or just use a little hand-held vac.

Whichever way you do it, first pick up all the pens, marbles, matchbooks, combs, Christmas tree hooks, pizza crusts, crushed candy, and the

▶ **Under-the-cushion cleaning** has solved many mysteries, including (after you've raked out all those candy bar wrappers) why your spouse's diet hasn't been succeeding, who really stole Grandpa's pocket knife, what happened to the other earring, and all those things you "set right there," or "were here this morning," the barrettes, needles, scissors, keys, and watches. If you can't find a toothpick anywhere, you know there's always a used one down there, along with the doilies and lost toys.

There's always cold cash under the cushions too. Remember that quarters slip out of pockets much more easily than dimes, so you should have a real incentive to go for it.

like and dispose of them so they don't injure your vac. If you really want to get it all out, carefully step on the rear of the seat platform after the cushions are off. It'll open up that crack between the seat and the back so you can get all the goodies that have fallen down there easily. See also "Under Cleaning."

Cutlery. See "Knives/Scissors."

D

Do it now! Three words that will cut any cleaning chore in half.

Decals. See "Label, Sticker, and Decal Removal."

Decoupage

These clear-coated paper-decorated plaques, paperweights, wastebaskets, and the like usually have a ure-

thane or acrylic plastic (or in older pieces, clear glue) finish. They should be wiped with a cloth dampened with Woolite solution—don't scrub or saturate, just wipe gently and then dry with a soft cloth. Abrasive cleaners will scratch, so take care with any valuable pieces. Many of these homemade masterpieces can lose their charm after a few years, so you might want to declutter rather than clean.

Deep Cleaning. See "Cleaning, Deep."

Degreasers

Degreasers are cleaners or solvents specially formulated to speed up the dissolving of grease and oil. Degreasers are usually quite alkaline—they have a high pH. (See "Chemistry of Cleaning.") A degreaser is worth buying and having as a specialized cleaner if you find yourself fighting grease often, especially in the kitchen. One of the most effective mild degreasers is ordinary hand dishwashing detergent, such as Joy. Extra-strength cleaners, such as Formula 409 and Top Job, are also good for the dirty devil, or you can go to the janitorial supply store and get some heavy-duty degreaser. (See "Butyl Cellosolve"; Cleaners, Citrus.")

Dehumidifiers

These devices must be cleaned regularly because their water collection tanks are a breeding ground for mold, mildew, and bacteria. You can circumvent the need to empty and clean out the tank if you have a floor drain or sump pump nearby. Position the hose so the water flows right into the drain or sump pump. Some models don't even have a hose—they can be set directly over a floor drain.

If you can't divert the water into a drain, you may have to empty the tank—up to several times a day. If you add a little bleach to the tank each time, you can postpone cleaning for a while.

But eventually you do have to do it. Remove the tank, add hot water and several drops of dishwashing detergent, and leave it in there for a few minutes. Then go over the inside with a brush or white nylon-backed scrub sponge. Rinse well. If hardwater deposits linger, fill the tank with a 2:1 solution of water and vinegar. Allow it to sit for an hour, then scrub with a brush. Rinse and dry. Add a bit of bleach to the tank, then replace in the unit.

Vacuum or dust the inside coils of *all* dehumidifiers once a year, and add a small amount of oil to the bearings of the fan motor to help keep it running smoothly.

Delimer (Descaler)

A delimer is a product designed to remove hard-water on "lime" scale (mineral deposits from hard water) and urine salts from pipes, plumbing fixtures, and other surfaces. Most delimers are largely acid. Industrial descalers usually contain hydrochloric acid, while products for home use are most often formulated with less-aggressive phosphoric acid. See "Cleaners, Acid"; "pH in Cleaning"; "Hard-Water Deposits."

Detergent

While a detergent is just about any cleaning product that performs the function of soap but is not a true soap, we tend to use the term for laundry detergents specifically. Soap's annoying habit of forming insoluble curds in hard water caused modern synthetic detergents to be developed. Detergents clean the same way soap does but are relatively unaffected by hard water. They are surfactants (wetting agents), which lower the surface tension of water and increase its ability to penetrate and dissolve soils and to hold them in suspension. (See "Surfactant"; "Emulsify.") Detergents also emulsify oils, and often contain water-hardness inhibitors as well as enzymes and other ingredients designed to digest protein-based soils. They may also contain chemicals to prevent loosened soil from being redeposited on surfaces, fabric softeners, suds suppressors, optical brighteners, colorants, and fragrances.

Laundry detergents come in both powdered and liquid form, with special formulas for use in cold water, boosted with enzymes, combined with bleach, and in both phosphate and nonphosphate forms. Liquid detergents usually do a better job of removing greasy, oily soils (this is one reason they make good laundry pretreatments; see "Pretreating"; "Prespotting"); powdered detergents are cheaper and remove mud and clay from clothes better. The powders are also usually better at preventing minerals such as iron in the water from staining your laundry. If you live in a no-phosphate area or have voluntarily taken the pledge, a liquid laundry detergent may do a better job for you than the no-phosphate powders. But if you're still using phosphates (and that doesn't necessarily mean you're

an insensitive slug—see "Phosphates"), you should be able to get acceptable results without paying extra for a liquid.

See also "Soap"; "Graying of Laundry."

Detergent, Dishwashing

There's a world of difference between dishwashing detergent (for hand dishwashing) and dishwasher detergent (for automatic dishwashers). The hand dishwashing liquids are mild detergents of almost neutral pH, formulated to cut grease and soil without being too hard on the skin. The automatic dishwasher detergents are much stronger, usually quite alkaline, and will leave your skin feeling like sandpaper if you give them a chance. Elsewhere I recommend powdered dishwasher detergent for certain heavy-duty cleaning jobs, such as soaking electronic air filter collector cells, but it's far too harsh to use as an all-purpose cleaner. Liquid dishwashing detergent, on the other hand, is so mild it makes a handy all-around cleaning product. It can be used safely on just about any washable surface, and it's designed to dry streak-free, without leaving detergent film or residues. It's great for washing the car, squeegee-cleaning windows, mopping floors, washing walls, and other light-duty cleaning where a neutral detergent is called for. The mistake most of us make when we use it for general purpose cleaning is in using too much of it—so we end up fighting mountains of suds. For mopping floors and squeegeeing windows, a little dab will do ya. See "Dishwashers, Automatic"; "Dishes, Hand-Washing."

When using dishwashing detergent to hand-wash dishes, don't forget to add it right at the beginning, right under the faucet, so the water action will mix it in well as the sink is filling.

Diaper Pails

Unless you're a body-builder, never fill a diaper pail all the way with water. Especially if you have to slosh down a flight of stairs to the laundry room with it (a great way for Dad to get involved). Instead fill it half full, add ½ cup of borax, and make sure it has a tight-fitting lid. Once you dump a pail of diapers in the washer, take a minute to wash out the pail—this will help control odors and germs too. Wipe the pail inside and out—lid too—with a borax and water solution, using a white nylon-backed scrub sponge or a brush, then rinse and fill 'er halfway up again and it's ready to go.

Diapers

Rinse soiled diapers immediately in the toilet, wring them out well, and soak them in a diaper pail half full of water and ½ cup borax (a great deodorizer and soil-release aid) until you accumulate enough for a full load. Heavily stained diapers should be presoaked overnight in a solution of ½ cup enzyme detergent (such as Biz) per gallon of water. To wash, empty the pail into the washer and turn to the spin cycle. Then add detergent according to package directions and 1 cup chlorine bleach to

▶ **Diamonds:** Anyone who has a diamond big enough to show dirt is rich enough to take it to the jeweler for professional cleaning. (Or see "Jewelry, Fine," if you insist.)

remove stains and kill germs (if the baby hasn't shown any sensitivity to it), and launder in hot water. A second rinse is recommended to make sure all the detergent is removed. You can add 1 cup vinegar to the second rinse to help ensure this. Dry in the dryer. Fabric softener may be used occasionally, but regular use will make the diapers less absorbent. There's nothing sweeter on the sideboard than a pile of freshly laundered nappies!

Diatomaceous Earth

Diatoms are microscopic, single-celled plants (algae), whose cell walls contain a sandlike compound called silica. When these tiny plants die and settle to the bottom of a body of water, their hard little shells stack up in layers. Dried-out deposits of this stuff form a light, loose, sharp-edged soil called diatomaceous earth, which is used in cleaning as an abrasive, in scouring powders, metal polishes, and toothpaste. It's also used to make poultices (see "Poultice") and to filter and clarify liquids, among other industrial and agricultural uses. Available at pharmacies.

Digestant

A digestant is a product that contains enzymes that remove stubborn stains by digesting them. Digestants are available from druggists as pure enzymes (pepsin, or papain, for proteins such as meat juice, egg, blood, or milk; amylase for starch and carbohydrates); or from your supermarket as commercially prepared bleach and enzyme detergent boosters, such as Biz and Axion.

Digestants can be used as a laundry presoak or as a paste for spotting dry-cleanables. Follow package directions; soaking time is usually thirty minutes to an hour; overnight for certain stains. Use warm water for soaking everything except bloodstains, which require cold. To make a paste, mix equal parts powder and water and pretest the fabric you intend to treat for colorfastness beforehand. The paste should be kept moist after application and left on the spot for fifteen to thirty minutes. Rinse thoroughly after removing. Don't use digestants on animal fibers such as wool or silk, or the fabric will be digested as well as the stain.

Dishcloths or Towels

A clean freak will point out that it's actually unsanitary to dry dishes with a cloth because it passes germs from one dish to another (especially because dishcloths are usually used to wipe not only the dishes but just about everything else in the kitchen). The most sanitary and efficient way to dry dishes is to let them air-dry.

You may have company, though, and need something to do while you finish discussing the price of potatoes, or have hard water and glassware that must be cloth-dried to pre-

vent streaks and spotting. Then be advised that superabsorbent cotton terry works the best. (Use plain cotton or cotton/linen for glassware.) Frequent visits to the washing machine—and declaring them off limits as *hand* towels—will keep your dish towels dainty.

Dish Drainers

Funny how often we're willing to stack our clean and sanitized dishes into an icky dish drainer. Go take a hard look at yours now. You'll probably want to plunge it right into a sinkful of hot water and heavy-duty cleaner. Let it soak in there awhile and then work the whole thing over with a stiff brush. Turn it upside down while you're doing this so you don't miss all the stuff on the underside that we never see from the top. When a drainer gets old and gray (from hard-water buildup), it's generally getting feeble too and the soft surfaces that protect dishes and silver are beginning to deteriorate. If a little phosphoric acid cleaner won't brighten it up, then replace it.

Here's a new habit that will help out here: When you're all set to start dishwashing—clean, hot soapy water in the left compartment of the sink and clear, hot rinse water in the right (or in a dishpan at the ready)—pick the dish drainer up off the counter and run it quickly through your wash and rinse water first. If you do this nightly, there won't be any grungies to get rid of.

Dishes, Hand-Washing

Almost a forgotten art! Hand-washing dishes is usually quicker than using the machine, and if you do it right it will even be easier on your electric bill. The big secret: Do those dishes while they're fresh and it'll go 86.3 percent faster than waiting until later when you have to chisel them off the counter.

Here too, soaking is one of the best ways to speed things up. So fill any crusted or sticky pots or pans with soapy water right away and get the dishes into the dishwasher where they can get the benefit of the detergent on them while you're refrigerating the leftovers.

Scrape the plates (a rubber spatula does a nice job here) and rinse. Make that a cold rinse for anything with egg, flour, oatmeal, or rare roast beef drippings on it. Pour off any loose grease in frypans and wipe greasy pots out with a paper towel.

Fill a dishpan or the sink with several inches of water, adding a squirt of liquid dishwashing detergent right under the faucet just as the sink begins to fill. Put the silverware and utensils in first so they cover the bottom of the sink or container and will be soaking and self-cleaning while you are dealing with the dishes themselves. In general, wash the cleanest things first; saving the grungiest ones for last. The usual sequence is: (1) glasses, (2) silverware, (3) china, (4) pots and pans.

When you put the plates in the water, set them in individually, not in a stack, so the water can come in around each one. Then be sure to let them soak a minute so the surfactant in the solution can attack and dissolve any grits or gravy on there.

If scrubbing is called for, the unequaled tool for dishes in my opinion is a sponge backed with a white nylon pad—3M Scotch-Brite is a good one. It cuts my dish-doing time in half. You can also use a dish mop, sponge, or cloth if you prefer. (We all have our own personal preference.)

Rinse each dish once quickly over the sink of soapy water and then lay it in the other side of the sink (or a dishpan) full of the hottest water around and let it sit. Do this until the rinse sink is full, then remove everything and set it in the drainer or even on a towel. If you have a double sink, you can also place the washed dishes in a dish rack set in one bowl of the sink. When the rack is full, spray the dishes all at once to rinse. If your dishes are hot-rinsed and well drained, you shouldn't have to wipe them dry unless they're clear glass and you have hard water.

Now that you have room in your sink again, load it up again with dishes, and repeat.

Problems

Burned-on food in pans: Fill with a solution of water and dish detergent, bring to a boil, then simmer until loosened, or soak overnight. Or scrub with baking soda (except aluminum), rinse well, and dry.

Baked-on food in ceramic or glassware: Soak overnight in dish detergent and water. Or you can soak for a short while in a solution of a small amount of automatic dishwasher detergent in hot water. Or scour with baking soda or powdered cleanser. Don't use steel wool—it may scratch the surface.

See also "Cookware"; "Glassware/ Crystal."

Dish Mops

Dish mops are essential equipment for the hands-out school of dishwashing, and the perfect rinsing and scraping tool when loading the dishwasher. For hand-washing, dish mops outlast sponges and leave your hands (well, at least one hand!) out of the mess and chapping medium. And they don't get dingy and smelly as fast as dish rags.

There are at least three species of dish mops: (1) sponge or sponge strips on a handle, (2) ministring-mop type, and (3) scrubbers (used mainly for pots/pans—either stiff bristles or a white nylon-backed pad used for Teflon, etc.). The kind that holds detergent in the handle really saves you money, because you don't end up dumping lots of detergent on everything you wash.

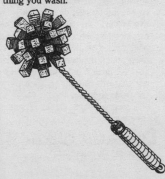

Dishpans

I first used a dishpan when we had a house with a single sink. The dishpan held the rinse water. And hand-washing dishes in a plastic dishpan does help protect against breakage. But today dishpans come in handy for all kinds of uses, the least of which is for dishes. When we need a cat litter pan, a toy organizer, a footbath, or a muddy-boot holder, there's one at hand. They even make a great, safe tray to cart all the egg coloring cups from the table to the sink at Easter-time. Thank you, Ms. Rubbermaid, wherever you are.

A plastic dishpan is the smartest way to carry the dirty dishes from the table to counter when you're mopping up meal mess. Then, as I mentioned, you can use the sink for soapy water and the dishpan for rinse water, and you can always freshen the dishpan by pouring it into the sink but not vice versa. Last, dump and swirl the rinse water around to clean the sink and finish the job.

Remember to fill dishpans only half full to avoid slopping when carrying. And when you're done with them, rinse and set them on their *side* to drip dry. (If you upend them, water will collect in the underside of the lip and give you a little surprise when you pick them up to put them away.)

Dishrags

The classical dishrag style is open weave for good reason(s): It gives them a little built-in scrub power, makes them easier to rinse out, and helps them dry faster. Rinse your dishrags well after each use and spread them out to air-dry, instead of leaving them in a soggy wad in the sink. And toss them in the washer with one of your "bleach *and* detergent" loads *before* they start getting dingy and smelly.

Dish Towel. See "Dishcloths or Towels."

Dishwashers, Automatic

Automatic dishwashers are one of the few cleaning robots at our disposal to date, and as we all know they do a better job of sanitizing than handwashing ever could. They're also a great place to hide dirty dishes and can even serve as additional cupboard space if you're one of the growing number of people whose dishes never see the inside of the cupboard.

To make sure you're taking full advantage of this mechanical wonder, see "Energy Saving While Cleaning." Be sure to reserve the top rack for small or plastic items that might be melted, misshapen, or otherwise damaged. And don't overlook the idea of using the dishwasher to sanitize and warm fruit jars before filling and processing.

To clean your dishwasher, spray and wipe the exterior, like most kitchen appliances, with all-purpose or glass cleaner and a cleaning cloth, and polish dry. While your cloth is still damp with the cleaner solution, wipe the control panel, knobs, and buttons clean. If your portable has a wooden top, see "Chopping Boards or Blocks" for care.

Occasionally check the drain for scraps of food and the edges of the door for splatters and eliminate them to avoid odors. The interior of a dishwasher cleans itself. Any darkening, browning, or scale you see there is caused by minerals in the water. You may need to try more than one of the following removal techniques for this:

• Scrub the spots in question with a white nylon-backed scrub sponge and a gentle cleanser like Bon Ami or Bar Keepers Friend—never use anything that will scratch and damage the finish. Run the rinse cycle when you're done.

• To remove light lime deposits in hard-water areas: Start an empty dishwasher on the rinse and hold cycle, open the door during the fill and add ½ cup white vinegar to the water, then let the cycle finish. If you have heavier deposits, start an empty machine at the main wash cycle, open the door, add 1 cup Lime-A-Way or phosphoric acid cleaner (see "Phosphoric Acid") to the water, and let the entire wash cycle finish.

• Brown, red, or black deposits may be caused by iron or manganese in the water. To remove, start the empty dishwasher on the rinse and hold cycle; while the machine is filling, open the door and add ½ cup rust remover from a janitorial supply store to the water; then allow the cycle to finish.

These procedures can be repeated as needed.

Disinfectant Cleaners. See "Cleaners, Disinfectant."

Disinfectants

The disinfectants commonly available for home use are quaternaries, phenolics, chlorine compounds, chlorhexidine, and pine oil products. *Quaternaries,* or "quats," are the safest to use, as they are the least toxic and not harmful to most household surfaces. They combine readily with detergents for good cleaning action and are effective against a broad spectrum of bacteria and fungi. *Phenolics* are good disinfectants but are more toxic and damaging to surfaces than the quats.

Liquid *chlorine bleach* (such as Clorox) is a good disinfectant, but its dangers limit it to the laundry room and to killing mildew on shower walls. (See "Bleach"; "Mildew.") *Chlorhexidine* is the active ingredient in a unique disinfectant used extensively by veterinarians, dairy farms, and pet handlers. Trade-named Nolvasan or Chlorasan, it's the safest disinfectant to use around animals, and is available through vets.

While not as good at killing germs as the other products, *pine oil cleaners* have the ability to clean, sanitize, and deodorize all at the same time. Some pine oil cleaners contain enough natural pine oil (20 to 30 percent) to qualify as fair disinfectants, and some boost their germ-killing ability with quats or other chemicals.

Read the label to know what you're buying: The active ingredient of quaternaries is some form of ammonium chloride, while phenolics will list the terms *phenol* or *phenyl* somewhere. (But don't be scared off by the term *phenol coefficient,* which is just a measure of a product's germ-killing power compared to phenol.)

Disinfecting

Disinfecting means "killing microorganisms." The fact that we call these little creatures *germs* indicates that we mean the harmful kind—those that cause diseases, create foul odors, spoil food, make stains, and destroy fabric. The microscopic creatures we want to control include bacteria, viruses, and fungi (molds, mildews, yeasts, and true fungi). A chemical agent that kills germs on inanimate surfaces is called a *disinfectant;* one that does the same job on living tissue is called an *antiseptic.*

To lay claim to the term *disinfectant,* a product has to achieve a 100 percent kill of the specific germ being tested for, within a certain time and temperature range in a testing lab. Many germs have dormant spores that are not affected by disinfectants. Processes that kill both germs and spores, leaving the surface completely free of life-capable forms, are called *sterilizers.* These are used primarily in medical facilities for sterilizing instruments and equipment. Chemicals that kill only 99.9 percent of the germs are called *sanitizers.* Sanitizers are used in the food-handling industry to reduce microbiological populations on utensils and food processing equipment to safe levels. For most home cleaning and deodorizing purposes, a simple sanitizing is adequate—we don't need to use su-

---

▶ Some general rules for using disinfectants:

1. Be sure to clean the area or object well first. A solution has to get to the surface of something to be able to disinfect it, and if that surface is covered with dirt and litter, it can't. Besides, the germ-killing powers of most disinfectants are seriously weakened by the presence of organic matter—things such as hair, feces or urine, dander, food, or milk. So scrape and brush and sweep first, but not so vigorously that you stir up a cloud of dust—that's an excellent way to spread disease germs through the air. Rinsing well after this precleaning is also important.
2. Don't mix a disinfectant with other cleaning products unless the label tells you it's okay—and then, use only the kind specified. Follow the dilution and other directions on the label to the letter—never make the solution stronger than it says.
3. Use disinfectants with care; many are irritating to the skin and can be absorbed through it. (You may want to wear rubber gloves.) Avoid spilling or splashing the solution on yourself or in your eyes. Likewise, don't mist a disinfectant solution or apply it in a very fine spray; it can be inhaled too easily. Avoid aerosols whenever you can—the mist from an aerosol can is finer and stays airborne longer. (If you must spray, squirt a small amount onto your cleaning cloth rather than filling the air with spray.)
4. When applying disinfectant, really saturate the surface with the solution. Don't forget the crevices, cracks, and corners. Where would you hide, if you were a germ?
5. Leave the solution on the surface for at least ten minutes.
6. Rinse well with clean water to remove the chemicals.
7. To disinfect fabric items, soak them in a bucket or tub of disinfectant solution for at least fifteen minutes before putting them through the usual washing process. Or you can add disinfectant to the final rinse cycle instead.
8. Air out or dry the disinfected articles or areas well before putting them back in use.
9. Store disinfectants in a secure place (preferably a locked place, well out of the reach of children and pets), and don't buy them in too large a quantity at one time.

---

perpowerful brew that will kill every last one of the little buggers.

Doilies

May I remind you that anything decorative is generally delicate? Hand-crocheted doilies are easy to distort when cleaning. Old and fragile or any handmade ones should be gently hand washed in Woolite or mild laundry detergent. The machine-made beauties available today are often acrylic instead of the crocheted cotton of the past and may even be machine washable. (Check the tag or wrapper when you buy them.) Their official title notwithstanding, dry cleaners do wash things too, so if you're in doubt about a particular doily, especially if it's stained, take it to a pro.

Grandmother used to dip doilies in starch or even (for superstiffness) sugar water after cleaning, then stretch them out flat and pin them in place—see "Blocking"—so they dried nice and straight. Sugar water is not actually such a good idea, because it will encourage mildew and encourage a doily to come undone when it's washed. People do, for some odd reason, like to pinch or fold back doilies, and the sugar-dipped kind often break under this treatment. Starch will help doilies keep their shape, and Faultless starch powder (mix according to directions) contains some bluing that will whiten white doilies. "Ready-to-use" liquid starches (such as Stayflo) should be mixed about 50:50 with water before using, especially if the doily in question has to curve around something like a chair arm or the back of a sofa.

If you need to iron a doily, use the lowest heat setting possible.

White doilies can be bleached, but coffee stains may not come out. The answer may be to dip the whole doily in coffee to give it a pretty off-white color. (If you want it darker, use strong tea.)

Doll Houses. See "Miniatures."

Dolls

Barbie and friends are subject to endless tea parties and even mud baths, so a true-to-life bath isn't out of the question. In general, cleaning will not

necessarily restore dolls to beauty pageant condition, but it's a better alternative than *not* cleaning them! Newer dolls come with cleaning instructions, but if you're unsure, surface washing is recommended for all but the most delicate (and expensive) of dolls. Any doll that talks, walks, or moves in any way or has electrical or mechanical parts should never be submerged in water. Older dolls with bisque or porcelain parts may not have had a sealer applied over the face, and water could wash the paint right off their faces. It's always wise to consult a specialist at your local doll hospital when it comes to delicate antique or valuable dolls.

To surface wash: Wipe with a sponge dampened in all-purpose cleaner solution. For really stained dolls, you can use a soft-bristled toothbrush. Ink often cannot be removed, but is sometimes bleached out by sunlight. It may be worth a shot to try dabbing some hair spray or dry-cleaning spotter on the ink, and then cleaning the spot with a soft toothbrush dipped in all-purpose cleaner solution. Rinse with a clean cloth dipped in water.

Machine washing: The only dolls that should be washed in an automatic washer are those that say so on the label. These are usually made entirely of cloth, stuffed with polyester or other washable fiber filling. Some dolls' heads can be removed and their cloth bodies run through the washer. For Cabbage Patch Kids, surface washing yields mediocre results. You can wash your little "Cabbie" in the machine (on gentle cycle with cold water and mild detergent) if you protect the head by first covering it with a pillowcase secured around its neck. Don't let your kids witness this—they may have nightmares! It might not be a bad idea to put the whole doll into the pillowcase—this will protect the stitching on the hands and feet as well.

Hair care: To wash synthetic and real hair, use a mild shampoo, rinse, and allow it to air-dry. Note that curly hair will not be nearly as curly after it is wet, and synthetic hair cannot be reset, so unless it's absolutely necessary, avoid washing doll locks. If you know for a fact that a doll's hair is made of human hair or mohair, don't wash it unless you're prepared to redo the 'do. For tangled hair, use a wig brush. Yarn hair should be hand-washed in Woolite solution.

Doll clothes: You will also want to use Woolite solution to hand-wash most doll clothes. They're generally not sturdy enough to withstand the agitator of an automatic washer. Clothes made of silk or old linen and the like should be dry-cleaned.

Don't forget to clean the cleaners

If there's one thing experts in any trade—from photography to dentistry to carpentry—learn, it's to have their equipment and supplies not only where they need them but in the condition they want them. Any rummaging or hunting you have to do for a tool, any repairing or reconditioning you have to do before you can use it, can put a real crimp in the cleaning impulse. The trouble is, we were so

relieved to finish cleaning last time we were all too likely to just toss the stuff somewhere. Then when we get ready to clean again we have to find, thaw out or untangle the mop, and get the now-rock-hard scum (which would have rinsed away in seconds at the end of the job before) off the bucket. So we end up depressed before we start.

• *Buckets*

Always empty and rinse a bucket when you're done with it. Buckets are great places for bacteria to breed—some nasty things can lurk in there when you get back if you leave dirty water in them. And even a few inches of water left in a bucket is a drowning danger to toddlers.

• *Mops*

Damp mops can also smell sour and support fine colonies of germs if you don't watch it. Don't think that a mop is disinfected even if it was used with disinfectant cleaner. Ideally, you should wash a mop head in the washing machine (without bleach, and in a mesh bag) after you use it, then hang it to air-dry. At least rinse your mop well and make sure it has a chance to dry completely. Never leave it in a bucket of water or crammed in a corner.

• *Cleaning cloths.* See "Cloth, Cleaning."

• *Sponges*

Rinse them well after each use, first squeezing a little detergent solution through them several times if you've done heavy-duty cleaning. Never bleach a sponge to clean it or you'll weaken it and speed its disintegration.

• Dust mops

If you live somewhere where shaking a dusty mop outside isn't possible (or would be an unfriendly act), just vacuum the accumulation from the strands when it seems to need it. Or you could tap the mop hard on the basement or garage floor, then vacuum up all the dropped debris. When a dust mop gets dark and dirty, take it off the frame and toss it in the washer, then air-dry and retreat it. You can bleach the head lightly if you want it to stay white, but *don't overbleach*, or you'll weaken the yarn.

• Brooms

Do get dirty. Dip the business end of a broom into a bucket of mop water every so often and swish it around well and shake the water off; the split-tip bristle brooms will also benefit from a good combing out occasionally.

• Treated paper dustcloths

These collect a lot of dust, since that's what they're designed to do. When they get bad you can rinse them with warm, clear water. They'll look a lot better and will still have some mileage in them.

• Wet/dry vacuum

If you use your wet/dry for wet work, especially dirty work such as cleaning

up an overflowed toilet or pet mess, mix up a bucket of disinfectant cleaner and suck it through the vacuum hose to clean it out. Just shove the hose into the bucket and empty the solution into the wet/dry pickup tank. This will eliminate odors and have the equipment all ready for the next use. If the attachments need cleaning, rinse them out in the bucket of cleaner before you vacuum it up.

Doodlebug. See "Scrubbee Doo."

Doors

Doors are some of the most heavily used parts of a house, yet we forget all about them when we clean. A spotless door really gives a house a lift, so let's do something about it! Ninety-nine percent of wood doors—varnished or painted, even elaborately carved—will have several protective coats of paint, varnish, or sealer, which means any moisture we use to clean them won't hurt the wood if we apply it the right way and then get it right off. I like to wash a door just like a wall, applying an all-purpose cleaner solution with a sponge on one entire side of the door, letting it sit for thirty seconds, then wiping it dry with a cleaning cloth. Don't forget that grimy area around the doorknob and the dusty top of the door too. If there are a few marks and nicks left, dip the corner of your cloth into the solution and rub the spot with some pressure; most (even black) marks will come out. If they don't, then I use the nylon side of a dampened white nylon-backed scrub sponge. Dip it into the solution and gingerly scrub the mark. If that doesn't do it, it's probably damage to the door rather than dirt. If the door is varnished wood you can clean it the same way using some oil soap (see "Oil Soaps") solution—it'll leave a nice low luster behind. Be sure to wipe and dry with the grain of the wood. You can use a squeegee on a smooth-surfaced metal door too.

Don't wash doors in the sunlight, when they're warm or hot, or they'll streak badly. See also "Tracks of Sliding Doors."

Drain Blockages

You don't have to call a plumber at the first sign of an overflow—many drain blockages are no big deal and can be cleared quite easily as follows.

The first line of attack is the familiar plumber's friend, or plunger. Run enough water in the fixture to cover the plunger and use wet rags to block off any other openings, such as the overflow tube in a basin or tub or the other side of a double sink. Then seat the plunger firmly on the drain opening, and pump vigorously ten or fifteen times. Try it several times before you give up.

If the plunger doesn't do it but the drain is partly open, you might try a chemical drain cleaner. (See "Drains—Using Chemical Drain Cleaners Safely.") But don't believe the advertising that says this or that drain cleaner works even in standing water—they seldom do.

If none of the above does it, try

▶ **Dough:** Does *not* make a good cleaner, as so many old wives' tales claim, nor does it do any better when baked and used in the form of bread crumbs. There was an old wallpaper cleaning dough that worked pretty well in the 1940s, but it left little mouse droppings all over the place. The dry sponge (see "Dry Sponges") does a much better job.

taking off the trap under a lavatory or sink—that's often where the blockage is, and it's not a big job. Just be sure to put a bucket or something under the trap to catch the water that will gush out when you take it off.

If the drain is still blocked, at this point most of us should call in a plumber. In the case of toilet and bathtub blockages, most people will want to call for help once they've plunged for a while without success. Clearing clogged drains in these fixtures usually means dismounting the stool or finding and opening up the cleanout in the tub drain. Handyman types may want to rent a plumber's snake and attempt such deeper clogs themselves, but if the blockage is in the main line, it'll probably require the efforts of a pro anyway.

Most drains will benefit from an application of the Big R every so often in their life. The Roto Rooter man or his equivalent will come with a sharp-bladed revolving head on a cable that passes through the "cholesterol" in the pipe and razors off the accumulated grease and scum and all the little tree roots that have invaded.

Drain Cleaners

Chemical drain cleaners are of three basic types: caustic, acid, and enzyme. Caustic types usually contain lye, which is fairly effective on fatty acids such as grease and body oil, but less so on hair and vegetable matter. (See "Caustic"; "Lye"; "pH in Cleaning.") Acid drain openers usually contain a strong concentration (sometimes 100 percent) of sulfuric acid, which is more effective against hair, soap, and other kinds of drain stoppages but is dangerous to use. (See "Sulfuric Acid.") Of the two, caustics are safer, but also slower and generally less effective than acids. Enzyme types contain friendly bacteria that produce enzymes that "eat" organic material. (See "Bacteria/Enzyme Digester.") These are by far the safest to use, both for you and for your plumbing fixtures and for the septic tank/sewer system/overall environment. Unfortunately, they aren't as effective as the harsher products and take longer to work. One big drawback is that the soaps, detergents, bleach, and sanitizers often found in drains tend to kill the bacteria that produce the enzymes. As scientists work to make ever better enzyme cleaners, these products will be able to replace the corrosive chemicals we now keep stashed under our kitchen sinks.

Drain Pans, Appliance

These drain pans are the plastic or metal pans under refrigerators and freezers and the below-the-burner area on the stove where you're likely to find fossilized macaroni, escaped peas, and dead gnats. Fortunately, cleaning them is not a daily task. It's easy enough to remove the pull-out pans and soak them in warm sudsy water until the dirt and grease come off. Then, unless the manufacturer's instructions say soap and water only, you can spray or wipe with disinfectant cleaner and put them back.

Stove pans are tougher. Many aren't easily removable and you have to do contortions to get to them. Whisk or vacuum up all the loose stuff first, and sponge on heavy-duty cleaner/degreaser (available at a janitorial supply store) or a product like Formula 409. Then go do something else for a few minutes and give it time to soak in. When you come back, wipe the worst of it off with paper towels and throw them away. Reapply cleaner, let it soak, and wipe away again and then rinse until it's clean. The key here is leave the cleaner alone to do the work for you.

Drains—Preventing Clogs

Dealing with clogged drains is no fun. Here are some simple precautions you can take to prevent the problem.
- Don't pour grease down the kitchen sink—this is the biggest cause of clogged drains.
- If you use a garbage disposer, run it with cold water (not hot) to keep any grease or greasy food particles in solid form, so they'll flush away without sticking to the pipes. Fill the sink with water before turning the disposer on, and run the cold faucet full force while the disposer

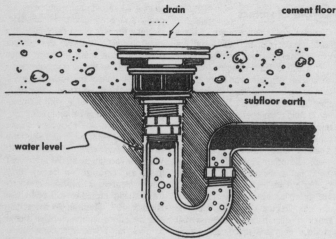

The P-trap of a floor drain is designed to keep bad odors from coming up the drain.

is running and for a full minute afterward.

- Don't pour coffee grounds down the sink or flush them down the toilet—put them out with the trash (or, better yet, compost them).
- Pull pop-up stoppers out of bathroom basins and tub drains regularly and clean off the inevitable blob of accumulated soap and hair.
- Keep toothpicks, hairpins, and the like out of toilets and sinks. If one gets in fish it out—don't flush it down the drain where it can jam in a pipe and start a clog.
- Don't flush disposable diapers or sanitary napkins down the toilet. (Toy trucks, dollies, and other little items a kid might chuck down there won't help either.)

Drains, Smelly

The seldom-used drain, such as a floor drain in a utility room or garage, will often get stale and smell. This is because most drains, down inside where we can't see, have a curve of pipe called a *p-trap* that holds some of the water we flush down to block sewer smells from coming up through the drain. But if it sits for a long time with no new liquid going down, the water in the trap will evaporate and let sewer gas seep up. To prevent this, you can pour a gallon of fresh water (maybe even with a little pine cleaner in it) down the drain at least once a month to keep the trap operating properly.

Drains—Using Chemical Drain Cleaners Safely

Don't use drain openers routinely in hopes of preventing clogs—too frequent use can damage pipes. But if you do have a partial blockage that plunging won't clear, a chemical drain cleaner may save you a plumber's bill. Here are some guidelines to follow.

- Don't put drain cleaner in a totally blocked drain—especially if there's water standing in the fixture. It won't clear the blockage, and you'll just end up with a sink full of caustic water. Plunge first to get any standing water to drain out.

- Always use rubber gloves, and be careful not to splash drain cleaner on your skin, in your eyes, or on surrounding surfaces.

- Follow the label directions to the letter, and turn on the fan or otherwise provide ventilation to clear toxic fumes. If you have pets or little people around, close the door to the room while the stuff is working.

- Never mix different types of drain cleaners together or use any other cleaning product with them—violent chemical reactions can result.

- Don't look into the drain after you've poured the cleaner in—the chemical reaction going on in there can cause the caustic to boil up and spatter. Toxic fumes are often produced too, so leave the room while the chemical works.

- Never use a plunger once you've put the drain cleaner in—it'll only splash caustic chemical around.

- Don't use chemical drain cleaners in a garbage disposer.

- Rinse the sink or fixture out well when the stuff has finished working, and flush the drain out with a full steam of water for several minutes.

Drapes. See "Curtains."

Drawers

The cleaning part of drawer cleaning (we're not talking about all the excess stuff—junk—in there, which is a separate problem; see "Junk and Clutter") is mainly the debris that sifts out and gathers in the corners. This stuff—lint, sand, crumbs, bits of paper, buttons, paper clips, broken parts of things, and other little odds and ends—is generally best dealt with by emptying the drawer. Then dump the fallout, wipe the inside of the drawer with a damp, not wet, cleaning cloth or sponge, let the drawer dry, and replace it and its contents. A limited-power vacuum (one—such as a cordless hand vac—that won't suck up the socks) held close to the bottom can clean out the corners without emptying the drawer.

If you have an old wooden drawer that's stained and dirty inside, clean it well first with all-purpose or heavy-duty cleaner solution, depending on how dirty it is. Let it dry thoroughly, use fine sandpaper to remove any remaining stains, and seal it (see "Sealing") with polyurethane or varnish to prevent further stain absorption and ease future cleaning. Never saturate wood drawers with water—it can warp them and make them hard or impossible to pull in and out. Go easy with moisture on metal drawers too, and dry them immediately after cleaning to prevent rusting. Sand and repaint any rust spots already there.

Driveways

The easiest way to clean a driveway is just to hose it off. But you don't want to hit it with water if it's super dirty—you'll just get a layer of hard-to-handle mud. Sweep it first to get the worst of the soil, then hose it down to leave a nice clean surface. Hosing is quick and efficient, if done regularly before heavy concentrations of dirt buildup. In below-freezing months, and anytime hosing isn't possible, sweeping with a stiff-bristled push broom is the best bet. A stiff broom will make short work of light snow too. For removing oil and other stains from concrete driveways, see "Oil Stains"; "Concrete." Oil stains on asphalt can be treated with an absorbent compound, but solvents shouldn't be used as they will dissolve the asphalt.

Dry Cleaning

We tend to think of dry cleaning in terms of clothing, but the term actually refers to any cleaning process where solvents (usually petroleum solvents) are used rather than water. Dry-cleaning systems are available for carpeting, resilient floors, and upholstered furniture, among other things. Fabrics and surfaces that water might shrink, warp, or cause to lose color are usually dry cleaned.

The dry-cleaning process for cloth-ing is much like laundering, except the washing machine uses volatile solvents (usually perchlorethylene) instead of water to dissolve and flush out the soil. To get the most out of professional dry cleaning, take soiled articles in promptly before stains can set, and point out any spots or stains to the cleaner. Let them know what the stains are and how old they are, if you know, and what you've done to try to remove them, if anything. Be especially sure to mention the following spots, which can leave permanent stains if not given special care: salad oil, coffee, tea, soft drinks, liquor, or fruit juice. Think twice about using the do-it-yourself coin-op dry cleaning machines at laundries. You give up the professional cleaner's expert evaluation and the often-necessary prespotting, to say nothing of the steaming, pressing, or other finishing touches that may be needed. Most of what we own that requires dry cleaning is too valuable to take a chance on for the sake of saving a few dollars.

Dry-Cleaning Fluid

A dry-cleaning fluid is any solvent used in a dry-cleaning process, whether for clothing, carpeting, furniture, or whatever. As used in this book, the term refers to the volatile solvent spotters used to remove oil and grease stains from fabrics. These are available in supermarkets and variety stores as Afta, Carbona, Energine, K2r or Thoro (an aerosol solvent spotter that you spray on and brush off after it dries). Janitorial supply stores also carry aerosol and liquid solvent spotters. Dry cleaners

▶ **Dry cleaners** are our friends, and generally the smart alternative for cleaning things we're unsure about or have no experience with. Dry cleaning is reasonably priced (I've never met a rich dry cleaner), and dry cleaners have better tools and chemicals and a thousand times the experience we do. In the long run, they can handle questionable stains and articles, especially, cheaper and better. Use them as one of your first, rather than last, resorts. Refusing to turn things over to them is like refusing to use electricity. Don't forget to praise and thank them when you can. People always expect miracles of dry cleaners; they take the positive for granted and make a big deal of any negative.

use *perk* (perchlorethylene) in their machines and a variety of other solvent spotters.

Go easy with dry-cleaning fluid on upholstery and carpet, as the solvents in it can damage the foam in upholstery cushions and dissolve the latex adhesives used to glue carpeting to its backing. (The "bubbles," or raised spots, you see on some carpeting are due to rash use of dry-cleaning fluid!) Always use dry-cleaning fluid in a well-ventilated place, and don't use it on clothing that you're still wearing. Keep out of reach of children!

Dryers, Automatic

For efficient drying, and to prevent fires, the lint filter or a lint screen of a dryer should be cleaned before each new load. Lint can also collect in the exhaust duct and inside the rear panel on electric dryers or around the burner on gas dryers and create a fire hazard. These parts of a dryer should be cleaned by a professional serviceperson every two to three years.

If the interior of the dryer has been discolored by dyes (baked on by heat!), it's probably a permanent discoloration. But try unplugging the machine and using heavy-duty cleaner, such as Formula 409 or Fantastik. If that doesn't do it, try a mild cleanser, such as Soft Scrub. Rinse with a damp cloth and then tumble a load of clean wet rags for twenty minutes or so to remove the last traces of cleaner residue. If the stains don't come out, at least you can find some consolation in the fact that they're very unlikely to have any effect on future dryer loads.

Exterior: See "Washing Machines."

Dry Sponges

Dry sponges are soft, foamlike rubber sponges used to "dry clean" wallpaper, acoustical tile and other porous ceilings, oil paintings, murals, and any surface where moisture would pose a problem or soak in and stain. Dry-sponging is also a popular professional way to clean smoked or plain old dirty wall paint. It's great for wood paneling and vinyl wall coverings too. Even if you intend to wash the walls anyway, ten minutes of dry-sponging the room first will cut your washing time in half. Dry-sponging is also a good way to clean walls before

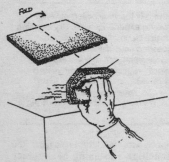

How to fold and use a dry sponge

you paint them. A dry sponge won't remove grease, fingerprints, jam smudges, or flyspecks—just the surface film of dirt.

Dry sponges come in two sizes, a 2- by 2- by 6-inch block and a 5- by 7- by ½-inch pad. The block can be mounted easily on a stick or pole to reach and remove heavy coats of dirt in high places. But I prefer the pad because it has more usable surface—it can be folded and used in such a way that you have eight fresh surfaces to clean with.

To use a dry sponge, just swipe it lightly over the surface in 4-foot lengths (or shorter if your arms are shorter). The sponge will absorb the dirt and begin to get black. It will hold the dirt as you clean along, but when it is saturated, switch to a new area of the sponge and keep going. When a dry sponge is thoroughly saturated with dirt—black—on both sides, toss it. And don't even think of using one wet—it isn't designed for that. Dry sponges can hold a ton of water, and it will all run out on you and the floor before you get to your work spot!

Dry Spotters. See "Spot Removers."

Dust Allergies

Most people aren't actually allergic to the contents of common house dust itself. (See "Dust and Dust Control.") Most of us with dust allergies are really reacting to the fecal pellets produced by *dust mites,* the tiny insects that thrive on the skin flakes present in almost all house dust. Experts estimate that up to 2,000 dust mites can live in 1 ounce of mattress dust, so there are plenty of them to go around. Interestingly enough, people with animal allergies aren't usually allergic to the actual animal hair either—the hair is just a handy carrier for the animal skin flakes (dander) and dried saliva that is the true source of the allergy problem. In any case, we've got to get rid of the hair and dust that carry the allergens, and that's a challenge, since the stuff is everywhere.

To reduce the amount of dust in a house, you have to eliminate the places it hangs out—carpeting, bedding, upholstered furniture, and dust-catching decorations. Give up the overstuffed, padded, and cluttered look and go lean and mean. Replace carpeting with hard floors; cover mattresses, box springs, and pillows with plastic covers, wash bedding and curtains often; and go to hard-surface rather than soft furniture. (Vinyl upholstery is okay.) Even if you just do your bedroom, you'll have relief for eight hours a day. Then keep those nice hard surfaces scrupulously clean. Wipe them regularly with a damp cloth to avoid stirring dust up into the air. (See "Dusting.") Vacuum any soft furnishings with a vacuum that doesn't leak particles back into the air. (See "Vacuums.") Installing a high-efficiency (HEPA) room air filter will probably be a help, but an electrostatic precipitating filter may not be. These high-energy electronic filters also produce ozone, which itself can cause breathing problems for asthmatics and people with hay fever. Keeping the furnace filters faithfully cleaned or changed can make a real difference. A humidifier will also help hold dust down, but keep it clean too, or it will build up mold, to which many people are allergic. Detailed instructions on dust-proofing are available by sending a self-addressed, stamped envelope to: Mothers of Asthmatics, 10875 Main Street, Suite 210, Fairfax, VA 22030.

Dust and Dust Control

More than 40 million tons of dust settle on the United States every year, about 40 pounds of it in your house. It's composed of everything from tiny particles of rock, sawdust, fabric, and paper, to salt from the ocean, carbon from smoke, and ash from volcanoes and cosmic dust. There's flakes of skin, little pieces of insect bodies, viruses, bacteria, pollen, and mold spores in there too, along with insect eggs and droppings, hair, and just about anything else you can think of. The air in the average home has about twice as much dust as the air outside (around a million tiny bits of particulate matter in every cubic inch of air), and many of the

particles are so small that they never settle—they just float around constantly. Since we're constantly breathing and ingesting this stuff, it's no wonder some of us have dust allergy problems. (See "Dust Allergies.")

If no one in the house has a dust allergy, one of the main reasons we fight dust is cosmetic—dust makes us look like bad housekeepers. And tiny as they are, many components of dust (such as silicates and volcanic ash) can be quite abrasive, so we want to keep it from scratching and grinding on things. Accumulated dust will wear away both carpeting and hard floors underfoot, and it wreaks havoc with such things as electronic equipment. We control dust by preventing it (door mats, weatherstripping, sealing concrete floors, etc.), by collecting it (dusting, sweeping, vacuuming), and by sifting it out of the air with the filters on our furnaces and air conditioners, and with special air filters. For removing dust, see "Dusting" and the discussions of specific types of dust removal equipment. For preventing dust, see "Mats, Walkoff"; "Sealing"; "Vacuum Care."

Dust Bunnies (Dust Balls)

In the space shuttle, when a wrench or a pair of pliers floats away and gets lost, astronauts have learned to go to an air intake or a quiet corner where things settle to look for it. It's the same with the household phenomenon called dust bunnies. Dust falls out of the air and settles into quiet places such as under furniture, in back of the fridge, and in out-of-the-way corners where it lays undisturbed and builds up into balls and clumps of fuzz. Poke your vacuum wand or a dust mop under the bed once in a while and wave it around—if you let the dust bunnies multiply under there unchecked for too long, they'll take over the world someday.

Dustcloths

A good dustcloth doesn't just move dust around—it traps and holds it. Some people dust with a damp rag or sponge, but this makes mud if there's much dust at all and you end up just smearing the stuff around and leaving streaks. And many of the things we dust (such as polished wood furniture) aren't going to benefit much from a wiping down with water. A better way to go is to make a real dustcloth by treating a piece of soft cotton (flannel is good here) with a good dust treatment. (See "Dust Treatments.") Ready-made dustcloths are also available, either retreatable or throwaway. Some of the best throwaways are made by Chicopee Mills, either Stretch-n-Dust or the original yellow Masslinn cloth, available at janitorial supply stores. There are also electrostatic dustcloths, such as the New Pig Dust

---

▶ In case you had any doubts, you dust first and vacuum last. Then all the dust and debris you flick off the windowsills, ledges, and furniture will be vacuumed up with all the rest, instead of arriving later to sully your freshly curried carpet.

Cloth, which attract and hold dust with static electricity. Cloths like these can be laundered and reused over and over. See also "Duster, Lambswool."

Dusters, Feather

Feather dusters offer a quick way to remove dust from things such as knicknacks, plastic philodendrons, and elaborately carved moldings, but they can present a dirt redistribution problem. If vigorously flicked around, the feathers just dislodge the dust and launch it into the air, where it's free to settle on other surfaces. A quality ostrich feather duster will actually hold a fair amount of dust if you're careful. Use a smooth wiping motion to gentle dust away and don't shake the duster around too much. The time-honored technique is then gently to tap the duster on the heel of your shoe, allowing the collected dust to settle to the carpet where it can be vacuumed up. Even this process tends to get quite a bit of dust airborne, however. To complicate things, good ostrich feathers are hard to find and expensive nowadays, and the cheap feather dusters aren't much good for anything but moving dust from one location to another. A smarter choice would be a lambswool duster, which collects and holds dust better. (See "Dusters, Lambswool.")

Dusters, Lambswool

A cotton-candy–looking puff of natural or synthetic wool attached to a long handle, lambswool dusters rely partly on the natural oils in the wool

A lambswool duster

(which is why real wool is better) and partly on static electricity to attract and hold dust. Professional cleaners have been using lambswool dusters for years—they make dusting and decobwebbing fast and easy, and you can do high and low dusting without stretching or bending. Some even come with an extension handle, which makes it possible to dust light fixtures, exposed beams, and ceiling corners without climbing. Lambswool dusters are much better than a cloth, and almost as good as a feather duster at dusting uneven and intricate surfaces, and dusting knickknacks and trophies. And they're much better at holding on to the dust they collect. Even so, you want to use them with a smooth wiping action (rather than flicking or waving the wand around) to avoid redistributing dust. Lambswool dusters are *not* the thing to use on rough wood or masonry surfaces—little wool tufts will get caught on slivers and protrusions and remain as mute testimony of your visit.

When your duster gets loaded with dust, it can be vacuumed or shaken outside. When dirty, it should be shampooed gently like human hair and rinsed well. Then spin the handle between the palms of your hands to throw off excess water, and hang the duster up to dry.

Dusting

Too often dusting is just moving dust from one place to another. A broom, for example, gets much of the dust off the floor, but it kicks a lot of the finer particles up into the air where they will soon settle on other surfaces. Dusting with a feather duster or untreated cloth also tends to clean the object we're working on but redistribute a lot of what we take off. A vacuum with leaking seals or a bad bag or filter can fling dust through the whole house. The key to dust control is using tools that *capture and remove* dust instead of just relocating it.

A good vacuum is one of the most effective dusting tools we have, because it traps and holds dust so it can be removed from the premises. You can use a vacuum dusting brush for everything from hard floors and furniture, to lampshades and woodwork. Just make sure bags, filters, gaskets, and seals are in good shape, so dust really is gathered up by the machine and not just blown back into the air as you vacuum. For those with dust allergies, a central vacuum system or a Rainbow water-filtration vac may be a good investment, as machines like these dispose of fine dust better than conventional vacuums. (See "Vacuums.")

When you hand-dust, you also need to collect and hold the dust, and you can't do that with a retired T-shirt. What you want is a treated or electrostatic dustcloth (see "Dustcloths") or a lambswool duster. A lambswool duster is better than a feather duster, but either can redistribute dust into the air if used too vigorously. (See "Dusters, Lambswool"; "Dusters, Feather.") Always use a gentle wiping action, being careful not to flick dust off the surface and into the air, and don't shake a duster out in the house. For dust on hard floors, you want a treated dust mop. (See "Dust Mop"; "Dust-Mopping.")

No matter what tool you're using, you always want to dust from top to bottom, and be sure to switch sides when one side of your cloth or duster gets loaded up.

To prevent dust, use good walkoff mats at entrances (see "Mats, Walkoff"), seal all raw concrete floors and masonry (see "Concrete"; "Sealing"), and use weatherstripping to seal windows and doors against dust infiltration.

Dust Mop

For removing dust and dirt from large areas of hard floor, a dust mop is much more efficient than a broom. Not only will a dust mop cover the area faster and need only one pass to do the job, it traps and holds fine dust better and won't kick dirt up into the air the way a broom will. The best dust mops are the professional models sold by janitorial supply stores. An 18-inch mop is a good size for

home use; you might want to go a 24-inch one if you have a lot of large, open areas. To work the way it's supposed to, the mop must be treated with dust mop treatment. (See "Dust Treatments.") Follow the directions supplied with the dust treatment, and be sure to use the right amount of chemical for the size mop you're treating. After each use, just shake the mop out and give it a light touchup spray of dust treatment. When badly soiled, the mop can be removed from the frame and laundered. (Put it in a mesh bag to keep the strands from tangling, and don't use bleach.) Pretreated, disposable mops are available from janitorial supply stores for those who don't want the fuss of treating their own.

Dust-Mopping

To get the most out of a dust mop, you have to use it right. The mop should be pushed over the floor in a smooth, continuous motion, with the same edge always leading. This can be done in long, uninterrupted swaths by simply pushing the mop in a straight line in front of you, or by using the efficient side-to-side S motion preferred by professionals (which enables you to get more sweeping done with less walking). The mop head should never leave the floor, and each time you change direction, swivel the head so that the same edge of the mop is still leading. This way you can be sure to carry all the dust and dirt along with you, without dropping any. Avoid hitting corners or edges of furniture legs because this too will cause the mop to drop some of its dirt load. At the end of a swath, the accumulated dirt can be gently shaken off into a pile, but avoid vigorous shaking, which will unleash dust into the air. To finish up, push all your little dirt piles into one, and pick up with a dustpan and whisk broom. See also "Dust Treatments."

Dustpans

What's more frustrating than a dustpan that won't pick up? To do the job, a dustpan needs a thin, flexible edge that will conform to irregularities in the floor and not allow dirt or dust to be swept underneath it. Plain metal and hard plastic dustpans are worthless for this. Metal ones with a flexible vinyl lip are better. Probably the best are the flexible molded pans,

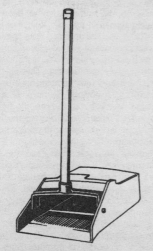

A long-handled dustpan

such as the professional-quality ones made by Impact, available at janitorial supply stores. They don't rust or get bent out of shape, they're deeper so you can use them to pick up water, and they're unaffected by most chemicals. Keep your molded dustpan hanging flat against the wall to keep it straight and even.

If you do a lot of litter pickup, a long-handled dustpan (the kind used in hotel lobbies and at Disneyland) lets you do a lot of dust-panning without bending. You can find them at a janitorial supply store too.

Dust Ruffles

Dust ruffles are those floor-hugging ruffles and skirts around the bottom of furniture thought to prevent dust, but really best at preventing efficient vacuuming. The truth is they *collect* and *hide* the stuff. If you want to declare war on dust, rip the dust ruffles off your furniture so you can see the dust bunnies forming and get at them before they multiply. Don't use a dust ruffle to hide the area under your bed, unless you enjoy conducting a minor expedition under there periodically to retrieve all your runaway socks and earrings. Leave these under areas open and exposed so they're easy to clean and aren't forgotten.

Dust Treatments

Dust treatments are usually oily or waxy compounds designed to attract and hold dust. Some water-based dust treatments are designed for floors (such as rubber and terrazzo) that can't tolerate oil. Applied to dustcloths and dust mops, dust treatments cause dust particles to clump together and cling to the cloth or mop rather than float around. Dust particles are like sheep—skittish and hard to round up individually, a lot more manageable when bunched up. Dust treatments are available as aerosols, such as the Drackett Company's Endust, or the liquid form available at janitorial supply stores that you put in your own spray bottle. Enough dust treatment should be applied to the mop or cloth to make it feel moist but not wet.

Dust mops should always be treated (ideally, dustcloths too), then wrapped up in a plastic bag overnight before using, to give the oil a chance to saturate the fibers evenly. This is especially important for mops, as most have an absorbent pad that acts as a reservoir, to which you apply the dust treatment. The mop is designed so that just the right amount of oil will wick down into the strands from the reservoir. If you try to hurry the process and spray the strands so you can use a mop immediately, they usually are too wet and you end up with oil on the floor. Most liquid dust treatments come with directions telling you how much of the product to use to treat different-size dust mops. After the initial treatment, an occasional light misting with dust treatment will keep your dust mop or cloth fresh and effective. (Do the misting after you finish today's dusting so the treatment will be well absorbed by the time you need to dust next.)

Be careful where and how you store treated mops and cloths—hang mops and seal cloths in a plastic bag—or you may end up with oil stains on the surface they've been leaning against.

E

"Eureka, I found it!" Deep cleaning is an excellent way to renew your supply of petty cash.

Earthenware. See "Clayware."

Edges (Floor, Carpet)

The last inch or so that the vacuum seems to miss isn't a panic piece of cleaning. Any floor surface right against the wall, fixture, or furniture is seldom stepped on. Whatever it collects (lint, fuzz, little bits of debris) doesn't get ground in, so it does no damage and comes up easily when you do clean it. Don't try to muscle your way right up to the wall with an upright vacuum—you'll only cause scuffs and gouges. Hit carpet edges quickly every week or so with an angle broom and maybe every month or so with the edge tool of a canister vac or a damp cloth. Or whenever you know an edge-checker is coming. Wax buildup on the edges of hard floors, on the other hand, is a major cleaning problem. See "Wax Buildup"; "Floors, Stripping for Waxing"; "Wax Strippers"; "Waxing Floors."

Electric Cords. See "Cords."

Electrolytic Cleaning. See "Silver."

Electrostatic Air Cleaners.
See "Air Cleaners, Electrostatic."

Emergency Cleaning

Cleaning up after a fire, flood, sewer backup, furnace blowup, or the like is a demanding job. Specialized equipment and expertise are often needed, and this is one time it's definitely smart to call in a pro. Fortunately, most such calamities are covered by homeowner's insurance, and the insurance adjuster can refer you to a professional disaster restoration specialist who know just how to handle them. When disaster strikes, call your insurance company right away. Then do what you can immediately to get fires put out, running water turned off, faulty appliances shut off or unplugged, furniture and other belongings up and out of standing water, broken windows boarded up to protect contents, and so on. The longer these kinds of situations sit the greater the damage, so fast action is critical. Bear in mind that your insurance company will expect you to protect the building and its contents from further damage, as far as possible. Don't allow a flood, for example, to run unchecked when it can be reasonably stopped. Be sure to tell the company the action you took to reduce their costs.

If the mishap in question is not covered, ask your insurance carrier whom you might use for that particular problem. Insurance companies deal regularly with competent professionals in all fields. Get competitive bids—three should be enough. Get some references and check the company out. Get the job estimated in detail, not just a total but an itemized list of the operations and the costs. You need to know what they will and won't do. It's also important to have a mutual understanding as to the expected results of the job.

If you're qualified to do a disaster cleanup yourself, you can rent equipment at janitorial supply stores or rental centers.

▶ **A salute to the emergency substitutes:** Let's show some respect (give a cheer!) for the emergency substitutes, the unsung heroes of cleaning:
The hanky . . . often the *only* thing available.
The human fingernail . . . has scraped at least 100,000 tons more than all the putty knives in the world put together.
The coin (edge) . . . always tougher than the hardest gum or gunk.
The credit card . . . it's never expired when it comes to shoveling up mini-spills and messes.
The old piece of cardboard . . . has picked up more dirt than any dustpan.
The shirttail . . . its cleaning battle scars are quietly tucked away.
The Q-Tip . . . tiny, but totally committed to the places nothing else can reach.
The diaper . . . the genius behind many a home cleaning chore.
The old toothbrush . . . the only mini-scrub brush most of us own.

Emulsify

Technically, *emulsify* means to cause one liquid (such as oil) to mix with another liquid (such as water) with which it normally wouldn't mix. This is how soaps and detergents in water solution are able to remove oily and greasy soils. Surfactants (see "Surfactant") in the soap or detergent break the oil into tiny droplets and then surround them, preventing them from getting together with other droplets to re-form as an oil slick. The detergent solution with all the little oil droplets suspended in it is called an *emulsion*. Mechanical action (scrubbing) is often used to assist the detergent in breaking up and dispersing the oil in the cleaning solution. The idea then is to hold the dirt suspended until you can dump out the bucket of dirty water. If you exhaust the cleaning power of your solution before you dump it, you'll notice oily deposits forming on the bucket as little runaway droplets of oil escape the emulsion and start clustering with others of their kind again.

Soap contains natural emulsifiers, and synthetic emulsifiers are added to detergents to help them perform this vital function.

Enameled Metals

The term *enameled metals* is somewhat unclear because of the confusion between the terms "enamel" and "porcelain." (See the box "Enamel versus Porcelain.") As used here, *enamel* means a vitreous (glassy) coating fused onto metal by firing in a kiln. Cloisonné jewelry is an example

of enamel work, but we find far more examples of this ancient art in our plumbing fixtures and appliances today than we do in decorations. Enameled steel is used for such things as washer and dryer cabinets, bathtubs, sinks, and cookware. Enameled cast iron makes by far the most durable and chip-resistant bathtubs and sinks.

Be careful not to confuse enameled steel, which has a glasslike coating fused onto the metal, with the baked enamel finishes used on many appliances. Baked enamel is just paint baked in an oven, and doesn't withstand chemicals and solvents as well as enameled steel. Many manufacturers will refer to enameled steel as "porcelain" or "porcelainized steel." Whatever it's called, a true enameled steel cabinet is superior to a painted one.

Whether the enamel is fired onto a cast-iron bathtub, a steel wash basin, or a dryer top, the care is the same. It will withstand just about any common cleaning chemical or solvent, with the exception of hydrofluoric acid, which eats glass. If you use a rust remover containing this potent acid, don't use it on your "porcelain" washer or dryer top. Harsh abrasives such as silica-based scouring powders and colored nylon scrub pads shouldn't be used on enameled surfaces either, or over time even their glassy surface can be scratched and dulled. (See "Abrasive Cleaners.") If a scouring cleanser must be used, get one with mild abrasives, such as the new-formula Comet. The safest approach is to use an all-purpose cleaner, with a white nylon-backed

► **Enamel versus Porcelain** (in case you've wondered): These terms have been used rather loosely by marketing people, creating a lot of confusion. Originally, *enamel* meant a vitreous (glassy) coating fused onto metal or pottery by firing in a kiln, for decoration and protection. Cloisonné jewelry is a classic example. When you buy an "enameled steel" or "enameled cast-iron" bathtub, this is the kind of enamel you're getting. Unfortunately, the paint manufacturers long ago began calling their hard, glossy, enamellike finishes *enamel*, and nobody was smart enough to stop them. Then, when people started curing paint jobs in ovens, the term *baked enamel* was born. To make matters worse, appliance manufacturers began referring to enameled metal surfaces as *porcelain*. So when these terms are used now, it's anybody's guess what they mean.

To sort it all out, here's how I use the terms in this book:

• When referring to paint, I use such terms as *semigloss enamel, latex enamel,* or *enamel paint.* (See "Painted Surfaces" for care instructions.)

• For true vitreous fired enamel finishes, I'll say *enameled steel* or *enameled cast iron.* (See "Enameled Metals.")

• I use the word *porcelain* only when referring to true porcelainware, which is a ceramic (clay) material fired in a kiln to produce fine china dinnerware and figurines and other decorative pieces as well as household and plumbing fixtures. (See "Porcelain.")

scrub pad to loosen hard deposits. Acid descalers can be used on enamel without damage, but be sure whatever you use is also safe for any metal or plastic fittings or trim.

Energy Saving While Cleaning

• Most of the electricity used in cleaning goes to heat water. Insulate the water heater (keep it at 120°F) and hot water pipes.

• Repair leaky faucets.

• Run cold, not hot, water down your garbage disposer when running or cleaning it. (This makes it operate better, anyway.) Hot water isn't necessary for many jobs; it turns room temperature soon after it hits the wall or floor you're washing, anyway.

• When vacuuming, save energy by clearing the clutter before you turn the vacuum on. Empty the bag when it's half full to increase your vacuum's efficiency. And make sure the belt and fan are replaced when worn. Use mats (see "Mats, Walkoff") to reduce the need for vacuuming.

• Utilize the self-cleaning feature of the oven after baking, while the oven is still hot.

• You usually save money and energy using the dishwasher instead of hand-washing. Most dishwashers will clean dishes that have been scraped, and there is no need to rinse, except casseroles, pots, and the like. It costs the same to wash a whole load or partial load, so fill 'er up! Let the dishes air-dry (usually by using the energy saver button on the machine). If you do hand-wash, rinse dishes in a sink or a pan of hot water, rather than one by one under the tap.

- Don't overload clothes washers or use too much or too little detergent, and carefully select both water level and temperature; warm-water washing with the right detergent will clean most clothes. Use a cold-water wash whenever you can and *always* use a cold rinse. Use a shorter cycle for lightly soiled clothes. Use high-spin speeds for such things as towels and jeans. This will remove more water and reduce that expensive drying time.

- Don't heat up the whole dryer for just one favorite shirt, and dry loads consecutively while the dryer is already heated. Don't keep opening the dryer door while a load is drying—it lets heated air escape. Don't overdry clothes. (It'll only wrinkle them and wear them out before their time, if it doesn't shrink them.) Use the automatic dry and permanent press cycles— they use less energy than the normal cycle. Keep the dryer filters free of lint. Install dryers with as short and straight an exhaust duct as possible.

- Once in a while, especially for very heavy or bulky things, consider the old clothesline instead of automatically tossing everything in the dryer. It gives you a little exercise and fresh air as well as that impossible to duplicate fresh-from-the-line aroma.

- Operate both the washer and dryer (and other cleaning appliances such as dishwashers) at nonpeak times in your area.

- Iron a bunch, or at least a batch, of clothes at once, instead of heating up the iron (and setting up the ironing board) for one desperately needed item at a time.

- Clean in the daytime whenever you can—you can see better and do a better job and you don't need all those lights.

A few ways you can save energy *by* cleaning:

- If you defrost the freezer and vacuum the dust from behind it, it'll run better and cheaper.

- Clean air conditioners (see "Air Conditioners and Heat Pumps") cost less to run too.

- Clean light bulbs, lampshades, diffusers, reflectors, and the like give you more light for your money.

Etching

Etching is the action of a corrosive chemical (usually an acid) eating away at a surface, leaving a porous, pitted area. Etching can be good or bad. Concrete floors are etched with an acid bath before sealing, to roughen the surface and assure a good bond for the seal. But when the rough, dull spot is on top of your new automatic washer, where you put the rust remover on your white jeans, it's another story. Restaurant owners have to replace their drinking glasses periodically because the surface of the glass becomes etched from repeated dishwashing. Showing first as an iridescent film and progressing to opaqueness, this kind of etching is accelerated by high pH dishwasher

▶ **Excuses for not cleaning:** *I fell
asleep. . . . I can't find my Don Aslett
book. . . . I got a late start. . . . I'm
teaching the kids what a dirty house
really looks like. . . . I'm letting my
fingernails grow. . . . The maid
quit. . . . I lost a contact lens. . . .
We're moving anyway. . . . I'm
pregnant. . . . My fairy godmother is
on vacation. . . . We had an
earthquake. . . . I ran out of paper
towels/vacuum bags. . . . I'm going to
do it right before Mother comes. . . .
No one ever goes in there anyway!
. . . Don't you want the house to look
lived in? . . . I'll do it tomorrow/on the
weekend/later. . . . I just did it last
week. . . . The vacuum is on the
blink. . . . It'll make the rest of the
place look bad. . . . Housecleaning
isn't aerobic. . . . What dirt?? . . . It's
been a rough week. . . . I don't want
to disturb the household ecology. . . .
My therapist told me to avoid
stress. . . . I'm allergic to lint/dust. . . .
It's your turn. . . . No one ever
appreciates it anyway! . . . I'm going
to wait till the dog finishes shedding/
kittens grow up. . . . I'm beat/too
busy. . . . It only gets dirty again. . . .
It's more efficient to do it all at
once. . . . I'm doing it a room at a
time. . . . I don't like inside work. . . .
What will the roaches eat?*

detergents and extremely hot wash
temperatures. The same process
happens at home, but probably not
enough to notice before the kids leave
the glass out in the garden, anyway.

Exhaust Fans

While there are several types of exhaust fans, the one we worry most

about cleaning is the kitchen fan,
which gets loaded with cooking
grease. This kind of fan is usually
ceiling or wall-mounted and vented to
the outside. For range hoods, see
"Hoods, Range." Many such fans
have a removable grease filter, which
can be taken out and washed separately. To clean a grease filter in the
sink, soak the degreaser solution or
steaming hot water with some automatic dishwasher detergent added.
Scrub with a brush, then rinse wth a
forceful spray of hot water. Aluminum
filters can go in the dishwasher, but
don't put them in with dishes. After
washing, shake out all the water you
can and set aside to dry before rein-
stalling.

Most of the motor and fan units can
also be unplugged and removed for
cleaning. Wipe off all the grease you
can with a dry paper towel, then carefully clean the fan blades with hot
detergent solution, being careful not
to get water inside the motor openings. The duct, grille, and surrounding area should also be washed while
the motor unit is out. Use a white
nylon-backed scrub pad to loosen
stubborn grease, but be careful not
to scratch polished surfaces.

Extension Poles

A must for modern cleaning. Extension poles have long, lightweight aluminum or fiberglass handles that enable you to reach high places quickly
without a ladder, from the floor or
the ground outside. The business end
of the pole is tapered or threaded so
that a window squeegee or window
scrubber, lambswool duster, paint

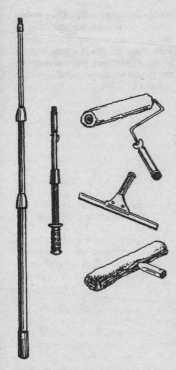

Extension poles and some of the tools they can be used with.

roller, or the like can be attached. With an extension pole you can do high work safely without climbing and reach over obstructions easily to paint walls or clean windows. Extensions come in all sizes. Best size for the average home is a 4-foot pole that extends to 8 feet.

Eyeglasses

You probably clean your glasses at least once a day . . . the wrong way. Here's the right way to do it, to protect those ever more expensive prescription lenses and make short work of any spots in front of your eyes.

Never wipe dry lenses with *anything*—your shirtfront, slip, or a scratchy paper towel. Most lenses today are plastic, and even if antiscratch coatings have been applied, it's all too easy to scratch them. Dragging the dust, dirt, and grit that's sure to be on the surface across it dry is a sure way to end up with little lines that weren't there before. If you're caught out somewhere with dusty glasses, resist the urge to start wiping—just blow hard on them to remove the worst of it, and wait until you're in a better position to clean them.

Don't use glass or window cleaner on plastic lenses and frames, because the ammonia in these products isn't good for the plastic. Don't use silicone-impregnated lens cleaning tissues on plastic lenses either—they're made for glass. Use a dampened soft cloth instead, or a squirt of the special alcohol-based glasses cleaner the optician gave you, followed by a soft dry cloth. Best of all is holding them under a running tap of lukewarm water, so all those tiny abrasive particles will be washed right off the lenses and down the drain. If they need it, you can then dab a little soap on with your finger, rub it around, and then rinse. If there's a bit of buildup caked on there, use a soft toothbrush to scrub gently all around the rims of the lenses and the nosepads too. For drying lenses, tissues may be handy but a soft cotton cloth or even a camera lens cleaning paper is a surer way of sidestepping scratches.

Oil the hinges, and rinse the entire frame from time to time too to remove the salt from sweat that will eventually whiten and roughen plastic frames. To restore life and color to plastic frames that are faded and dull from oxidation, rub in a little vegetable oil or petroleum jelly and then rub the plastic as dry as possible with a soft cloth.

F

Forty percent of housework is just picking up, working around, and tending junk, litter, and clutter.

Fabric Softener. See "Laundry."

Fabrics

NOTE: The following table lists the fibers home cleaners deal with every day. Use it as a guideline for the general care of fabrics that have no care label. If an item does have a care label, follow it!

Fiber, Common Trade Names, Main Uses	Cleaning Characteristics	Cautions
ACETATE (Airloft, Avron, Celanese, Estron, Lanese, Loftura, etc.) Used in clothing, lingerie, linings, draperies, upholstery fabrics. Also as fiber fill for quilts, pillows, and mattress pads.	Stain, moth, and mildew resistant, but susceptible to color fading and dye running. Most acetate fabrics must be dry-cleaned; some can be washed as delicates in cool water. If ironing is necessary, press on wrong side at low heat setting.	Damaged by acetone, alcohol, and acetic acid (vinegar); can't tolerate high heat; weakened by long exposure to sunlight. Weak when wet.
ACRYLIC (Acrilan, Creslan, Fina, Orlon, Pa-Qel, etc.) Found in all kinds of clothing (especially sweaters) and in pile fabrics, blankets, robes, carpeting, draperies.	Stain and mildew resistant, good dye fastness. Machine-wash and dry on low heat. Block acrylic sweaters out flat on a towel to dry. White and light colors will usually tolerate chlorine bleach. Use only low iron settings.	Heat sensitive. Lack of resiliency and abrasion resistance in acrylic carpeting makes for grayed-out and crushed traffic lanes, permanent furniture indentations.
BROCADE. See entry.		
COTTON (a natural plant fiber) A favorite for apparel because of its comfort, long wear, and colorfastness. Also used for linens, slipcovers, curtains, etc. Often blended with polyester in permanent-press fabrics, and treated with various finishes to improve handling and care characteristics.	Untreated cotton is susceptible to staining, wrinkling, and mildew, and deteriorates in sunlight. Strong and long-wearing, will withstand aggressive laundering, including hot water, chlorine bleach, and scrubbing. Wash whites and coloreds separately. Follow label directions for cotton treated with specialty fabric finishes.	Sensitive to acids— don't use vinegar or acid spot removers.

Fiber, Common Trade Names, Main Uses	Cleaning Characteristics	Cautions
COTTON *(continued)*	Iron damp with a hot iron. (Corduroy is a form of cotton fabric with some special requirements: Turn inside out before washing to minimize lint and wash in warm water to prevent shrinking. If you dry until only half dry on permanent press setting, then hang dry the rest of the way, you can avoid ironing.)	
LINEN (a natural plant fiber) Durable, drapes well, and has a soft luster; comfortable in hot weather—used for blouses, dresses, and summer suits, and for households linens.	Resists soiling and staining better than cotton; moth resistant; tends to wrinkle easily. Launders well, becoming softer with repeated washing. Washes best in hot water, and white linen can be chlorine-bleached. Press while still damp with a very hot iron.	Shares cotton's sensitivity to acids.
MODACRYLIC (SEF, Verel) Fake fur, deep-pile coats, blankets, children's sleepwear, stuffed toys.	Stain and mildew resistant. Most modacrylics (especially the fake furs) should be dry-cleaned. If laundered, air-dry without heat.	Very heat sensitive— will not tolerate hot air–drying or ironing.

Fiber, Common Trade Names, Main Uses	Cleaning Characteristics	Cautions
NYLON (Anso, Antron, Cantrece, Caprolan, Celanese, Cordura, Crepeset, Qiana, etc.) A popular fiber, widely used in carpeting, apparel, sporting goods, hosiery, and home furnishings.	Strong and long-wearing; resists abrasion, nonoily stains, mildew, and insect damage; washes easily and dries quickly. Fabric softener recommended. Wash colors separately to avoid dye transfer; use medium dryer setting.	Attracts oily stains, develops static cling, picks up other dyes easily, whites yellow in sunlight and chlorine bleach. Don't dry whites in sun. Use a warm iron if needed.
OLEFIN (Herculon, Marquesa, Marvess, Vectra, etc.) A member of the polypropylene family, olefin is used primarily in carpeting, especially outdoor carpeting (synthetic turf), both as face yarn and backing material. Used to a lesser degree in upholstery fabrics, blankets, and apparel.	Not as abrasion resistant as nylon, but extremely resistant to stains, chemicals, insects, mildew, sunlight, and perspiration. Solution-dyed olefin is very colorfast. Withstands aggressive cleaning methods, including chlorine bleach, but should not be ironed or subjected to high heat.	Most heat sensitive of all synthetics—melts at less than 300°F; lack of resiliency leads to crushing and matting in carpeting.
POLYESTER (Avlin, Caprolan, Dacron, Fortrel, Hollofil, Kodel, Shanton, Trevira, etc.) Blended with cotton, rayon, and wool for use in all types of garments, especially permanent-press; also used as fiber fill in pillows, jackets, and sleeping bags. Occasionally used in carpeting.	Strong and colorfast. Resists wrinkling, abrasion, stretching, shrinking, mildew, moths, sunlight and perspiration. Wash in warm water and dry at medium heat, using fabric softener. Remove from dryer promptly. Iron at permanent-press setting if needed.	Attracts oily stains, develops static cling.

Fiber, Common Trade Names, Main Uses	Cleaning Characteristics	Cautions
RAMIE (a natural plant fiber) Often blended with cotton for sweaters and other garments.	Ramie fibers make strong, lustrous fabrics that are colorfast and resistant to alkali and mildew. Withstands hot laundering, drying, and ironing, but some dyes or finishes may call for dry cleaning.	Sensitive to acids—use no vinegar or acid spotters.
RAYON (Avril, Coloray, Durvil, Fibro, Zantrel, etc.) A man-made fiber of regenerated cellulose, used alone and in blends for apparel, lingerie, rainwear, linings, draperies.	Comfortable, colorfast, and static-free. Some rayons are dry clean only, others can be machine-washed and tumble-dried. Iron on the wrong side while still slightly damp, or use a press cloth.	Susceptible to acids and mildew, and weakened by long exposure to sunlight. Untreated rayon will shrink. Ironing without a press cloth may leave shiny spots. Resin-treated rayons shrink less, but may be damaged by chlorine bleach.
SILK (a natural animal fiber) Used for garments, linens, handkerchiefs and scarves, decorative uses.	Luxurious look and feel, resists wrinkling and soiling but is sensitive to many chemicals. Most silk requires dry cleaning, but some types can be hand-washed or machine-washed as delicates. Follow care label directions. Test for colorfastness before washing. Press on the wrong side with a warm iron while damp.	Sensitive to acids, alkalis, enzyme digesters and chlorine bleach; weakened by perspiration and exposure to sunlight. Many silk fabrics water spot, and some are subject to dye running.

Fiber, Common Trade Names, Main Uses	Cleaning Characteristics	Cautions
SPANDEX (Lycra) Elasticized fabric used for foundation garments, swimwear, athletic apparel, support hose, etc.	Resistant to stains, body oils, perspiration. Most spandex garments can be machine-washed and tumble-dried on low heat; some may require dry cleaning, depending on other fibers blended in.	Damaged by chlorine bleach; very heat sensitive. Don't use chlorine bleach. If ironing is necessary, use lowest temperature setting and keep the iron moving.
TRIACETATE (Arnel) Used for permanent-pleat garments, flannel, jersey, taffeta, textured knits, tricot, sportswear.	100 percent triacetate fabrics can be machine-washed, dried, and ironed at hot temperatures. Whites can be chlorine-bleached. Pleated garments should be washed and dried on medium heat and laid flat for drying.	Damaged by acetone, alcohol, and acetic acid (vinegar). Susceptible to moths, mildew, and static cling.
WOOL (including alpaca, angora, camels hair, cashmere, mohair, and vicuña—all natural animal-hair fibers) Used for garments, blankets, carpeting, decorative uses. Wool is comfortable, wrinkle resistant, colorfast, and naturally water-repellant.	Because of the potential for shrinkage, most wool garments should be dry-cleaned. Some woolen knits tolerate gentle hand-washing, using a product such as Woolite (never a detergent). Wool garments labeled "machine washable" can be washed in an automatic washer on delicate but should not be tumble-dried unless the label specifies it. Knitted woolens should be blocked out to air-dry. Use no chlorine bleach.	Damaged by moths, chlorine bleach, strong alkaline cleaners, and enzyme digesters.

Fall Cleaning

Fall is the best time for deep cleaning—the time to rid your house of "dirt weight" for the largely indoor living months ahead. Here's what I'd do, in order of priority.

1. Vacuum everything thoroughly—under, over, behind too. Pull all the dust out from everywhere, and don't forget the drapes.
2. Deep-clean rugs and upholstery.
3. Clean all inside and outside door mats.
4. Wash windows and light fixtures.
5. Clean drapes and blinds.
6. Wash or spot-clean walls and ceilings.
7. Scrub (or strip) and wax all floors.
8. Wash cabinets, baseboards, woodwork, vents.
9. Clean or change furnace filters and declutter the furnace zone.
10. Clean the garage, right down to the floor.

Fans

Your ceiling fan may look okay as you gaze up at it from the floor, but did you ever look at the *top* of those blades? No wonder the poor thing wobbles as it turns: The blades are out of balance from all those bug bodies and all that built-up gunk! Spray a little all-purpose cleaner solution on, let it sit on there a few minutes, then polish dry. Turn off the power to the fan before you start, and be careful not to spray into the motor openings. Use metal polish on brass parts only

if the metal is uncoated. (See "Brass.") If the brass has been lacquered to keep it from tarnishing, just wipe it gently with the all-purpose solution or with glass cleaner.

Portable fans can be damp-wiped with all-purpose cleaner, after removing any grilles or cages that enclose the blades. (Be sure to unplug first.) If the motor assembly is removable, you can speed up the chore of cleaning the grille by soaking the whole thing in all-purpose or degreaser solution for fifteen minutes after removing the motor. Don't immerse or hose down fans with nonremovable motors, though—moisture will damage them. Any cooling vents in the motor should be vacuumed to remove lint and dust, and vacuuming off the grille every time you pass it with a running canister vac isn't a bad idea either.

Faucets

In areas where mineral scale isn't a problem, Windex-type glass cleaner will put a nice shine on chrome fixtures. For areas with hard water, a mild acid cleaner is a better choice. (See "Hard-Water Deposits"; "Cleaners, Acid.") Many pro cleaners use a spray bottle of phosphoric acid or tub and tile cleaner diluted 5:1 with water to spray-clean their bathroom fixtures and never have any mineral scale buildup to contend with. Just spray it on, hit any stubborn soil with a white nylon-backed scrub pad, then polish dry. Once a week or so go after the edges and cracks and crev-

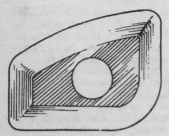

A small plastic scraper is a good way to go after the grunge that collects around faucet hardware.

ices that fill up with soap scum with an old toothbrush, a plastic putty knife, or a flexible plastic scraper. If you have faucets with serious mineral scale buildup, use full-strength delimer straight out of the bottle to get the stuff off, then maintain with the dilute solution. Most delimers contain mild acids that won't damage chrome, plastic, or porcelain fixtures as long as you rinse after using. If you have brass or gold faucets or other high-society hardware, make sure the product you use is approved for use on those metals and follow the manufacturer's cleaning instructions.

Feather Dusters. See "Dusters, Feather."

Feather Pillows. See "Pillows."

Feathering

Many fabrics show a water spot or ring after a wet spot dries on them. The reason this happens is that any soil and fabric treatment (sizing, etc.) in the fabric migrates to the wettest part of the spot as it dries, accumulating and depositing at the part of the spot that dries last—usually the outside edge. A spot from which a stain has just been removed is also often slightly cleaner than the surrounding fabric, so it will show up unless blended in. To avoid both of these effects, professional cleaners usually finish spot-cleaning by "feathering" the edge. Spotters in dry-cleaning plants do it with a steam gun. We home stain removers feather as follows:

• When you finish working a spot and rinse it, brush the spot with a dry towel, working from the center out toward the edge with light, lifting strokes to blend the wet area in with the dry. Instead of a marked boundary between wet and dry, you want it more wet in the center and fading to dry at the edges.

• Blot the spot and force it to dry from the outside in. This can be done by rubbing briskly around the edges of the spot with a dry towel or by drying from the edge in toward the center with a hair dryer.

Fiber Rush. See "Cane."

Fiberglass

Everything from sinks and skylights to campers and canoes is now made of fiberglass, a plastic resin reinforced with glass fibers. The surface layer, or "gel coat," is smooth and shiny and quite soil-resistant if you keep it intact. So don't use cleansers or abrasives of any kind on it—many of them will dull and scratch fiberglass, making it harder to clean. If you do find it necessary to use a cleanser on fiberglass, make sure it's one of the new gentler formula ones, such as Mr. Clean Soft Cleanser or Comet. (See "Abrasive Cleaners"; "Cleansers.") Also avoid using strong alkaline cleaners and solvents such as acetone and lacquer thinner. The safest way to clean fiberglass is with a neutral cleaner and a white nylon-backed scrub sponge. This will remove just about any soil and keep the surface smooth and shiny. If hard-water scale is a problem, use a phosphoric acid cleaner to dissolve it. (See "Hard-Water Deposits"; "Phosphoric Acid.") The acid won't hurt the fiberglass as long as you rinse it off right after use. To help worn fiberglass resist soiling and make it easier to clean, wax it with car wax—this seals up the tiny pores in the surface and makes it slick and soil-repellant again. If you wax the bottom of your tub or the floor of the shower, you'll want to use a rubber bath mat to avoid slips and falls.

Fiberglass fabric is indeed woven of glass fibers, which is why it's not machine-washable or -dryable. The agitation of a washer will damage the fibers and small particles will remain in the tub and stick to fabrics washed in later loads, causing serious skin irritation. If you toss fiberglass in a dryer you'll have itchy fiberglass hair in your clothes for thirty-one years afterward (or the life of the dryer, whichever comes first).

Since it is glass, fiberglass doesn't absorb much soil, so you may actually be able to just wipe it clean with a damp cloth. If it needs deeper cleaning, dissolve laundry detergent in a tub full of warm water. Add the item and let it soak in the solution for half an hour, then swish it around gently by hand, being careful not to rub or twist the fabric. Then rinse both the item and the tub well and air-dry—you can hang drapes over the shower curtain rod or roll them in towels to remove most of the moisture. Then, if it is a curtain, hang it back up on the window to finish drying, smoothing a little by hand as you do so. Don't use clothespins on fiberglass—they could injure the fabric—and never iron it.

Filters, Appliance

We have a way of forgetting about filters, those low-profile items that collect and hold dirt that would otherwise get all over everything. Many appliances, including automatic washers, clothes dryers, and dishwashers, have filters that need regular cleaning. Otherwise, they won't be able to continue to trap and remove undesirables from the stream of air or water moving through them. The lint traps on automatic washers are usually found either on top of the agitator or in a slot just under the lid. Flush the trap out under the faucet, using a stiff toothbrush to dislodge stubborn particles. Dryer lint screens are found in a slot just inside the door or behind a small door on top of the cabinet. The layer of accumulated lint can be peeled out easily with your fingers. Both washer and dryer lint filters should be cleaned after every load. Dishwasher food traps should be checked after each use and cleaned as needed, but a good prerinsing of dishes will save a lot of filter cleaning. For range hood filters, see "Hoods, Range"; "Exhaust Fans."

▶ **Filth:** The "f" word of the cleaning profession.

Filters, Heating and Cooling System

Furnace filters remove airborne soil from indoor air as it passes through the furnace. Filters should be cleaned or replaced at the beginning of the heating or air conditioning season, and about once a month while the system is operating. Dirty filters not only allow airborne soil to be circulated throughout your home, they also seriously diminish the heating and cooling capacity of the furnace's air-handling system. Dirty filters make the motor work harder to pull the air through them, so they waste heating and cooling dollars. There are three basic types of filters: dispos-

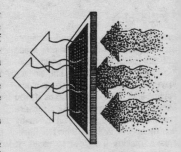

Filters remove airborne soil from indoor air.

able, permanent, and electronic. Locate the filter by removing the access panel or filter drawer on the front of the furnace. (Some filters just sit in open slots and you don't have to remove anything to get to them.)

Disposable filters are just a mesh pad in a cardboard frame, and these should be replaced whenever they appear clogged. (Hold them up to the light and you'll know.) Simply throw the old filter away and replace it with one the same size. (The size is stamped on the edge.) Most filters also have an arrow stamped on the edge that indicates the direction of air flow. Since air moves toward the blower, the filter should be installed with the arrow pointing toward the blower.

Permanent filters are usually a foam pad mounted in a metal frame. The foam must be removed and cleaned with hot detergent solution and rinsed, then sprayed when dry with a filter-coating chemical sold at hardware stores and home centers. The foam filters in portable or window-mounted air conditioners, humidifiers, and air cleaners are not usually sprayed. If in doubt, consult your owner's manual.

Electronic filters clean the air by imparting an electrical charge to dust particles and attracting them to a collector plate. This is the most effective type of air filter available. Once a month, or when the indicator light shows the unit needs cleaning, turn off the switch on the cleaner's power supply door and remove it. If there is no power switch, turn off the circuit breaker to the unit. Pull the collector cell(s) out by the handle, then slide out the aluminum prefilter. These units can be washed by themselves in the lower section of your dishwasher. Or you can put the collector cell and prefilter in a plastic tub or bathtub with ½ cup automatic dishwasher detergent and enough hot water to cover them. Let them soak for twenty or thirty minutes, then scrub with a brush to loosen the accumulated dirt. Take the units out, rinse with a garden hose, and let them dry before returning them to service.

Fireplace Ash

You'll clean the firebox ten times as much as the outside of the fireplace and a hundred times as often as the chimney, so take the time to learn how.

1. Clean it more often—don't wait until the ashes are so deep they're spilling out on the hearth. If the firebox is lined with metal, a hole will eventually burn through the metal—faster if it's always full of ashes. And you'll get more heat if you have less ashes!

2. Take it from the man who once burned down the dock at Sun Valley: Make sure the fire is totally out before you start this operation! If there's even a flicker of a chance that a live coal or two is left, *wait.*

3. Open the damper as wide as possible when you're cleaning the firebox. Doing so will generally (unless it happens to be a low-inversion day) cause all that fine ash dust to filter up the chimney and out of your house as you work, and not into your lungs.

4. Set a container such as a cardboard box or plastic bucket as close as possible to the opening, and line it with a plastic bag.

5. Proceed slowly. (This is one job even I do slowly.) Scoop the ashes up with a small dustpan and don't pour or dump, but *set or lay* them in the container. Do this until all the ash is gone. Don't worry about scooping up every last speck; your goal here is to get rid of the bulk of the ashes.

6. Before moving (dumping, carrying, etc.) the container, tie the top of the bag. If you don't, ashes will snort out of there like a whale spray.

(The ashes make a nice addition to the compost pile or fertilizer for the garden.)

Fireplace Facing

Cleaning the face of a fireplace is a project that demands patience. The dirt and stain have usually accumulated over the course of years, and most of us want to wipe it away in five or ten minutes. Unlikely. Fireplace stone and brick may be hard, but they're also porous. This means plenty of tiny holes for soil to accumulate in.

First mix up a warm solution of high-alkaline cleaner (see "Cleaners, Heavy-Duty"; "Degreaser") and 1 ounce of chlorine bleach per gallon of water. There's bound to be some fallout, so make sure the floor around the fireplace is well covered with dropcloths before you start. Wet the surface of the fireplace well with the solution, but don't put on so much that it runs. Dirty water running down the face may cause hard-to-get-out streaks. Then scrub the solution in with a brush—you should see the suds getting dark and dirty as the buildup comes off. Rinse well. If the surface is shadowy after cleaning, a light cleaning with a phosphoric acid cleaner may be enough to brighten it up the rest of the way. Don't use any acid stronger than phosphoric—it will attack and damage the brick or stone.

If the results still aren't satisfying, make a poultice of heavy-duty cleaner, bleach, and diatomaceous earth and apply it to the areas needing attention. This should draw out any remaining residue. If necessary, repeat these steps until you get the result you want. The color of the brick or stone determines how aggressive your use of bleach can be. Heavy bleaching will whiten a dark surface and cause it to look out of place. You can use a stronger solution on white or light surfaces.

Fishing Reels

Reels see a lot of fast action, so they need to be kept free of salt, grit, and sand that corrodes and grinds away at the working parts. A reel used for saltwater fishing should be rinsed in fresh water right after each use. If you drop a reel in the sand or in salt water (or in dirty fresh water), it's a good idea to open it up and flush it out with clean water on the spot, before continuing to use it. When you get it home, take it apart and wash all the parts in solvent (see below) and wipe dry, then lubricate as needed and put it back together. Once a year, preferably before packing it away in storage, a reel should be completely disassembled, solvent-cleaned and relubricated.

Better reels come with an instruction manual containing disassembly instructions and a lubrication chart showing which lubricants to use where. Your reel dealer or any quality sporting goods store can supply reel cleaning services if you don't want to do it yourself, or advice and the supplies you need if you do. You can use a special parts washing solvent for cleaning, or any nonvolatile solvent, such as kerosene or paint thinner. Most moving parts require a light oil, such as sewing machine or gun oil, while the gears need a lightweight grease. As you reassemble, make sure the gaskets that seal the gear box are in good shape, to keep out damaging grit and moisture.

Fishing Rods

If you still lure the lunkers with a venerable old bamboo fly rod, caring for your favorite fish stick can be a little involved. You have to worry about the varnish cracking, the glue joints drying out, the ferrules coming loose, and getting the cane too wet. When cleaning a bamboo rod (mild detergent solution is the best thing to use), don't let water sit on the surface long, especially if the varnish is cracked.

Use fine steel wool to gently rub corrosion off the metal ferrules and reel seat. A light coat of oil after that will help retard future rusting. A soap-filled steel wool pad will make grungy cork grips look like new too; just go easy on the water.

Most of us, fortunately, are dealing instead with a modern composite rod made of fiberglass or graphite fiber. Cleaning and maintenance of these babies is a cinch. Just rinse your rod with fresh water after saltwater fishing, and wipe with a damp cloth to keep it free of dust and dirt. Keep it in a hard case so it won't get crunched by a wayward boot or car door, and replace the guides at the first sign of line grooving. Old, worn, scuffed rods can be brightened up a bit with car wax.

Flock and Foil Wall Coverings

Flock is that raised fuzzy material you first saw in a three-dimensional storybook where you could feel the fur on the tigers and the spots on the dogs. The flocked wallpaper made now generally has a vinyl or vinyl-coated base. First wipe it with a dry sponge. (See "Dry Sponges.") Then, only if necessary, wring a cleaning cloth dipped in all-purpose cleaner solution almost dry, and use it to gently wipe the surface of the flock itself. Blot dry immediately with a thirsty towel. Don't get the surface wet or rub or use aggressive cleaners.

Be even more careful never to scrub or use harsh or abrasive cleaners or tools on the reflective wall coverings called *foil*. Use a dry sponge or cautious damp-wiping here too, when unavoidable, and if you do use water on it, polish the surface dry immediately with a cleaning cloth to avoid streaks.

Floor Finish

While the term *floor finish* can be used loosely to mean any type of floor polish, I use it to refer to the synthetic polymer water-emulsion finishes. These are actually tiny spheres of plastic suspended in a water base. As the water evaporates, the plastic coalesces into a tough, uniform film that protects and beautifies the floor. Modern floor finishes like these are clearer and glossier than the old waxes, as well as more durable and resistant to yellowing and scratching. Most are self-polishing, which means they dry to a nice gloss without buffing, and after they get scratched and worn, most of them can be brought back to a shine by buffing or burnishing. Finishes designed to be maintained by high-speed burnishing are called *thermoplastic*, since they are softened and smoothed by the friction and heat of the polishing pad. (See "Buff"; "Burnish.") Very hard finishes that are essentially unchanged by buffing are called *nonbuffable*—they resist wear better, but can't be repolished.

One of the best finishes sold in supermarkets is Johnson's Future—this acrylic finish wears well, doesn't yellow, and is relatively easy to remove. If you go to a janitorial supply store, ask for a metal cross-linked self-polishing finish.

Most floor finishes are quite water resistant but they can be dulled by strong alkaline cleaners, so use only neutral cleaners or mild detergents to damp-mop them. And keep solvents including alcohol away because they will dissolve wax.

See also "Waxes."

Floor Machines. See "Floor Polishers."

Floor Polishers

(Also known as *buffers, waxers, scrubbers,* and *floor machines.*) These machines range in size from small household units with 6-inch brushes to big commercial units with 28-inch brushes. Just squeeze a switch on the

A professional model 12-inch single-disc floor polisher.

handle and an electric motor turns a disc that scrubs or polishes the floor. The newer nylon pads are much better than a brush on the bottom of the machine—different colors are available with different qualities. Yellow and white are soft polishing pads, and red is for buffing. Green and blue are moderately abrasive, and black or dark pads are downright vicious. The small twin-brush units (including those that hook to a vacuum) aren't strong or heavy enough to be effective. They just float over the deep dirt. They also splash badly, and the twin brushes make them difficult to control. If you want a polisher for your home, the best size is a 12- or 13-inch single disc machine. You can get a pad and drive block perfectly tailored to your home, and simply by changing pads you can scrub, polish, spray buff, shampoo, or sand with them. Floor machines like this are available at janitorial supply stores for around $300. Or watch the local want ads or auctions for a going-out-of-business sale—you might pick one up for a lot less. Operating them is tricky until you learn that to make them go right, you need to lift on the handle; to go left, you move the handle down. Pushing during either operation makes it go forward, and pulling makes it go backward.

Floor Squeegees

Available at janitorial supply stores, floor squeegees are a great way to expedite water roundup and removal on all types of hard floors. They'll also speed the drying of sidewalks and garage floors. Similar to a window squeegee, only larger, these have a rubber blade set in a frame attached to a handle, and the best ones are made so you can either push or pull them to clear a floor of liquid—floods or overflows, scrubbing or stripping water, even light snow or slush. A squeegee is superior to a mop for this purpose, because after that blade passes over it, the surface is almost dry. Instead of endlessly wringing a mop into a slop bucket, with a floor squeegee you can gather it all up quick and slick as a whistle. If you remember the first time you ever used a rubber spatula to scrape the last of the batter out of the bowl, you'll understand why. You can squeegee the puddles you collect into a dustpan, sweep them down the floor drain, if there is one, or wet/dry

A floor squeegee used with the push motion.

vacuum them up. I like an 18-inch push/pull Ettore myself, with a 5-foot handle.

You'll find yourself using the pushing motion most often, because when you push liquids away from you, there's less chance of flooding your own footsies. Push with a slow, steady motion—the blade has to curl under a little so it won't skip or chatter and throw water up in the air. Pushing or pulling, set yourself a target (drain, doorway, whatever) where you're going to get rid of the water and then push the water toward the target.

Floors, Cork

Cork floors may be either tile or cork sheeting, and though quiet and comfortable underfoot, they don't hold up

▶ **Floors clean enough to eat off of:** Says more about how hungry you are than how clean things are.

well in heavy-use, high-traffic areas. They will wear better, however, if sealed. Some cork tiles are sealed at the factory and others upon installation. Most cork floors are too resilient to put urethane on—the cork flexes underneath and causes the urethane to crack. Unless you have unusually hard cork, it's probably better to maintain it with paste wax.

If the floor is finished with paste wax, clean and polish with fresh paste wax, using a floor polisher with a steel wool pad.

If the floor is sealed with penetrating sealer, lightly sand worn areas and recoat. Like hardwood floors, cork floors can be sanded and refinished, but be careful: Cork is so soft it can easily be oversanded and permanently damaged.

Cork floors are maintained much the same as wood floors. Neutral cleaner solution can be used sparingly on a sealed cork floor. Avoid ammonia and other harsh alkaline cleaners or flooding the floor with water; either can easily damage cork. Spirit or solvent paste waxes are better for the floor than water-emulsion finishes. Pick up spills immediately and stay away from oily sweeping compounds or strong solvents such as paint thinner or lacquer thinner.

Use soft, wide furniture glides under furniture legs to help avoid denting this soft flooring. Place walkoff mats at all entrances and keep grit swept or dust-mopped up so it can't abrade the finish.

Floors, No-Wax. See "No-Wax Floors."

Floors, Resilient

Resilient floors are those with a little give or resiliency to them, such as linoleum, vinyl composition tile, sheet vinyl, cork, or rubber, as opposed to nonresilient or hard flooring, such as stone, concrete, terrazzo, or earth tile. Resilient floors need a flexible finish ("wax") that will move with the floor as it compresses under foot traffic. Harder, less flexible (and usually more durable) finishes can be used on nonresilient floors.

Floors, Rubber. See "Rubber Floors."

Floors, Scrubbing and Waxing

Waxed floors need to be swept and mopped regularly to keep off damaging grit. (See "Sweeping"; "Mopping.") When the traffic areas start to look dull and lifeless, it's time to scrub and rewax. Just mopping before waxing isn't enough—you need to scrub to remove stubborn embedded soil. If you don't scrub, you'll be waxing over dirt, and the floor will darken and require stripping sooner. You're not trying to remove all the wax here, just shave off the dirty surface layer, so be sure to use a mild or neutral cleaner. (See "Cleaners, Neutral.") Strong cleaners soften the wax and take off too much.

- After sweeping, wet the area with detergent solution, then scrub with a floor polisher or a Scrubbee Doo long-handled floor scrubber with a blue or green pad. (See "Scrubbee Doo.")

- Pick up the scrub water with a mop, then give the entire floor a fresh-water rinse.
- After the floor is good and dry, apply new wax or finish to the traffic areas only, avoiding edges, corners, and underneath things. (See "Waxing Floors.") The finish in these areas doesn't get walked on and should stay shiny, so you really want to rewax only the dull areas.
- If there's a marked difference between the freshly waxed area and the nontraffic areas when you're done, you can buff it out with a floor polisher or with a white pad on your Scrubbee Doo.

Floors, Stripping for Waxing

For stripping wood floors, see "Wood Floors."

After many applications of floor finish (or wax), floors will usually get a buildup of discolored old wax. When the whole floor starts looking dark and dirty and you can no longer ignore those ugly edges, it's time to strip. This means taking off *all* the old wax, right down to the bare floor. Stripping is one of the most dreaded cleaning operations, but a professional approach can make it much more bearable.

- First, sweep or vacuum the area, and don't ignore the corners, or under and behind things.
- Mop a generous amount of stripper solution (see "Wax Strippers") onto an area about 10 feet by 10 feet and

let it sit for five to eight minutes. It's critical to give the chemical time to work before you start scrubbing. You may have to rewet areas that start to dry out.

- Scrub the softened wax or finish with a heavy-duty floor polisher (see "Floor Polishers") if it's a large area, or a long-handled floor scrubber (see "Scrubbee Doo") if it's average size, using a black or brown stripping pad. I go over the floor twice: once to loosen the wax and help the stripper penetrate it, then again to really rake off the old wax. Apply fresh stripper as needed to keep the entire area wet while you're scrubbing—if the sludge dries, it will readhere to the floor.
- Squeegee the loosened goop into a puddle with a floor squeegee, and scoop it up with up with a dustpan. Or vacuum it up with a wet/dry vacuum. This is a lot faster than trying to mop it up.
- Quickly rewet the entire area with rinse water (don't let it dry out) and check to be sure all the wax is gone. If you see dark patches of remaining wax, or if your fingernail or the edge of a coin will still scrape some up, repeat the stripping operation. For heavy buildup, several strippings may be required.
- Rinse thoroughly. For no-rinse strippers, one final rinse with clear water will do. For highly alkaline strippers, at least two rinses are required, and the first one should have 1 cup vinegar added to each gallon rinse water.
- Let the floor get good and dry, and

it's ready for rewaxing. (See "Waxing Floors.")

Floors, Stripping Wood.
See "Wood Floors."

Floors, Vinyl Sheet.
See "Vinyl Sheet Floors."

Floors, Waxing.
See "Floors, Scrubbing and Waxing."

Floors, Wood.
See "Wood Floors."

Floppy Disks

The best procedure with floppy disks is simply to keep them clean at all times. Keep them in their dust jackets in a floppy disk file. Disk drives are designed to clean the floppy as it's used. You can buy a disk to clean the disk drive at your computer dealer.

Flowerpots (Clay)

Before potting a plant in a previously used pot, it's a good idea to sterilize it to discourage plant diseases and fungi from passing from the old plant to the new. You can accomplish this by rinsing the pot with boiling water, or immersing it in a warm solution of 1 part chlorine bleach to 10 parts water for twenty minutes. If you use bleach, be sure to rinse well.

Moss or algae can be scrubbed off pots with a stiff brush or nylon scrubber, but those crusty discolorations known as mineral deposits may call for steel wool.

For glazed flowerpots, see "Clayware."

Flowers and Plants, Artificial

Silk: Containers of compressed air that blast the dust off these dirt-loving lovelies are available at craft supply stores. Just follow the instructions on the label. A blow dryer set on low or cool will do the same. For actual dusting, a feather duster or small sable paintbrush is best, or for jumbo leaves, an electrostatic dust cloth.

If you're really ambitious, or your grimy flowers are one step from the garbage can, you take the arrangement apart and wash each flower. Dip each flower into a bucket of cool Woolite and water solution and swish it around a few times, then dip in a container of cool rinse water. Shake well and hang by the stem to dry. If you're less adventurous, you may want to try gently wiping each bud in place with a well-wrung-out cloth dampened with the same solution. Be careful not to distort the petals or fray their edges.

Plastic: Weekly dusting with a lambswool or feather duster will go a long way toward preventing the need to ever actually clean plastic plants, flowers, and fruits. Plants and flowers in the kitchen will inevitably acquire a coating of greasy grime (the same stuff that settles on top of the fridge). Fill your sink with a solution of warm water and liquid dish detergent and swish those blossoms back and forth a few at a time until you think the grease is gone. Then rinse in clear water and spread out on terry towels to dry. You may have to let the solution sit on the flowers a few minutes if they're heavily soiled, or even work them over with a soft-bristled brush.

Flowers, Dried

Dried flowers are one of the least cleanable things around. Not only are many of the inhabitants of dried arrangements incredibly fragile, many have 10,000 tiny parts, or are highly textured or prickly (which means they not only trap dust, they hold on to it with a vengeance). Depending on what a bouquet is made of, you could try gentle dusting with a feather duster; if it's heavy on dried baby's breath, foxtail grass, and aged goldenrod, you might not even want to try. The best solution is simply putting dried bouquets under or behind glass—immediately, right after you get them, if you intend to keep them indefinitely. At least try to locate them in places that aren't too dusty and prone to cooking vapors. Otherwise just replace them with a new arrangement.

Fluorocarbons

Fluorocarbons are chemical compounds similar to hydrocarbons, in which some or all of the hydrogen is replaced by fluorine. Because fluorocarbons are slippery and repel water and oil, they're used in lubricants, nonstick coatings, and soil retardants. (See "Cookware"; "Soil Retardants"; "Gore-Tex.") A group of fluorocarbons containing chlorine has been found to cause damage to the vital ozone layer of the earth's atmosphere. Before this connection was made, chlorofluorocarbons were widely used as propellants in aerosol cans, but most manufacturers have now switched to safer propellants. Fluorocarbons are still used widely as refrigerants, where they are in a closed system and much less likely to have any impact on the atmosphere. Freon is Du Pont's trade name for a group of fluorocarbons used as refrigerants and aerosol propellants. Teflon is a Du Pont trade name for a fluorocarbon nonstick finish.

Flush

As used in stain removal, flushing means applying enough liquid to flow through the fabric and carry away a stain or the spotting chemical used to remove a stain. You can use a squeeze bottle, spray bottle, or even an eyedropper to flush, and you want to do it from the back side of the fabric. This will wash the stain back out the way it came, instead of forcing it in deeper. If you're in a situation

FLUSHING

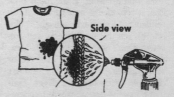

Always flush from the back side of the stained material.

Absorbent cloth soaks up the stain as it is flushed through.

where you can't flush the solvent all the way through to the other side—working on a carpet or upholstery, for example—keep applying it and blotting it out.

To avoid enlarging the wet area when you flush, put a pad of absorbent cloth on the face of the spot and apply the liquid through the back no faster than the pad can absorb it. Some stains require running water from the faucet or even boiling water to flush them out. (See "Red Fruit Juice" in "Spot and Stain Removal.") To flush carpeting, sponge liquid on and blot it back up with a clean towel.

Foam Rubber

Foam rubber often means the foam cushioning made of natural or synthetic rubber used in upholstered furniture, mattresses, pillows, and the like. The term is also loosely used to refer to foams in general, including those made of other synthetic materials, such as urethane. While we rarely clean naked foam, we often shampoo furniture cushions with foam padding inside and wash pillows filled with the stuff. If the foam in an item is actually made of rubber, it can be damaged by heat, sunlight, chlorine bleach, harsh cleaners, and solvents. Don't wash or dry with heat, dry-clean, or expose to sunlight or strong alkaline cleaners. Foam rubber can even catch fire in a dryer. Synthetic foam is less sensitive to chemicals and heat, but it still should not be treated with solvents.

Foam rubber can absorb odors, and if this happens, removing the covering and giving it a chance to air out

well (out of sunlight) is about the best thing you can do. See "Furniture, Upholstered"; "Pillows."

Foil Wall Coverings. See "Flock and Foil Wall Coverings."

Food Graters. See "Graters, Food."

Food Processors

First, unplug your food processor. Second, follow manufacturer's directions for cleaning. Third, for those of us who've long since disposed of the box and warranty card along with the care and cleaning instructions: Rinse all food-contacting parts immediately after use to avoid ending up with dried, stuck-on food. All those little attachments will harbor shreds of food if you let them—most unsanitary. If you rinse after each use you'll look forward to pulling out this cook's helper instead of letting it collect dust on the shelf. Most removable pieces and blades are dishwasher safe in the top rack only, or you can hand-wash them in sudsy water. Be careful of sharp edges, and don't use abrasives, they will scratch. Wipe the base (electrical housing) with a damp cloth after every use, and polish dry—never immerse in water.

Formica. See "Plastic Laminates."

Foxtail Brush. See "Counter Brush or Broom."

Freezers. See "Refrigerators/Freezers."

Frequency of Cleaning

How often should you clean things? First determine the desired result. Do you want to be able to eat off the floor or just stay a few steps ahead of the Health Department? Do you want a lintless carpet or just not to break your ankle crossing it? Do you want the dining room ready for surgery or for unexpected guests? Do you entertain frequently (including business clients and prospects) and have people popping in all the time? Other criteria to consider when determining how clean your home should stay are the number of people living in it, the type of furnishings you have, the amount of help you're getting, and how friendly your users are. Only you can determine the level you want to maintain. If you set your standard too high, you're only going to be frustrated and disappointed. If you have a large family and a densely furnished house and you're not seeing a lot of help or friendly users, either increase your cleaning frequency or reduce your expectations. Otherwise the burden on you may be pretty unrealistic. What degree of spit and polish do you actually need, feel comfortable with, and have time to achieve?

Let's take a look at what it takes to achieve cleaning standards of 95, 80, and 70 percent, for example. The frequencies that follow are just a general guide. Climate and environment have a bearing on frequency, for example. Dusty areas demand more dusting. Cold climates call for more frequent wall washing because more heating means more airborne soil. Damp climates usually require more floor care and carpet cleaning. Rural areas mean mud and windblown powdery soil, urban areas black gritty airborne dirt. The more members in your household or the larger your family, the more frequent cleaning (or at least policing and spot-cleaning) you'll usually have to do.

Cleaning Frequency Chart

Task	95%	80%	70%
Policing (straightening up)	7×/wk	4×/wk	2×/wk
Trash removal	3×/wk	3×/wk	2×/wk
Routine dusting	3×/wk	1×/wk	EOW
Dusting—high (above 6′)	1×/wk	EOW	1×/mo
Spot-clean light switches, doors, walls	3×/wk	1×/wk	EOW
Vacuuming—traffic lanes	4×/wk	1×/wk	2×/mo
Vacuuming—details and edges	1×/wk	2×/mo	1×/mo
Vacuuming—complete	3×/wk	1×/wk	1×/wk
Carpet spotting	7×/wk	2×/wk	1×/wk
Carpet shampooing—traffic lanes	1×/mo	1×/3mo	1×/4mo

EOW = every other week

Cleaning Frequency Chart

Task	95%	80%	70%
Carpet shampooing—complete	1×/6mo	1×/yr	1×/yr
Spill cleanup	As needed	As needed	As needed
Window washing—first story	1×/mo	2×/yr	1×/yr
Window washing—upper stories	2×/mo	1×/yr	Every 2 or 3 years
Blinds—dust	1×/mo	1×/2mo	1×/3mo
Blinds—wash	2×/yr	1×/yr	1×/yr
Walls—wash	2×/yr	1×/yr	1×/yr
Bathroom			
Spot-clean sinks	7×/wk	7×/wk	7×/wk
Mirrors	7×/wk	2×/wk	1×/wk
Toilet	2×/wk	1×/wk	1×/wk
Shower wipe down	7×/wk	4×/wk	2×/wk
Shower sanitize	2×/wk	1×/wk	1×/wk
Spot-clean walls, doors, switches	2×/wk	1×/wk	1×/wk
Kitchen			
Sink	7×/wk	3×/wk	1×/wk
Spot-clean walls	5×/wk	2×/wk	1×/wk
Floor—sweep and spot-clean	5×/wk	3×/wk	1×/wk
Floor—sweep and mop	2×/wk	1×/wk	1×/wk
Floor—scrub and wax	1×/mo	1×/mo	1×/mo
Stove—wipe	As needed	As needed	As needed
Oven	As needed	As needed	As needed

Frypans, Electric

Most electric frypans on the market these days are immersible and dishwasher safe—they will often say so right on the bottom. Never immerse electric appliances you're uncertain of, but if they are dishwasher safe it's a good idea to run them through oc-casionally for a thorough cleaning. Check your owner's manual carefully—some frypan covers, for example, should not go in the dishwasher.

For ordinary cleaning, turn the control to *off*, unplug the fryer, and when it cools, remove the heat control plug. Wipe it with a damp cloth if necessary, but never put the plug in

water. After the pan is cooled, soak
it in hot soapy water. Caution: Putting a hot pan in cold water will warp
it. Metal or green nylon scrubbers or
abrasive cleansers will mar the finish,
so scrub only with a plastic scrubber
or white nylon-backed scrub sponge
as needed. Rinse in hot water and
dry.

For stuck or burned-on food, heat
water to boiling in the pan with a
squirt of liquid dish detergent and
gently scrape the spot with a wooden
spoon. Use a coffeepot destainer
such as Dip-It to remove stains inside
the skillet, following package directions.

Nonstick finishes may need conditioning after washing (or when you
start to notice food sticking). This
usually means putting a teaspoon of
vegetable oil on a paper towel or soft
cloth and wiping the pan well all over.

Fuller's Earth

Fuller's earth is an absorbent clay
that gets its name from the process
of fulling (thickening and cleansing
cloth during its manufacture) for
which it is used. It is employed in
cleaning as an absorbent for removing
grease and oil from fabrics, and in
poultices. (See "Absorbents"; "Poultice.") You don't have to use a Fuller
brush with it!

Fur, Genuine

Genuine fur is not something to clean
at home, unless you're the family cat!
Fur should go to professional cleaners at least every couple of years,

not just when it looks dirty. They will
remove the lining and clean the fur
chemically, either with a dry powder
or other process that will remove
dust and dirt and help condition and
restore the sheen of your pelts. The
best thing you can do for your furs
otherwise is to avoid wearing them in
situations where soiling is almost certain, such as standing too close to a
crowd of animal rights activists or to
the champagne bottle at a ship chris-
tening. Store them at a furriers' during the nonwearing months, where
they'll be put in a climate-controlled
room at 38°F, where humidity won't
collect, mildew won't flourish, and the
fur won't dry out.

If you're keeping your fur at home,
store it apart from other garments in
a cool, dark place and don't crowd
it—give it plenty of room. Make sure
it's on a good sturdy hanger and put
a clean old shirt—not a plastic bag,
which doesn't allow it to breathe—
over it to keep the dust off. Take it
out every few months and fluff it up:
Shake it gently from the shoulders as
you would a throw rug (but not so
hard that you snap or pop it).

When you're wearing a fur or fur-
trimmed garment, wear a scarf
around your neck under the collar to
keep makeup and skin oils off the fur.
If fur gets water on it, shake it and
let it air-dry—don't blow-dry or use
heat of any kind.

Wall hangings or rugs made out of
fur can be dusted by blowing them
with cool air from your vacuum or
blow dryer. That's about it, because
they're not washable. You can take
them to your dry cleaner or local
furrier, though.

Fur, Imitation

Imitation fur is made of synthetic or natural fiber, or sometimes a blend of both, on a woven or knit backing. It may be dyed, airbrushed, or highlighted, or have "hairs" of different lengths to more closely simulate the real thing. And both the "fur" and the backing are often treated: The former with resin finishes to make it thicker, softer, and shinier, the latter with stiffening agents.

All of the above make cleaning it a tricky business. Fake fur is sensitive to heat, and it also can be crushed, matted, or shrunk easily. So to be on the safe side, dry-clean these fake fluffies, especially anything with long pile. Some of the shorter pile furs are hand- or machine-washable. (Follow labels very carefully—you usually want to avoid hot water and machine drying.) When in doubt, take your fake fur to your local dry-cleaning professional. The agitation of a washer and heat of a dryer could easily cause the fur to mat and fall out before its time. And a hot iron will *melt* it!

If you get a spot on fake fur, take it to the dry cleaner. Many spot removal preparations will melt or disintegrate fake fur, and it's all too easy to create a bald or scroungy spot by scrubbing. (Don't cram that faux fox jacket in the closet, either, when you get it home, or it'll look more like squashed possum when you go to wear it.)

See also "Stuffed Animals/Toys"; "Furniture, Plush."

Furnaces

While most furnace repairs require a trained technician, there are several important cleaning and maintenance tasks you can do yourself. Three parts of a furnace need regular attention: the filter system, the blower, and the motor. Keeping the filters clean is probably the most important thing you can do—for directions on how to clean them, see "Filters, Heating and Cooling System." To gain access to the blower and fan assembly, first turn off the electrical power to the furnace, then remove the front access panel. Most fan units mount inside the blower housing on tracks, held in place by set screws. Loosen the screws and slide the fan assembly out. Disconnect the motor wiring if necessary.

With hot soapy water and a toothbrush, clean each blade of the squirrel cage fan and wipe it dry with a cleaning cloth. Use a vacuum crevice tool to suck up any loose dirt and dust. Dirt accumulations on the blades disrupt the air flow and seriously hamper the blower's efficiency, so make sure you get the entire blade and the headers in between blades. Vacuum and damp-wipe the blower housing and the motor to remove any dust or debris, but don't get any water in the motor. Be especially sure to get any dust and lint out of the motor's ventilation holes, or it will run hot and die before its time. Look for oil cups on the bearings at the ends of the motor. Most newer motors have sealed bearings, but older motors have bearings that must be oiled. For units with belts and pulleys, lubricate the blower

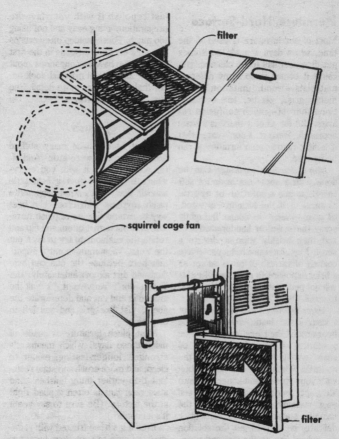

Filters are located differently in different models of furnace.

drive shaft bearings as well, and check the belts for wear. Put everything back together, but make sure it's all dry before restoring power to the unit.

In addition to the furnace itself, the ductwork and vents need to be checked and cleaned periodically to make sure nothing is interfering with the free flow of air.

Furniture, Hard-Surface

Most of our furniture is used all the time, seven days a week, so it does get dirty and has to be cleaned. Because it comes in so many different materials—wood, imitation wood, metal, glass, plastic, and combinations thereof—much confusion results. But for all of it there is a basic approach: Wash it. I don't care what it is, if it's hard-finish furniture it can be washed.

Minor touchup washing: Can be done with a spray bottle and a soft towel, using a solution of neutral cleaner, or if the furniture is wood, oil soap. (See "Oil Soaps.") Lightly spray the soiled or handprinted area and then briskly wipe it dry to a shine. Most furniture has a protective coating of varnish or other sealer so a brief exposure to moisture like this will not penetrate and cause the wood to swell. (See "Wood.")

Major washing (deep cleaning): Put a canvas or plastic cover over the floor around the piece, and sponge on a solution of neutral cleaner or oil soap, wiping with the grain of the material. Then remove the solution with your sponge and squeeze it into an empty bucket, so you don't soil your washing water with it. If the furniture surface is at all absorbent or delicate, be sure to get the solution on and off fast so the dirt and moisture won't have time to sink in. Then polish the surface dry immediately with a terry towel.

The full luster may not return the minute furniture is cleaned, because you probably removed some of the wax and polish that was on there. So just repolish it with your favorite preparation, going easy and not using too much. Polish buildup often causes the need for deep cleaning in the first place. If you have any questions about a particular type of material, look under that heading for more detail. See also "Furniture Polishes."

Furniture, Plush

Did you have a nice fuzzy stuffed animal when you were little? And after you'd carried it with you everywhere a while, was it a bald little animal? Well, that's what happens to plush anything with time. The best way to extend the life of plush furniture is to vacuum it often, and flip and rotate the cushions to try to even out the wear. Vacuuming is extra important here because the pile can hide dust and dirt almost indefinitely. But if you don't remove it, it will be ground in and cut and deteriorate the fibers, just like grit and soil left in carpeting.

Most plush furniture is made of nylon these days, which means it's stronger, longer-lasting, easier to clean, and more crush and stain resistant than earlier fluffy finishes. And stain retardant is often applied right at the factory. (Be sure to say yes if it's an option.)

Even if it's been treated with retardant, be sure to spot-clean furry furniture when it needs it. All furniture gets smudges and spills. Though they may be disguised better on plush fabrics, they'll eventually mat and deteriorate the fur. Spot-cleaning with dry-cleaning fluid and a terry towel is best for oily spots on plush fabric.

Water-based spots should always be wiped up the minute they happen, and be sure to rinse the area lightly with a damp cloth after you mop up the spilled fruit juice or formula. If the spot has been on there awhile, or if you have a grimy armrest or head-rest area, work up a lather of uphol-stery cleaner or Woolite and water solution. Sponge a little of the *suds only* on the spot and let it sit on there a brief while, then blot it off with a towel. Use another sponge dampened in plain water to rinse, so the area won't dry sticky and soapy. You never want to flood the piece with the solu-tion; use as little as possible. Dry immediately with a clean towel, wip-ing with the nap.

When it's finally time to deep-clean furry furniture, you should probably assign this to a pro, since napped finishes are trickier than plain fabric. Whether you or a professional does it, dry (solvent) cleaning is far less likely to cause matting, pile loss, and other problems. If you must wet-clean, see "Furniture, Upholstered." Remember that there's lots of fabric there to absorb and hold soap resi-due, and if you don't rinse well that's what will happen. Those soap-laden strands will begin to mat flatter than a pancake the minute you're finished cleaning and will attract dirt like a magnet. If you don't have access to extraction equipment (which is what you need to do a proper job of rins-ing), be sure to use an upholstery shampoo that dries to a crisp powder that can be vacuumed away.

Furry furniture, just like long hair on a human head, also takes a while to dry. So give it a good long time

▶ **Fur on fur:** If you need to make the furry couch Fido spends all his spare time on look good in a hurry, lightly dampen a washcloth and wipe it over the surface.

(and good ventilation) before you re-sume lounging on it. And before it dries, be sure to brush the nap all in one direction. Textiles have a mem-ory, and if you let the nap dry in exotic swirls and random patterns, you'll be looking at them until the next shampooing.

Furniture, Upholstered

Most upholstered furniture can be cleaned with water (shampooed) if you're careful not to get it too wet. You can do it yourself unless the piece is heavily soiled, very delicate, or a valuable antique, in which case it's better to call in a professional. First, look to see if there's a care label on the piece: "W" means safe to clean with water; "S" means use dry-clean-ing solvent only; "WS" means either method is okay; "X" means clean only by vacuuming or light brushing. If there's no care label, before proceed-ing test shampoo a small patch in an inconspicuous place with a white cloth to see if any color bleeding or damage occurs.

Before shampooing overall, vac-uum thoroughly to remove loose dust and dirt. Heavily soiled chair arms and backs should be spot-cleaned first with dry-cleaning fluid to remove oily soils, and other types of stains should be pretreated with all-purpose spot-ter. Then mix up a gallon or so of upholstery shampoo in a bucket (or use one of the aerosol foam shampoos). Squeeze a sponge out in the solution several times to make some foam, and use the foam to clean with, not the water. You don't want to soak the fabric and the filler material. Just pick up a dab of foam with the sponge and apply it to the fabric as evenly as possible. Then scrub with the sponge until the fabric is evenly damp and clean. Clean entire panels or sections at a time to avoid leaving water lines or rings. When finished with a section, use a wet/dry vac or blot or rub with a dry cleaning cloth to remove as much of the moisture as possible. For napped fabrics such as velvet or velour, brush the pile in one direction while it's still wet and let it dry that way. And make sure that newly shampooed piece is good and dry before putting it back in service!

Furniture Polishes

Advertising claims aside, furniture polishes do little to "protect and preserve" furniture. The varnish or lacquer finish applied to the wood is what preserves and protects it; polish only enhances its appearance. I think it's the smell of the stuff as much as anything that convinces us (or our guests) that we've really cleaned. Dusting your furniture regularly is important, but you really don't have to use a polish at all unless the furniture is starting to look seedy and you

want to spiff it up a little. Lacquer and varnish finishes can get scratched, dulled, and worn from use, and furniture polish will bridge the tiny scratches and leave a smooth, glossy film on the surface that helps it look better for a while. Deep scratches can also be darkened and made less noticeable with one of the scratch cover polishes.

Paste-waxing furniture is a lot of work, and I see no benefit to it. I would even avoid polishes that contain a lot of wax—it just builds up over time and has to be removed eventually. The best bet is to use a cloth impregnated with a waxless product such as Endust for regular dusting, and use oil or wax polishes only as necessary to cover a scratched or dulled finish. If you do decide to polish, use the polish only as often and as liberally as necessary; slathering it on too thick just leaves an oily, dirt-attracting film. Stick with one brand of polish too; different types aren't always compatible, and mixing types often results in streaks or white patches. If you use an aerosol, spray the cloth rather than the coffee table to prevent overspray. And don't expect polish to resurrect a cracked, crazed, or chipped finish—if it's that bad you should consider refinishing. Oil-finished wood will benefit from an occasional application of lemon oil or Danish oil, but be advised that if the piece has been waxed, the oil will remove the wax.

G

Guest mess: a contagious plague that comes with company. Symptoms include empty glasses and half sandwiches left around everywhere, candy wrappers under the couch cushions, cigarette burns on carpets and counters, spills in hidden areas of the house, and enough dirty dishes to make the emergency light come on in the dishwasher.

Garages

The problem here isn't so much cleaning as dejunking. (See "Junk and Clutter.") If something doesn't fit in the house, it usually ends up in the garage. A good rule of thumb for garage keeping is this: If you haven't ever used or even thought about using something that's been deposited there, get rid of it. With every passing year our time becomes more valuable and more of the things we might someday use are less likely to get used. But we strain and injure and just plain tire ourselves out moving them, falling over them, cussing them out, and, in general, carrying this excess baggage through life.

Another prerequisite for a clean garage is a well-sealed concrete floor. You've no doubt noticed how futile it is to sweep an ordinary cement floor because the broom actually flakes off more concrete dust in its wake. Once the floor is sealed, it has a finish that you can sweep, dust-mop, wet-mop—clean—like a regular floor. Then the dog piddle won't seep into the pores, the oil from the leaking crankcase won't stain, and it will be 100 percent easier to keep clean. (See "Sealing.")

After you've dejunked and sealed, *organize.* Hooks, hangers, shelves, and cupboards are a necessary evil in here. I paint a silhouette or outline of tools and garden equipment on the wall behind the hook so it's easy to see where it goes and what's missing. At least one lockable cupboard or cabinet is critical for safe storage of hazardous chemicals so kids can't get to them. Any yard equipment that is gas-powered would be better stored in a yard shed, if possible.

Organize a corner of the garage for your recycling center with easy access to containers to accommodate your household flow of recyclables. A planned area for this purpose makes recycling more inviting and easier to accomplish.

Garbage Cans

These are easy to clean, it's just a matter of getting up the gumption to do it. Right after the garbage people have emptied them is the best time. Bring the cans up onto the driveway and spray them out hard with a hose; anything left clinging will seriously interfere with the action of the disinfectant you'll want to use. After getting all the grungies out, dump out any water and spray 'em down, inside and out, with a good disinfectant cleaner. Let the disinfectant sit on the cans ten minutes or so, while you pick up all the bits of stuff slopped around in the garbage storage area. Go back to the cans then and give them a good scrubbing with a stiff brush or nylon pad, then rinse them out with the hose. Set them upside down to dry before returning them to service—liquid in the bottom of a garbage can is the perfect incubator for all kinds of revolting little life forms. For this same reason, as well as for pet- and pest-proofing, well-fitting watertight lids with tie-downs are a must.

Garbage Compactors. See "Trash Compactors."

Garbage Disposers

If you use your disposer correctly, it cleans itself with every use. The problem—*odor*—comes when we don't run enough water through while we're disposing. Instead of just giving it a trickle that will only mix those potato peelings into a soup that can settle and molder on the sides and under the baffle, give it a good wide-open cold-water tap run and finish by filling the sink with several inches of water, the pulling the plug and letting it all flush down at once. The water pressure will fill the chamber and clean the blades and rinse any lingering particles down the drain.

If your disposer already has the ickies, use a disposer cleaner such as Ajax's Disposer Care to get rid of that slimy smell, then start your full-flush campaign.

Glass

Glass is easy to clean because it's so hard and shiny nothing soaks in—any dirt on glass is just resting on the surface. In cleaning glass all you really have to do is break the surface tension of the soil with the right solution, and the foreign substances will float off. If the glass isn't too dirty, a spray-and-wipe glass cleaner such as Windex is okay, but if it's filthy inside or out, from rubber dust, smog, heating and cooking fumes, flyspecks, whatever, mix up a bucket of warm water and 4 or 5 drops of dish detergent, such as Joy, or a capful of ammonia. Then, if something is clinging tightly to the glass and the solution

won't remove it, a little aggression with a wet sponge or cloth will be necessary. You can also use a white nylon-backed sponge. If that doesn't do it, you might want to go to a razor blade scraper. (See "Razor Blades.") If you keep the surface soapy and wet and scrape in one direction only (just forward, never backward), you can remove almost anything without scratching.

If glass doesn't sparkle and shine after cleaning, the problem is probably detergent residue left behind or hard-water scale (see "Hard-Water Deposits"), so rinse well with clear water or water with neutralizer or vinegar added. (See "Residue.") Glass that's been pelted with hard water or blowing sand for decades may never come clear or shiny; it's damaged, not dirty.

Tinted glass: If the tint is right in the glass, you can clean it the same way as clear glass. If the tint was applied to the glass in the form of a stick-on film, great caution should be used, to the extent of, yes, reading the manufacturer's recommended procedures for cleaning the product, should you still have them. If not, use the mildest cleaner and the softest cloth, and don't try to clean a tinted window film in the sunlight.

Etched or textured glass: Is still glass, it just has more hiding places for dirt. Once you've applied the cleaning solution to the glass and let it sit on a minute or two, use a stiff brush to work the dirt loose if necessary, then rinse it off.

Stained or cut glass: Can be sprayed with glass cleaner and then dried and polished with a soft clean cloth. Don't use a scrubber or scraper on any stained or cut glass.

Glass Cleaners

Forget newspaper and vinegar and all those brew-your-own glass cleaners. Clean windows the way the professionals do: Use a spray-and-wipe glass cleaner on the itty-bitty panes and a squeegee on the larger ones. For squeegeeing, all you need is a bucket of lukewarm water with a dash of liquid dishwashing detergent, such as Joy, in it. A little dab will do it—½ capful is plenty. Too much will leave streaks. Ammonia works too, but it doesn't lubricate the squeegee blade as well.

For small windows and mirrors, use a prepared Windex-type glass cleaner. These products usually contain a little ammonia to cut the dirt and some alcohol to speed drying, plus various wetting agents and emulsifies to help the water penetrate the soil and dry without streaking. They work better than anything you can mix up at home, and for the small amount you'll use on small windows and touchup jobs, they're worth it. Janitorial supply stores sell inexpensive window cleaner concentrates that go a long way—you just mix it up as you need it.

Spray glass cleaner is also a fast and effective way to clean and polish chrome, stainless steel, and other brightwork, and the porcelain enamel of appliance fronts. For some of the cleaning jobs described in this book you will want a spray glass cleaner without ammonia, and Sparkle is one such product.

Glassware/Crystal

Ordinary glassware: The glasses you'll let the kids use can just be cleaned in the dishwasher or in the sink with dish detergent—scrub, rinse, and dry. Your everyday glassware is probably machine-made and therefore dishwasher-safe. Sometimes glasses will develop a white film caused by detergent working its way into the glass surface. To remove it, soak the glass in vinegar or ammonia for a while and then wash as usual. When hand-washing dishes, always do the glassware first, and rinse with water as hot as you can tolerate.

Some clear drinking glasses aren't glass but plastic, and will cloud as they collect fine scratches over time, from exposure to hot water and scouring in attempts to remove dried-on gunk. The label will say *glassware* rather than *glass.*

Hand-blown glassware: Should ALWAYS be hand-washed. (See directions for washing crystal.)

Crystal glassware: The nice company's-coming stuff with delicate stems, designed to be broken, should never be trusted to the dishwasher. Don't be fooled by the weighty feel of lead crystal; the more lead content in a glass, the more delicate (breakable) it is. Never put cut glass in a dishwasher or subject it to extreme temperatures. Fine glassware with metallic trim shouldn't be put in a dishwasher either, or soaked in hot water or strong cleaning solutions.

Wash fine crystal in the sink, using hand dishwashing liquid and a few drops of ammonia. Do them one at a time, by hand. (As you age you'll pray for them to break.) Put a rubber mat in the bottom of the sink and a rubber guard on the kitchen faucet. Don't stand stemware upside down to dry (the rims of the glasses are fragile too); hand-dry with a *clean* cotton towel.

On any glassware, using detergent rather than soap and making sure that rinse water is hot will help prevent spotting. You can also add ¼ cup white vinegar to the rinse. If you prefer to use soap, be sure to add a drop or two of ammonia to the wash water. If you use a dishwasher, be sure to keep a rinsing agent in the machine when you do glassware. These agents contain ingredients that cause the water to "sheet" over the surface of the glass and drain away, rather than lingering in droplets that turn to spots.

Gloves

There are as many different ways to clean gloves as there are types of gloves. For those made from more than one material, such as knitted gloves with leather or vinyl palms, follow the directions for the most delicate component. It's best to err on the side of caution. When in doubt, take them to a dry cleaner.

Machine Washing

Gloves that can be washed in the machine include sturdy fabric work gloves, acrylic knits, and any gloves whose care label indicates it's safe. Be sure to detach the string that keeps kids from losing their mittens before washing, or wash them string and all in a lingerie bag, so it won't get tangled in the washer.

Work gloves can be tossed in the machine with the rest of the work clothes. For all other machine washables, use a mild detergent and a gentle cycle. Tumble dry on medium.

Hand Washing

Most gloves can be safely hand-washed. Leather gloves should be washed *on* the hand, except for doeskin and chamois, which are too fragile when wet, and leather work gloves, which need only to be oiled with a good leather conditioner. Suede is best taken to a dry cleaner, although you can sometimes remove water stains by rubbing suede on suede.

Special leather cleaners are available at shoe repair shops—follow the directions on the container. Or you can make a solution of lukewarm water and mild soap or detergent. Squeeze and press the suds through the leather, using a soft brush on stubborn spots; avoid rubbing. Remove the gloves by rolling from the wrist (don't pull off by the fingers) and then rinse several times in lukewarm water. Press out any moisture using a soft dry towel—never wring. Reshape the gloves by blowing into them and then gently stretching them. Dry them flat, away from sunlight or heat.

To soften your gloves when dry, you can knead them; put them on your hands and rub them together; or fold them in a damp towel and gently press them.

To hand-wash off the hands, use a

mild detergent or Woolite and luke-warm water and squeeze the suds through the gloves, using a small, soft brush for stubborn spots. Rinse thoroughly, reshape, and dry flat on a towel. When the top is dry, flip the gloves over to dry the other side. To help woolens keep their shape, trace the gloves' outline before washing, and then place washed gloves over the outline and stretch into place. Never dry anything made of wool in the sun or near heat—it will shrink. A pair of woolen gloves particularly dear to your heart might even be allowed to dry on your hands, so you don't have to pass them on to munch-kin-size relatives.

For shearling and fleece gloves, see "Shearling/Fleece."

Gold and Gold Plate

Gold is chemically inert and doesn't oxidize or tarnish as some metals do, but it still gets dirty and has to be cleaned from time to time. Small objects such as gold jewelry can be cleaned at home or taken to a jeweler. Most jewelry stores have ultrasonic cleaning tanks that get all the little cracks and crevices clean without damage to the metal (see "Ultrasonic Cleaning"), and many stores offer the service free to their customers. Larger items, such as gold-plated flatware or bathroom fixtures, should be cleaned with a neutral cleaner solution and a soft cloth, then rinsed and polished dry. Don't use abrasive cleansers, steel wool, colored nylon scrub pads, or metal polishes on gold—it's a very soft metal, and gold plating is often very thin. Hard scrub-

bing and strong cleaners will scratch the metal and wear it away, obliterating subtle patterns in solid pieces and exposing the base metal underneath. Keep chlorine bleach away too—it can cause pitting. Fine china with gold trim should be gently hand-washed immediately after use. Some foods will stain the trim if left standing on it, and the harsh detergents used in automatic dishwasher detergents can deteriorate and discolor it.

Golf Clubs

If you watch the tournaments on TV, you know that golf pros do a lot of cleaning—because clean equipment performs better. They wipe their clubs after every shot, for example, because dirty grooves can't put the right spin on the ball. You may not want to be as meticulous about your equipment, but there are some steps you won't want to skip for long club life and peak performance. They may even put a little extra spirit in your swing!

Covers for the club heads are a must. The bunny ears and pom-poms are debatable, but some soft cover is needed if you want to keep your clubs from being scratched and chipped as they bang against each other in the bag. Keeping them dry is important too—always dry wet clubs before putting them away to prevent rusted metal and delaminated woods. Rust on the metal parts of your clubs can be gently rubbed off with fine steel wool. Golf pro shops have special cleaners to remove ball marks, grass stains, and mat marks from your clubs, and waxes to keep irons and

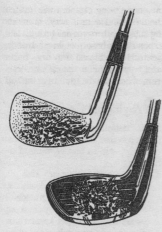

Dirty iron and driver.

woods protected and looking sharp. A stiff toothbrush does a good job of scrubbing out impacted grooves. Grips should be kept clean and free of skin oil so they don't get slippery. If they do get slick and smooth, a wire brush or a little fine sandpaper will roughen them back up again. Leather-wound grips should be cleaned with saddle soap.

Gore-Tex and Similar Materials

Gore-Tex is one of several trade names for a type of fabric often used in sportswear that has the ability to shed water, yet still "breathe." This fabric is created by laminating a thin layer of Teflon to an outer fabric, usually nylon or polyester. The pores in the Teflon are smaller than a water molecule but larger than a water *vapor* molecule. Fabrics of this type will shed liquid water while allowing perspiration vapors to escape, making for a waterproof garment that's a lot more comfortable to wear than the old rubber jackets.

After five or six times through the washer, however, most fabrics of this type start to lose some of their waterproofing. Garments made of Gore-Tex and the like should be protected from soiling as much as possible, in order to avoid too-frequent laundering. When it comes time to wash, most manufacturers recommend a cold-water wash using the gentle cycle and regular laundry detergent. No bleach should be used, and the fabric shouldn't be dried with heat or ironed. Avoid laundry pretreatment as well. Don't try to dry-clean fabrics of this type, as most of them won't tolerate the solvents involved. Only gentle methods and chemicals should be used on stains—no acids, solvents or harsh alkalis, and no aggressive tamping.

Graffiti

Since graffiti artists express themselves in so many different media, it's hard to recommend a single cleaning method that works in every case. One thing you can be sure of, however: It's tough to remove spray paint, pencil, pen, marker ink, or crayon from rough, porous, unsealed surfaces. Most janitorial supply stores sell a graffiti remover that is effective on all of the above and more, as long as the underlying concrete, cinder block, or whatever was sealed before the primitive artwork struck. On unsealed surfaces, any graffiti remover is bound to be only partially effective.

One key here is to give the chemical time to work. Apply the remover and let it soak, giving it time to soften the offending stain. Use a scraper, wire brush, sandpaper, steel wool, or whatever the surface will stand to agitate the stain from time to time. Patience is a virtue in graffiti removal. To be better prepared next time, you can buy a sealer at janitorial supply stores that makes the surface stain resistant and also withstands the solvent action of the graffiti remover.

CAUTION: Don't use graffiti removers on plastic, paint, or varnish unless the label says it's okay—most graffiti removers will damage such surfaces.

Modern cave drawings can sometimes be removed from painted surfaces without damaging the paint by gentle application of a mild solvent such as paint thinner. In most cases, though, it's quicker and easier to just cover the offending message or mural with a fresh coat of paint. Rough, unfinished masonry surfaces such as concrete block can be lightly sandblasted to remove graffiti.

Grass Cloth. See "Wall Coverings, Woven."

Graters, Food

These handy gadgets need thorough cleaning after each use so that food particles won't contaminate your next shredding. This is best done right after grating, especially cheese, before it has a chance to harden. Soak in soapy water for a while first, if necessary, and use a scrub brush (on both sides!) to remove stuck-on bits. Then run warm or hot water over the grater to rinse and drip dry. Easier still is tossing it in the dishwasher—remember, plastic graters in the top.

Graying of Laundry

What "tattletale gray" laundry is telling you is that all the soil hasn't been removed, due to one or more of the following:

1. *Not enough detergent.* Use extra detergent if your loads are large, water is hard, or the load is extra dirty. If you live in a no-phosphates area, get a water conditioner and/or wash in hot water with a liquid detergent.

2. *Not hot-enough water.* Detergents, even the cold-water ones, don't work as well in cold water, especially on greasy and oily soils. Even warm water is much more effective than cold.

3. *Overloading the washer.* If there isn't room for the fabric to flex and for water to circulate, clothes won't come clean.

4. *Using soap in hard-water areas.* True soap (as opposed to detergent) forms insoluble curds with the minerals in hard water, and will make clothing gray and dingy. Don't use laundry soap unless your water is truly soft—less than 3 grains hardness.

Grease Removal

Nothing is safe from that insidious grease buildup, as dirt is trapped and glued to things by airborne oils from cooking, heating, smoking, candles, auto emissions, and the like.

Scrubbing won't do much to remove grease—you have to dissolve it. Grease is an acid, so you need a strong alkaline cleaner, such as ammonia or heavy-duty cleaner, to dissolve it. (See "Chemistry of Cleaning.") Ordinary hand dishwashing detergent is fully up to the job of much of the grease-removing we have to do at home. (It was designed to deal with greasy dishes.) Whether you use heavy-duty cleaner (for heavier deposits) or dish detergent solution (for lighter oil slicks), be sure to give it *time* to do its dissolving. Spray it on, let it soak for ten seconds or so, and presto, you can wipe it away.

For major-league grease cleanup, degreasers are available at janitorial supply stores. (See "Butyl Cellosolve"; "Cleaners, Citrus.") An excellent citrus-based product is Soilmaster—a nonbutyl cleaner, which means it has no petroleum solvents or noxious odors, and is quite safe to use.

Greasy machine parts and tools can be cleaned in solvent degreasers. (See "Solvents.") Don't use gasoline—it's too flammable. For grease stains on concrete, see "Concrete." For greasy spots in fabrics, see "Spot and Stain Removal." For greasy plastics, see "Plastics."

Griddles

Any griddle (even those with nonstick finishes) should be allowed to cool to avoid warping, then washed in hot

sudsy water, rinsed, and dried. Many are dishwasher-safe. To recondition the surface after cleaning, follow the manufacturer's instructions or wipe on 1 teaspoon vegetable oil with a paper towel or soft cloth.

For cast-iron griddles, see "Cast Iron." For electric griddles, see "Frypans, Electric."

Griddles are bound to get something on them occasionally that has to be scrubbed off, and a plastic spatula or (on other than nonstick finishes) a curly metal scrubber such as a Chore Boy wielded vigorously on a wet surface is the best approach to this. If that doesn't do it, you can use a pumice bar on it, or let it soak in sudsy water for an hour—or even overnight. You'll save a lot of elbow grease and the crud will wipe right off. But this will definitely mean reseasoning afterward.

If a griddle has been allowed to accumulate burned food and grease, you may need to use a heavy-duty commercial degreaser such as Sokoff. This is a pastelike product that you apply with a brush, allow to sit on the surface for ten to fifteen minutes, then brush off. Repeat applications may be necessary to remove heavy buildups.

Grills, Barbecue

Chances are that faithful grill was put away grimy last fall. To make that first (or last) cleaning of the year less painful, proceed as follows.

On the grill itself, if it's plated or stainless steel (not aluminum, which will pit) you can use oven cleaner. Remove the grill from the unit, spray both sides of it well, and seal it in a plastic bag overnight. The mess should slide right off the next day. Or you can soak the grill (if you can find something big enough to soak it in!) for several hours or overnight in a solution of degreaser or heavy-duty cleaner. Whichever you use, wash and rinse well afterward. Or after the cooking is done and the grill is still nice and hot, lay out two thick layers of newspaper on the lawn and soak the paper down with a hose. With gloved hands, lay the hot grill on one of the stacks, then place the other stack of papers on top, turning the sides and corners under to form an airtight seal. This will allow the heat and moisture to steam and soften the cooked-on crud. After about thirty minutes (enough time to finish eating dinner), the grill is ready to be washed in dishwashing detergent and rinsed.

Don't feel obliged to sanitize the grate or grill after each use. The fire sterilizes it every time you cook. And a certain amount of blackening (carbon) on the grill helps it heat more evenly and keep food from sticking.

I just keep a wire brush handy to scrape off any encrusted food or juice after the last hamburger is served. If I'm cooking for a party of fifty, I scrape the grill after each round of chow to prevent buildup.

If you do deep-clean a grill, be sure to oil it afterward with cooking oil to retard rust, especially if it's cast iron.

Now a few specifics.

Kettle grills: You can use oven cleaner on the inside, but keep it off the painted exterior, and any alumi-

num parts. A degreaser solution can also be used inside, to reduce the greasy deposits that collect around the top of the bowl, but never attempt any kind of cleaning of a kettle until it's good and cool. Apply boiled linseed oil to wooden parts occasionally when they start looking weathered. The outside of a kettle can be shined up with glass cleaner.

Gas grills: Removable lava rocks can be boiled in dish detergent solution. Flavorizer bars can be cleaned with a wire brush or run through the dishwasher. DON'T use a self-cleaning oven to clean any barbecue part. The extreme heat would remove chrome plating and cause premature rusting.

Clean the burner with hot dishwashing detergent solution or a wire brush to get rid of hardened spills or rust. Wire-brush the entire outer surface of the burner to remove loose corrosion. Unclog the burner holes with a thin wire or opened paper clip—be careful not to enlarge the holes. Tape gas openings closed to keep water out, then clean inside the grill with a stiff brush and detergent solution, using a wet scraper for really gunky spots. Then run a damp sponge over the whole thing and rinse with a hose.

Don't use oven cleaner on any plain or anodized aluminum grill parts, or abrasive pads or cleansers on painted or nonstick surfaces.

After the barbecue has dried, oil any wooden parts with boiled linseed oil to keep from cracking. And to ease cleaning next time, spray the inside with nonstick cooking spray. You can also line it with heavy-duty aluminum foil, but be sure to make holes in it to allow the air vents to function.

When you're done cooking for the day on a gas grill, close the cover and blast it at the highest setting for five minutes. This works like a self-cleaning oven, burning off anything sticking on there. Wipe away any ash that results when the grill is cool and close the cover. Follow your owner's guide for checking and cleaning venturi tubes, valve orifices, and pressure regulator vents.

If your grill has side burners, clean and inspect these frequently, especially if you haven't used the burner in the past week. Insect nests and cobwebs could accumulate and block the venturi tubes, causing the fuel mixture to back up and catch fire at the control panel. Follow the directions in the owner's manual on how to clean.

To cure flare-up: If you're getting excessive flare-up, clean your grill by burning off the accumulated grease. Close the cover, and leave it on at the highest temperature setting for five minutes. You might also check to be sure the grease drain isn't clogged. If lava rocks get covered with grease, turn them over and then turn the grill on to burn away the grease.

Grinders and Slicers

Grinders, in the very act that so endears them to us, create a lot of tiny particles that can easily go all over and lodge anywhere. And this food-dust is worse than most because it will not only get stale and rancid and

pollute the flavor of later grindings but also attract insects and other pests, and spoil and pose a health hazard.

Coffee grinders: Every once in a while take a brush and whisk out any grounds or coffee powder that remains on or in the grinder. Coffee grinder brushes are available, but any soft clean brush will do.

Wheat grinders: Whether your grinder uses stones or stainless-steel heads, the best way to clean it is to blow any debris away with a blow dryer on cool or the blowing end of your vacuum; you can also use a soft brush. Clean after each use, following the manufacturer's directions. Newer machines rely on air flow to adjust the degree of coarseness or fineness. If they're not cleaned, you may not get the grind you had in mind. Also, if the air passages get clogged, the flour will heat up in the grinder and lose much of its nutritional value. Stone grinders are a lot harder to get completely clean—you almost need to take the stones out to do it. You can wipe the motor housing with a damp cloth, but remember water and flour don't mix—except into a paste that clogs the works. So keep your machine dry. An excellent way to clean stainless-steel heads is to grind rice; rice is harder than wheat and will clear out any flour residue stuck on the milling heads. Flour with a high moisture content will stick to the heads.

Meat grinders: These usually push the ground meat through tiny holes, and they are a challenge to get clean. The minute you're done grinding, hold all the parts that come in contact with the meat under a wide-open tap; this will remove most of the residue. Be sure to brush out any meat particles that remain or they'll spoil and rust the parts. Wash the stainless-steel parts in clean dishwater and dry thoroughly. Don't put them back together until they're dry.

Meat slicers: Watch your fingers, that blade is sharp! Remove the blade and any parts that come in contact with the meat after each use and wash thoroughly. Some parts may be dishwasher safe. Never use abrasives—wash parts in clean dishwater and dry completely before reassembling. Wipe the housing with a damp cloth and be sure all cracks and crevices are clean, but never immerse.

Grout

Ceramic tile would almost be a maintenance-free surface if it weren't for those gruesome grout lines! It's the grout that usually gets stained, dirty, and mildewed and creates all our cleaning problems with tile walls, floors, and countertops. If you're putting in new tile, be sure to specify grout with a latex or acrylic admix—it's much harder and more stain resistant. For old grout, scrub with wax stripper or heavy-duty cleaner solution and a grout brush (see "Grout Brushes") to get it as clean as possible. Use bleaching cleanser on stubborn spots. Rinse well. After it's good and dry, apply a coat of masonry sealer to keep it from absorbing so many stains and dirt in the future. For countertops, lemon oil (see "Lemon Oil") also works well as a grout

sealer. Put on three coats with a small paintbrush, allowing each coat an hour to dry, then wipe off any excess oil. Reapply about once a year. For mildewed grout in tub and shower enclosures, scrub with a 1:5 solution of liquid chlorine bleach and water, then rinse. See "Ceramic Tile"; "Mildew."

Grout Brushes

If you find yourself with lots of things you need to clean with a toothbrush, go down to the janitorial supply store and get the professional version of this. It's called a *grout brush*, but it works on anything.

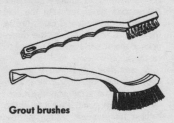

Grout brushes

A grout brush is small enough to clean tiny things and fit in tight or narrow places, and has just the right stiffness of bristle for scrubbing. It's inexpensive and heavy-duty enough for tough jobs and resistant to strong cleaners and acids. A grout brush looks a lot like a toothbrush, but it's a little bigger and the bristles are much more effective.

Guitars. See "Musical Instruments."

Guns

Firearms need frequent cleaning not only to look good but to function properly. Each time a bullet is fired, it leaves tiny fragments of metal and powder in the barrel and on the working parts of the action. As these residues build up, they affect accuracy and can even cause the action to jam or the barrel to explode. Powder residues also attract moisture and promote rust and corrosion, which will quickly ruin the barrel of any rifle, shotgun, or pistol. Fingerprints also will speed rusting. To keep a firearm in good working order, it should be thoroughly cleaned and moisture-protected after each use.

To make the job easy, get a gun-cleaning kit. A proper kit will have a cleaning rod, fittings and bore brush for the specific caliber of gun you're cleaning, plus powder solvent and cleaning patches, rust-inhibiting lubricant, and gun grease. Follow the instructions in the kit and the firearm manufacturer's directions for maintenance of your particular gun. You can even get stock refinishing and gun bluing kits to touch up both the wood and metal parts of your favorite shooting iron.

H

Home Brew! No, it's not more prudent, practical, or patriotic to concoct your own cleaners. See "Cleaners, Concentrated" for the only home mixing it pays to do yourself.

Hair Cleanup

One little piece of hair in an otherwise clean area or in our food is a real red flag. We'll never accept hair. Even if it was boiled with the beef so we know it's sanitary, it *looks* bad. It's elusive and hard to remove too, which is why it's so often left behind. Any hair not captured in the cleaning process will be all too apparent after everything is clean and dry. Human and animal hair alike poses the same

problems and is removed the same way.

1. Hair in *tubs and sinks* rolls right under many a good cleaning tool. For those "sink snakes" in the basin or the tub, before you start washing, snatch up a bit of toilet paper, dampen it, and wipe the hairy area. The hair will cling amazingly well to the soft wet paper. Then toss the paper in the toilet or the trash.

2. Hair in *drains*. Hair combed near

176

sinks or shampooed off in showers washes down the drain, where you may think it's flushed away to the big sewer in the sea—wrong. Go right now to your favorite sink and twist the stopper out and pull it up—be prepared for a monster movie, a slimy snake of hair at least 4 inches long. That's why the water was draining sluggishly and the sink was getting smelly. Clean off the hair, wash away the soap deposits that have collected in it, and reinsert the stopper. Then don't panic and opt for a flattop, but do be more considerate as to when and where you groom.

3. On *fabric or upholstery*. Instead of seventeen passes with the vacuum, it'll go much faster if you get a pet rake (a brush with crimped nylon bristles—see illustration) and go over the area with light, even strokes. The velour-type brushes work fairly well too, as do wide tape rollers or a couple of wide bands of packaging tape wrapped around your hand.

4. On *carpets*. You need a vacuum with a good beater brush or brush roll. A plain vacuum without one can't generate enough lift to pull

up all the hair. (Hair has strong static cling.)

5. *Baseboards, woodwork,* and similar small hard surfaces can just be wiped with a damp paper towel or cloth.

6. Hair is light enough to float, and you will find it in the *filters* of your heating and cooling system. Keep them clean and they'll be an asset in dehairing the place.

Hairbrushes

Even hair washed daily will eventually produce a dirty brush, especially with all the gels, sprays, lotions, and other hair potions we apply these days. Clean hair and lint out of a brush daily or as needed, with a comb or another brush. (Fuller Brush even makes a special little rake just for this purpose.) If you're using a comb, run it through gently, especially on natural-bristle brushes, or you'll soon have a bald brush. You also want to be careful not to scratch the varnish on the bristle bed of a wooden brush, or water can seep in and ruin it.

After dehairing, dip the brush face-down into a solution of warm water with a little hair shampoo added and swish it around well. You can also massage the bristles a little with your fingers. On rubber-cushion brushes use a toothpick or a wooden match to plug up the air holes before you get the brush wet, so water won't get in and rot the cushion. Rinse thoroughly, smack the back of the brush in the palm of your hand to shake clinging water loose, then set it somewhere facedown to air-dry. This

Pet rake

is especially important for brushes with wooden handles, so water doesn't run down the bristles and collect on the wood. Never soak brushes—especially wooden brushes —in anything.

Handbags/Purses

The biggest problem with handbags is the inside, which I encourage you to declutter when they get too heavy to tote. To keep the outside looking as good as something that's almost part of us should look, you do have to clean it occasionally. Overall, handbags are pretty durable (think of the everyday beating they have to take), and most of them are hard to hurt. Ninety-five percent of them can be cleaned, inside and out, with a cloth dampened in a mild soap or detergent solution, then wiped dry. Just don't overwet them and they'll be fine. Bear in mind that the grip, handle, or shoulder strap gets extra-heavy body contact, so leave the solution on there a minute to dissolve and remove all that skin oil, hand lotion, perspiration, and the like.

Since handbags are made from everything from leather and vinyl to seashells and straw, a few specifics now.

Leather bags. These need the gentleness of a saddle soap or a cream leather cleaner, available at any shoe repair shop. Use a soft cloth to rub it in as well as wipe it off. Buff with a clean cloth. For patent leather (which scratches easily), use a patent leather cleaner applied with a slightly damp, very soft, cloth.

Vinyl bags. These can be cleaned with a cloth dampened with all-purpose cleaner solution, or patent leather cleaner. You might want to use a vinyl conditioner on them occasionally.

Suede. A suede brush will remove mud and surface dirt, but once it's really dirty, there isn't much you can do for suede except have it professionally cleaned. As a precaution, spray on suede protector (available at shoe stores or shoe repair shops) when it's still brand new, and reapply afterward according to manufacturer's directions.

Straw. Just vacuum to remove trapped dust. If necessary, wipe with a cloth lightly dampened with neutral cleaner solution, followed by a damp cloth rinse. Then hang to dry—but avoid the sun, because it will shrink straw.

Fabric bags. Anything from canvas to tapestry to crewel to, yes, carpet bags. Most of them can be safely cleaned with a solution of Woolite or Ivory Snow and warm water, applied with a cloth. Rinse with a damp cloth and air-dry.

Handles

Handles of tools, doors, drawers, suitcases, steering wheels, refrigerators—anywhere hands hit or hold— usually have heaven knows how many germs as well as heavy deposits of skin oil (and sweat, jam smears, hand lotion, dirt). Yet seldom are they a cleaning target. Wipe them with all-purpose or disinfectant cleaner and let it sit on there for thirty seconds, then buff dry with a cloth. (Don't faint when you look at the cloth.)

Hard-Water Deposits

Most tap water contains dissolved minerals (rock). When the water from a drip or splash evaporates, it leaves minerals behind, mostly salts of calcium and magnesium. As they build up, they form a layer of hard-water scale that is literally as hard as a rock. Since this is an alkaline deposit, it takes an acid cleaner to dissolve it. (See "Chemistry of Cleaning.") Phosphoric acid is the one professionals favor, since it works fairly well on hard-water scale yet is safe for most surfaces. The tub and tile cleaners available in supermarkets contain 4 to 6 percent phosphoric acid and work rather slowly. The lime scale removers available from janitorial supply stores usually contain 8 to 12 percent phosphoric acid, so they get the job done faster. This concentration is safe for most household surfaces as long as you rinse it off afterward. Let the acid sit for a few minutes after you apply it to help it break down the scale, then

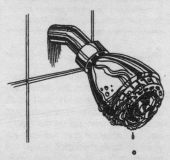

A shower head with hard-water buildup

▶ Refrigerators that dispense ice and water from the door have created a new problem—very visible hard-water deposits under the spouts. To help prevent this install a charcoal filter (available from water softener suppliers) in the water line from the refrigerator to the water supply.

rinse. If you're up against stubborn deposits, you may have to reapply the acid, leave it on for a while again, and do some scrubbing with a white nylon-backed scrub sponge. If it took months (or years) to make the deposits, you may have to spend a little time removing them. Any product that would remove them in a single application would probably rip the fixtures off with them.

For heavy toilet bowl ring, another hard-water deposit, you may have to use a strong bowl cleaner. These often contain hydrochloric acid, which will damage metals and fabrics. They're meant for the inside of the toilet bowl only and shouldn't be used on sinks, showers, or bathroom fixtures. For instructions on removing toilet bowl rings, see "Toilet Bowl Ring" under "Toilets." See also "Cleaners, Acid"; "pH in Cleaning."

Hats and Caps

For all those wash-and-wear and give-away caps and hats, I'd do just that. Wash and wear them or just chuck the expendable ones before the next state fair or home show where they are giving away fresh ones. If you have a favorite baseball-type cap worth keeping, you have a couple of cleaning choices. You can gently hand-wash the cap in cool water and Woolite, according to the instructions on the label, rinse and let it air-dry on a clean dry towel. A small bowl or a rolled-up towel will help reshape the hat before the drying process begins. Many hat manufacturers also recommend placing a hat like this in the top rack of the dishwasher, without the dishes, and running it through the normal cycle with a small amount of dishwasher detergent added. Don't let the hat dry in the dishwasher, place it on a towel to dry as described.

Dust hats with a vacuum dust brush or, if they're really bad, a clean slightly damp cloth—but better yet, avoid leaving or hanging them out where they can collect airborne soil. You can spot-clean a hat with supermarket dry-cleaning fluids, such as Carbona or Energine. Remember to feather or blend the spot in a little so as not to leave a cleaning ring. Saddle soap will work on leather and vinyl hats; just remember to use mostly the foam and not to prolong the exposure to moisture. Don't soak, just lightly dampen them!

Serious hat cleaning, however, can't be done at home. Brims, for example, with or without interior stiffeners such as buckram, are a touchy business. An inexpertly cleaned brim may never again have that jaunty angle so essential to your image. If you want to wear a hat for dress and not feed your horse out of it, take it to a professional hatter. Such people have professional extraction equipment and highly effective (but also highly flammable and poisonous) cleaning fluids that will take hair oil and other soils out without shrinking the hat, solvents that aren't available to the general public.

Straw hats can only be surface-cleaned as described above. If you get a straw hat wet, you'll be sorry. A good Panama or other handmade straw hat can be cleaned just like a felt hat, but most straw hats around these days aren't of that quality. It depends on the stiffener used. If it's a water-soluble one, a professional hat cleaner can wash the hat, reblock it, restiffen it, retrim it if necessary, and reshape it. See "Straw."

Wearing your hats only on a clean head will lengthen the time between cleanings. Hats should be stored in a clean box, not a plastic bag, because the bag can transfer plastic smells and colors and hats can also sweat inside the bag, causing them to mildew, especially in damp or humid climates.

▶ **Hawaii:** A place to send that demoralized cleaning member of the family. It works every time. Aloha.

Heaters, Space

Electric: To clean your electric space heater, unplug it from the outlet, then vacuum it out, using the dust brush to remove dust from around the wire grille. Don't take the heater apart, and don't immerse it in water or use water to clean the inside. Clean the outside with a slightly damp cloth. Make sure the heater is thoroughly dry before plugging it back in.

If you have one of the little electric disc furnaces, be sure to wash or vacuum the foam-rubber filter on the back when it gets dust-clogged and dirty.

Kerosene: The most important way to keep your kerosene space heater clean is to use high-quality fuel, with no water added. Using the proper K-1 Kerosene will prevent your heater from giving off messy fumes, which leave nasty films and deposits inside the heater and inside your house.

Follow your manufacturer's direction for cleaning and maintenance of your specific model. What may be good for one unit may ruin another! In general, on the outside, an ammoniated glass cleaner such as Windex and a paper towel will remove fuel spills, along with your average dust and grime.

You want to clean the inside too, occasionally, or eventually the heater will get too choked up to work properly. You'll know it's time to clean if your heater starts to smell or takes a long time to heat up. Use a scraper of some sort to remove carbon deposits inside, then follow up with a *dry* green nylon-backed scrubber (without any cleaning product on the scrubber).

Using good fuel will also keep the wick in shape. If the wick is burned down or burned on the ends, it needs to be replaced. Check your manufacturer's instructions carefully—on some models the wick must be burned dry periodically (without any fuel in the heater) to burn off any carbon deposits on it.

Heat Pumps. See "Air Conditioners and Heat Pumps."

Heat Registers. See "Heat Vents/Grates/Registers."

Heat Types and Cleaning

Oil burns cleaner than coal, gas burns cleaner than oil, and electric is cleaner than any other kind of heat, but that's talking only about the combustion products that go up the chimney. The type of fuel you heat with may make a difference in the cleanliness of the outside air, but unless you heat with wood, it doesn't affect the amount of dirt inside your home.

Unless there's something wrong with your furnace, the combustion chamber where the fuel is burned is sealed off from the air that circulates inside the house. Whether you have a forced air or a radiant heat distribution system, the dirt you often see above the heat registers or vents doesn't come from the heat-generating part of your furnace, it's simply interior airborne soil that the distribution system causes to be deposited in certain locations.

Forced air systems tend to circulate airborne soil and deposit in on drapes and walls near where the blast of air comes out of the hot-air vents. The solution to this is to keep the furnace filters scrupulously clean so they can do their job of removing airborne soil. To get really clean inside air, an electronic air filter can be installed. (See "Filters, Heating and Cooling System.") Diffusers that direct the hot air into the room help keep the area right around the heat vents cleaner, but they don't reduce the overall amount of soil in the air.

In radiant heating systems, whether electric, hot water, or steam, the air is circulated not by a fan but by natural convection. The radiators draw cold air to them and radiate hot air upward. This gentle flow of air attracts soil to the radiator and deposits it on the relatively cooler surfaces around it. Poorly insulated walls will attract dirt faster than well-insulated ones. There are no air filters to trap circulating dirt in a radiant system, so the answer is to simply keep the house interior cleaner and try to reduce major sources of soiling, such as cooking grease and cigarette smoke. Of all the radiant heat types, electric ceiling cable heat circulates and deposits the least amount of soil, but it doesn't change the total amount of airborne soil present in a home. While a forced air system often seems the dirtiest because it deposits soil around the heat vents, it has the potential to be the cleanest because of its ability to filter out airborne soil and trap it.

Woodstoves create a lot of ashes to dirty things up when you go to dispose of them, and deposit soot on interior surfaces from the smoke that escapes from the stove door and from leaky stove pipes. Not to mention the mess (chips, bark, bugs), of the wood handling. Newer pellet stoves are easier on both the interior of a house and the environment.

Heat Vents/Grates/ Registers

Heat vents are like a house's pearly gates. Eventually everything passes through them. And grease and grime and then lint and hair will stick to them, gradually reducing the air flow as well as looking bad. Give all vents and grates an occasional stiff vacuuming, rubbing the dust brush nozzle briskly against the grille. If you do this regularly, you shouldn't have to deep-clean vents and grates more than every three or four years, when vacuuming won't take off the clinging fuzz or when they seem to reach a point of impaction. While floor vents are held in place by gravity and can be simply lifted out, wall or ceiling units generally have a couple of screws to remove. Be sure to have a cardboard box or other container ready to set them in immediately, because all that dirt and dust lodged around the seal will crumble off the instant you take them out. Have a vacuum with you too, to vacuum around the edges and reach into the hole (a dustcloth alone will never do it).

The condition of the vents after you get them out will determine how you clean them. You can soak them in degreaser solution—give the grease maybe fifteen minutes to loosen, then scrub the grille with a brush until it's fuzz-free. (Don't soak a painted vent too long in degreaser solution, or you could remove more than the grease.) Rinse and let drip dry thoroughly before replacing.

Heavy-Duty Cleaners. See "Cleaners, Heavy-Duty."

▶ **Home brew (homemade cleaner):** Several different ingredients mixed together to make something capable of ruining your favorite furnishings. Usually done to save money, but always ends up costing at least three times what something off the shelf would have. Much safer cleaning chemicals that work far better are available for a minimal cost everywhere, so there's no reason or excuse to ever make home brews to clean with. Doing so is only asking for trouble.

High Chairs

Lash that high chair to the hood of the car and run through the car wash. . . . Just kidding, but the thought has crossed every mom's mind. A hose isn't out of the question, though, especially for the plastic models. Spray with all-purpose cleaner, then let the cleaner work for a minute or two to soak off the dried-on plum puree and Fudgsicle drips. Scrub as necessary with a plastic scrubber or soft brush. Don't forget the underside of the tray, where little hands reach, and you're sure to find a few surprises. Rinse well to remove all the cleaner residue, then wipe and polish dry. Straps can be cleaned with a toothbrush if necessary or removed and run through the washer.

Wooden high chairs should be treated like wooden furniture and cleaned with a cleaner made especially for wood, such as oil soap. (See

"Oil Soaps.") Leave the cleaner alone to work a minute or two here. If the mess doesn't come off with the first wipe, reapply the cleaner and leave it on again.

Avoid abrasive cleansers and pads that will scratch plastic, wood, and metal.

In general, while feeding Baby, a quick wipe when food first drops beats having to scour or chisel it off later. (Just keep a damp rag at the ready whenever you're shoveling those goodies in.)

Here again you run into a whole gamut of special features such as pop-out cushions, removable straps, nonimmersible trays, wheels, and the like, so read the manufacturer's booklet for the particulars on your chair.

Hoods, Range

There are two basic types of range hood: the kind that exhaust cooking aromas and grease to the outside through a duct system, and those that simply recirculate the inside air, after filtering out odors with an activated charcoal filter. In both cases, there will be an aluminum mesh grease filter that must be removed and cleaned. The recirculating type of hood also has a disposable charcoal filter that needs to be replaced periodically.

Remove the grease filter and the light's lens diffuser, if any, and soak them in a tub of hot dishwashing detergent solution—stubborn deposits might require a strong degreaser solution. After soaking awhile, the accumulated grease should melt away under a forceful spray of hot water. Or just wash the filter by itself in the bottom rack of your dishwasher. While the grease filter is bathing, wipe all the grease you can from inside and outside the hood with paper towels, or scrape it off the inside with a wide-bladed scraper. Then wash the hood down, inside and out, with hot heavy-duty cleaner solution. If your motor and fan assembly is removable, unplug it and take it out of the hood to make cleaning easier. Fan blades should be wiped down and grease and lint removed from the motor housing, but don't immerse the motor or allow water to drip inside. After everything is clean and dry, put it all back together. Downdraft range exhaust systems are essentially the same, except that the fan and filters sit down inside the range instead of in a hood over the top. Downdraft systems do a better job of collecting cooking grease because they have gravity working for them. See also "Exhaust Fans."

Hot Tubs. See "Spas and Hot Tubs."

▶ **House:** A place we should live in, not for.

Houseplants

Plants do need to be cleaned. Dust and dirt gradually coat and clog the little pores in the leaves, which is why houseplants often grow slowly. If they're dirty, they can't (remember Biology 101?) photosynthesize, or feed themselves. This doesn't mean you want to shine up the leaves with plant polishes or skim milk. You want to clean, not decorate, your greenery. So fill a plastic spray bottle with plain old water, set the nozzle on gentle spray, hold it about two feet away from the target, and spray till the leaves are dripping wet. Be sure to do the undersides too, and keep at it till you know all the dirt is gone. Large sturdy plants can also be hosed down with a fine spray from the hose outside or set in the tub under a gentle shower. If they're extra dirty and grimy, you could add a tiny bit of soap or detergent, such as hand dishwashing liquid, to your spray bottle and shower the plant down with this first. When you flush and rinse it off with clear water right afterward, the detergent will actually act as a mild fertilizer. You can also apply a mild detergent solution to the leaves with a paper towel or a soft cloth, but use a different cloth for each plant to prevent spreading diseases.

To keep dust from accumulating on large leaves, and then being glued on by airborne grease, you can run an electrostatic dustcloth, lambswool duster, or feather duster over them.

Caution: Always apply liquid or dry fertilizers and insecticides to houseplants carefully. To prevent drips and spills, do things like this in the sink or a basin. Many plant treatments can permanently stain carpet and fabric, and the stains may not show up until the carpet is cleaned!

Humidifiers

The best way to eliminate potentially harmful bacteria and mold spores in the reservoir is to clean your humidifier before every use, though most of us won't do that. The water sitting in there stagnates between uses and becomes a breeding ground for germs, which are made airborne and inhaled when you turn it on. Clean your humidifier according to manufacturer's directions and recommended frequency. *At least* clean it when you go to fill it.

In general, this means first unplug it, then lift out the water tank, wash with a solution 1:10 of bleach and water to kill bacteria; rinse well. Use descaler according to the manufacturer's directions to remove minerals, or soak in 2:1 vinegar/water solution. (Using soft water will cut down on mineral buildup.)

Filters can be rinsed in water or soaked in the vinegar solution if necessary, but don't wash them with detergents or other cleaners. Ultrasonic models may have a demineralization filter that needs to be replaced.

Disinfect the other parts of the humidifier, as recommended by the manufacturer, with a cloth dampened in the bleach solution. You can clean the exterior and grilles with the same cloth and polish dry. Most of the parts are plastic, so avoid harsh chemicals and abrasive cleaners or pads that will mar the finish.

Hydrochloric Acid

Hydrochloric acid is a powerful acid (hydrogen chloride—HCl) used extensively in toilet bowl and drain cleaners. Even though there's some dilute hydrochloric acid in our very own gastric juices, this isn't a user-friendly product. It can cause eye damage and skin burns, respiratory irritation if inhaled, and all kinds of unpleasantness and even death if swallowed. It will bleach nylon and deteriorate cotton and other natural fibers, so you don't want to get it on carpeting or clothing either. Hydrochloric (also called muriatic) acid is also very corrosive to metals, and shouldn't be used on chrome bathroom fixtures or stainless steel. We've all seen flush valves and faucets in public rest rooms with little black or green specks all over them. The specks are pinholes eaten in the chrome plating, usually by acid bowl cleaners. Always use rubber gloves and be very careful how you use and store products containing this potent stuff. And don't use a concentration stronger than 9 percent in the home. See "pH in Cleaning"; "Cleaners, Acid."

Hydrofluoric Acid

Hydrofluoric acid is a solution of hydrogen fluoride (HF) in water used widely in professional rust removers and also in some rust and lime-scale removers for home use. Hydrofluoric acid attacks silica and silicates, which means it will etch glass, porcelain, china and the like, so don't use rust removers containing HF on your procelain washer top or on fabrics containing glass threads (or on red fabrics—it causes red dye to bleed). The big danger with hydrofluoric acid, though, is skin burns. This acid penetrates skin swiftly and easily, and can cause second- and third-degree burns, so always be very careful not to splash it on your skin or in your eyes. Oxalic acid is a slower but safer rust remover. See "pH in Cleaning"; "Cleaners, Acid"; "Oxalic Acid."

Hydrogen Peroxide

Hydrogen peroxide is an oxidizing agent, which means it gives up its extra oxygen molecule rather easily to other chemicals it comes in contact with. When this happens, a new compound called an oxide is formed. In the case of bleaches like hydrogen peroxide, the oxides that result are often white or colorless—the stain material may still be there, but it's a lot harder to see. Hydrogen peroxide finds use not only as an oxidizing bleach but as an antiseptic. As a bleach, H_2O_2 is mild yet effective, safe for almost all fabrics. It's a great help in removing tough stains such as blood and scorch marks from chlorine-sensitive fabrics such as wool, silk, and spandex. For stain removal, use the 3 percent solution sold as an antiseptic, not the stronger solution sold for bleaching hair. Putting a few drops of ammonia on the fabric after applying peroxide boosts its bleaching action. See also "Bleach."

I

If you're old enough to mess up, you're old enough to clean up!

Ice Makers, Automatic

You'll know when this baby needs cleaning by the taste of the cubes! After sweating in the field, I've run into the house for a glass of ice water only to gulp down metallic or garlic-tasting brew. To clean, first, if the ice maker has a switch, turn it off. Dump the ice bin and wash it with baking soda solution (4 tablespoons per quart) of sudsy water, then rinse and dry thoroughly before replacing the bin in the freezer section—make sure it's all the way in. Then switch it back on. That's it! Keep the ice fresh by

dumping the bin regularly if you're not using all it's producing.

Still have funny-tasting cubes? Food in your refrigerator or freezer could be the cause of the problem. Very cold surfaces, such as ice, are quick to pick up odors. Our (often aged) cold-storage array offers a variety of smells from which to choose—and even cans and metal containers can taint the cubes. Foods should be wrapped securely in freezer-designated materials—forget flimsy bread wrappers, margarine cartons, wax paper, and the plastic wrap the supermarket put the meat in. Hard water or water containing minerals can make ice taste bad too. Ice made with water like this absorbs odor faster than ice made with softer water.

If all else fails, you can call a plumber and have him or her check to be sure the connections to the ice maker are right for your model, or see if the plastic tubing to the refrigerator might need to be cleaned.

Ideas, Bright (Yours!)

Have you found a new, better, or faster way to clean something than I've recommended in these pages? I'd like to hear about it. If it's a good one I'll get it out to the world. Sharing means caring, curing waste, and changing lives and our world for the better! Write to Don Aslett, New Ideas, P.O. Box 39-E, Pocatello, ID 83204.

Instruments, Musical. See "Musical Instruments."

Irons, Steam

Mineral deposits (that white crusty stuff) are the main problem with steam irons. To avoid mineral buildup you can use only distilled water in your iron, especially if you live in an area where the water is very hard. But at least be sure to drain the iron after each use. Turn it off, unplug it, and invert it over a sink while it's hot and let the water run out of the fill hole. Watch your hands—the water will be scalding! Check the manufacturer's instructions before using vinegar solution or commercial iron-cleaning products in your iron—they can damage the insides of some irons.

Many irons have a self-cleaning feature that flushes the vent holes and

---

▶ Inventions, Cleaning

On or about:

1774 A patent was granted for the first mangle iron.

1792 The automatic washing machine was invented.

1814 The average homemaker fetched (carried) all household water over half a mile.

1859 The first American patent was granted for a vacuum cleaner using pneumatic air.

1860 The first washing machine manufactured in quantity was offered for sale.

1900 A British civil engineer made the first successful suction vacuum.

1910 The first electric vacuum hit the market.

1911 The first built-in vacuum was made.

1922 The average washing machine lasted twenty years. The life span of most of them today is more like seven years.

1945 The aerosol dispenser was developed to help soldiers in jungles combat mosquitoes.

steam passages at the touch of a button, to prevent clogs from mineral deposits. Other steam irons can be cleaned this way by filling them, heating the iron to high, holding it over a folded terry towel, and pressing the steam button until all the water is spent.

The soleplate—the business end of an iron—is likely to develop starch buildup. Never scrape it with a knife or scour it with an abrasive pad; the resulting scratches will snag clothing. Wipe soleplates—nonstick finishes too—with a damp cloth when cool. Otherwise soleplates with nonstick finishes should be cleaned as the manufacturer recommends only. If necessary, scrub aluminum soleplates gently with a paste of baking soda and water, a mild cleanser such as the newly formulated Comet, or a steel wool soap pad, with light, uniform strokes lengthwise on the plate. Rinse well and iron over a piece of wax paper or cloth-covered paraffin to slick the surface back up. If fabric or plastic is melted on there, heat the iron up and iron off as much of it as you can onto a disposable cloth. Store the iron upright on its heel to prevent water seeping out the steam holes and pitting the soleplate.

The outside of an iron can be wiped with a soft cloth dampened in all-purpose cleaner solution. Never use heavy-duty cleansers or scouring pads here either.

Ivory. See "Bone/Ivory."

J

Jumping Germs—what's the dirtiest place in the house? The doorknob! Imagine what the average person's hand goes through in a day, before they grab that doorknob at home. Spray knobs with a shot of disinfectant cleaner, wait a minute, then wipe with a towel. Don't faint when you look at the towel.

Jackets. See "Coats/Jackets."

▶ **Janitor:** A name for professional cleaners, derived from the Roman god Janus who was doorkeeper and custodian of the treasure. Janus had two faces to see both ways, a feat any mom can easily manage.

Janitorial Supply Store

These stores are places where professional and industrial cleaning products—chemicals and equipment—are sold, generally geared to the large economy and even skyscraper size (5 gallons, 55-gallon drums). As more and more homemakers visit them in search of quality items that clean fas-

More and more janitorial supply stores are also serving the informed consumer.

ter and better (and cheaper), some of these professional outlets are catering more to them. Janitorial supply stores have better products and more knowledgeable answers to tough cleaning questions than any supermarket or hardware store in the country. Look in the Yellow Pages under "Janitorial Supplies."

▶ **A sure source of pro tools and supplies:** If you're panting for pro tools and supplies, and you can't find them locally in a janitorial supply store (under "Janitorial Supplies" in the Yellow Pages), write to me and I'll send you a free copy of my "Clean Report" newsletter from which you can order them by mail. "Clean Report," P.O. Box 39-E, Pocatello, ID 83204.

Jewelry, Costume

The best way to clean costume jewelry is with an ultrasonic cleaner (see "Ultrasonic Cleaners" under "Jewelry, Fine"; "Ultrasonic Cleaning"), something your jeweler is more likely to have than you. If it's not a high-cost or -risk item, I advise you to treat costume jewelry with a quick dip, a light scrub (with a soft toothbrush) if needed, and a fast rinse to remove the residue and then dry by blotting, not rubbing. Use a mild cleaner such as hand dishwashing detergent and avoid ammonia and solvents, as they can harm plastic, discolor plated metals, and cause setting glues to release. Avoid hot solutions for the same reasons.

For fun and funky jewelry, the cleaning is trickier. Papier-mâché, for example, popular for earrings, cannot be safely wet-cleaned. Plastic jewelry can be wiped with a damp cloth, but avoid commercial jewelry cleaners and keep it away from heat and sunlight. As for those 10,000 tiny-shell necklaces, peach pit or pheasant feather earrings, hand-blown miniature unicorn pendants, and zebrawood bracelets, use caution and common sense. Consider what it's made of before attempting to clean it. Do clean the metal posts of all pierced earrings with alcohol occasionally. If you've ever worn pierced earrings for any length of time, I don't need to tell you why.

Storing your collection in a closed container instead of in a wide-open jewelry box or hanging out on a rack will cut the need for cleaning considerably. And applying hairspray, perfume, and cosmetics before, rather than after, adding adornments will do a lot to keep them attractive too.

Jewelry, Fine

All that glitters isn't gold, and even gold won't glitter forever without a little help from you. All fine jewelry loses its sparkle after a while and needs cleaning and polishing to restore its beauty and luster. Stones and settings get coated with skin oils, soap, cosmetic residues, and airborne soils, and precious metals get scratched, dull, and tarnished. Regular care will keep your fine jewelry turning heads for a long time to come.

The first order of business is to protect jewelry from damage. Storing and transporting valuable pieces in separate lined compartments of a jewelry box or in protective flannel or chamois bags is a must. Thrown together in a box or drawer, the diamonds and hard stones of one piece can nick and scratch the precious metals and softer stones of others. Set stones should be inspected by a jeweler periodically for worn or loose settings that could let a precious stone slip away unnoticed. Having pearls restrung whenever they get loose, with a knot between each pearl, is good insurance against lost pearls.

For regular cleaning, most jewelry can simply be washed. Use a commercial jewelry cleaner, or make your own by mixing 1 part hand dishwashing detergent, 1 part clear ammonia, and 3 parts water. Soak the piece in the solution for a few minutes, then brush soil loose with a soft toothbrush. A toothpick can also be used to remove stubborn soil from cracks and crevices. After washing, rinse with warm water and pat dry with a soft cloth. Wash jewelry in a small pan, not the sink, or you could lose stones down the drain. After washing check for any loose or dislodged stones before emptying your wash water.

NOTE: Some gems and settings are delicate and require special care. Check precautions for specific types below before cleaning. Don't immerse stringed necklaces, pearls of any type, ivory, shell, or any of the soft gemstones in jewelry cleaner.

Ultrasonic cleaners: These clean by passing high-frequency sound waves through a cleaning solution, so that soil-scouring vibrations reach into all the little cracks and crevices. They're great for plain metal pieces and diamond sets, but the high-frequency sound can damage certain stones. Check with a jeweler before using ultrasonic cleaning on any jewelry other than diamond. See also "Ultrasonic Cleaning."

Closed settings: Before washing old jewelry, check to see if the setting is closed in behind the stone. If it is, don't wash it—at one time, foil was used to back stones with this type of setting, and washing can discolor the foil and ruin the piece. Check with a jeweler if you're unsure. These settings should be simply polished with a dry silver-polishing cloth or chamois leather.

Pearls: Pearls are more prone to damage than the hard mineral stones because they're "organic"—the product of a living shellfish. Acids are particularly bad for pearls, even the acid naturally found on human skin and in products such as perfume and cosmetics. For this reason, after wearing you should wipe pearls off with a chamois, or else wash them in warm soapy water, rinse, and dry. Don't use heat, ammonia, detergents, abrasive polishes, or any harsh chemicals on pearls; just pure soap and warm water. Put pearls on *after* you've applied hair spray, perfume, and cosmetics, as these can damage their lustrous surface.

Precious metals: Because gold and platinum don't tarnish, all they need is occasional cleaning to restore their natural beauty. (See "Gold and Gold Plate.") If they become scratched and dull, they can be polished with silver polish or rebuffed to a brilliant shine by any jeweler. Sterling silver doesn't usually tarnish when worn regularly, but it if does the tarnish can be removed with a commercial silver dip or silver polish. (Before using a dip on silver settings, make sure dipping is safe for the stone. See also "Silver and Silver Plate.") Be careful of abrasive polishes on plated pieces—you can rub right through the plating and down to the base metal! See "Metal Polishes." Because chlorine can pit and corrode gold and gold alloys, don't wear gold jewelry in a swimming pool or allow it to come in contact with chlorine bleach.

Soft stones: Opals, turquoise, coral, jet, amber, ivory, lapis, onyx, and peridot are fairly soft substances, and can be scratched and damaged easily. All can be washed with mild soap and warm water, but nothing stronger. Some experts recommend against washing opal. Since opals actually contain water, they should be kept away from heat to prevent them from drying out. Some people recommend rubbing oil into opals to keep them from drying, but natural skin oils should be sufficient if opal jewelry is worn regularly. *Don't* rub them down with glycerine, as some recommend. Elaborate methods have been devised to keep ivory white, but most experts advise against bleaching and other harsh treatments. It's better to let the ivory develop its own natural color as it ages and avoid damaging it with chemicals. Most of the softer stones can be repolished if they get scratched and dull.

Emerald: Emerald (beryl) is a special case. Even though the gem itself is fairly hard, emerald is more susceptible to flaws than other gemstones and is often soaked in a green oil to hide small imperfections. Once filled with oil, the flaws become almost invisible, but washing can remove the oil and expose the flaws. Cleaning emerald jewelry is best left to an experienced professional.

Jugs, Picnic. See "Coolers and Jugs, Picnic."

Junk and Clutter

The single biggest multiplier of cleaning is the amount of clutter in, around, and underfoot in a dwelling place.

Our rooms, closets, drawers, and cupboards are full of it, and our cars don't even know they belong in the garage. (You couldn't even fit a bike in there.) And clothes—there are plenty of sixty-year-old women out there who still have their maternity clothes and seventy-year-old men who still have their starting jersey lined up in the closet. (You never know!) Dejunking eliminates cleaning—at least 40 percent of cleaning is just coping with junk, litter and clutter. Get rid of it, and almost half your housework will disappear. Too much of your cleaning otherwise is just wading through, working around, and repositioning junk and clutter, not actual cleaning. *Get rid of it!* What are you waiting for? It will never get easier. Start today! It doesn't cost a dime!

Here's a short course to get you started: Get up early in the morning, the earlier the better; you're cold-hearted and objective then. (And there are fewer people around to interfere with the process or restash the junk.) Wear clothes with no pockets or you will toss two and save one. Play some rousing dejunking music such as Sousa marches or "I got along without you before I got you, I'm gonna get along without you now." Get five big cardboard boxes and label them : JUNK, SORT, CHARITY, EMOTIONAL WITHDRAWAL, and PROBATION. Now you're ready to go; put your boxes down somewhere and start sorting. I promise you that great surges of victory and self-esteem will come over you with each piece of worthless junk you cast away. When you reach the point of exhaustion, relax for a while and read a few pages of *Clutter's Last Stand* or *Not for Packrats Only*, then get back

▶ **Dejunk:** Unneeded (or unwanted) stuff increases housework and cleaning, even if it does cover up floor square footage. Clean it out and watch cleaning time and expense disappear from your life!

on the job. And from now on when you see a garage sale, take a cold shower immediately!

Some Junk-sorting Guidelines

(by permission from *Clutter's Last Stand*)

It is junk if:
it's broken or obsolete (and fixing it is unrealistic)
you've outgrown it, physically or emotionally
you've always hated it
it's the wrong size, wrong color, or wrong style
using it is more bother than it's worth
it wouldn't really affect you if you never saw it again
it generates bad feelings
you have to clean it, store it, and insure it (but you don't get much use or enjoyment out of it)
it will shock, bore, or burden the coming generation

It's not junk if it:
generates love and good feelings
helps you make a living
will do something you need done
has significant cash value
gives you more than it takes
will enrich or delight the coming generation

Jute Browning

A yellowish or brownish tint or stain that appears in the carpet after flooding or cleaning. This becomes less of a problem each year, as more and more jute-backed carpets are replaced with new ones made with polypropylene backing. But enough jute backing is still around that jute browning will continue to haunt us for a while yet. Most browning is the result of overwetting the carpet during cleaning, which gets the backing material damp. The jute in that backing is often cured with (believe it or not) cow manure or urine, and as water evaporates from the tips of the fibers, moisture wicks up from the backing material carrying traces of this, and it colors the tips of the fibers a pale brown or yellow. This condition is aggravated by excess alkalinity in the cleaning solution, and can almost be cured by giving the carpet an acetic acid rinse (1 part of 10 percent acetic acid to 10 parts water).

K

Kamikaze cleaning; a point in the cleaning process when you see the battle is going badly and you're willing to give all for a clean win over housework.

Kerosene

Among the old wives' tales still circulating nowadays, we sometimes hear kerosene recommended as a cleaner. It's not really very useful as a cleaning solvent. Its flammability makes it a poor choice for washing oily machine parts and such, and its aroma and the oily residue it leaves rules it out as a spot remover. One of the dry-cleaning fluids made specifically for the purpose would be a much better choice for fabrics, and mineral spirits are a safer degreaser for metal parts and the like. Kerosene as a cleaner may have made sense in Grandmother's day, when it was one of the few solvents widely available.

Kettle Grills. See "Grills, Barbecue."

Kitchens

If you have to suppress a shudder, you're not alone. Even the pros would like to dodge the kitchen, because it's one place that can really slow you up and bog you down. The kitchen is the most heavily used part of most homes—it gets more handprints, footprints, crumbs, drips, spills, splatters, stains than anywhere else. The key to less painful kitchen cleaning is staying on top of it. Not only because food mess ages less gracefully than most other messes, but because the airborne grease problem is worst in the kitchen. If you give it a chance to accumulate, you'll have a truly major job ahead of you.

There are at least three levels of kitchen cleaning. The first is *KP or culinary cleaning*. This is the everyday cleanup that has to be done in the aftermath of meals, snacks, and general grazing.

KP cleaning doesn't just mean dishes. After every meal, the table and countertops should be damp-wiped to remove all the dinner debris. You'll also want to clean the sink and the working parts and exterior of any appliances you used. Damp-wipe and remove any spills or drips from the stovetop and front and inside or outside the refrigerator. Be sure to take advantage of the presoaking technique here rather than wearing yourself and the surface out scrubbing. Finally check the floor for crumbs and pick them up with a hand vac or broom and dustpan. Keeping faith with this clean-as-you-go routine will do a lot to keep kitchens liveable.

The second phase of kitchen care is *weekly cleaning*. If KP is kept up, this will be no big deal. For the weekly cleaning you need all-purpose cleaner, glass cleaner, a mild degreaser, and possibly a mild phos-phoric acid for any mineral deposits in the sink. Do not use bleach or abrasive cleaners to clean kitchen surfaces. A white nylon-backed scrub sponge will safely provide as much aggression as you need for routine cleaning.

Before you start, remove all the trash from the kitchen.

The biggest cleaning challenge in kitchens is that film created by dust, moisture condensed from steam, and airborne grease from cooking. This stuff falls on and sticks to everything, and the best way to approach it is with a degreaser. Mix up a spray bottle of mild degreaser solution, or even hand dish detergent and water, and spray it on a soft cloth, then wipe. Don't use even mild degreaser on any wood surface in the kitchen—use oil soap solution instead. All the flat surfaces, such as shelves, the tops of refrigerators, stoves and microwaves, the kitchen cabinets, and the doors and sills should be cleaned (or at least dusted) weekly. This will do a lot to forestall the need for a big kitchen cleanup. Don't forget the tops of the cabinet doors! First wipe with the damp cloth, then buff dry immediately with a terry cleaning cloth. This will prevent streaks.

Then spot-clean the range and around the range, and all the other appliances large or small, doorways, handles, light switches, and so on. Knock down any cobwebs, and dust any decorations and high fixtures or chandeliers, as well as moldings and baseboards, with a lambswool duster.

Weekly you want to wash the *whole* counter—so start at the back and move canisters and appliances out as you go and replace them. Now do a quick wipe of chairs and any other furniture that needs it. Check out the legs and the backs of the chairs (where you grab them to move them around) too—you'll be amazed what you find there.

After that, all that's left is the sink, and then to sweep and mop the floor.

Phase three is *remedial or deep cleaning* of the kitchen—what we pros call *project work*. See "Floors, Scrubbing and Waxing"; "Waxing Floors"; "Walls"; "Windows"; "Ovens"; "Ranges"; "Hoods, Range"; "Furniture, Hard-Surface"; "Junk and Clutter." Then heave a sigh.

Knickknacks

They come out at 2:00 A.M. and breed, that's why you have so many of these little trinkets. You set them high so the baby or the dog can't get them, but they're in the grease zone. And they're such a mixture (everything from cheap souvenirs to fine china) that no two can be cleaned exactly alike. There are five principles to knickknack maintenance overall:

1. Limit your inventory. Have and display only what you really like and cherish. Rotate if you have to. We notice and appreciate fresh sights more anyway. Excess is always a low blow to cleaning. Cut the ranks from a division to a company, then you and your company will enjoy them more.

2. More and more people are going for glass-covered or enclosed display cases. It's the only truly sen-

sible solution. It keeps dust, dirt, and insects off and protects our little treasures from pets, children, and overly curious visitors, and even from our own inept handling.

3. If they're exposed, dust them frequently using either a lambswool or feather duster. The more you dust, the less of a sticky dirt film will accumulate, and dusting is a lot easier than cleaning. If you leave dust there airborne grease will settle on it and bind with it.

4. Eventually you may have to break down and give them a deeper cleaning. Many figurines and other knickknacks can be washed. Don't put them in a dishpan and let them sit like dishes, or water will seep inside and loosen glue, peel finishes, and even swell or disintegrate some materials. If an item seems water-safe, just dip it in hand dishwashing detergent solution and sponge it off or use a soft scrub brush or grout brush on it if necessary. Line all your knickknacks up like old-time Saturday bath night and go at it. This is a good time to accidentally drop the ones you hate.

5. Before you buy (or give) any knickknack, ask yourself, "How will I/they clean this?" and "How

---

▶ If you enclose your knickknacks, you'll only have to use one cleaner (glass cleaner) on one surface, and you'll be done in two minutes. You can spend the rest of your time gazing at those marvels instead of dusting or washing them.

long will I/they enjoy looking at it?"

Knives, Electric

Careful cleaning after each use will keep you a carefree carver. Before cleaning, unplug the cord from the outlet and from the handle. Remove blades—watch out, they're sharp—and wash in the sink or the dishwasher, as most are dishwasher safe. Wipe the handle and cord with a cloth dampened with nonabrasive cleaner, never immerse them in water.

▶ **KP:** The army's "kitchen patrol," many men's first exposure to the facts of life.

Knives/Scissors

Usually knives are either stainless or rolled ("carbon") steel. Carbon steel can be resharpened more easily when it gets dull, but it corrodes and discolors very easily. Carbon steel, hand-forged or hand-stamped knives, and any knives with wooden handles *must* be washed by hand and always dried immediately or the blade will rust.

Stainless-steel table knives without wooden handles can be safely washed in the dishwasher. If the handle is made of wood, hand-wash.

Cutlery is best cleaned right after use, because acids and salt from food left on the blades can discolor or even pit them. Do your good knives in the sink like dishes, with just a bit of water in there so you can see and find them easily and not get cut feeling around for them. Use a white nylon-backed scrub sponge to scrub if you need to and always rinse and dry well. For safety, always dry knives from the spine side with a soft terry cloth towel and put them away as soon as you're done (not in the silverware pocket of a dish drainer to bump against other things). Likewise, store cutlery in a wooden block rather than loose in a drawer, to avoid dulling and chipping the blades.

Never put fine cutlery in a dishwasher. Intense heat and radical temperature changes affect the temper of steel blades, and the finely honed cutting edge can be easily damaged.

Scissors: To clean gunked-up scissors, use WD-40 or paint thinner on a soft cloth. Water-based soils can be removed with all-purpose cleaner. Dry thoroughly and then wipe the blades and screw with a cloth dipped in light machine oil. For longer wear, use a separate pair of scissors for different uses: paper, cloth, icky things like tape, and general use.

You can use a metal polish such as Flitz to brighten your knives and scissors, but well-used tools of this sort usually shine themselves with constant use.

L

Love nothing that can't love you back.

Label, Sticker, and Decal Removal

You can lift some labels and stickers by rubbing cellophane tape onto them firmly and then jerking it off quickly. Some stickers and decals are applied with water-soluble glue and can be loosened by soaking in warm soapy water. If the item can't be submerged, cover the sticker with a wet cloth and leave it on there awhile. Stickers and labels with solvent-based adhesives can be safely removed with an orange-oil solvent such as De-Solv-it. Strong solvents such as lacquer thinner and acetone can be used on glass and metals but may damage paint, plastics, and some fabrics. Resist the urge to attack stickers with metal scrapers, razor blades, and screwdrivers, as these can scratch and damage surfaces. Gentle scraping with a fingernail or a plastic scraper should easily remove adhesive residues after you've softened them with the right solvent. Large plastic stickers such as bumper stickes can often be pulled loose after heating with the hot air from a blow dryer, but be careful not to get the underlying surface hot enough to damage it.

Lace

Lace always looks better than it feels (even in lingerie), so keeping grubby hands off it will save a lot of lace cleaning. If you have a lace tablecloth made by your great-grandmother, it was painstakingly crocheted or "tatted" by hand from cotton, linen, or even silk yarn. Most modern lace is made on a machine, from one of the natural fibers Grandma used or a synthetic such as nylon or rayon. Any lace or lace-trimmed garment or domestic item should be treated delicately—it doesn't take much to make lace unravel or tear loose from what it's attached to. Follow care label instructions if available. If you have valuable heirloom lace, a museum textile curator can advise you on its care. Ordinary old pieces should be gently hand-washed in lukewarm water and soap such as Woolite. (See "Soap.") Remove any metal hooks or fasteners first to prevent rust stains. Small items can be placed in a jar with lukewarm water and soap and shaken until the lace is clean. Rinse lace thoroughly after washing and let air-dry on a flat clean surface. Be sure to squeeze, rather than wring, the water out, to avoid distorting or damaging the lace. Don't use chlorine bleach, rust remover, heat, or harsh chemicals unless absolutely necessary. Take stained lace in to a pro for stain removal. If ironing is needed, use a warm iron and put a press cloth over the lace to keep the tip of the iron from catching in the loops.

Antique lace items and doilies are often blocked out (see "Blocking") to air-dry.

To block a lace doily or tablecloth in the traditional way, after washing dip in a mixture of 2:1 water to sugar or liquid starch, roll in a towel to get rid of excess water, and lay flat on a clean towel on the floor. Then smooth

it out into the exact shape you want and use stainless-steel straight pins to hold it in place until it's dry.

Ladders. See "Safety in Cleaning."

Lambswool Dusters. See "Dusters, Lambswool."

Lamps

Weekly dusting is the best way to keep your lamps and their shades clean. Vacuum the shade and wipe the base. Use a Masslinn dust cloth (see "Dusting") on hard surfaces such as brass, glass, wood, and ceramic (you can dust cool bulbs with it too); use the upholstery brush attachment on your vacuum to dust fabric. Intricate designs or carvings or cut glass can be dusted easily with a lambswool duster. If a lamp needs more than that, use the right cleaner for the material it is made of; for example, glass cleaner on glass; oil soap on wood; all-purpose cleaner on pottery, china, plastic, and so on. If you're going to do any wet-cleaning, be sure to unplug the lamp first. Then spray the cleaning cloth—not the lamp itself—with cleaner and wipe and polish dry. Caution: Certain exotic species can't tolerate cleaning solution of any kind, so use your best judgment and dust only.

As for those hanging fixtures, don't fight them. It's impossible to clean them properly while you're teetering on a chair or standing on the bed—stretched to your limit, swiping at them with a wet rag. Not one in a hundred can be cleaned well in place. Unscrew them and take them down, dump the bugs, and wash removable glass parts in dish detergent and water in the sink. Polish them dry and put them back.

Lampshades

The heat and light of lamps draws airborne soil, flying insects, fingers, and even socks draped over them to dry. Most lampshades are made of materials that absorb flyspecks, dust, and grease like mad too. They're about as uncleanable as anything in a home—it's no wonder so many of us just ignore them until they have to be thrown away and replaced. Weekly dusting (especially of paper or fabric shades) can ward off the need for thorough cleaning. Vacuum inside and out with the dust brush or upholstery attachment. Dry sponges (see "Dry Sponges") work well on many shades. The trick is to lift the dirt lightly from the surface rather than rub it in. Grease or oil spots may be blotted out of fabric shades with dry-cleaning fluid. K2r should take spots out of paper.

For the hard-surface variety—glass, metal, or plastic—use a cloth spritzed with glass cleaner or all-purpose cleaner; wipe and polish dry. A sullied fabric shade that is sewn rather than glued onto the fame may be washable (if you can remember the instructions that came with it). Some of the hazards of lampshade washing include water spotting, glue separating, color bleeding, fabric shrinking, trim falling off, and the frame getting out of shape—or just plain making it look worse than it was to begin with! But if the shade is at the point of being tossed if it can't be cleaned, try this method. Make a sudsy solution of mild cleaner such as Woolite and water in your tub, dip the shade in repeatedly, and let the soiled water drip off; rinse the same way until the water remains clear. Quick-dry in front of a fan to prevent the metal frame from rusting into the fabric.

Fluorescent panel covers are easily cleaned out on the lawn with a white nylon-backed scrub sponge or scrub brush and all-purpose cleaner solution. After scrubbing both sides, rinse with the hose to flush the muck and gnat bodies away, then let them drip dry. An alternative is a scrub in the bathtub.

Chimneys from your chandelier, kerosene lamps, candleholders, and the like are a delicate hand job all the way. Wash in a sink of warm water and dishwashing detergent. Do each one separately so they don't bump together and break, and you might want to put a rubber mat or towel in the sink bottom too. Rinse, then polish dry with a soft clean cloth to prevent water spots.

Lattice-type Things

Lattices were designed to drive cleaners and painters to the rubber room. Things like this are neglected forever because we somehow have the notion that anything we can see through, such as screen, mesh, bars, or grates, doesn't get dirty. The light shining through fakes us out. But whenever there are lots of holes and spaces, there is actually far more area to be cleaned than if the thing just had a simple flat surface. So any okclcton structure not only gets dirty more thoroughly, but quicker.

The most efficient way to reach all the little holes, corners, edges, and hard-to-get-at places in something like this is by flooding or dousing with plenty of solution. Take the article outside first if at all possible. Then pour the cleaning solution (all-purpose or heavy-duty cleaner, depending on what you're up against) on and let it run and drip at will. Then take a stiff-as-the-surface-will-stand brush and hit it from both sides and all angles. Then flood equally with rinse water. Don't skip the scrubbing step because rinsing alone will *not* remove things like longstanding dirt film.

If excess water would create a problem, work the cleaning solution into a foam and apply it to the surface, then scrub with a brush. Absorb the dirty foam with a towel—blotting usually works best. Then lightly wet the brush and use it to rinse, and blot the surface dry.

In between washings, go over lattice-type things well with a vacuum dust brush attachment. This may seem unnecessary because you can't see anything on it, but trust me, it's there. Getting rid of all that clinging dust and hair will prevent it from being glued on by airborne grease.

Since intricate designs are hard to paint, they've often been given only one coat. Next time the item is clean and you have a chance, grab a long-nap roller and paint it again—with

semigloss enamel. Future flyspecks will come off a lot easier.

Laundry

Automatic washers and dryers have done a lot to lighten the laundry load, but you can still waste a lot of time and money and actually damage clothes by using these tireless helpers incorrectly. So take a few minutes to read the little booklets that came with your washer and dryer and the care labels in your clothes. You'll be amazed how much information is there, and then you only have to remember the following basics.

Sort

Sorting before you start will not only ensure better results, but save you the extra work of trying to restore damaged clothes back to normal.

Ideally, have four separate laundry baskets or hampers and train your family to sort on the spot, into the appropriate basket. Label them:

1. WHITES (includes white-background prints that are colorfast)
2. MEDIUMS (includes pastels, medium and bright colors, as long as they're colorfast)
3. DARKS (dark colors that tend to run)
4. FUZZIES (lint-makers such as towels, flannels, sweatsuits, chenille rugs, etc.)

Consider also the weight and nature of the fabric and the degree of soil (that is, try to keep light with light and heavy with heavy) when sorting for either washing or drying.

The five basic International fabric care symbols.

means
Washing

means
Bleaching

means
Drying

means
Pressing or
Ironing

means
Dry Cleaning

means
Do Not
Wash

means
Do Not Use
Chlorine
Bleach

means
It may be
dried in a
tumble drier

means Do
Not Press or
Iron

means
Do Not Dry
Clean

means
Hand
Washable
Using
Lukewarm
Water

means
Use
Chlorine
Bleach as
directed on
Container
Label

means
It should be
hung to dry

means
Can be
ironed, note
temperature
setting

means
Machine
washable,
note
temperature
setting

means
It should be
hung soak-
ing wet to
drip dry

means
It should be
dried on a
flat surface

Things to Wash Separately

Next take out any delicates: loosely knit or loosely woven fabrics, sheers, anything with delicate trim or unfinished seams (which will fray). Delicates need a shorter wash time and/or gentler agitation.

If an item says "wash separately," you can be sure it will run at least the first few times it is washed. Even the tiniest amount of dye in the water can transfer to other fabrics, especially whites and nylon.

Wash really grungy or greasy items separately too, or they may dirty the rest of the load. Presoak if necessary. See "Presoaking."

Preparing the Clothes

After sorting, take a minute to close zippers and Velcro patches, bra hooks, and the like (so they won't catch and snag other clothes); tie drawstrings and sashes loosely to prevent loss or tangling; empty pockets; unwad socks; brush dirt and lint out of cuffs; remove unwashable belts, ornaments, and trim. Don't forget those pinned-on bows on girls' dresses—they never look the same after being washed.

▶ **Ring around the collar:** A manmade soil line usually blamed on the washing machine (for not getting it out). The cure is either washing your neck or pretreating the collar in question fifteen minutes before washing.

Laundry Cleaners and Aids

PRETREAT

Pretreat with a commercial pretreatment or liquid detergent, or even a paste of powdered laundry detergent. See "Pretreating and Presoaking."

DETERGENT OR SOAP

Follow the directions on the label and measure, don't just pour. Bear in mind however, that the label instructions are based on an average load, which means 5 to 7 pounds of laundry, with moderate soil, moderately hard water, and average water volume (17 gallons in a top-loading washer; 8 gallons in a front-loading washer).

If your load of laundry is smaller, larger, dirtier, or otherwise different, then you must adjust the amount of detergent accordingly. For example, smaller, less dirty loads need less detergent. Be careful not to use too little detergent, which may leave your clothes dirty and cause grime to redeposit on them.

Don't use soap in hard-water areas, or you'll end up with whitish deposits (soap scum) on your finished load. And while powders are generally more economical, liquid detergents are better to use in hard water. See "Detergent."

Always use a detergent for flame-retardant items. If you do wash them in soap, rewash using a detergent to restore flame retardancy.

BLEACHES

It's almost impossible to wash clothes over and over and keep them sparkling white and colors bright without using some kind of bleach or brightener. Adding bleach separately is by and large more effective than using a detergent with built-in bleach.

Bleaches help remove stains that detergent can leave behind. There are two types of bleach—chlorine bleach and oxygen bleach. While you'll probably always want to use one or the other with each load of laundry, don't mix them—this cancels their effectiveness.

Chlorine bleach. Chlorine bleach is a good germ-killer (keep this in mind for the launderette) and removes stains best, even in cold water. Although generally used for white loads, if used as the label directs chlorine bleach is safe even on most colored synthetic fabrics. But used too often and too heavily on natural fabrics such as cotton, especially, it can weaken and deteriorate them. Always check the fabric care label and test first! Don't use on silk, wool, mohair, leather, spandex, or flame-retardant fabrics. Never pour undiluted bleach directly on fabrics!

Oxygen bleach. Is generally okay to use on fabrics that can't take chlorine bleach. Check the labels—if an item says "no bleach," it means that even oxygen bleach should not be used. However, it's still best to test first, especially on such sensitive fabrics as acetate, nylon, silk, and washable wool. Oxygen bleach also makes an excellent presoak. (See "Presoaking.")

FABRIC SOFTENER

Today's detergents are so good, they wash clothes almost too clean—the fibers are stripped so bare the fabric can feel harsh and scratchy afterward. The old-time laundry *soaps* left a bit of oily residue on the fibers (which meant they were less clean, but a little softer).

Fabric softeners help combat this by giving fabrics a softer, smoother finish and reducing static cling, so our laundry looks and feels better, wrinkles less, and collects less lint. Two basic kinds of softener are available: liquid, which is added to the rinse or wash water, and the type that is added to and activated by the heat of the dryer. Dryer softeners come in sheets, which are added to each dryer load, or packets, which attach to the dryer drum fin. Certain detergents also have built-in fabric softeners.

The liquids generally get clothes softer; the dryer sheets do a better job of controlling static. The combination detergent/fabric softener products usually sacrifice quality for convenience, neither cleaning nor softening as well as individual products.

Whichever kind you use, don't overdo it—too much softener of any kind will cause towels and diapers to lose absorbency, and create a dirt-attracting buildup on fabric surfaces. And follow the directions on the package carefully or your clothes may end up with oily spots on them, especially from dryer sheets. Too hot a dryer setting with synthetics, for example, will often cause the sheet softeners to leave oil spots. Oil spots will also appear on clothes if liquid softener is poured directly onto the wash (where it collects in pockets). It's better to dilute liquid softener in about a quart of water before you add it, so it distributes itself more evenly in the washload. If you do end up with softener spots, use a little laundry pretreatment on them and then relaunder.

Never put softener in the same water with soaps, detergents, or other laundry aids or you'll end up with a sticky, gooey mess!

Setting the Controls

WASHING MACHINE

Set the water level: To match the load size, then check to make sure there is enough water to allow free movement of the clothes. If not, reset the water level higher and add more detergent.

Choose temperature setting: This depends on the amount of soil, type of fabric, and colorfastness. Use a cold rinse for all loads; it saves energy and prevents wrinkling of permanent press fabrics.

- HOT—130°F or above: No two ways about it—hot water cleans best. Use for white and colorfast items, heavily soiled or greasy loads, diapers, and disinfecting washes.
- WARM—90–110°F: Use for moderate soil, noncolorfast items, knits, silks, woolens, synthetic and permanent press fabrics. (Note: Grimy permanent press should be washed in hot water, using the permanent press cycle.)
- COLD—80°F or colder: Use only when necessary, for lightly soiled

loads, items that shrink easily (or that you aren't sure you got all the stain out of), and dark or bright colors that bleed.

▶ **Shrinking:** The process of getting smaller, as in your housemate washed your sweaters again.

Cycle selection: Determines the amount of agitation (the modern equivalent of beating with a rock to loosen dirt) your clothes get. Most loads require normal/regular agitation for good soil removal. For lingerie, sheer or rayon fabrics, and quilted or padded items, set for gentle or delicate.

Wash time: Depending on your machine, the wash time can be adjusted anywhere from a minute or two up to eighteen. What you choose here depends on how dirty and sturdy the items are.

Spin speed: Some washers let you choose either regular or slow/gentle spin. The regular spin removes most of the water from clothes, shortening the drying time.

For permanent press, use a slow or gentle spin—this leaves clothes a bit wetter, which prevents wrinkling. Washable woolens should be given a regular spin after gentle washing.

Loading the Washer

Don't overload the machine. Doing so is false economy, because your clothes won't come clean and they'll come out wrinkled.

ADDING DETERGENT AND BLEACH

If your machine doesn't have a detergent dispenser:

1. Add your detergent (either powder or liquid) and any oxygen bleach as the washer fills with water. Add clothes after agitation has started and any powder product has dissolved. OR:

2. Fill washer with clothes and water. After agitation begins and clothes are circulating freely, add detergent and oxygen bleach. Be careful not to spill bleach directly on wet fabrics.

SPECIAL INSTRUCTIONS FOR CHLORINE BLEACH

Many machines have an automatic liquid bleach dispenser, which adds the bleach at the proper time in the cycle.

If there is no dispenser, dilute chlorine bleach (1 part bleach, 3 parts water) and add five minutes after the cycle starts. Some detergents contain optical brighteners that work in the first five minutes of the wash cycle, and chlorine bleach attacks these brighteners.

ADDING LIQUID FABRIC SOFTENER

Use the machine's dispenser: Pour in correct amount and add an equal amount of water to prevent clogging.

If the machine has no dispenser, buy one! (An appliance dealer will know if one is available for your model washer.) Otherwise you'll have to dilute the fabric softener and hope you catch the final rinse.

Drying Clothes in an Automatic Dryer

Sorting is important in drying too. Items that were washed together may be dried together in the same load. Don't overload the dryer or be tempted to mix the "wash separately" items with regular loads of laundry in the dryer—the color can transfer there and the heat will permanently set the stain. Small loads will tumble better if you add a couple of clean dry towels.

Shake each piece out before putting it in the dryer.

See also "Clotheslines."

DRYER FABRIC SOFTENER

Dryer sheet: Add one with each laundry load.

Packet type: Attach to a fin of the dryer drum. Replace according to instructions on package.

SETTING THE CONTROLS

Cottons: Choose the regular cycle if most of the load is all-cotton fabrics.

Synthetic or permanent press: Choose the permanent press cycle if the load contains mostly synthetic or permanent press fabrics. This provides a cool-down period to prevent wrinkling. Don't overdry: Doing so will worsen static cling and make your clothes wrinkle and shrink. Fold or hang clothes immediately to avoid unnecessary ironing.

Ironing

Steam ironing helps prevent heat damage to your fabrics and makes the job easier. Be especially sure not to overdry items to be ironed, and if you can iron immediately it helps a lot to take them out of the dryer while they're still damp. To avoid adding wrinkles, iron small areas first, such as collars and cuffs and sleeves, then proceed to larger areas. Use a starch product to restore body to fabrics as needed. See "Starch."

You want to sort here too, and iron in this order if at all possible:

* Low heat: Silks and synthetics
* Medium heat: Permanent press, wool
* High heat: Cottons and linens

(And my favorite: If it needs to be ironed, get rid of it!)

A Few More Facts About Ironing

1. Turn the iron to the proper heat setting. Do read that little label on the garment, or you'll read it later and weep. The iron itself—the print on the temperature selection—will help you out here.
   * Don't be unduly impressed by the labels "drip-dry" and "permanent press." You will probably, in the famous house-cleaner's term, have to "touch these up a bit" with the iron at a low setting, unless you're into the rumpled look.
   * Don't use too hot an iron on synthetics or delicate fabrics unless you're looking for an excuse to never wear them again.

2. Place the article to be ironed on the ironing board (or pillowcase or towel if there's no ironing board in sight). Corduroy and wool are ironed inside out—unless you

want crushed corduroy and shiny suits.

3. Dampening might be desirable if the item is severely wrinkled or made of cotton or linen. Dampening simply means spraying the item all over with a fine mist from a spray bottle, and then rolling it up and wrapping it in a towel or plastic bag for a while to give the moisture a chance to disperse itself evenly throughout.
   * Steam is almost as good as sprinkling—and actually better on some things—for banishing wrinkles. You do have to put water—preferably distilled—into the iron, to get steam.

4. A standard man's shirt should be ironed in the following order:
   * Collar—back of collar first, then front
   * Shoulder area or "yoke"
   * Cuffs—inside first, then outside, then sleeves
   * Front pieces—it's best to iron the button strip or "placket" on the reverse side first
   * Back or body, including that wretched "pleat," which you can iron or not depending on whether (a) it will show and (b) you are scrupulous.
   * If you're of the stiff-collar school, send a blast of spray starch before you as you iron each piece.

5. Place the shirt on a hanger, fasten a top button, and hang it in the closet.

Leather

Finished leather, which has a paint-like coating of dye on the surface, is quite soil resistant and easy to care for. Many spots and spills can just be wiped off with a damp cloth. Finished leather furniture should be cleaned with saddle soap once a year or so. Don't use a lot of water, just work up a lather with the soap and rub it in with a damp cloth or sponge. Wipe off the lather and soil with a cloth dampened in clear water, and polish the leather back to a soft glow with a dry towel. If leather is starting to dry out or crack, use a leather conditioner designed for furniture to restore the moisture. Don't use neat's-foot oil, mink oil, shoe polish, or waxes on leather furniture or garments—they'll make a mess. If leather gets a serious stain such as ink or grease on it, take it to a pro, don't try to remove it yourself. Leather garments should be taken in for professional cleaning at least every other year. Be sure to inspect the garment carefully with the leather cleaner when you take it in, and ask about any problem areas. The cleaner will probably explain to you that some leather garments may undergo changes in color, shading, and texture with the cleaning process.

Unfinished smooth leather, such as that found in work boots, saddles, baseball gloves, and Clint Eastwood's holster, should be cleaned with saddle soap, allowed to dry, and then oiled. This is where the neat's-foot oil, mink oil, and similar leather preservatives come in. The oil keeps the leather soft and flexible, and protects it from water damage. Suede (and split leather of any kind) is another story. These rough-surfaced leathers have no protective finish, so they absorb soil and stains very easily. You can remove dry soil and some marks with a rubber eraser or suede brush or even fine sandpaper, but any serious cleaning or stain removal on suede is best left to a professional leather cleaner. No oils, waxes, or leather preservatives should be used on suede except the clear water-proofers specifically recommended for rough and split leathers. Never try to speed up the drying of leather by placing it near a heat source. Keep it away from moisture and sun, and store it where it can breathe, never in plastic bags. Wear a scarf under a leather coat or jacket to protect the collar from makeup and body oils.

Ledges

If you remove the dust on ledges regularly with a lambswool duster or Masslinn cloth (see "Dusting"), dust won't have a chance to accumulate and get glued on by airborne grease. One secret of ledges (including the tops of doors and door casings) is to make sure they have a good smooth coating of paint or varnish to help dust and debris slide off. Dust low ledges at least once every two weeks, high ones about monthly. As for washing them, that depends on your energy level (maybe every five years?). At least get all that junk off the ones wide enough to set things on!

Lemon Oil

Forget those visions of a lemon press—lemon oil is very likely to be a high-grade paraffin derivative (petroleum solvent) with lemon scent added. Some "lemon oils" may also contain kerosene, alcohol, coal oil, or silicones. There *is* at least one lemon oil that lives up to the name—Swenson's Golden Crown, available at fine furniture stores.

Lemon oil is useful for "feeding" (moisturizing and helping to protect) dry or bare wood. On varnished or sealed wood such as most furniture finishes, a light coat of lemon oil helps restore the gloss and depth of the finish and highlight the grain of the wood. If put on too heavily and not wiped off, however, it just lies on the surface and collects dust, free of charge.

Lemon oil can also be used to help protect ceramic tile from soap scum, to brighten stainless steel, and to restore the gloss and deepen the color of faded and dulled plastic laminate (Formica), anodized aluminum, even fake-wood finishes. When using it on tile, apply it generously to both tile and grout, leave it on for a half hour or so, and then wipe it off the tile.

Lexan. See "Plexiglas."

Light Fixtures

Light fixtures attract bugs, dust, and airborne grease, and it doesn't take long for them to develop a five o'clock shadow. All that dirt and grime seriously affects a fixture's ability to put

▶ **Lick and a promise:** A cleaning process that leaves you with both a sore tongue and the work undone.

out all the light you're paying for too. You should take a moment to clean the fixture every time you change a light bulb, and some need it more often than that. Most fixtures have easily removable glass diffusers, bowls, or chimneys, which can be taken down and washed in the sink. The safest way to clean these is by hand (be sure to let them cool first) with hand dishwashing detergent solution. Don't put them in the automatic dishwasher or use harsh scrub pads—some fixture glass has decorative coatings or designs that can be damaged by overly enthusiastic cleaning.

While you have the glass off, wipe the fixture down with a damp cloth, making sure the power is turned off at the wall switch first. Chrome, glass, and other shiny surfaces can be made to sparkle with glass cleaner and a dry terry polishing cloth. For fixtures made of brass or other metals, see the entry for that specific metal for proper cleaning procedures. Ornate fixtures with hard-to-reach cracks and crevices can be vacuumed with a vacuum dust brush. Before putting any glass back on, make sure the felt or cork washers are in place that hold it firmly without breaking it. Screw the nut on hard enough to keep it from working loose when the door is slammed, but not hard enough to break the glass. See also "Lamps"; "Lampshades"; "Chandeliers."

Linoleum

While linoleum hasn't been manufactured at all since the 1970s, and not in any quantity since the '60s, it's still found in older kitchens, bathrooms, and commercial buildings. Even though all sheet flooring manufactured in the U.S. today is made of vinyl, a lot of us still refer to it as linoleum because that's what sheet flooring was called for nearly a century. True linoleum was made by pressing fillers, such as ground-up cork and wood dust, along with pigments, into a binding material, usually boiled linseed oil and resins. All this was then applied to a canvas or felt backing and formed into tiles as well as sheet goods.

Linoleum is easily damaged by oil, hot water, solvents, and strong alkaline cleaners, so it must be protected with a water-based floor finish. It should be swept and damp-mopped regularly with a neutral cleaner solution, and additional finish applied as needed. (See "Waxing Floors.") If linoleum isn't protected by a floor finish, don't use an oil-treated dust mop on it. When it becomes necessary to strip off all the old wax, don't use a harsh alkaline stripper, especially an ammoniated one—it can turn linoleum yellow and degrade the bonding oils. Test the proposed stripper in an out-of-the-way place to make sure it doesn't damage the floor. Use only lukewarm water, and don't let the solution sit on the floor any longer than necessary.

Linseed Oil

This extract of flax seed, or linseed, is used to help seal and condition bare wood, especially outdoors, to make it less porous and protect it from the elements. When used to create an oiled finish on fine furniture, it's usually thinned with turpentine and applied in many thin coats, well dried and buffed between coats. When using boiled linseed oil as a protective coating for exterior and/or any raw wood, apply it liberally with a brush and then wipe away any excess after you're done with a cloth. Be aware, however, that linseed oil dries *slowly*. Unless the surface you've applied it to is extra absorbent, don't be surprised if it takes several days to fully dry. And be careful what you do with the oily rag(s) afterward—they don't need a match to catch fire!

Linseed oil is also an important ingredient in paints, varnishes, and wood preservatives as well as some furniture polishes and oil soaps used to clean wood.

Lint

Some lint (those short fluffy fibers that come out of nowhere and stick to everything) is inescapable. But don't make matters worse by any of the following.

Reckless disregard of laundry sorting: Always separate such lint generators as towels, chenille, flannel, sweaters, and the like from the lint takers like corduroys, permanent press, and synthetics. And turn these lint grabbers inside out before washing them with anything. Be sure to separate lights from darks (see "Laundry") so that if a fabric does pick up lint, at least it'll blend in.

Before laundering, shake clothes out, turn down cuffs, and brush away lint and dirt. Take an extra moment to check pockets too—one forgotten tissue can cover everything in the load with fuzzies.

Overfilling the washer: Cramming the washer too full causes clothes to rub together, creating more lint and pilling. And there won't be enough room for the water to carry loosened lint away either.

Forgetting the lint filter: Face up to emptying the lint filter after each load—on your dryer (and your washer too, if the filter needs manual cleaning).

For washers with no lint filters or automatic filters, save your plumbing: Slip an old panty hose leg over the drain hose that empties into the tub or sink so that the foot is hanging free. Tie the leg part to the hose or

slip a tight rubber band over it to hold it in place.

Many of the things we do to reduce dust (see "Dust and Dust Control") will also reduce lint. For less lint, tumble clothes dry—this shakes lint loose so it can be caught on the lint screen. But remove things from the dryer while they're still slightly damp—overdrying causes static electricity and attracts lint.

Fabric softener (used in either the washer or dryer) reduces lint's fatal attraction. Throwing a yard of nylon netting into your dryer with the wet clothes may help—dark net for dark clothes, white for light ones. It'll loosen lint from the surface of the clothes and hold it by static attraction.

Brush lint-infested laundry with a clothes brush while it's still damp—all the lint will come off. (The clothes must be damp for this to work.) If you've already dried them, pat them with a piece of masking or packaging tape wound around your hand, sticky side out. If it's still impossible to get off, rewash, using fabric softener in either the washer or dryer.

In an emergency (you're already on your way to the meeting or the job interview), a dampened hand can do a lot to remove lint. Slip into the rest room, put a few drops of water on your hand (don't get it dripping wet), and use it to brush all the lint on your blazer into a ball. If you're really desperate, you can even lick your hand and use it to delint—primitive but effective.

As for lint on hard surfaces, drying a glass coffee table or hallway mirror is a frustrating experience. No matter how we try, lint clings and ruins the effect. You can limit the lint in this situation by using a soft cotton cloth rather than a paper towel and using long, nonstop strokes from edge to edge with a final pass around the entire outside. This catches the little lint piles at the end of each stroke and corrals them all together for disposal. The best way to delint glass or mirrors is with a Masslinn dustcloth (See "Dustcloths"); it's perfect for glass shelves. Another good lint getter is the used dryer softener sheets often recommended for computer screens. Cleaning agents with drying agents such as alcohol in them can help control lint too. Dampen (don't wet) a cloth with the solution; the cloth will pick up the lint and the alcohol will allow the surface to dry without streaks.

See also "Paper Towels."

Litter

Our home's biggest cleaning problem is our country's biggest cleaning problem—the containment of litter. Litter can even consist of good and useful things, left around instead of placed where they belong. Picking up and putting away (or throwing away) accounts for about half of the housework we do, and sadly, when we're finished removing litter, we're right where we should have been before we started! The litter stream *can* be reduced, as follows:

1. Dejunk and declutter! Much of the stuff that's all over shouldn't even be around. Weed through it and keep only the most worthy.
2. Make sure there's enough shelf or storage space, inside and outside, for the things you do want and use.
3. Make sure you have (adequate!) waste containers everywhere they're needed: kitchen, bedrooms, bathroom, workshop, sewing room, garage, outdoors.
4. Refuse to be your spouse's or children's or anyone's janitor. Teach and coach (unceasingly) each person to be responsible for his or her own mess. This will also help cure the national debt of stuff strung out all over our streets and parks and highways.

Litter Boxes

The trademark of a cat household seems to be "that ammonia stench." Caused by (surprise!) cat *urine*, this odor is avoidable if you clean the box regularly. Your cat will then use it more surely, eliminating accidents elsewhere in the house, and worm eggs and other parasites in the stool won't have a chance to reach the infectious stage.

How often "regularly" is depends on the number of cats, the location of the box, and your personal pet mess tolerance level.

When finished cleaning the litter, wash your hands well. If you are pregnant, *do not* perform cat box duty. Toxoplasmosis, transmitted by spores that can easily become airborne during box cleaning, can harm your unborn child.

For a One-Cat Litter Box

The key tool is an *unslotted* metal serving spoon, so that you can remove urine-soaked litter clumps and even loose stools without anything falling through the slots and getting mixed with the clean litter to smell up the box. Remember, it's the urine that usually causes the odor.

Daily: Pan out the solid wastes (first urine clumps, then feces). To keep spills down, stand with the box up against the toilet or waste container. Tilt the box gently to one side and any urine deposits will stand out as darkened masses of wet litter, stuck to the sides or bottom of pan. Try to remove the clump intact. If you do break a clump, scoop out as much of it as possible—don't mix it back into the clean litter.

Weekly: Change the litter completely, and wash the box, using the hottest water possible, then disinfect the container with a non-phenol disinfectant. (See "Disinfectants.") Mop the floor under and around the box with a deodorizing cleaner solution and rinse. Occasionally apply disinfectant cleaner solution to the area; let stand for five or ten minutes, then rinse off with a mop dampened in clean water.

For a Multicat Household

A different approach is called for here because in digging for clean, dry waste space, the cats will disturb the urine clumps anyway. Scoop feces out every day, with a slotted litter scoop that allows you to sift a lot of

litter at a time, and has a good long handle to keep your hand above it all. Don't worry about stirring up the litter—the clumps will probably be broken up anyway. Change the litter and wash the box at least twice a week to keep odor down.

Living Rooms

Living rooms are designed to be user friendly, and the key to living-room cleaning is friendly users. We professional cleaners call this *user education*. At home you can call it *teaching the messers to clean up after themselves.* Cleaning the normal dust and dirt out of a living room is no big deal. But you have to get the family to help you keep it that way. Living rooms can all too easily become a reservoir for old newspapers and magazines, dropped shoes, sweaters, and books, popcorn bowls, pop cans, shoes, half-eaten sandwiches, and just about anything else the family can haul in. So as they do in the national forests, encourage packing out what they pack in. If they won't help clean up the mess they leave, cut the plug off the TV set, cancel the cable service, or don't shop for a while. You have to get their attention. It takes mental toughness and determination, but if you have to shovel out the living room before you clean it, you're allowing yourself to be blitzed. Once you win the battle of user education, the job becomes easy.

Living rooms should get a weekly once-over. This includes spot cleaning, dusting and vacuuming, and trashing. Begin with dusting. Use a

Masslinn cloth (see "Dustcloths") and dust all flat surfaces, such as windowsills, tops of furniture, shelves, desks, TVs, what have you. Don't wax, polish, or oil your wood furniture weekly. Monthly or even less often is enough. You can also use a lambswool duster. (See "Dusters, Lambswool.") These are good for reaching the high places as well as hitting the cobwebs in the corners and hanging from the ceiling. As you dust around the room, keep a spray bottle of all-purpose cleaner and a dry cloth in your cleaning caddy (see "Caddy, Cleaning") to spot-clean fingerprints on furniture, doorknobs, doorframes, and light switches. Spray the cleaner on the cloth, not the thing you're cleaning, and move around the room in a circle, either right to left or vice versa, and high to low. This process should be quick and easy if the friendly users have already removed the debris from the scene. After you finish dusting and spot-cleaning, spot-clean the carpet. After the carpet spotting is complete, brush the pet hair from the carpet and upholstery, if applicable. Vacuum the carpet and you're done. Detail vacuuming around the edges and under everything should be done every other week or monthly. The knickknacks and other shelf inhabitants can be cleaned monthly. Windows can be washed two to three times a year and walls once a year.

Long-handled Floor Scrubber. See "Scrubbee Doo."

Louvered Doors/Shutters

Who would have invented something with so many hard-to-reach crevices! Keeping louvers well dusted is the key, especially anywhere near the kitchen, so dust won't have a chance to blend with airborne cooking grease and become stuck-on dirt. Louvers can be dusted fairly quickly with a lambswool duster, but you have to pay special attention to the corners and the upper parts of the slats to keep dust from accumulating there. When it's time to give the beast a thorough cleaning, remember the basics of smart cleaning and soak before you scrub. Spray the whole unit with all-purpose cleaner solution, making sure you spray up into the openings to get those hidden tops of the slats and all the corners. (A thick towel slid under the door before you start will keep your cleaning solution from running onto the floor.) Give the chemical a minute or two to soften the soil, then scrub each and every slat with a thick damp terry towel wrapped around a paint stirring stick or a wire coat hanger. Spray with clear water in a spray bottle to rinse the soap and loosened dirt away, then polish with a dry cloth. To make sure the louvers dry quickly, you might want to return to the paint-stick routine, using a dry towel this time. Don't treat louvered doors and shutters with furniture polish or wood oils, as this only makes them better at attracting and holding dust!

Lucite. See "Plexiglas."

Luggage

If you've ever gotten a bag back from airline baggage handling, you understand the need to clean luggage, especially to keep spots and smears from becoming permanent stains. How to go about it depends on what you're lugging.

Hard-sided molded plastic or soft vinyl: Remove any spots as soon as possible with a cloth dipped in all-purpose cleaner solution. If that doesn't do it, use the same solution with a white nylon-backed scrub sponge or a nonabrasive cleaner such as Fantastik or Formula 409. Wash the entire outside of the bag off from time to time and apply a silicone conditioner such as Armor All to help keep your luggage looking good.

Nylon and other synthetic fabrics: Use carpet and upholstery shampoo according to directions, or sponge lightly with the solution, working from the middle to the edges. Do the whole panel, or you'll end up with water rings. Don't get any piece too wet, or you run the risk of some inner part of the bag that *isn't* water resistant bleeding through and creating a stain. Apply Formula 409 or a laundry pretreatment to nongreasy spots before you wash, and dry-cleaning fluid, K2r, or degreaser should take care of any greasy or oily ones.

Canvas: True canvas (cotton) can be washed in the washing machine in warm water, cotton cycle, then tumble-dried long enough to get the wrinkles out and air-dried the rest of the way. Don't leave your duffel wadded up somewhere damp or wet or you'll be rewarded with mildew or rust stains from metal zippers and rings. Be sure to treat (or re-treat) all fabric bags with a soil repellent such as Scotchgard after cleaning. Keep the spray off black painted locks though, or it will discolor them.

Leather: Use saddle soap according to the instructions on the can, but try wiping away surface spots first with a damp cloth. Never saturate leather, and if it does happen to get caught in a cloudburst, dry it well away from heat sources.

Aluminum: When your Halliburton case stops getting envious glances, work it over gently with a mild cleanser. Rinse well and let dry. To slow down the course of retarnishing, you can then wax it with a nonsilicone car wax (but I wouldn't do it, since I know all too well that even an unwaxed metal suitcase is slicker than a sled runner).

Suitcase interiors (often quilted satin): Vacuum and air out after each trip. Blot up spills as soon as possible and use carpet and upholstery cleaner or dry or wet spotter as needed, testing in an inconspicuous spot first. See also "Spot and Stain Removal." Pack spillables in Ziploc bags or even more securely waterproof containers. When the inside of your Amelia Earhart gets to looking awful, bear in mind that you can send a bag back to the manufacturer to be relined. To deodorize inside a suitcase, stand an open box of baking soda inside (yes, just like the fridge). Leave for a day or more, depending on what broke in there.

Before you finish, take a spray bottle of all-purpose cleaner and a cleaning cloth and hit your suitcase handles and those little roller wheels that take the weight off you!

Lunchboxes

Metal or plastic, these are easy. And if you've ever left a lunch leftover moldering for a few days, you know why it's worth doing. A quick wipe with a cloth or sponge wrung out in clean dishwater will keep that little larder appetizing. A more thorough cleaning to remove odors or mold means plunging into soapy water and scrubbing with a sponge (a white nylon-backed scrub sponge if necessary), and drip-drying. Metal boxes will stay rust free and last longer if you towel them dry immediately.

If your work is greasy and dirty, your plastic lunch cooler (minipicnic coolers too) will get greasy and dirty. Spray and wipe the outside with heavy-duty cleaner, such as Formula 409. Every two weeks or as needed, fill the inside with water, add 4 capfuls of bleach, put the lid on facedown, and leave overnight. The bleach not only degerms but bleaches out the stains. You can also use a baking soda or vinegar and water solution.

Lye

Lye is a generic term for caustic alkalies, either sodium hydroxide (caustic soda) or potassium hydroxide (caustic potash). Lye is used in the manufacture of soap and is a common ingredient in oven and drain cleaners. It can cause severe skin burns, so keep it well away from your skin and eyes. The fumes are dangerous and it's a powerful internal poison, so store it safely out of the reach of children. Lye will also damage natural textiles, such as silk and wool, and will darken aluminum. Handle lye products very carefully, and add no other chemicals to them. See "Caustic"; "Soap"; "Drain Cleaners"; "Oven Cleaners."

M

HONEY! DOES THIS THING PLUG IN, OR TAKE BATTERIES?

Men are better at housework than they let on.

Macrame

The nylon cord most popular for macrame is highly washable and can just be tossed in the washer (in a net bag to minimize tangling, please) and air-dried. However, any attached beads, ceramic decorations, driftwood, or the like aren't likely to come through the washer unscathed. I've been advised that most macrame cord is pre-shrunk, but there's always the possibility—especially if the piece contains several colors or types of yarn—that one will shrink or bleed into another. The conservative approach is to fill a tub or sink with a solution of Woolite and cool water and soak the piece for ten minutes and then agitate gently by hand for a minute or two if necessary. Rinse repeatedly until water is clear and dry flat on terry towels—hanging while wet will surely stretch it. If there's a big raveled nylon poof at the end, tie a small piece of string tightly around the end of it before washing.

Jute is the second most popular cord for macrame. It must be dry-cleaned, or it will shrink and dry funny.

Marble

All rock isn't as hard as a rock. Just because marble is smooth and shiny and we know it's stone, we tend to think it's impervious. Not so. On the hardness scale, where diamond is 10 and steel is 6, marble is only 3—just half a point harder than your fingernail! A marble floor may look ritzy, but it can be scratched and marred by tracked-in soil and by abrasives such as steel wool or powdered cleanser. And since it's easily damaged by strong alkalies, only mild cleaners can be used on it. Acids *dissolve* marble, so when using any acid around it (especially bowl cleaners) be CAREFUL! Being a fairly porous stone, marble also tends to stain easily.

To clean this sensitive stuff, use a neutral cleaner solution, then polish dry. Marble floors can be protected with special stone sealers and floor finish. Scratched and dull surfaces can be revived with Marble Restorer (available from janitorial supply stores), which covers up the smaller scratches and restores the gloss. Oil stains will often respond to a poultice of kaolin or whiting and paint thinner. (See "Poultice.") For rust or other stains, use one of the specialty stain removers made especially for marble. See also "Stone."

Marble, Cultured

Cultured marble is made from a mixture of marble dust/chips and plastic resins and is denser than real marble and more resistant to staining. It will and does lose its luster after being cleaned for years, however, especially with strong or abrasive cleaners. We professionals clean it with a spray bottle filled with all-purpose or disinfectant cleaner and a soft cloth. Always keep it wet while working on it. Never use powdered cleansers, steel wool, metal scrapers, or colored scrub pads on cultured marble. If the surface is worn and looks dull even after cleaning, polishing compound (such as auto polishing compound) may bring back the glow. A little appliance wax, car wax, or silicone sealer (see "Silicone Sealers") will also help fill fine scratches and restore the shine. Small surface injuries such as burns or cuts can be sanded out with fine, then ultra-fine sandpaper, followed by polishing compound.

Masslinn Cloth. See "Dustcloths."

Mats, Walkoff

Eighty percent of the dirt in your house walks in through the door—on people's feet! The right kind of mats placed inside and out of all entrances will cut your cleaning (vacuuming, dusting, and mopping) in half. It's a lot easier to clean dirt out of a little mat than out of all your household surfaces and furnishings. When I say mats here I mean the professional kind you see at the entrances to hospitals and supermarkets. You can buy these in a janitorial supply store. They're called walkoff mats because they give the dirt a chance to be walked off before it gets in and all over. Walkoff mats are usually nylon or olefin with a rubber or vinyl back

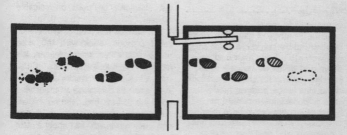

A doorway matted with walkoff mats. To do their job well, both the inside and outside mats need to be at least four strides long.

for inside the door, and rubber or vinyl-backed synthetic turf for outside on the step. They're available in a variety of colors, and to do their job well, both the inside and outside mats should be four strides long.

Vacuum your mats regularly or shake them outside. Hose them down and scrub with all-purpose cleaner solution as needed. You can also use upholstery shampoo or a wet/dry vacuum to clean them. I've even draped mine over a clothesline in a rainstorm to get out collected debris. The most important thing is to always hang them until they're COMPLETELY DRY so that moisture (which can

---

**NEW CARPET
$1,100**

After a few years a carpet does get dirty and worn out—mainly from debris tracked in from outside.

I'd rather spend $15 on a commercial walkoff mat, wouldn't you?

---

damage your floor) isn't trapped under the vinyl backing.

Mattresses. See "Beds."

Melamine. See "Plastics."

Metal Polishes

Although many claims are made for all-purpose metal polishes, no one polish can perform perfectly on all kinds of metal. Differences in metals and the way they tarnish call for at least two and maybe three types of polish—a gentle one for silver; a medium-duty one for brass, bronze, and polished copper; and perhaps a more aggressive one yet for heavily soiled copper cookware. As a rule, you don't need to polish nontarnishing metals such as stainless steel, aluminum, chrome, tin, and pewter.

Most metal polishes contain solvents and detergents to remove the tarnish, mild abrasives to polish the metal, and oils or other coatings to retard future tarnishing. Polishes like

▶ **Medallion mess:** It's pretty, it's intricate, it's made of gleaming metal or silver-colored plastic, it holds soap and water to release later and run down and streak whatever you've just cleaned and polished. What is it? Those little logos, badges, medallions, and insignias, mounted on furnaces, appliances, vehicle interiors and exteriors, fine furniture and fine instruments, and countless other manufactured items, placed there to boast of their quality. They also manage to break fingernails and snag clothes and cleaning cloths and cause rust. The solution (besides ripping them off or taping over them) is to spray them with all-purpose cleaner and scrub them well with a grout brush first—before you clean anything else—and then clean around the object they're attached to. (When you go to dry them, bear in mind that wiping over them won't do it, you need to press a thirsty cloth hard against them and hold it there awhile to absorb. Then complain to Ralph Nader.)

these rub away a little of the metal's surface each time you use them, so they shouldn't be used on plated objects. Most polishes are in paste or cream form, which is wiped on, allowed to dry, then polished off. The polish-impregnated cotton rope types, which incorporate gentle polish and polishing cloth all in one ready-to-use form, come as close as anything to an all-purpose metal polish. Dip-type liquid cleaners, which remove tarnish but don't polish or protect, can be used on utility items but shouldn't be used on valuable pieces.

If a surface has a lot of grooves or relief designs, stick with the rope polishes or a clear metal cleaner. It's hard to remove every trace of the cream types from cracks and crevices, and this can cause an otherwise good job to look bad. And no matter what type of polish you're using, don't use too much. Just apply a little with a clean cloth, massage the surface with it, allow it to dry, and buff to a shine. If you use too much you won't just waste polish, you'll have to work a lot harder to polish it all away.

See also "Brass"; "Chrome"; "Copper"; "Pewter"; "Silver"; "Tarnish, Metal."

Microwave Ovens

You don't have to spread out the newspapers or don rubber gloves, barricade the kitchen, and hyperventilate before heading in—we're cleaning the microwave oven. Microwaves are a cinch to clean compared to conventional ovens! And if you just get in the habit of wiping yours out after each use, you may never need to do a serious cleanup. It's not a bad idea always to cover dishes with a paper towel to keep spatters off the walls. But if you share yours with your brother or a roommate who isn't quite so conscientious, you can still get that glob of cheese off with no trouble. Just hit it (according to how hardened the criminal) with a paper towel, cloth, or white nylon-backed scrub sponge damp with dish detergent and water. Still there? A tough hunk of pizza, huh? Boil a ½ cup of water in there for several minutes and then let the water stand without opening the door for several more minutes to loosen any remaining goo. Add a little lemon juice or a dash or two of pumpkin-pie spice to the water to remove lingering odors.

Many microwave parts are plastic—even the windows on some models—so don't use metal scrapers, steel wool, or powdered cleansers that could scratch or damage. Treat the outside of your microwave and the seal around the door with non-abrasive care too. Spray and wipe with all-purpose or glass cleaner and a soft cloth. Never use abrasive pads or cleansers; they can mar the finish and may damage the seal. And push the CLEAR button when you're done to erase any instructions you may have cleaned in.

Mildew

Mildew is a growth produced by a tiny plant of the fungus family that often leaves black, white, or bluish-green specks or blotches on the surface of the affected item. Mildew thrives in warm, damp, dark, poorly ventilated environments, such as cellars, crawl spaces, closets, bathrooms, and laundry rooms. Since it actually eats its host, it's usually found on organic materials, such as cotton, linen, silk, wool, leather, wood, and paper. But almost any material or fabric can sprout mildew if it's dirty enough to provide this mini-fungus with something to eat. Most synthetic fabrics are mildew resistant, for instance, but mildew can grow on the soil in them, especially if

they're left damp. Wadding or bunching things up (especially wet things such as shower curtains) is a real invitation to mildew. Mildew grows on tile shower walls by feeding on the soap scum and body oils trapped in the grout, and on painted surfaces by eating the oils and organic compounds in the paint. As mildew grows, it leaves a musty odor, and as it consumes its host it often causes it to weaken and fall apart.

To control mildew, you need to decrease the humidity and increase the air circulation and amount of light. You can do this with fans, vents, dehumidifiers, air conditioners, or even a heat cable or bare light bulb installed near the floor of a damp, dark closet. If you opt for the latter, leave it burning day and night but don't go higher than 100 watts and be sure to place it in such a way as to prevent a fire hazard. Repairing any sources of outdoor moisture coming inside—such as basement wall cracks—will also help. To dehumidify small or enclosed areas—for example, storage lockers and closets—you can add bags or containers of water-absorbing chemicals such as silica gel, activated alumina, or anhydrous calcium sulfate or calcium chloride. Most of these can be dried out in the oven and reused. Several poisonous chemicals used for moth protection—such as paradichlorobenzene and paraformaldehyde—can also be used to help prevent mildew in storage, but be sure to use according to the instructions that come with them to prevent accidental poisoning or injury to certain plastics.

Remove mildew from clothing

▶ Stephen Gibson, a poetic janitor from Denver, tired of cleaning the ever-reappearing mildew, etched this fine verse in a crop of it:

Mildew, mildew on the wall,
In the sink and down the hall.
You think it's gone? It comes creeping back,
In blooming blue, orange, and black.
How must I deal with that sporey villain
I fondly call bathroom penicillin?

quickly, before fabric damage occurs. First dry-brush and vacuum to remove as much as possible, then launder or dry-clean as appropriate. Bleach laundered clothing with as strong a bleach as the fabric will tolerate. Then air-dry in the sun. Shoes and leather goods can be wiped with diluted denatured alcohol (1 part alcohol to 1 part water), then polished. Shoe stores have fungus-inhibiting sprays for leather that help retard future growth; keeping shoes well waxed will help too. To kill mold and remove mildew stains on tile shower walls, scrub with a stiff brush and a 1:5 solution of chlorine bleach in water. Mildewed hard surfaces such as painted or paneled walls should be cleaned with disinfectant cleaner. Mildew-resistant paints are also available.

Mineral Spirits

Also known as *paint thinner,* mineral spirits are a petroleum distillate used extensively as a solvent for oil-based paints and varnishes. While the two terms mean essentially the same thing, products labeled "Paint Thinner" are generally a lower grade of distillate (not as powerful a solvent, slower evaporating) than those called "Mineral Spirits." These solvents are used not only to thin paint but to clean up the equipment you put it on with and to wipe up any drips or spatters. Some cleaning tipsters recommend using mineral spirits as a spot cleaner to remove grease and tar from carpeting, fabrics, and other surfaces. This is okay for hard surfaces such as flooring and Formica, but mineral spirits can leave a ring on fabrics, so dry-cleaning fluid would be a better choice. Mineral spirits or paint thinner is fine for removing oil and grease from machine parts, metal, concrete, and other such nondelicate surfaces. (See "Oil Stains.") The more powerful—and flammable—solvents can be used for degreasing too, but don't use them unless it's absolutely necessary. See "Solvents."

Miniatures

Many of the at least 9 million different kinds of miniatures available fall into the dollhouse furniture category. Since they're usually made of the same materials as their full-size counterparts, you can clean, dust, and polish them just like regular furniture.

For general doll housekeeping, a paintbrush of the right size will remove dust from floors and furniture. Or there are mini vacuum cleaners the size of a small flashlight made just for this purpose, complete with mini vacuum bags. They can either vacuum or blow the dust off. These are available through miniatures dealers and office supply stores. (They're also used to clean keyboards.)

Miniature ceramic or pewter items can be cleaned like the full-size versions. Washable miniatures can be washed in dish detergent solution, then rinsed. Some people do this by putting them in a metal tea ball and shaking it up and down in sudsy water. (This is a good way to clean them thoroughly.) Cotton swabs dipped in sudsy water can clean even the most intricate details.

Stained or soiled rugs and other fabric items can be treated the same as regular-size furnishings made of the same fabric.

For dollhouse windows, rubbing alcohol or mineral spirits work well. To remove glues that may remain on glass windows, try nail polish remover.

Mirrors

A mirror may be just a piece of glass with a reflective silver coating on the back, but don't clean it like any old piece of glass. When you're cleaning the front, you have to be careful not to damage the backing in the process. Mirrors with black edges or black specks in them are usually victims of careless cleaning. Here's what happens: If you overwet a mirror so that the cleaning solution puddles at the edges, it begins to wick up onto the silver coating, oxidizing it and turning it black. Harsh chemicals such as ammonia or acids oxidize the coating very quickly, but even mild cleaners will affect it over time. The key is to avoid wetting the edges. The best

way to clean a mirror is with a fast-evaporating Windex-type glass cleaner and a soft cloth, but don't spray the mirror! Instead, lightly spray the cloth, then use it to clean and polish the mirror.

Drying is important too. Always wipe a mirror (especially those edges!) dry with a lint-free cloth before the air does it.

Mixers, Electric

Never immerse an electric mixer, and make sure it's turned off and unplugged before cleaning. Beaters and attachments should be removed to clean and can be hand-washed (rinse and dry well!) or run through the dishwasher. Just dampen a cloth with all-purpose cleaner to wipe down the mixer body (and bowl housing if yours has one)—and don't forget to wipe the beater shaft or shafts, beneath the bowl turntable if removable, the *underside* of the motor head or case, and the cord—those spatters get everywhere. Wet down any dried-on batter blobs and let them soak a few minutes, then wipe and rewet as necessary until they come off. Go after the powdered sugar in the crevices with a cotton swab or a grout brush. (See "Grout Brushes.")

Mohair. See "Angora."

Mop Buckets

Mop buckets distinguish themselves from ordinary buckets with an attachment to wring or squeeze water out of a mop. This is an important feature as it not only speeds up the mopping

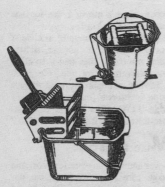

Mop buckets suitable for home use.

process and gets the mop drier, it also saves our hands from cut and puncture wounds. A professional-quality metal or plastic mop bucket is a good investment. Eighteen-quart is a nice size for the home. I prefer a built-in roller wringer to the wringers that mount on the side. Even the smallest of the side-mounted type is topheavy and awkward for a home. The smaller versions of the commercial handle squeezer type are good too. You don't necessarily want wheels on a bucket for home use. Most of us don't have big expanses of hard flooring to roll one around on, and we don't move a bucket much in home mopping anyway.

(P.S. Don't leave your dirty mop water sitting around in the bucket when you're done—it settles, hardens, and smells.)

Mopping

Small floors can be spruced up with a sponge mop, but a large floor is eas-ier to do with a regular string mop (see "Mops") and a wringer bucket. Use only a neutral cleaner to mop floors, and not too much of it—using too strong a detergent or in too strong a concentration can leave floors dull after mopping. A short squirt of liquid dishwashing detergent in a bucketful of water is plenty.

Make sure the floor is well swept, vacuumed, or dust-mopped before you start. Quickly mopping over the floor just once with a damp mop may be enough for a lightly soiled floor, but if it's heavily soiled you'll have to do it twice. Lay a thin film of solution out on the entire floor (don't flood it) when you go over it the first time. This will allow the cleaning solution to emulsify and soften the soil so it will come off easily on the second pass. Mop all around the edges first, then do the middle, using overlapping figure-8 strokes. For a thorough job, push the mop strands into corners and tight places with your fingers. Be sure you get up all the little bits of stray macaroni, cat food, dead bugs, and the like we seem to miss no matter how carefully we sweep first. Always flop your mop over to a clean side when one side gets dirty. And when both sides are dirty, wash and wring out the mop in the bucket, before it loads up and starts losing stuff like this all over your floor.

After the initial wetting, and before your second pass over the whole floor, scrub up any stuck-on or stubborn soil wth a long-handled floor scrubber. (See "Scrubbee Doo.") See also "Black Marks." Then remop the floor with clear rinse water, wringing the mop out as dry as pos-

▶ **Mop flop:** An important procedure you shouldn't forget to perform while mopping, whereby at intervals you flip (or flop) the mop over to get to a drier or cleaner side.

sible each time you rewet it in the bucket. Anytime you can't see a quarter dropped in the bottom of the mop bucket, your rinse water is too dirty. When it gets murky, you're just putting dirt back on the floor. (This is the other big reason for the dull look.)

Mops

A mop is meant for light washing and rinsing, to remove surface soil. You should scrub with a long-handled floor scrubber (see "Scrubbee Doo"), which is ten times faster than a mop. Gather water and stripping slop up from a floor with a floor squeegee (see "Floor Squeegees"), and pick it up with a dustpan.

If I had only a little kitchen- and bathroom-worth of hard flooring, I'd just own a sponge mop. (See "Sponge Mops.") If you have half an acre of vinyl, tile, or hardwood floor as I have, pick up a 12- or 16-ounce commercial mop and a mop bucket (see "Mop Buckets")—a $30 or so investment, but this will keep you off your hands and knees. Make sure the mop head is a rayon/cotton blend so it won't start shedding strings on every chair leg. Layflat is a good brand, for the reason its name suggests. Remember I said 12- or 16-ounce—commercial mops also come in 32-ounce (like a wet lion mane) and 24-

ounce sizes, both too big for the home.

Don't bleach your mop to clean it or it will suffer premature balding. Hang mops from the handles to make sure they dry after use. The head needs air and it can't get it wadded up in a corner.

Mother of Pearl. See "Shell/
Mother of Pearl/Coral."

▶ **Mouth Cleaning!** You've tried it in a moment of desperation—blowing, spitting, maybe (if no one was looking) even licking something to try to get it clean. The mouth really is a wonderful instrument for getting cleaning done, but the way to use it is to say a few words to guests and others who ask "Can we help?" What do 99 percent of us say? "Oh, that's okay." Next time say **yes** instead.

Muriatic Acid. See "Hydrochloric Acid."

Musical Instruments

I never thought much about this until the day a clerk in a music store handed me an extension mouthpiece to try out a new harmonica: With all the mouth and hand contact they get, of course they need cleaning!

Musical instruments should be cleaned according to the manufacturer's directions and the particular materials used in their construction. The general word here is caution, since these are not only delicate and valuable objects but *working* ones whose sound and function can be damaged by careless handling or cleaning. The fine wood finishes on instruments should never be soaked or exposed to moisture for any length of time. Plastic parts can be cleaned with neutral all-purpose cleaner. Be extra careful with surfaces close to electronic components, and don't use silicone polishes on *any* part of a musical instrument. Keep other cleaning chemicals, including alcohol, ammonia and ammoniated cleaners, bleach, abrasive cleaners, methylene chloride, trichloroethylene, MEK, acetone, and ketones, well away from your musical instruments unless the manufacturer specifically recommends them. *(Read the label!)*

There are so many different types of instruments, each with its own specialized cleaning requirements, that I will only consider a few of the most common.

Guitars and like instruments: Perspiration can damage the lacquered or polyurethaned finish of a wooden guitar, so always wipe your guitar off with a clean, soft cloth after each use. You can also use a cloth lightly dampened with water or neutral cleaner or oil soap solution, if you buff dry immediately afterward. Don't use any type of oil soap on unfinished parts of a guitar such as the fingerboard, as oil will soften raw wood. To clean the fingerboard, use a fingerboard dressing such as Petillo Fingerboard Dressing, available at music stores. Commercial guitar cleaners, which often contain waxes like carnauba, are available at music stores. You can also apply a thin coat of a nonsilicone

car polish, but be sure to use it with a soft cloth and only on a clean surface. And use it sparingly, because wax or polish buildup on a guitar will affect its performance.

Wipe off the strings with a soft cloth after every use. Perspiration and dirt collected on the strings will not only accelerate oxidation but cause problems with sound quality. Change strings regularly and relax the tension on them if you put your guitar into extended storage.

Guitars, like most musical instruments, are sensitive to temperature, so never subject them to sudden changes such as suddenly taking them out of the case in a warm room, after they've been in a cold car for hours.

Pianos: Maintain and clean the outside as any fine furniture. Dust weekly with a Masslinn cloth or lambswool duster. (see "Dusting.") The surface of a piano is well sealed with varnish or lacquer so it doesn't need oiling. Give it a quick wipe, instead, when it seems to need it, with a cloth very lightly dampened with nonsilicone furniture polish, and then buff dry immediately. Don't get any polish on the keys and keep them covered when not in use to prevent dust from settling into those crannies. Most keys nowadays are plastic; unless your piano is a classic, you'd be hardpressed to find ivory. Never use spray cleaner or anything on the keys; instead *lightly* spray neutral cleaner on a cleaning cloth and wipe. Never allow drips to slip down between the keys. For hard-to-remove stains on plastic keys, dip a damp cloth into baking soda (don't let the powder fall between the keys). Use another cloth to wipe off, then buff dry.

If you do have real ivory keys, be sure you don't use anything but neutral cleaner on them, never acids or alkaline cleaners like ammonia. To help keep ivory keys white, make sure they're regularly exposed to light—steady darkness will accelerate the yellowing all ivory undergoes with age. Trying to whiten ivory keys with lemon juice or the like is risky. See "Bone/Ivory."

The inside of a piano (the metal strings and hammers) is best left to a professional, who should clean it during the twice-yearly tuning pianos should receive.

If it's a grand or baby grand, be sure to close it when not in use.

Organs: According to the only certified organ technician in my neck of the woods, Milo Price, a thirty-five-year veteran, there's nothing a home organ owner *should* do to today's electronic organs but maintain the exterior of the cabinet like a piece of fine furniture—dust it regularly and keep wet glasses off it.

Especially do nothing—not even

vacuum—*inside* an organ. Far more damage than good is done by attempts to clean inside. If a wire is pulled loose it'll take hours of detective work to find where it went, so it's just not worth tampering with. It's not dust that usually causes problems, anyway—the culprit is a chemical reaction from moisture in the air and the metals and materials in key contacts, which creates corrosion.

No regular maintenance has to be done by a professional, but if you take your organ in for repair it will be cleaned as well. It's okay to wait till something goes wrong.

Once a year clean the outside of your organ with a good nonsilicone furniture polish—it'll bring out the richness of the wood grain. But don't do it too often, such as every week, and don't get any polish on the keys, just wipe them with a barely water-dampened (not dripping!) cloth as needed. Clean the keys as you would piano keys.

▶ **Good cleaning music:** Anything that can be heard over the vacuum.

N

Haney!
I'm Going
to need
a BIGGER
BROOM!!

Nasty things come out of places we fail to clean regularly

Neat's-Foot Oil

Neat's-foot oil is a light yellow fatty oil made from—yes—the feet of cattle, used primarily as a dressing for unfinished leather to keep it moist and pliable. It can be used on finished leather as well, but will leave a dull, matte finish. See also "Leather"; "Shoes/Boots."

▶ **Neatnik:** The title less neat people give to the more neat. No relation to beatnik.

Neckties

Even professional dry cleaners have trouble restoring soiled silk ties, especially, to their original appearance. The best thing to do is to keep them looking as good as possible for as long as possible by taking care of spots as soon as they happen, then just retiring a tie when it starts looking ratty. Oily and greasy spots can be removed with dry-cleaning fluid; just be sure to feather out the edges as you finish. (See "Feathering.") Water-soluble soils are a problem on silk because the fabric tends to water-spot so easily. A procedure that often works is to wet the spot and a large area around it with dry-cleaning fluid, then immediately (before the solvent can dry) work the spot itself with all-purpose (water-based) spot remover or mild soap and water. Blot as dry as possible and feather the wet edges. Polyester ties are a little more workable, and wool and knit are downright enjoyable to work on; just follow the instructions in "Spot and Stain Removal," following any precautions listed for that particular fabric under "Fabrics."

Needlepoint. See "Needlework."

Needlework

The word *needlework* encompasses many crafts. For crocheted or knitted items, check the content of the yarn before washing so you know what water temperature and washing method to use. Cool water, hand-washing, Woolite or Ivory Snow, and air-drying is always the safest approach when in doubt. Soap can leave a residue that eventually yellows, so be sure to rinse well. Some newer items can be machine-washed, but if the age and content of fibers are not known, stick with hand-washing and air-drying.

As for the art needlework, the nicer it is, the more we want it out and about (and exposed to soiling!). The safest way to display needlework is behind glass, as this protects it from most kinds of abuse and just about eliminates the need for clean-

ing. Unfortunately, it's hard to appreciate the texture of a cross-stitched thistle when it's covered by glass, so much handcrafted work has no protection from spots, smudges, and airborne pollutants. Treat needlework with a soil retardant such as Scotch-gard to help resist dirt and make cleaning easier. This is especially important on heavy-use items, such as needlepoint seat cushions. Be sure to test the retardant you intend to use in an inconspicuous place to make sure it won't affect any of the dyes in the piece.

For needlework on its own in the open, vacuuming is the preferred method of cleaning. Frequent and thorough vacuuming will help stretch out the time between deep cleanings. Use a vacuum dusting brush attachment, but clean it off or even wash and dry it carefully first to get rid of the dead flies or unmentionable muck you vacuumed out of the sliding window tracks last week. Don't rub and scrub the bristles around on the piece—just lightly flick the threads with the tips of the bristles and let the suction do most of the work. On delicate embroidered pieces, it's best not to let the bristles touch the threads at all. On handcrafted upholstery, a more vigorous vacuuming may be in order, but take care not to snag or distort any decorations or loose threads.

When accumulated soil makes deep cleaning necessary, the method to use depends on what the piece is made of. Most art needlework is a combination of materials (such as wool or silk thread on a canvas or linen base). *Dry cleaning* is the answer for antique pieces, needlework with stains or spills on it, or any needlework containing noncolorfast threads (some threads, especially silk, bleed color badly) or needlework done on backing material that tends to shrink. You might consider dry-cleaning any art needlework, since it's so small and valuable. Take it (removing it from the pillow or chair seat first if necessary) to a knowledgeable cleaner who has experience with needlework and tapestries. *Some pieces* can be gently hand-washed in cool water and a mild product such as Woolite. Before washing any piece you're not sure of, test by pressing a clean white cotton cloth moistened with warm water to the piece. If any color transfers (bleeds), don't wash it! When washing, always vacuum away any dirt you can first and be careful not to rub, scrub, or distort the fabric and stitching. Be especially careful on the back of the piece where all those loose threads are. Just let the needlework soak for a while and then gently flush the water back and forth through it, coaxing the dirt out with your fingers. Roll the piece up in a dry towel to blot most of the water out, then block it out to dry. (See "Blocking.") Return to the stretcher frame, if there is one, when dry. You can also shampoo washable pieces by wiping the surface lightly with some upholstery shampoo foam on a sponge or a thick terry towel. Washing or dry-cleaning will remove part or all of any retardant that may have been applied, so retreatment will be necessary for continued protection.

▶ **Nonstop chores** (Including dishes, laundry, and bedmaking): theologians and philosophers have always sought the perfect definition of *eternal* and at last we have it: "housework," for it has no beginning and no end. And it's so essential to the maintenance of mankind that our approach to it can result in heaven or hell around the house. Bathing, eating, rocking babies, and other inescapable chores we've found a way to look forward to or even love; the never-ending housework jobs can be the same. We just need to consider the fact that our cleaning efforts can change the *quality* of our own and others' lives.

Neutral Cleaners. See "Cleaners, Neutral."

Nonstick Cookware. See "Cookware."

No-Wax Floors

This is a not-entirely-accurate term coined by the flooring manufacturers to describe sheet vinyl flooring (and tiles) with a thick protective layer of clear vinyl or polyurethane over the top. No-wax floors do shine without waxing, and the gloss layer will keep them looking good for a while. But with time and use, especially heavy use, the gloss layer will develop worn or dull areas and need to be coated with a floor finish (alias: *wax*) to maintain a uniform shine. If you have a new no-wax floor that doesn't see much action (you never wear shoes

▶ **Nook and cranny:** A design factor incorporated by architects to compound cleaning inconvenience.

and you don't have kids), with good care you can keep it looking good for years without wax. But if you have a lot of foot traffic and tracked-in dirt, or if the floor is showing signs of wear, it's best to keep it waxed to protect it from further deterioration. You can choose one of the major brands of floor polish sold in the supermarket or get a self-polishing, metal-interlock floor finish from a jan-itorial supply store. After the initial waxing, recoat the traffic areas as needed to maintain a good protective layer. See "Waxing Floors."

Whether you wax your no-wax floor or not, daily maintenance is the same. Sweep and damp-mop (using plain water, or water with a dash of neutral cleaner added) regularly to keep abrasive soil off the surface, scrubbing as needed with a white nylon-backed sponge to loosen stubborn or ground-in soil. (See "Sweeping"; "Mopping.") Good walkoff mats (see "Mats, Walkoff") at entrances will help keep damaging grit out of the house.

O

Old wives' tales: Cleaning facts and finds that were hot news before 1900, or early in this century, and they're still being passed around as gospel. Some did work fairly well in their day, but they're no match for modern cleaning tools and chemicals.

Odors

To get rid of odor you have to remove the *source*, not just cover the odor up with perfumed air fresheners. That means get rid of the dead mouse behind the dryer and the rotten banana under the garbage can liner—and then wash the areas where such things have been with disinfectant cleaner. (See "Disinfecting;" "Clean-

► No matter how well meaning the men in your house, there's always a misfiring problem in the bathroom. If you go after those errant shots with disinfectant cleaner, the bathroom will be fresh-smelling and germ free.

ers, Disinfectant.") Disinfectant cleaner will kill the microorganisms or "germs" that cause most unpopular household odors. Bacteria working on forgotten food, spills, or organic waste in kitchens or bathrooms, for example, give off gases that smell bad. Musty smells usually come from the tiny funguses called mold or mildew.

Organic messes such as vomit or urine, human or animal, especially those that have penetrated absorbent materials like carpeting and upholstery, should be treated with a bacteria/enzyme digester. (See "Bacteria/Enzyme Digester.") Cooking odors and cigarette smoke respond best to airing out with fresh air and an odor-neutralizing spray. Most of the supermarket air fresheners just mask bad odors with perfumes, but janitorial supply stores have odor neutralizers that actually eliminate the bad odor. They chemically convert the odor molecule into a new substance that doesn't smell bad. These products also have pleasant masking fragrances that help out while the neutralizer is doing its job.

The quicker you get after odors, the easier they are to remove. The longer you leave a bad odor around, the deeper it sinks into your clothes, hair, furniture, drapes, and carpets.

Oil Soaps

The term *oil soaps* can mean superfatted soaps, such as the saddle soap used for cleaning leather, in which some of the tallow or fat is left unconverted to soap. However, the term is most often used to mean vegetable oil soaps, made of vegetable oils such as linseed (flaxseed), cottonseed, or pine oil. Oil soaps are mild true soaps used to clean such things as finished wood and natural stone, which benefit from the thin film of oil residue this type of soap leaves on the surface. This helps keep wood finishes from drying out, helps seal and protect stone, and can be buffed to a nice shine.

A popular brand is Murphy's Oil Soap, available in supermarkets and elsewhere either as concentrate or in a ready-to-use bottle.

Oil Stains

Oil on hard surfaces usually isn't a big deal; just wipe up all you can and scrub away any remaining traces with a detergent solution. It gets to be a problem when oil soaks into a soft, porous material such as raw wood, concrete, carpeting, or fabric. The first rule is: Act promptly. Many oils oxidize over time and become much harder to remove. An oil stain "set" in a piece of clothing by ironing or hot-air drying can become impossible.

For fresh oil, using an absorbent is the first step. (See "Absorbents.") For drips and spills on a garage floor, use a handful of cat litter. Sprinkle it on the spill and grind it in with your foot, then let it sit for several hours to absorb the oil. For carpeting, upholstery, and dry-cleanable clothing, use fuller's earth (see "Fuller's Earth") on dark-colored fabrics; cornmeal or K2r on light colors. For washable clothing, just spray the stain with laundry pretreatment and wash it in the hottest water safe for the fabric. Make sure the stain is completely gone before you tumble-dry or iron, though, or it could be with you forever. If in doubt, air-dry the garment.

For old, dry oil, or for residues left after using an absorbent, blot the stain with dry-cleaning fluid. (See "Blot.") Oil stains can often be coaxed out of porous surfaces, such as concrete, raw wood, cinder block, and marble, by applying a solvent poultice. See "Poultice."

Optical Brighteners

Also called *fluorescent whitening agents*, optical brighteners are chemical compounds added to soaps and detergents to help whiten and brighten fabrics. They coat the fibers and work by fluorescence, in which invisible ultraviolet light is converted into visible blue light, lending a blue-white brightness to treated fabrics, both white and colored. Optical brighteners are added to laundry products and carpet and upholstery shampoos, and are also applied to some fabrics at the mill. (See "Yellowing.") Optical brighteners are also what give many cleaning demonstrations much of their drama.

Order of Cleaning

What's the best order to clean in? You might think that's like what order should you eat the food on your plate. As long as you get it down, does it really matter? When you're cleaning by yourself it does make some difference, and with more than one person, or a crew, it's critical. With a crew, it's important to schedule so you keep out of each other's way and everyone finishes at the same time.

Within a room:
• First remove all the junk, clutter, and trashables (scattered clothes, wilted flowers, dropped pop cans and newspapers, etc.).
• Then do any dust-, debris-, or fallout-producing jobs, such as high dusting or shoveling out the fireplace.
• Dust first, before you vacuum or sweep—and dust from top to bottom.
• Spot-clean the walls and other hard surfaces next if they need doing.
• Polish furniture and the like as needed.
• Do mirrors, glass, and windows next.
• Floors (vacuum, sweep, mop, etc.) last.
• Do the sides, edges, and corners before the middle—of anything. Get the slow, tight, tricky, awkward places first—and leave the wide open spaces for a fast, freewheeling finish.

Within the house:
• Clean the easiest rooms first (usually the bedrooms and the living room).

- Save the kitchen (which is usually where we get our water and cleaning supplies from, and where the garbage depot is) last. Otherwise you'll dirty it up again before you're through with the rest of the house.
- Do all the hard floors at once if you can.

A couple of rules that apply anywhere: We don't want to reenter and resoil areas that have been cleaned—that is, you don't want to be dragging a drippy garbage can across a freshly finished floor. So start at the back of the room and work to the front; or circle the room in a clockwise motion; Always move from a clean area to a dirty area. The second rule is that if the furniture is moved out of the way for any reason, clean that empty spot—the floor or carpet under there—immediately, while it's visible.

Organs. See "Musical Instruments."

Oven Cleaners

Most oven cleaners rely heavily on lye to break down those burned-on fatty deposits. Lye is highly alkaline, which is why it's able to dissolve highly acid grease. Lye is not only poisonous and damaging to paint, fabrics, aluminum, copper, and other surfaces but the fumes are toxic and it can cause severe skin burns. If you use lye products, be sure to wear rubber gloves and protective clothing (long sleeves) to avoid contact with skin. If using an aerosol, wear a dust mask to avoid inhaling toxic fumes.

Easy-Off Non-Caustic Formula, though not quite as effective as the lye products, is much safer to use. Another alternative is to leave a pan of ammonia in the oven overnight— this will help soften oven soil so that it can be wiped out with all-purpose cleaner. Caustic oven cleaners should never be used on self-cleaning ovens—under the high heat of the cleaning cycle, they can damage the porcelain coating. Oven cleaner should be kept away from the heating element and door gasket in any type of oven, because not only will it injure them but the whole house will reek of oven cleaner when you turn the oven back on. See "Lye"; "Caustic."

Ovens

The most hated job in the house, because we usually wait to do ovens until it's either clean it or buy a new stove. If you clean your oven regularly, it won't take much longer than the morning shower. And you won't mind even heavy-duty oven cleaning so much if you remember to let the chemicals do the work.

Most commercial oven cleaners contain lye and must be handled with great care. Oven cleaner will eat your fingers right to the quick—if you get it on your skin, rinse it off right away with plenty of water. Protect yourself (long sleeves and rubber gloves at least, and you might even consider safety goggles and a paper mask). Protect your kitchen too, with newspapers or better yet an old tarp or dropcloth on the floor and surrounding surfaces. Then paint or spray the cleaner on according to directions. Put on a good thick coat and leave it there a good long time. (I go all the way and leave it overnight.) Most oven cleaners will work faster on a warm oven. Keep the spray off wires, light bulbs, thermostats, and elements—I wrap strips of foil around such things before I spray. The oven door is the first thing I clean. Then I take off the door and set it somewhere to make the rest of the job easier. Most oven doors can be removed by pulling straight up. (Some have a latch.)

Be sure to don your protective gear again before you start removing the cleaner. First use paper towels to get off the worst of the gunk and stuff them right into a garbage bag. You could also use a rubber spatula or even a small squeegee to scrape off that initial thick layer of icky stuff. After you've removed the bulk of the mess, wipe with a water-dampened sponge or cloth until all the oven cleaner is gone. If it's dried up a bit overnight, a light new application of oven cleaner will resoften it and it should come right off. If you still have some stubborn spots, just reapply cleaner to the holdouts and leave it on for at least thirty minutes—that (or a third application if necessary) will get 'em. If it doesn't, call in a welder and have the spot cut out with a torch, or learn to live with it.

You can use my famous two-bucket system (see "Walls") to good advantage in this messy operation. You want one bucket full of water, the other just a quarter full. Each time your sponge gets loaded up, squeeze it into the quarter-full bucket and

rinse the heavy soil out of the sponge in that one too. Then dip the sponge into the full bucket to refill it with water. Repeat by always squeezing the sludge into the slop bucket. This will keep your cleaning water—and your sponge—cleaner to work with.

Going over the surface with a cloth dampened in vinegar water after most of the sludge is gone will neutralize the alkaline residue and make rinsing easier.

After the inside is done, wash the outside of the stove and around the oven with all-purpose cleaner or degreaser solution. Don't forget the edges and underside of doors and drawers where the drips like to collect.

What about the racks? Don your protective gear and place them on newspapers outside and spray them well on both sides with oven cleaner, then place the whole mess in a garbage bag and set it up somewhere high safe from kids and pets. Next day hose them off, wipe them dry, and deliver them to your shiny oven.

All that's left to do is remove the foil on the elements and replace the door.

Ovens, Gas

This is one place you have to rely on manufacturer's directions—there are many different kinds. In general, don't start cleaning until you turn off the gas valve. The interior of the oven can generally be cleaned like a conventional oven (see "Ovens"), but there's an additional range drawer for broiling that usually slides out and

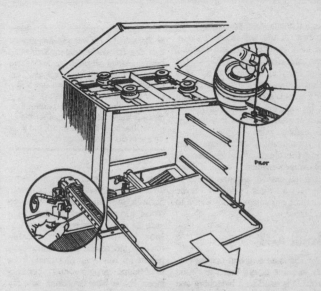

When cleaning gas stoves, be sure to unclog the burner holes, if necessary, in the oven burner and pilot as well as on the rangetop.

usually needs oven cleaner and serious degreasing. Removable pans and other parts, as long as they're not aluminum, can be soaked in ammonia water (4 ounces per gallon) for several hours. Ammonia will discolor aluminum.

When you finish cleaning you'll need to relight the pilot light(s). Be sure that the oven burner jet holes aren't clogged. If they are, turn the oven off and unclog them by poking with a wire, such as an open paper clip. Turn the oven on again to make sure that all holes are unclogged.

Ovens, Microwave. See "Microwave Ovens."

Ovens, Self-Cleaning

These blessed inventions get so hot during their self-cleaning cycle that they turn any drips, spatters, or spills to ash that can just be wiped away with a paper towel. Do check your owner's manual to see if the racks should be left in during cleaning. No part of a self-cleaning oven should ever be cleaned with caustic oven cleaners—some traces of the cleaner will always be left, which will damage the oven lining when you turn on the high heat of the self-cleaning cycle. Also bear in mind that self-cleaning ovens can't clean the area outside the gasket but they will heat it up, so if you leave smudges and spills on there they'll be baked on but good. Prevent this by cleaning outside the gasket with a degreaser before you use the self-cleaning cycle.

If your oven doesn't come clean during the cleaning cycle, consult your owner's manual. Maybe it's not getting hot enough and just needs to be set for a longer cycle. Or maybe the gasket is damaged and needs to be replaced.

Oxalic Acid

Oxalic acid is an acid that occurs naturally in some plants (such as wood sorrel). It is used as a bleaching and cleaning agent, and in the making of dyes. Oxalic acid is a good rust remover and is available from pharma-

▶ **Overkill** is cleaning something that doesn't need cleaning. Scrubbing the paint off after the dirt is long gone, or putting in five glugs of cleaning concentrate when one will do the job fine (in fact, better). Overkill is the deep-seated belief that more is better. It doesn't bother the germs because they're dead, but it sure can do mean things to us.

cies in either liquid or crystal form. To remove rust stains from bathroom fixtures, wet the area, sprinkle on oxalic acid crystals and let it dry. Be sure to rinse it away after it dries. Most janitorial supply stores also have liquid oxalic rust removers, helpful for removing rust stains from hard floors, carpeting, and other surfaces. Follow label directions carefully and keep oxalic acid in any form well away from pets and children, as it is a powerful internal poison.

P

Pack Rat (two-legged variety): Comes in both male and female form and can transport more stuff to more places and use it less than any creature in the universe.

Paintbrushes and Rollers

No matter how tired you are, the time to clean painting tools is right when you finish using them. When you're done painting, just set your jaw and clean 'em up; putting it off only makes it harder (both the paint residue and getting around to it!). If you're in the middle of a job and will be using your roller again within a day or so, you can just sop it up good with paint, lay it flat in the roller tray, and seal it up well with plastic wrap. If it's a brush, give it a good dip in the paint bucket, wrap it in plastic wrap, and lay it on a flat surface; putting it in the fridge will keep it fresh for up to a week. Don't ever stand brushes on end in a can or bucket—the bristles will warp. And don't leave paint tools soaking in water or solvent for long periods either—the handles as well as the bristles will be damaged.

When you do start to clean up, be sure to select the proper solvent—warm water and detergent for latex paints, mineral spirits for oil-base and alkyd paints and varnishes, lacquer thinner for lacquer, alcohol for shellac. The can label should resolve any doubts you have about this. The easiest way to clean tools used for water-based (latex) paints is to work them with your hands under a stream of warm running water. Those requiring solvent can be cleaned in the roller tray or in a tin can.

• First, scrape all the paint possible out of the roller or brush with a paint paddle or putty knife.

• Pour an inch or two of solvent into the tray or can and work the brush up and down against the bottom—run rollers through the solvent and roll out on the dry part of the tray a few times. Work solvent into the bristles or nap with your hands (using rubber gloves) and squeeze it back out, and keep doing this until no more paint seems to be coming out. Flex the bristles of the brush from side to side by pushing hard against the heel of your hand to work out the elusive paint deep in the roots. If you don't get it all out, the heel of the brush will harden and leave you with only 2 inches of working bristle. This is important to do even if you're just changing colors, lest the original paint work its way out as you paint and contaminate the second color.

• Pour the dirty solvent into a catch jug and replace with fresh solvent, then continue as before until no more paint is coming out of the tool. It may take three or even four separate rinses before the tool is com-

pletely clean. I know you want to, but don't give up too soon. Persevere until *all* the paint is out of that brush or roller, or it'll be stiff and unusable when you need it next. Whether to try and get the hardened drips off the brush handle is a matter of taste—attacking them too vigorously with solvent will remove the factory-applied paint on there too (which is why professional brushes often have bare wood handles).

• Finish by washing the brush or roller in warm water and detergent under the tap; spin excess water out of brushes by holding them in a bucket and spinning the handle between your hands. Give rollers a brisk spin on a post or board outside.

• Hang rollers up or stand them on end to dry; put brushes back into the wrapper they came in to keep the bristles straight and properly shaped.

• Save dirty solvent in a (labeled!) catch jug for future brush and roller cleaning—the paint will settle to the bottom and you can pour off the used solvent to use for the next series of first and second rinses.

Painted Surfaces

The type of paint largely determines how cleanable it will be. Here's how the paints rank:

1. *Baked enamel (such as most appliance finishes), epoxy enamel, and automotive paints:* These are the most durable and stain-resistant of paints, their finish is so slick and hard it resists not only stains but dirt penetration. Paints like these tolerate scouring with mild abrasives and will withstand heavy-duty

cleaners and degreasers if needed. But even these finishes can be scratched and dulled by harsh abrasive cleansers, steel wool, or colored scrub pads, and harsh chemicals such as oven cleaner, drain cleaner, toilet bowl cleaner, and strong solvents should never be used on them.

2. *General-purpose enamels:* These are the enamels used in most interior painting—the kind you'll find on your kitchen or bathroom walls. These resist stains well and tolerate moderate scrubbing, but heavy-duty cleaners and even gentle abrasives may scratch and dull if used with a heavy hand. The best bet here is a neutral cleaner solution and a white nylon-backed scrub pad. Use heavy-duty cleaners or abrasive cleansers carefully and only when absolutely necessary. Latex enamels shouldn't be soaked for more than a minute or two, or the paint may begin to soften. Oil-base enamels are generally harder and more water-resistant. In general, gloss enamels are the most durable, washable, and cleanable, followed by semigloss and then satin finishes.

3. *Latex flat:* This is the flat wall paint used in many homes. Different brands and grades vary in their washability, but all flat paints absorb stains more readily than gloss paints and are harder to clean. Heavy-duty cleaners and hard scrubbing will often remove the paint right along with the soil. Mild detergents and gentle scrubbing are the order of the day here, and never let the solution sit on the surface for more than a minute. They may look rich and classy, but flat paints are so hard to clean that many

people are now using semigloss or satin enamel throughout their homes.

4. *Exterior paints:* Whether oil-base or latex, exterior house paint should be scrubbed only with a mild detergent solution and rinsed with a hose. A long-handled brush can help remove stubborn soil on those hard-to-reach sections. Using pressure washers or harsh chemicals on exterior paint can loosen its bond to the surface and cause it to flake off.

For the right way to wash painted walls and ceilings, see "Walls."

Paint Thinner. See "Mineral Spirits."

Paneling

Both real and imitation wood paneling can be cleaned the same way, as long as it has a protective coating (such as varnish) on it. If it doesn't, if it's just raw wood, washing is risky—I'd just dry-sponge (see "Dry Sponges") it down, damp-wipe it lightly and, once it's dry, oil it with the wood treatment recommended by the manufacturer or a local cabinet maker.

Paneling that does have a finish on it we clean with an oil soap (such as Murphy's Oil Soap). Clean from the top down. Apply the solution sparingly with a sponge, and squeeze the sponge into an empty bucket each time it gets dirty, not back into your cleaning water. Then buff the paneling dry with a clean cotton terry cloth, wiping with the grain so an occasional streak or skip won't be noticed. The bit of oily residue left by the oil soap will shine up the paneling and save you from applying gunky panel polishes, which only leave a sticky surface to collect and hold dust, dirt, and handprints. Any sealed wood surface can be cleaned this way, just don't leave the solution on for more than a minute or so.

Raw, natural wood and unfinished paneling should be coated with a finish (see "Sealing"; "Wood"; "Varnished Surfaces") so moisture and stains won't penetrate the wood. You'll then be cleaning the finish, not the surface of the wood itself—it's faster and much easier on the wood!

Paper Towels

Paper towels are certainly convenient (*too* convenient, some say): You don't have to hunt for a cloth, or clean it up after you use it. Cloth, however, is actually better to use in most situations—it's more absorbent, stronger, protects your hands better, leaves less lint, is softer than paper (which, after all, is made of wood fibers), and more environmentally sound because it can be reused. See "Cloth, Cleaning."

The main problem with excessive use of paper towels is environmental. It takes a lot of trees to clean the windows and mirrors of America. Those used paper towels have to be disposed of too. And the chlorine used to bleach paper towels leaches into our water supplies in the form of dioxins and furans. Paper towels made from recycled paper are gradually becoming available and are just as good as the one-timers at what paper towels *are* good for.

You'll save not only the environment but money too if you use cloths to wipe up most spills and save the paper for the truly disgusting messes. The best use for paper towels is for removing greasy, gloppy stain-making messes, such as blackened oven cleaner, spilled paint, the half-inch layer of grease on the kitchen exhaust fan, or pet manure. You can just toss them without having to clean the mess off cloths afterward. (Most of this kind of stuff never comes out anyway.) Paper towels are good to have handy for emergencies, and for this, location is everything. Stash or mount a roll anywhere you're likely to be caught unprepared. And on ceramic cooktops (see "Cooktops, Ceramic"), paper towels are the only thing you ever want to use.

When you do buy paper towels for cleaning, the features you want to look for are: absorbent, double ply, and without a pattern. (Patterns can bleed onto light surfaces.) For

---

▶ Few of us have ever quite gotten over the ease and let's face it—fun—of using paper towels. They twirl so neatly off that big thick roll it's easy to overuse them. In public rest rooms, too, we always snatch two out of the dispenser even if one will do. Try to use them a little more thoughtfully. Install a hand towel in the kitchen, for example, and get people to dry their hands on that instead of heading for the paper towel dispenser. Use paper towels for small spills and messes only. When you need to blot up a Mississippi flood, use a sponge. (P.S. For drip pickup, a crumpled towel works better than a folded one.)

grungy-stuff pickup, the heavier, more clothlike towels such as Heavy Wipes or Teri Towels are better.

For those of you who like to use paper towels to wash windows, *surprise!* The most expensive paper towels also leave the most lint. The best brands for lint-free cleaning of windows and mirrors are: Marcal (rated the best by *Consumer Reports*), followed by the following five-way tie: Viva, Truly Fine (Safeway), Hi-Dri, A&P, and Mardi Gras.

Particle Board

Everything I say about plywood (see "Plywood") is true for particle board, only more so. Moisture causes most particle board to swell and fall apart, so it should always be well sealed before using any water on it. With a couple of coats of durable enamel paint or clear urethane finish on it, particle board makes a very durable, cleanable indoor surface. Exposed to the elements outdoors, you'll never get it sealed up well enough to be serviceable. Its only real use outdoors is as an underlay for siding, roofing, or other weatherproof coverings.

Patios

Patios are our casual living headquarters, and they go a long time between cleanings, so they're usually pretty dirty when we do get there. I'd keep a push broom handy, one with good stiff bristles on the inside to get the glued-down food globs and flattened bug bodies, and finer, softer bristles around the outside for fine dust. Most patio materials will tolerate moisture,

so spread a generous supply of mop water (made with all-purpose cleaner) over the floor and let it sit almost to the point of drying. Then a quick pass with your long-handled floor scrubber (see "Scrubbee Doo") with a heavy-duty brown nylon pad on it should finish off any stubborn residue. I'd whisk the dirty water right off the edge with a floor squeegee — don't worry, it won't hurt the plants or the lawn. You might want to give the surface a quick hose-down afterward, or if that's not possible rinse with a mop. I'd keep 3- by 5-foot walkoff mats (see "Mats, Walkoff") on the patio at the most likely entrance and exit, to pick up and hold the dirt and debris, so it won't be tracked all over.

For stains on masonry patios, see "Stone"; "Oil Stains"; "Concrete."

Wood patios need to be swept and hosed at the beginning of each season, then keep them clean through the summer with a fine-bristle broom.

Pests

Pests are uninvited insects, rodents, and birds that infest living areas and create cleaning problems. Some of these creatures (clothes moths, carpet beetles, silverfish, weevils, flour beetles, termites, mice, rats, squirrels, etc.) eat and destroy things—fabrics, stored food, and even the very structure of our home. The droppings and nests of others (mice, flies, spiders, pigeons, box elder bugs, etc.) leave a mess. Some pests do both, and some (especially mice, rats, flies, fleas, and mosquitoes) also bite and/or spread diseases. And some, such as ants and cockroaches, don't really do any harm other than carrying off our spilled food, but most of us simply don't like sharing our living quarters with scurrying things.

It's a lot easier to avoid infestations than it is to fight them. The first step is to deny access to the invading hordes. Caulking and stopping up exterior and interior cracks and holes, making sure doors and windows fit properly, and using screens will do a lot to keep flying pests and the bigger critters out. For the smaller crawlers, spraying a barrier of Diazinon on the ground for a foot or two around the foundation and into all cracks and entry points in the exterior walls will help.

The next thing to do is deny them bed and board. Eliminating the dust, dirt, litter, and clutter these little creatures live in and feed on goes a long way toward making your place an unfriendly environment. A regular vacuuming program, including cracks, corners, and crevices, will remove a great deal of bug breeding material. Proper storage of not only food but woolen and starched fabrics, leather, and anything trimmed with fur or feathers will keep them from falling prey to devouring invaders. Cleaning up crumbs and food spills promptly and proper disposal of garbage is important too.

If you've done all this and still haven't gotten rid of them, you may want to consider using poisons or traps to control the little beasties. Get advice on the proper chemicals to use from a qualified distributor, and be especially careful when using pesticides around children, pets, and the ill or elderly. Don't hesitate to call in an exterminator for termites, rats, mice, or any serious infestations.

Now a few pointers in cleaning up after pests: Flyspecks can be wiped off windows easily with alcohol. Go after those mouse droppings and nests with a shop or canister vac. Dispose of any contaminated stored foods immediately, and then clean the shelves well with disinfectant cleaner. Make sure any food you return to the area is in tightly sealed containers. Always remove vacuum bags you've used to vacuum flea-infested carpeting immediately and dispose of them in sealed plastic bags to prevent further problems. (When those vacuumed-up eggs hatch, you don't want it to be in your closet.)

Pewter

Pewter is an alloy of 75 to 85 percent tin with other metals—usually lead or copper—used for eating and serving utensils and decorative items. Pewter is a soft metal that can be scratched easily, so forget about using abrasive scouring powders and steel wool on it. Simply wash in mild detergent and warm water, then rinse and dry with a soft cloth. If you have to scrub, use a white nylon-backed scrub sponge or a plastic Chore Boy. Some foods, especially party dips, eggs, salad dressings, oils, salt, and fruit juices, contain acids and other chemicals that attack pewter. Remove such foods immediately after use, and don't use pewter containers to store food of any kind. Silver polish can be used to remove tarnish and stains from polished pieces, and a paste of rotten-stone (see "Rottenstone") and linseed oil will do the same for those with dull finishes. Be sure to wash food service articles thoroughly after polishing. See also "Metal Polishes"; "Tarnish, Metal."

pH in Cleaning

pH is a chemical symbol that expresses the degree of alkalinity or acidity of a solution. The pH scale runs from 0 to 14, with 7 being neutral. The higher the number, the more alkaline; the lower, more acid. Most of the soils we clean up every day, including fats, oils, greases, proteins, body discharges, and most foods, are mildy acid (have a pH below 7). Because acid soils are more easily removed by alkaline solutions and vice versa (remember Chemistry 101, how acids and alkalies neutralize each other?), the majority of soaps, detergents, and cleaning products are alkaline (have a pH above 7). There are some alkaline soils and stains, however, and these are most effectively dealt with by acid cleaners. Alkaline soils include lime scale (hardwater deposits), rust stains, tannin, and food stains such as coffee, tea, mustard, and liquor. See also "Cleaners, Acid"; "Cleaners, Alkaline."

Phonograph Records

If you put on your favorite recording and the lead singer sounds like a snake with a sore throat, you're probably not taking proper care of your records. The vinyl used to make phonograph records creates a lot of static electricity, so floating dust particles are attracted to it the minute you take the disc out of its jacket. Dust and dirt in the grooves of your records not only interfere with good sound reproduction but can permanently scratch and damage the delicate playing surface. Improperly cared for records tend to develop a lot of pops and hisses, and lose tonal quality with each use.

To keep your records in good shape, always store them vertically in the dust jacket, and never handle the playing surface with your oily fingers. Get one of the antistatic record-cleaning cloths sold by music stores, and lightly press it to the surface of the record as it turns on the turntable for three of four turns before you play it. Keep the turntable dust cover down while playing records to prevent

pH AND CLEANING

Clean with ALKALINE cleaner   Clean with ACID cleaner

Fats, oils, grease, proteins, body discharges, most foods

Lime scale, rust, tannin, coffee, tea, mustard, liquor

accumulation of airborne dust. This will keep damaging grit from being ground into the grooves by the stylus as it plays. It's important to keep the stylus clean too—see "Phonograph Stylus (Needle)." When a record gets really dirty or smudged, you can wipe the playing surface with a cloth dampened in a mild solution of hand dishwashing detergent, rinse with a cloth dampened in cool water, and dry. Be careful not to get the label wet; some of them aren't very water resistant. Or you can use one of the special record-washing solutions or kits sold by audio shops, such as Discwasher or Orbitrac. Never use solvents, abrasives, or strong cleaners of any kind on phonograph records.

Phonograph Stylus (Needle)

Those tiny specks of dust on your turntable stylus might not be visible to the naked eye, but in the little valleys of the grooves on your records they're as big as boulders. It's just as important to keep the stylus clean as it is to keep your records themselves free of dust and dirt. (Go back and read "Phonograph Records" if you skipped it.) Don't try to brush dust off the stylus tip with your fingers—even if you don't bend the needle, you'll do a poor job of cleaning and leave dirt-collecting oil all over it. Trying to blow the dust off won't get it all either. Use a stylus-cleaning brush or a soft artist's paintbrush, moistened with a little rubbing alcohol, and wipe the tip of the needle from back to front. Don't brush it from side to side, as this can bend

the stylus. Those cute little dust-catching brushes that mount directly on the phono head aren't recommended, because they interfere with proper balancing of the tone arm.

Phosphates

Phosphates are salts of various phosphoric acids. The ones you hear about on the evening news are the complex phosphates used as builders in laundry detergents. They boost the cleaning ability of detergents, mainly by counteracting the adverse effects of hard-water minerals and helping to maintain alkalinity. Not long ago almost all laundry detergents were fortified with phosphates, because they worked so well. Then the concern was raised that adding unnatural amounts of phosphorous to lakes and rivers could stimulate runaway algae growth and lead to smelly, oxygen-starved waters. Even though laundry detergents account for only a small part of the phosphorous added to surface water, the use of phosphates has been banned in some areas of the country, and manufacturers are working on ways to enhance the cleaning power of their detergents more safely. Some consumers have voluntarily switched to phosphate-free detergents. But if you have to wash with hot water to overcome the ineffectiveness of nonphosphate detergents where you were getting by with cold before, the net environmental impact could be negative because of the extra energy consumed. In hard-water areas, installing a water conditioner will usually provide satisfactory cleaning with nonphosphate formulations, even in cold water.

Phosphoric Acid

Phosphoric acid is a versatile acid used extensively in tub and tile cleaners, lime descalers, denture cleaners, and metal polishes. (It is also the ingredient that gives many soft drinks their bite, by the way.) It does a good job of dissolving hard-water mineral scale and metal oxides (tarnish). It is safe for most surfaces in concentrations of 9 percent or less, if rinsed immediately after use. Phosphoric acid is a mild skin and mucous membrane irritant, so use rubber gloves and avoid breathing the fumes. To use phosphoric acid to descale windows or bathroom fixtures with heavy lime-scale buildup, see "Hard-Water Deposits." See also "Cleaners, Acid"; "pH in Cleaning."

Photographs

Ah, nostalgia! All that time spent ogling our favorite photos is bound to result in an occasional stain or blotch on a favorite. If you keep your photos protected in an album or a frame, you'll never need the following cleaning information.

Water spots: Unless blotted up immediately, water spots will leave a mark (either staining or buckling, depending on the age of the photo). Anytime you touch a cloth to a photo, make sure it's soft, absorbent, and nonabrasive. Remember, when you touch it you're going to be wiping off emulsion, permanently changing the surface. Water damage isn't as no-

▶ What do we do if we drip a teardrop on the picture of our first love; blob some blueberry jam on the only existing copy of Great-Grandma and Grandpa surrounded by their 198 heifers; or drop the negative strip containing the only picture of the charging grizzly under the kitchen table?

ticeable on matte finish photos as it is on glossy; it also depends on the age and condition of the photo.

If it's an antique photo, blot off the water or stains as best you can, and leave it at that. If it looks bad and is a very valuable photo, take it to a photo restorer who will airbrush it and re-photograph it. Just bear in mind that you will be going a generation away from the original image, with resultant blurring.

To clean a newer picture or negative, blow off any crumbs and super-carefully chip off any blobs or specks of foreign matter, then place it in a shallow tray filled with a mixture of Photo-Flo and warm water for a few minutes. Follow the package directions for amounts. With a small photo squeegee, remove any excess water from the photo or negative's surface—be extremely careful since the surface emulsion is very susceptible to scratches when wet. Allow the photo or negative to air-dry by hanging from a clothespin or two, to avoid curling. Any of the foregoing equipment is available at any camera store with darkroom supplies.

If this technique fails, or if you are faint-hearted, take the photo to a professional photo lab or photo refinisher who will basically do the same things, except with better equipment and more expertise.

Pianos. See "Musical Instruments."

Pilling

Pills are those little fluffy nubs or balls that seem to grow on the surface of some fabrics. Pilling is caused by abrasion—skin rubbing against fabric, or fabric against fabric. Collars, cuffs, and sleeves of permanent press, woolen, and synthetic fabrics are especially pill-prone. These little nuisances won't come off in the wash, and worse yet, they trap lint.

Better than brushing or picking them off is to shave them off with one of those battery-operated sweater shavers that look like electric razors. Second choice would be a regular electric razor, or one of the special "stones" (available in mail-order catalogs) that pull off pills. Be prepared to repeat this, because just like a heavy beard, pills will grow back.

You can do a lot on washday to minimize pilling. Don't overload the washer. It's a bad idea anyway, and it crowds the clothes and causes them to agitate against each other. Turn pill-prone things inside out before washing, and don't wash soft-surface things with harsh fabrics such as denim. Ironing clothes with a starch product containing cellulose polymer will help too. (See "Starch.") Cold wash temperatures may increase pilling on some fabrics.

Pillows

Pillows are such a pain to clean, the best thing to do is to keep them from getting dirty in the first place. So use a pillow cover over the ticking and under the pillowcase. You don't want a plastic one though, because then the pillow can't breathe and if it's a feather pillow it will develop a slight odor.

Launder or dry-clean pillows every couple of years—they should have labels identifying the filling and care instructions. If not, a synthetic-filled pillow can be washed as follows: Look over the ticking first and stitch up any holes. Dissolve a low-sudsing detergent in the water before adding pillows to the machine. Squeeze as much air as possible out of the pillow and be sure to submerge it when you put it in. Use a short, delicate cycle, warm and high water setting. Wash two pillows at a time to balance the machine. Check occasionally to make sure the pillows are still submerged. Don't expect a pillow to have exactly the shape it did before washing.

Hand-washing a pillow (the more conservative approach) can be done in a tub of lukewarm water with low-sudsing detergent mixed into the water well before you add the pillow. Hold the pillow down till you're sure it's soaked, and squeeze the solution through it gently several times. Drain the tub and add rinse water and repeat the squeeze play. Use the spin cycle of your washing machine to get that wet pillow weighing less than 20 pounds, then air-dry it the rest of the way.

Machine-dry one pillow at a time

for sixty-to-ninety minutes on hot. (This restores the fluffiness.) Or drip-dry, but don't expect quick drying.

Feather or foam rubber bed pillows should be dry-cleaned for best results.

If you must wash a foam rubber pillow, confine it to washing the case—washing can cause the foam to disintegrate, and machine-drying can cause it to catch fire.

Throw pillows take a beating, especially if they're actually used, not purely ornamental. My best advice is to put the washable ones in the TV room and save the satin showpieces for the guest room. Include the pillows when you vacuum your sofa cushions, using the upholstery tool. For spots and stains, see "Furniture, Upholstered"; "Spot and Stain Removal."

Fluff up pillows when you make the bed. You can restore the loftiness of fiberfill or feather pillows by putting them in the dryer on fluff (no-heat setting) with a clean tennis shoe or a couple of tennis balls.

Pine Oil Cleaners. See
"Cleaners, Pine Oil."

Place Mats

I was surprised to find that even my wife's most intricate holiday place mats were machine-washable. It stands to reason—they're meant to get dirty, so they're meant to be cleaned. At my house after a meal we stack the mats, carry them to the sink, and shake them over the sink.

Plastic, vinyl, bamboo, and other woven mats can then be sponged off and returned to the table. As needed, toss the washable ones in the washer and dryer. Be sure to pretreat any spots first. And don't forget one of the other big secrets of stain removal: Scrape off all you can before commencing chemical warfare. In this case it means chipping off the drips of dried gravy or ice cream with your fingernail or a blunt tool, such as a spoon or spatula.

Plaster

Although plaster is rarely used today, there's still a lot of it around. Sooner or later you may run into bare plaster in an old house or basement, and it will be dirty, I guarantee it. I would first dry-sponge and then wash it. (See "Walls.") Plaster isn't like raw sheetrock or texturing compound. They look a lot the same, but plaster won't disintegrate or dissolve the minute moisture hits it. When bare it won't clean up worth a darn either, so when you do get it clean, paint it with a good hard enamel. Once plaster is covered with paint or finish, it can be cleaned and treated like any other painted wall or ceiling. (See "Walls.") Nicks, holes, and cracks in plaster can be patched with modern-day spackles and crack menders. Once you've patched, be sure to shellac the patches so the paint you're applying won't soak in and leave highly visible matte spots when it's dry.

Plastic Laminates

Or the old familiar Formica (the best-known trade name) so many of our counter, table, and furniture tops are made of. To create this kind of laminate, layers of paper and plastic resin are bonded by heat into a single tough sheet. Though durable and easy to care for, plastic laminates can be damaged by heat and strong solvents, and scratched and cut by such things as abrasives and kitchen knives. Don't set hot pans on plastic counterparts or use them as a cutting board, and avoid the use of powdered cleansers, steel wool, or colored (abrasive) scrub pads.

Plastic laminate is so soil resistant all you need is an all-purpose cleaner or dish detergent solution for everyday cleaning. Stubborn soil can be soaked for a few minutes with the solution, then scrubbed with a white nylon-backed scrub sponge. For stains, just have patience—most of them will lighten and disappear with repeated cleanings. Tenacious stains can be gently scoured with either baking soda or new-formula Comet (one of the mildest powdered cleansers). Or squeeze on lemon juice and let it sit to remove grape juice, Kool-Aid, and Jell-O stains. White laminate can be safely bleached with a 1:1 dilution of chlorine bleach and water, but be sure to rinse well afterward and test before using bleach on colors and patterns. Mild solvents such as alcohol and dry-cleaning fluid can be used to remove meat label ink-stains and the like, but avoid such strong solvents as acetone and lacquer thinner. Never use strong acids or caustics, including toilet bowl cleaner, drain opener, tub and tile cleaner, or oven cleaner on laminate. To brighten dull or scratched laminate, rub down with Johnson's Jubilee, car wax, or one of the silicone sealers.

Plastic Tile

Plastic tile is a rare commodity these days, but there's still some around. It's pretty delicate stuff compared to ceramic tile. Like all plastics it's fairly soft, so stick with a white nylon-backed sponge and never use abrasive cleaners or harsh scrub pads on it. Many solvents will also mar it, and acid cleaners that safely descale ceramics will deteriorate plastic over time. Frequent cleanings are the best answer to mineral buildup here. Just use all-purpose cleaner and polish dry with a soft cloth.

If you must use a bleach solution to remove mildew from the grout in plastic tile (see "Mildew"), try to keep it off the tile itself and leave it on only briefly.   •

Plastics

The term *plastics* easily includes at least 10,000 if not 100,000 different items, from cooking utensils to construction materials, tent pegs to toothbrushes . . . and the types and textures of plastic available account for at least another 40,000 variations. There are even plastic corral poles now so the cow manure will come off easily. No doubt about it, for many things plastics are tougher, better, and safer than anything ever used in the good old days. You do have to be a little careful with them, though.

Most of us have learned the general rules that apply to plastic the hard way: Most plastics are heat-sensitive and the surface is soft enough to be scratched easily by abrasives (which means everything from powdered cleanser, to steel wool, to most scrub pads). And many solvents will permanently mar plastic.

As anyone who's ever stored pickles in a plastic container knows, plastics can also absorb odors, and certain kinds of plastic stored up against certain other materials such as other plastics and some fabrics will create a chemical reaction that ruins one or both.

Some plastics, such as car vinyl tops, fade and deteriorate when exposed to sunlight and ozone in the atmosphere. (See "Silicone Sealers.")

Don't put plastic containers in the dishwasher unless specifically recommended by the manufacturer, because the high heat can warp or even melt them. Hand-wash them instead. Plastic cooking utensils can usually go in the dishwasher however, because most are designed to withstand high heat. The plastic dishes called Melamine are dishwasher-safe because they're made of plastic resin hard enough to withstand the heat. But be sure to put them on the top rack only.

That greasy film that clings so stubbornly to plastic can be removed with Dawn dishwashing detergent. Use a white nylon-backed scrub sponge to remove sticky spots. Stains can be scrubbed with a paste

of baking soda, or the stained object can be soaked in a solution of 1 tablespoon chlorine bleach per cup of water. To get rid of odors, soak in a baking soda solution for several hours. Leave the lids off when you store your plastic containers to minimize plastic odor.

See also "Vinyl"; "Vinyl Sheet Floors"; "Wall Coverings"; "Toys"; "Plexiglas"; "Plastic Laminates"; "Furniture, Hard-Surface."

Plexiglas (and Lucite, Lexan, and Other Sheet Acrylic)

You'll stay out of trouble here if you just remember that these items are called "glass" not because they are hard as glass, but because they *look* like glass. We're always tempted to clean Plexi the same way we do glass, usually with disastrous results. Plexiglas, Lucite, and Lexan are trade names for acrylic (polycarbonate) plastic sheet material, and it's found in everything from storm doors and picture frames to shower doors and small appliance parts. Despite its resistance to shattering, acrylic is a fairly soft material—very sensitive to abrasion (scratching!) and chemical attack.

Acrylic sheet should never be wiped when dry, because even tiny particles of dust and grit on the surface can scratch. (And with plastic's propensity for static, you can bet there will be dust clinging to it—see "Static.") Clean it instead with a neutral cleaner solution and a soft cloth, and flood the surface with plenty of water to remove surface dirt before you start. Keep switching to clean sections of the cloth as you wipe, to keep any dirt you've picked up from rubbing or being ground into the surface. Don't use razor scrapers, steel wool, scouring cleansers, nylon scrub pads, or abrasives of any kind. (See "Abrasive Cleaners.") Even some paper towels are harsh enough to leave fine scratches, making clear plastics look old and dull before their time. Avoid using ammonia, acids, alcohol, acetone, dry-cleaning fluid, lacquer thinner, and other volatile solvents too. (Most ready-to-use Windex-type glass cleaners are not good for Plexi because they contain ammonia and/or alcohol.) Mild solvents such as paint thinner can be used sparingly if they're rinsed off immediately.

Special Plexiglas and plastic cleaners are available that leave a static-reducing coating on the surface. Some of these also contain waxes that fill in tiny hairline scratches and improve the clarity of slightly dulled clear acrylic. Windows and other large surfaces can be cleaned with a squeegee, but be sure to flood with water to remove dust first and be sure the window stays wet the whole time—any little piece of grit you drag across the window with your squeegee is sure to leave a scratch.

Plush Furniture. See "Furniture, Plush."

Plywood

Plywood is like any other wood—it needs to be sealed with some kind of paint or finish to make it cleanable. Left unfinished, most any kind of wood is a veritable sponge for stains, and water will make it swell, crack, and deteriorate. Because plywood is a "sandwich" of thin layers of wood glued together, the edges are particularly susceptible to moisture—make sure the edges are well sealed to prevent them from coming unglued and coming apart. Exterior plywood will hold up better outdoors than interior plywood, but it too must be sealed or it will soon be damaged. Once plywood is coated with paint or varnish, you're not really cleaning wood anymore, you're cleaning the finish, so just follow the cleaning directions for painted or varnished surfaces. With wood, and especially laminated wood, it's always smart to use limited amounts of water and never let it stay wet for more than a few minutes.

Polishes, Furniture. See "Furniture Polishes."

Polishing Compound

The term *polishing compound* refers to any of a number of fine abrasive powders or pastes used to smooth and polish metals, plastics, and other materials. Polishing compounds come in varying grits, depending on the material being polished and the degree of luster desired. Automotive polishing compound, for example, will remove fine scratches, road film, weathered and oxidized paint, and many surface blemishes from vehicle finishes. It can also be used to buff small scratches out of Plexiglas, cultured marble, and fiberglass. Three common buffing compounds, bobbing, tripoli, and jeweler's rouge, are available through jewelry supply dealers. (See also "Rottenstone.") With a small buffing wheel and a supply of polishing compounds, you can give all kinds of scratched or dulled household surfaces a new lease on life. Just put a little compound on the wheel, and buff the surface until the shine comes back. Many compounds can also be applied by hand with a dampened cloth.

To remove deeper scratches, start with a more aggressive compound (or even ultra-fine sandpaper) and move up to progressively finer ones.

When using compounds, remember that, like sandpaper, they actually remove part of the surface you're using them on, so take care that you don't do more than you intended. Follow the instructions that come with them (such as keeping the surface wet while you're working on it, not using too much of the compound or rubbing any harder or longer than necessary, rubbing more gently as the compound dries, etc.). If you're compounding by hand, make light, even strokes, and don't bear down too heavily on any single spot. Stop and rinse frequently to see exactly what you've accomplished so far.

Porcelain

I mean true porcelain, which is clay-fired in a kiln to produce fine china dinnerware, figurines, and the like, as well as the fired glazed household plumbing fixtures some manufacturers call *vitreous china*. Glassy fired

coatings on metals should properly be called *enameled metal*. (See "Enameled Metals.")

True porcelain, such as that found in some toilets and bathroom sinks, is tough stuff. It might chip or break if you drop your pipe wrench on it, but other than that it's pretty impervious. You can use just about any common cleaning chemical or solvent on it without fear. Don't use harsh old-style abrasive scouring powders or colored nylon scrub sponges on it, though, for even hard-as-glass porcelain can scratch and dull after a while. (See "Abrasive Cleaners.") If you have to use a cleanser, use one with mild abrasives, such as the newly formulated Comet. The safest approach is an all-purpose cleaner, with a white nylon-backed scrub sponge to loosen hard deposits. Acid descalers are okay as long as whatever you use is also safe for any metal drain or faucet fittings that may be attached.

It's hard to generalize about fine china and decorative porcelain pieces. The ceramic part may be durable enough, but then there's the question of what it's decorated with. Painted parts of figurines and the decorative glazes and gold rims on china can be delicate and easy to damage. The safest bet is to hand-wash in neutral cleaner solution, rinse, and hand-dry. Avoid rough handling and don't use an automatic dishwasher unless the manufacturer says that it's safe for the item in question. (See "China, Fine.")

Poultice

A poultice is a paste used to draw stains out of hard surfaces. It is made from absorbent material mixed with a solvent and possibly other cleaning agents. A poultice of lemon juice and baking soda is great for removing stains from plastic laminate (Formica) countertops. Put the lemon juice on first and let it sit for ten minutes, then mix in the baking soda and leave the paste on until it dries. Poultices for removing stains from marble and other porous stone can be made with chalk, talc, or whiting, mixed with the appropriate solvent. (For oil or grease: paint thinner or lighter fluid. For ink: alcohol or Ditto fluid. For food stains: hydrogen peroxide and a few drops of ammonia.) Commercially prepared poultices are also available from stone care specialty dealers. (See "Stone.") To draw oil stains out of concrete, pour on paint thinner until it puddles, then cover with crushed cat litter. Put a damp cloth over the litter for three or four hours, then remove it and let the poultice dry.

Poultices do have to be left on until they dry—from several hours to overnight. If a poultice is made from a volatile solvent, you'll usually want to cover it with a damp cloth or with plastic wrap for a while to keep it from drying out too quickly, and to give the solvent a chance to penetrate the surface and emulsify the stain.

After a poultice has done its job, wipe or vacuum it away. If the stain isn't completely gone, you may want to apply a second or even third poultice, till you're sure you've removed all you can this way.

Premeasured Cleaners.
See "Cleaners, Concentrated."

Presoaking

Presoaking is the long form of laundry pretreatment and will greatly up your success rate with badly soiled or stained items. If your washer doesn't have a presoak setting, here is how you presoak:
1. Fill the washer tub with water and add a normal amount of laundry detergent and oxygen bleach for your load size (check package); soak clothes for thirty minutes, longer for dirtier clothes. For really serious grime, soak clothes overnight in a plastic pail or tub.
2. Drain the water from the machine, sink, laundry tub, or pail. Add fresh water, new detergent, and bleach.
3. Wash as usual. Check to be sure stain is gone before drying. (Heat sets stains.)

Prespotting

Prespotting means removing spots, spills, and stains before you start the normal cleaning operation. It's important to do this, because the heat from the cleaning process, and even the cleaning chemicals themselves, can set certain kinds of stains. (See "Set.") Be sure to make the dry cleaner aware of any spots on clothing when you take them in, so he or she will be able to prespot anything requiring it. Ditto for carpet and upholstery cleaning. If you fail to do this, you can end up with permanent stains. When you do laundry, pretreat any stains, and unless they're grease stains avoid using hot water for the wash. After washing, check garments to make sure the stain came out before hot-air drying or ironing them.

Pressboard. See "Plywood."

Pressure Cookers

Pressure cookers have their share of nooks and crannies, and keeping them clean is a matter of not only sanitation and taste but *safety*. Do familiarize yourself with the manufacturer's instructions for your individual model, but the following is what you generally need to be concerned with here.

Interior: Before using your cooker for the first time, wash it thoroughly inside and out with detergent and hot water, then rinse and dry it thoroughly. After you cook in it each time afterward, pour warm water inside, letting it sit if you can't clean it immediately. Don't soak either the outside of the pot or the cover in water. Wash as directed above. To remove cooked-on food or hard-water stains, break out the steel wool soap pads, but use them on the interior only. If that doesn't help, try filling the cooker with a solution of 2 tablespoons cream of tartar per quart of water, and letting it boil on the stove for a few minutes. Or you can try a

strong vinegar solution. Rinse and dry thoroughly.

Exterior: Normal washing and drying should do it. The outside needs a workover only occasionally with silver polish to keep it shiny. This will also remove any water stains on the cover. Don't put the pot or the cover in the dishwasher—doing so will dull the finish.

Cover: Always wash the cover thoroughly after each use. Flush away any grease or food particles from the lift pin and lock lever by running hot water through all the openings in the handle. Remove the gasket from inside the cover and wash it well in hot water and dish detergent. Dry it well too, then slip it back into the cover.

Vent tube: Each time you go to use your cooker, hold the cover up to the light to make sure the vent tube is clear. Remove any obstruction with a piece of wire or pipe cleaner, then rinse with hot water. Failure to do this could result in the cryptic "overpressure condition" described in the manufacturer's directions, which you don't ever want to experience firsthand. (You'll be relieved to know that your pressure cooker is equipped with an overpressure plug to help prevent such emergencies.)

Pressure control: The pressure control valve is virtually self-cleaning because the steam cleanses it while the cooker is operating. If it makes you feel better, washing it in hot, clean suds and rinsing thoroughly won't hurt it, and will ensure that it's free of obstructive particles.

Storage: Don't store your cooker with the cover and gasket locked on.

Doing so will flatten the gasket and also cause it to stick to the pan and tear when they're taken apart.

Pressure Washers

Only a few homeowners take advantage of pressure washers, but pros have used them for years in cleaning. They're compact pump machines that attach to a garden hose. The water comes out of a spray nozzle under tremendous (up to 3,000 or more pounds per square inch) pressure—enough to do some tough cleaning jobs. Pressure washers can clean even the roughest and most uneven surface easily and can actually strip off and wash away old peeling paint. If you pressure-wash the outside of the house, bird manure, moss, maple sap, mud, and all kinds of dirt and debris will be whisked right away. Sidewalks, driveways, stone walls, gutters, all can be done far better and faster than you could ever do with your thumb over a hose nozzle. Pressure washers can usually be rented inexpensively at local rental stores, and directions come right with them.

Anything this powerful has to be used carefully, of course. The pressure is adjustable on most pressure washers, so check the instructions to be sure the pressure setting is where it should be for the job you have in mind. (1,000 p.s.i. will clean your car, 3,000 p.s.i. will take the paint right off.) If you're merely washing not trying to strip the surface, don't get the nozzle any closer than 2 feet to what you're washing and don't keep it in one spot long. (This goes even if you are stripping paint—hovering over the same place can actually gouge wood siding, for example.) If you're washing siding, make a light pass over the surface first with detergent solution and leave it on five or ten minutes before you do the main wash.

Several different types of nozzle tips are available, so use the right kind for the job at hand. Keep the spray off entryways and windows (especially old wooden ones). Wear safety goggles when you're using a pressure washer and keep the spray *well* away from people, including yourself. (A close-range blast can cut a 2 by 4 in half!) And get some practice with it before you start using it on a ladder!

Pretreating

Or how to make stains a lot less likely to still be there when the article in question emerges from the washer. Apply one of the pretreatment products (liquid, spray, or stick) designed to dissolve problem soils and spots. When you pretreat it's a good idea to place the item facedown on paper towels and rub the pretreatment into the back side of the stain—this will help assure that you push it out of the fabric instead of pushing it in. If you don't have a laundry pretreatment on hand, you can also try enzyme detergent, ordinary liquid laundry detergent, or a paste of powdered laundry detergent and water, stain remover, or bleach (oxygen or diluted chlorine bleach). See "Spot and Stain Removal" for instructions for specific stains. It's important to give the chemical time to work, so don't fail to wait the recommended amount of time after pretreatment before washing.

▶ **Pristine:** Name of one of the clean sisters. (Her siblings are Annie Septic, Mae Tickulus, and Betty Betterhouse.)

Professional Help with Housework

The best way to reduce housework is, and always will be, HELP. Some of us might be a little apprehensive about someone else dinging around in our dirt, but there's no way around what a difference it can make. Housework lasts minutes instead of hours, hours instead of days, a day instead of a week when you take advantage of a little help. And there's plenty of help available.

Today is truly a new world of cleaning help available for rich or poor or in between. Open your Yellow Pages to "Cleaning, Janitorial," "Maid Service," or "Carpet Cleaning" and right at your fingertips you'll see a cast of characters capable of cleaning anything, anytime. And for all of these, there are easily twice that many small mom-and-pop companies around. If your circumstances and economies allow or force you to use a professional cleaner of any kind, the following are some guidelines for getting a good job. The cleaning business has an enormous turnover rate (new, inexperienced people are entering it all

the time) and a high failure rate. These two facts mean lots of people are coming and going in the business all the time, and you *do* have a chance of getting a bad deal.

1. Find out how long they've been in business. If it's less than two years, I'd consider someone else.
2. Always check references. Call and ask other customers. Don't just believe all the propaganda in the ad or the brochure.
3. Get proof of insurance. If an accident happens to the cleaners or to your premises and they aren't properly insured, *you* could be in big trouble. Make sure they have professional liability insurance.
4. Get a bid or price quote before they start. Anyone who really knows their business can tell you (to the penny) what something will cost before they start. Get it in writing and hold them to it.
5. Never pay in advance. Only about 6 percent of a cleaning job is material, so paying in advance isn't necessary (or wise).
6. Find out who is coming to do the job. A clean, sharp, convincing manager might sell it and set it up and then unshaven, surly people (whom you have to instruct) show up to work. Ask who is coming. It's a good preventive.

Pumice

Pumice stone is actually hardened foam (what a natural cleaning tool!) from volcanic lava. When we really do need an abrasive, pumice is gritty yet soft enough to be safe for certain purposes. Pumice is ground into a

---

▶ **How much will it cost?** If you're thinking of hiring a pro to do some of your cleaning, the following figures will give you an idea of the cost. Keep in mind, though, that the size of the town or city in which you live, the part of the country you're in, and how much competition there is all make a difference in the price.

Windows:	about 11¢ per sq. ft. (varies with style and condition of windows)
Carpet cleaning:	12¢–23¢ per sq. ft.
Walls:	6¢–12¢ per sq. ft.
Floor care:	about 11¢ per sq. ft. (stripping and waxing an average kitchen floor)
Upholstery cleaning:	
Couch:	two-cushion $35, three-cushion $55
Chair:	easy chair $35, recliner $40
Maid service:	$10–$12 per hour is an average figure. In large cities or resort areas, however, the cost can almost double.

A pumice stick

powder used for grinding and polishing as well as for cleaning. The grit in he-man hand soap is usually pumice. Quarried blocks of pumice are also cut into bars that are used to remove stains and lime scale from toilet bowls, urinals, ceramic tile, and concrete. Pumice bars are helpful in scrubbing graffiti off brick and masonry and for scouring cooking grills and cast-iron cookware. Pumice stone has a hardness of 2. Generally your toilet is 5 or more, so it won't scratch, especially if you keep the stone wet while working with it. Wet it and then just rub it on the ring—that calcium (hard-water) buildup should come right off. Then rinse and feel the area—if it's totally smooth, any ring that remains could just be a permanent stain. To speed up the removal of toilet bowl ring, you can apply acid bowl cleaner and scrub it in with the pumice bar. (Be sure to wear rubber gloves when you do this.)

Use pumice only on vitreous china (but not on colored fixtures), ceramic tile, masonry, cast iron, and other such hard, durable surfaces. It will scratch enameled metal, plastics, fiberglass, cultured marble, plastic laminate (Formica), and softer materials.

Purses. See "Handbags."

Q

Q-Tips: If these are your main cleaning tool, it's a good clue that you're overdoing it.

Quarry Tiles

Quarry tiles, fired terra cotta tiles, are usually reddish-brown squares or rectangles. They are unglazed, so are somewhat porous and absorbent if left unsealed. Since they hold up extremely well under heavy traffic, they are a popular choice for entries, lob- bies, and kitchens. For maintenance, see "Tile, Clay."

Quilts and Comforters

While cotton/polyester or all-syn- thetic batting is probably the most common quilt or comforter filler and is very machine-washable (the newer synthetics are even treated to prevent lumping during the cleaning process), it's the cover fabric that will dictate how you clean a quilt. If it's a patchwork quilt, clean it as you would the most delicate fabric used in it. If it's made of a dry-clean-only fabric such as satin, taffeta, velvet, or wool, then it must be dry-cleaned. A lot of old quilts need to be dry-cleaned. You can test a quilt for washability by rubbing a clean, white cloth dampened in cool water over each different color in it. If no color runs, repeat using a lukewarm cloth. If the color still doesn't run, it can probably be hand-washed. If in doubt, dry-clean. But when you bring a quilt home from the cleaners, be sure to air it out well to get rid of the solvent fumes before you put it back in use.

If it's a quilt you've made (and all your fabrics were preshrunk), or a store-bought comforter whose label advises you so, it can be machine-washed. But for this you want one of the large-capacity machines at the laundry. If you crowd it into a regular-size machine, it will stay dirty and come out wrinkled and lumpy. Pretreat any spots or heavily soiled areas, make sure the detergent has already dissolved before you add the quilt, arrange it loosely in the tub, and use warm water and a short delicate cycle. Don't use detergent with bleach or brighteners/whiteners. If

the comforter in question is down-filled, make sure it's actually submerged in the water before washing begins—down things have a tendency to collect air and float. Check it a couple more times during the washing process for the same reason. Dry in a large-capacity dryer on warm or air only with a couple of big dry towels to act as a buffer and a couple of clean sneakers or rubber balls. Remove the quilt before it's completely dry, shape it flat on a sheet, and let it finish drying at room temperature.

If you decide to hand-wash one of the more fragile types, fill the bathtub with lukewarm water and dissolve a light-duty detergent or gentle soap such as Woolite in it, following label directions. Lower the quilt slowly into the tub and let it soak for thirty minutes or as label directs. Drain and refill the tub several times to rinse well. You can also hand-wash in the washer. Fill the tub with warm water and a mild soap, arrange the quilt evenly in the washer, and spin. Fill the washer with cool water and rinse by hand, then arrange evenly and spin out water. Repeat rinse if soap is not all removed. Do not put antique or valuable quilts in a dryer. A dryer's intense heat will overdry the fabric and make it brittle. To dry, gently roll the quilt up in towels to remove excess water and spread out over a sturdy double clothesline to air dry.

R

Rump print: What you're left with when someone sits on your velvet chair or couch and perspires. Some people run around, fluffing up the mashed fiber. I'd leave it. Ditto for vacuuming footprints out of carpets.

Radiators

(House, not car!) You younger cleaners may not even know what radiators are. In the old days when homes were heated with hot water, the water ran up from the boiler into heavy steel accordion-shaped consoles in each room called *radiators*. They not only radiated heat, but burned hind

ends, melted crayons, warmed soup, and got tons of dirt and dust behind them because they were piped to the floor, thus immovable. Special long-handled brushes were made, with which you raked the stuff out from under and behind and then swept it up. Anyone who still has an old-style radiator should approach it now with a vacuum and lambswool duster. It'll

263

go faster and make less mess. First run the duster in between the baffles, then behind, then under, then turn on the vacuum and whatever's left in the area will soon be gone. If you want to wash radiators, wait until summer when they're cool and spray them with all-purpose cleaner solution. Let it sit on there a minute or two, then scrub everywhere you can reach with a brush. Spray again with clear water to rinse. (If you don't, the odor of the soap residue will surprise you when the unit is fired up next year!) Then wipe dry. If they look a little shabby, they can be painted with heat-resistant paint.

Modern radiators are sleek, smooth, inconspicuous baseboard-hugging units with all their heat exchangers, or "fins," down inside. The outside is usually painted metal that can just be dusted, vacuumed, or wiped (when cool!) with all-purpose cleaner as needed. Reach down inside every so often with the dust brush or crevice tool of your vac to remove the dust that accumulates on the fins and louvers.

Rags

We pros refer to rags as cleaning cloths, much more couth and motivational. Most rags aren't much good to clean with as most fabrics today (nylon, rayon, polyester, etc.) are designed *not* to be absorbent. Yet because they are still good and in one big piece, we use them. Rags serve far better for making rag rugs, wiping up paint spills, and flagging antelope in the Wyoming desert. Toss out those old T-shirts, curtain and uphol-stery pieces, those torn sheets, worn Levi's, and old windbreakers. Do anything you want with them, but don't clean with them. The best cleaning cloth is a terry or Turkish towel, which consists mostly of nice absorbent cotton. See "Cloth, Cleaning."

Range Hoods. See "Hoods, Range."

Ranges

If it looks like the deer and antelope have been playing on top of your range, you probably don't wipe down your stove as often as you should. With a mere 1,200-some types of ranges around with all kinds of features, you'll have to rely on your owner's manual for specific cleaning instructions. In general, however, wipe the stovetop and burner rings every day, while you're finishing up the dinner dishes, and spills and spatters are still fresh enough to come right up. Don't skip that grease-splattered backsplash! If you've let it go awhile, spray and wipe the stovetop with a degreasing cleaner such as Formula 409, and let it sit on the tough spots for five or ten minutes. Use a white nylon-backed or other plastic scrubber on it after that if it still needs a little persuading. Reflector pans ("rings") and drip pans can soak in degreaser solution overnight. Pull those icky knobs off and clean them too—don't soak them though, because the lettering might come off.

You're really lucky if you have one of the flat-surface ranges that eliminates drip pans altogether. (See "Cooktops, Ceramic.") Some of the solid elements on these, like the cast-iron ones, can take abrasive cleansers and scouring pads, but most require a gentler touch, such as glass cleaner and a fresh paper towel to avoid scratching the surface.

Don't forget down under—under the range top. Some of you are lucky enough to have a top that props up like the hood of a car so you can get underneath easily. It's usually so awful under there—full of dropped, desiccated tidbits, matchsticks, and the like—you almost need to sweep or vacuum before you start. Degreaser's the best chemical attack here too. Apply and let soak, then wipe. Scrub if necessary, and repeat until clean.

The grates on indoor grill models need to be cleaned after each use. (Check manufacturer's directions.) Many have rocks that need cleaning and a drip pan or grease container to empty.

Wipe the front of the range when you make the counter pass in your after-dinner routine. Clean dishwater or glass cleaner will serve the purpose, just be sure to polish dry with a cleaning cloth to eliminate streaks.

Rattan and Bamboo

Rattan is a palm and bamboo technically a grass, but both produce long, tough stalks used to make furniture. Only the outer sheath of bamboo is used, but three different forms of rattan are used in furniture. The entire stalk, or cane, is used as a framework for tables, chairs, and so on.

This frame may be covered with woven reed or rush to make a wicker piece, or the rattan left exposed and finished with woven seats of cane or rush or removable cushions. The joints of exposed rattan furniture are usually wrapped with cane fiber or leather, and the frame is often sealed with a clear finish or paint.

Reed, the round flexible fiber often used for woven furniture, is cut from the smooth core of the rattan stalk. Some woven furniture is made from marsh reeds or rushes, but reed made from rattan is most common. Cane is the third rattan material. It's strips from the tough outer shell of the rattan stalk, often woven into seats and backs for chairs. For care of cane, rush, and sea grass woven seats, see "Cane."

Rattan is fairly durable in humid climates, but in dry areas it tends to dry out and deteriorate. The smaller canes and the wrappings, especially, tend to break and fray. Unfinished rattan can be wet down with a hose or in a shower once or twice a year to keep it moist and supple, but this shouldn't be done to lacquered or painted pieces. The latter should simply be regularly dusted and wiped down occasionally with a damp cloth. You can get materials from craft shops to repair frayed wrappings and replace small broken canes if that becomes necessary. Even though rattan patio furniture holds up well outside, it shouldn't be left out in the weather all the time, especially not in the sun. For care of woven furniture, see "Wicker."

Rawhide. See "Leather."

Razor Blades

You can use razor blades for cleaning but *be careful*—they cut people and property so quickly it's always too late to think about it. Single-edge blades are handy for removing paint specks and stickers from window glass and mirrors and for other light-duty scraping jobs. But don't ever use double-edge blades for scraping, or hold any razor blade in your fingers. Always use it in a holder!

Get the heavy-duty, single-edge blades made specifically for scraping and a holder that keeps the cutting edge well away from your fingers—and enables you to retract the blade when not in use. If you have a large area to cover, janitorial supply stores have razor scrapers in 3- and 4-inch widths that really cover the glass.

When using a razor scraper, always keep the surface wet, and scrape in one direction only. Press down firmly and scrape as you *push* the blade away from you, then lift it from the surface when you pull it back for another stroke. If you pull the blade back toward you while it's still in contact with the surface, bits of grit trapped under the blade can scratch even the hardest of glass. Don't use a razor scraper in extremely cold temperatures because the blade will

become brittle and can break or chip. Don't ever use a razor to scrape wood, vinyl, plastic, Plexiglas, or similar soft materials. A plastic or nylon scraper is what you want for these easily scratched surfaces.

▶ **"Redd up":** Old Scottish slang for straightening up the house.

Refrigerators/Freezers

Once again it would sure be nice to have that little booklet that came with the appliance, but for all of us who can't lay our hands on it or never got one, here are directions you can adapt to your frost-free refrigerator/freezer or freestanding freezer.

First, unplug that hummer before any thorough cleaning. Vacuum the back or underneath behind the pop-off grille of the freezer—the condenser coils and fins, louvers, whatever yours has—at least twice a year (more often if you have pets), using the crevice tool or upholstery attachment for your vacuum and a brush. (Long narrow brushes made just for this purpose are available at appliance stores.) Brush off the accumulated dust and vacuum it up..

Spray and wipe the exterior of the appliance as needed with all-purpose or glass cleaner. Automotive wax or an appliance wax will help protect the finish by helping to prevent sweating—this is important in hot, humid climates. Keep wax off any plastic pieces.

A lot of people like to wash the inside of the refrigerator and freezer with baking soda (about 3 tablespoons in 1 quart of water) to deodorize, but any mild neutral (not heavy-duty) cleaner is fine too. Either way, sponge the solution on, rinse with clean water, and dry. NEVER USE ABRASIVE CLEANSERS OR PADS or strong, harsh cleaners. Carefully wipe the folds in the gasket around the door free of crumbs and stuck-on splashes. Don't be surprised if you find mildew in there. Wash removable parts—bins, shelves, racks—in sudsy water, then rinse and dry them before replacing. Don't ignore all those awkward little places, such as the egg trays, door handles, underneath the vegetable drawers, the shelf supports, shelf "railings," and undersides of shelves. Last in your cleaning campaign should come the drip pan, since it's usually the worst. See also "Ice Makers, Automatic."

All done? Plug it back in!

Freezer defrosting: Called for at least when the accumulation in the cabinet becomes thick enough to interfere with the proper closing of the door but no less than once a year. Too much frost means food freezes too slowly, which will do nothing for the taste or texture of that food when you eventually use it. It also wastes energy and interferes with the general efficiency of the unit. Transfer your frozen treasures to your refrigerator, or place them, well wrapped in newspaper, on a nearby table. Scrape off the frost with a wooden paddle or plastic scraper and scoop it out with a piece of cardboard or a dustpan. Don't use any sharp instrument that might damage the interior. You can speed up defrosting by using

pans of hot water set inside the freezer or by aiming a portable fan into the freezer. Once you can actually see the original freezer walls, wipe them (and any shelves, trays, dividers in there) with neutral cleaner solution and then dry. Don't forget the freezer door gaskets!

▶ **Refrigerator fuzz:** Something that forms on most food left in the fridge for more than five weeks. Cultures superior to any grown at U.S. government experiment stations are grown in the home refrigerators of America. Moldy stuff is not usually chucked until it moves. And then 50 percent of us will try to scrape it off and leave the source to grow another head of mold.

Residue

Residue is the term used for any soap scum, dirt, cleaning chemical, etc., left on a surface after it's cleaned. Residue is usually the result of failure to rinse or to rinse enough. On hard surfaces it kills the shine, and on fabric or carpet it acts as a sticky magnet to attract dirt and speed up resoiling. Residue also contaminates and affects the bonding of things we often want to apply after we clean—wax, floor finish, paint, or soil retardant. Most residue is alkaline, so to remove it, a mild acid rinse such as vinegar water (see "Vinegar") is what you need.

Resilient Flooring. See
"Floors, Resilient."

Rinse

Of the four basic steps described in the "Chemistry of Cleaning," rinsing accomplishes step 4—removing the soil loosened or dissolved in the cleaning process. Once the particles of dirt and grime are suspended in the cleaning solution, you have to get the dirty solution off the surface before it can evaporate and redeposit the soil. We usually do this by rinsing with clean water (or whatever solvent we're using) or by a combination of rinsing and other methods. We spray off the car with a hose, mop the kitchen floor with clear water, and the washing machine simply runs through its rinse cycle.

Failure to rinse will leave a streaky dull finish on hard floors, a sticky film on carpet or upholstery that attracts new dirt quickly, and detergent residue on clothes that can cause allergies. Rinsing agents (see "Rinsing Agents") are often used to improve the performance of the rinse solution. An important point to remember is that porous surfaces may take a lot more rinsing than you think to remove all the soil and detergent residues. One of the most common reasons newly applied floor finish ("wax") doesn't hold up well is contamination of the finish by detergent residues left on the floor when we stripped off the old wax. If you don't use a neutralizing agent, it takes at least three good clear-water rinses to remove all stripper residues from vinyl flooring.

▶ **Rinse makes sense:** If you just sudsed your hair and walked out of the shower, you'd have a mighty stiff hairdo. Such is the case with all surfaces that are cleaned with a heavy-cleaning solution and not rinsed. A soap or detergent residue remains that can cause ugly streaks, damage the surface, and cause any coating you're trying to apply—wax, floor finish, paint, or polish—to fail to adhere or to powder (slough) off early. Because most cleaners are alkaline, they can be neutralized with a mild acid rinse, so a vinegar solution (see "Vinegar") will do the trick. You can also buy "neutralizer" at a janitorial supply store. In some situations, you can rinse by flushing—just spraying the object or area down and letting the water run off onto the ground or drain away.

Rinsing Agents

A rinsing agent is a surfactant or wetting agent (such as Jet Dry) usually added to the final rinse cycle in automatic dishwashers, and car washes. The wetting agent reduces the surface tension of the rinse water, so that it "sheets off," or drains evenly and quickly, instead of lingering in droplets. This eliminates spotting, streaking, and filming caused by dissolved solids in those droplets remaining on the dishes or the car finish as the water evaporates. Rinsing agent can mean acids (such as floor neutralizer) added to rinse water to neutralize alkaline detergent residues, and alkalies used in the same way to neutralize acid residues. A quarter cup of white vinegar per gallon is often added to the final rinse water when mopping floors to eliminate detergent haze, especially on glazed ceramic tile.

▶ **Robots to do all your cleaning?**
D-O-N-'-T C-O-U-N-T O-N I-T U-N-T-I-L A-T L-E-A-S-T 2-0-6-5.

Rollers, Hair. See "Curlers/Rollers, Hair."

Rottenstone

Rottenstone, a gentle abrasive used for polishing, is decomposed limestone. It is often used to buff out scratches, polish away stains or marks, or to bring dulled areas on finished furniture back to life. It's also used for the final polish following treatment by stronger abrasives such as pumice. It is mixed with linseed oil into a slurry and rubbed by hand until the desired degree of luster is obtained. Rottenstone is available at furniture repair outlets and some furniture stores. See also "Polishing Compound."

Rubber

We find both natural (from rubber trees) and synthetic rubbers in everything from boots and waterproof clothing to bath mats, shower curtains, and refrigerator gaskets. Rubber may be versatile, but it's also

sensitive. Don't attempt to dry-clean anything made of rubber—solvents shouldn't be used to clean it because they cause rubber to soften and swell. Oil will too, so don't use oil on it and be sure to clean body oil and perspiration off it regularly. This stretchy stuff is also affected by heat and shouldn't be left in direct sunlight, washed with hot water, or dried in a hot dryer. Wash with cool or warm water and a mild detergent, and air-dry. All-fabric bleach is okay, but avoid chlorine bleach. Don't use strong alkaline cleaners such as ammonia or degreaser on rubber either. Steel wool soap pads are fine for scrubbing whitewall tires, and silicone protectors can be used to perk up the color of black tires and bumper guards.

Rubber kitchen equipment tends to pick up stains and hang on to them, and most chemicals that would take out the stains would also damage the rubber. So like it or not, that spatula will remain chili-colored. And here's more bad news: When you feel creek water seeping into your waders from dry-rot cracks, there's not much you can do about it. Ozone in the air causes rubber to dry out and crack after a few years.

Sprinkle a little cornstarch or talcum powder on large rubber items before folding them away for storage, and keep them in a cool, dry place.

Rubber Floors

There are two basic types of rubber floors: rubber tiles and the studded rubber (Pirelli) sheet goods. Both are made of synthetic rubber and are sensitive to strong chemicals. Don't use oily dust-mop treatments or solvent waxes on rubber—they can soften it. Sweep or vacuum and mop regularly with a neutral cleaner solution. Don't use harsh alkaline cleaners or soaps. Softer, buffable floor finishes can be applied to rubber flooring, but hard, brittle nonbuffing waxes and seals will powder off. The Taski company makes a special cleaner/polish (available through janitorial supply stores) for Pirelli floors that can be buffed to a nice shine and that won't build up on the floor. When it comes time to strip off old finish, use a low-pH stripper (available at a janitorial supply store) and don't allow it to sit on the floor for more than ten minutes. Highly alkaline strippers and long dwell times can damage rubber.

Rubber Gloves

Rubber gloves are a must in today's world of ever stronger and more specialized cleaning products. Don't clean the oven, dip your hands in hot solutions, or use heavy-duty cleaner, degreaser, ammonia, or acid cleaners without them. Even mild cleaners eventually cause drying and cracking of the skin. (You may not care about this now, but you will ten years from now, believe me!)

Our household name for them is *rubber gloves*, but protective gloves are actually available in a variety of natural and synthetic materials, from latex to neoprene to PVC. If you are handling a truly hazardous chemical, be sure to find out and use the type that will protect you from it. Nitrile gloves are effective against just about all home-cleaning products.

I like the flannel-lined kind (which eliminate that clammy feeling), one size larger than my hand for easy on and off—only for delicate work is it worth corseting your hands with snug gloves. Rubber gloves really sweat inside and can smell like the Oakland A's locker room after you've used them awhile. Drop them in a dishpan of clean soapy water and let the solution lay inside a few minutes, then rinse and dry well.

When you're finished with an icky job such as pet cleanup, leave the gloves on and simply wash your hands with a bit of the cleaning solution you've been using. Then dry the outside of the gloves with a terry towel just as you would your hands. Remove the gloves in such a way that they peel off inside out. Store them this way, so the inside dries completely. When you go to use them next, turn them right side out by blowing air into the glove and pushing the fingers back in, then following with the rest of the glove. To reduce

---

▶ **Rubber glove recycling:** When canning, my wife uses a pair that must be very clean. When they're no longer good enough for that, she passes them on to me for household cleaning. The last rung in my ladder of rubber glove cleaning use is oven cleaning, because it's impossible to bring gloves back to pristine condition after that kind of punishment. I keep one pair—several shades of brown now—just for applying wood stain.

moisture and make putting them on easier, dust the insides lightly with cornstarch or talcum powder, just don't overdo it!

P.S. A rubber glove with one little hole is worse than no rubber glove, because the bad stuff will get in and be held against your skin! Throw them out!

Rugs, Area

The first step in caring for any type of rug or carpet is to keep it well vacuumed and remove spots and spills right away. (See "Carpet Care Basics.") Removing damaging grit and soil regularly and keeping spots out will make deep cleaning a once-in-a-while thing. Valuable and delicate rugs such as Oriental, Persian, and Navajo should be cleaned by a professional dry cleaner who is equipped to do fine rugs. To avoid having colors run, always have hooked rugs professionally cleaned too: Even within the same brand of yarn, colorfastness varies, and your beautiful vibrant design may become a muted mess if you try to wash the rug at home.

Large area rugs and carpets that tolerate wet cleaning can be cleaned in place using the procedures outlined under "Carpet Cleaning—Deep." The edges usually have to be cleaned by hand, both to avoid slopping over onto the surrounding floor and to keep the edges of the rug from being twisted and distorted by the carpet cleaning equipment. For rugs laid on wood floors, use one of the dry-cleaning procedures or move the rug to a surface that will tolerate water for wet cleaning.

Smaller water-safe rugs can be laundered in a washing machine—the commercial washers at laundries will accept larger rugs than will home washers. Pretreat any spots or stains, and use the gentle cycle. Proceed cautiously with rubber-backed rugs—use no hot water, chlorine bleach, heavy agitation, or hot dryer cycles. Dry either outdoors in the shade or on the air/fluff cycle in the dryer. Never dry rubber items in a hot dryer, unless you want to make smoke signals.

As always follow the manufacturer's directions when you have them!

Rust

Rust (ferric oxide) is an oxide of iron that forms on iron and steel in the presence of moisture. We get rust stains on surfaces that come into contact with rusting metal and on clothing from iron in the water and from rusty washer and dryer drums. If iron in the water is causing severe staining, a water conditioner or iron filter may be a good investment.

Several acids will dissolve iron rust and other metal oxides. Hydrofluoric acid is the most effective but also dangerous to use. (See "Hydrofluoric Acid.") Oxalic acid is safer but slower acting. An oxalic rust remover is the best choice for delicate fabrics or anything with red dye or glass fibers. Oxalic acid is also best for removing rust stains from porcelain or enamel plumbing fixtures and appliances. (See "Oxalic Acid.") Some scouring powders, such as Zud and Bar Keepers Friend, contain oxalic acid to help them dissolve rust stains. For stubborn rust stains inside the toilet bowl, a pumice scouring bar can be used, but be sure to wet the surface first. For removing rust (and keeping it off) iron and steel, see "Wrought Iron."

▶ **Tool TLC:** Any dirt or debris you leave on a tool when you put it back in storage will only harden and reduce its efficiency on its next outing. Scraper, paintbrush, lawnmower, trowel, saw, shovel—clean it off right after use. It will only take seconds when the mess is moist and fresh. Four thousand people a minute in the United States mix paint with their screwdriver and leave it on there. Now the paint is next to impossible to get off, the screwdriver scarcely fits the screws, and it's ugly to look at. Rinsing or wiping off your tool—or drying it if it's wet—takes just one or two swipes more, and it will even improve your attitude about cleaning and maintenance. You'll look forward to using it again if it's clean and inviting.

S

Sheer idiocy! (See "Design Cleaning Out.")

Saddle Soap

Saddle soap is a mild soap used to clean and condition leather. The reaction of animal fat (tallow) with alkali to form soap is called *saponification*. In saddle soap, some of the fat remains unsaponified (not converted into soap), resulting in what's called a *superfatted soap*. Such a soap is what you want for leather because tanned animal skins need to be treated with oil from time to time to keep them from drying out. Used properly, saddle soap not only cleans but reconditions the leather, keeping it soft and supple. The key is to use only a little water and work the soap up to a rich lather in the container. Rub the lather into the leather well, rinse quickly

273

and thoroughly with a damp cloth, and buff when dry to bring out a nice sheen. Saddle soap works well on finished (shoes, purses, furniture) or natural (saddles, ball gloves, tack) leather. Don't use it on suede, shearling, leather garments, or rough leathers.

Safety in Cleaning

Bandages: You won't have to wear them if you're careful.

Bottle contents: If in doubt as to the contents of a bottle or container of a cleaning chemical, dispose of it and start over. Safety is more important than saving a few cents.

Cuts: Big cuts come from a lot of dumb little things (including using your hands instead of the tools intended for the job).

Directions: Take the time to read them. Then *follow* them.

Floors: Cause the majority of cleaning accidents. Slick floors mean slips and falls; clean, dry, clutter-free floors save lives.

Footwear: Cleaning means climbing and stretching and working on wet floors. Shoes that tie stay on better, and rubber soles provide traction as well as some protection from electric shocks. Forget sandals and high heels!

Help: Get it when you need it. Stick with jobs that suit your age, strength, size, and physical limits.

High places: Our imaginations can work wonders when we're trying to figure how to reach them without going all the way to the basement or garage to get the ladder. Don't do it!

Chairs and benches are made to sit on, not stand on, cardboard boxes crush, and containers skid or collapse when you set foot on them. Standing or sitting on plumbing fixtures or fireplace mantels to reach something is a bad idea too—they weren't made to take the weight!

- Stepladders: One of the best all-round cleaning aids. A 5-footer of sturdy aluminum is best for indoor use. Be sure it's fully open and locked when you use it, so it won't scissor shut when you step on it.
- Extension ladders: A good height for the home is 16 feet. Fiberglass is best (lighter and stronger) but more expensive, wood and aluminum are okay too. Don't use metal ladders around electricity. Make sure the legs are on solid footing, and angle one foot away from the wall for every 4 feet of height. *Never* stand on the top rung.
- Plank: Inexpensive, available, and safe. A good sound 8- or 10-foot long 2 by 12 board stretched between two ladders or a ladder and a good sturdy wooden box (see following) lets you reach a lot of area without constantly climbing up and down. Redwood is especially good because it's light as well as rot resistant. Place a bucket or something at the end of the plank so you won't accidentally walk off the end.
- Scaffolding: Go rent it if you need it, don't try to rig something up out of old boards and cinder blocks.

Kids: Keep all cleaning products out of their reach. (See "Storage of Cleaning Equipment.")

Labels: Make sure everything has one, so that when you pour there won't be any doubt as to what's coming out.

Laundry: Keep small children away from washers and dryers, and make sure the mechanism that shuts them off when the door is opened is working.

Lifting: Furniture, heavy equipment, or oversize containers of cleaning solution, especially up or down stairs, can cause slips, falls, spills and serious injuries. Get HELP or a dolly or cart—it only takes once to cripple you forever. Be careful when you lift, and lift with your knees, not your back. Drag it, don't heave it if it's too heavy—a heavy towel or plastic garbage bag under the legs of heavy appliances and furniture will help them slide easier without damaging the floor.

Light: Make sure there's enough, so you can see where you are and what you're doing.

Mixing: Cleaning chemicals mixed together can create poison gas clouds right in your own home. Read the *cautions* on the label.

Place: Buckets, brooms, and other equipment where you won't fall over it—we all daydream while cleaning and forget where we set things. A bucket placed near the foot of a ladder is a guaranteed disaster; one of the safest spots is against the wall in a corner.

Reach: A five-letter word that ruins a lot of us. Anything that requires tiptoes has a very good chance of tipping over on you. Don't store heavy things up high.

Sharp: Eliminate or take real care with anything sharp—furniture edges or cleaning tools.

Shock: Where there is electrical power, there is a chance of electrocution. Steer clear of anything electrical when you're doing wet cleaning—water and watts don't mix! And make sure any electrical equipment you use is properly grounded with a three-prong grounding plug.

Short: Housework can overload more than your brain circuits—don't push your luck with extension cords and too many appliances in the same outlet. Watch for frayed wire and damaged plugs too.

Storage: Sloppy storage is full of surprises—all bad. Any place that is crammed, jumbled, and piled up is an accident waiting to happen.

Splash: A little splash of acid, ammonia, or many other cleaning chemicals (or a flying particle of abrasive) can do a lot of damage. Don't take a chance on spatters or stray drops of dangerous chemicals; wear safety glasses or goggles and protective clothing and rubber gloves.

Stairs: Don't store or set stuff on stairs—even seldom-used stairs. Don't leave stairs wet after cleaning them either, or leave your vacuum at the top or bottom. Go clear off those stairs right now!

Throw rugs: Are well named—they can throw you. Carpet scraps, rag rugs, tire-link mats, and any mat that curls, slides, or catches your heel can trip you up.

Tubs and buckets: Or anything you fill to clean with can be life-threatening. Be sure to drain them the minute you're done—you never know when toddlers or pets will come upon them.

Vacuums: Never feel under the beater bar to see if it's working, and

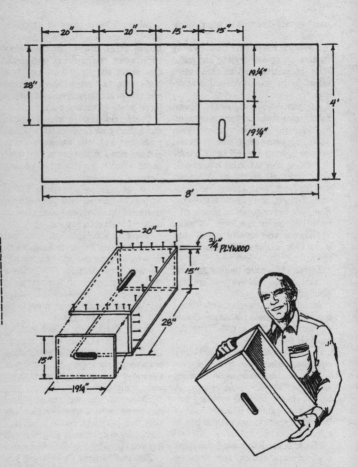

Illustration of how to make a cleaning box

The box, plank, and ladder system enables you to reach a lot of area without constantly climbing up and down. Be sure to put something on the end of the plank to keep you from accidentally walking off the end. See "Plank," "Stepladder," and "Box, to use for high cleaning" under "Safety in Cleaning."

► **Box, to use for high cleaning:** Better than a ladder! People are always trying to stand on boxes to reach and clean, and that isn't a bad idea *if* the box is made for standing. The Bell System developed something called a three-position stool, designed to enable you to reach three different heights safely. Better yet, it can be used in conjunction with a plank and stepladder (see "Safety in Cleaning") to enable you to reach even higher places safely. Alone or with a plank and ladder, it'll provide a quick and firm foundation whenever you need to reach to clean or repair.

Here is a plan for your own home box. You can make it in less than an hour for around $30. And you can use it to store tools or to cover your cleaning caddy when you aren't cleaning with it.

Materials: 1 sheet of ¾-inch exterior plywood; 1 pound of no. 8 finishing nails; 1 small bottle of wood glue; sandpaper; 1 pint of varnish or polyurethane. Just lay out and assemble as shown. You can alter the measurements to fit you or your stepladder, but if you're using it just to stand on, don't make it more than 28 inches long.

turn the machine off before you try to untangle a caught rug fringe. And if your vacuum cord is frayed, fix it now! Don't use a dry vac on a wet floor either.

Wet: Slips and shocks are the uninvited guests you'll get when it's wet. Warn everyone off wet floors—make signs—or create a blockade till it's good and dry.

Wringing: Mops by hand invites injuries from pins, tacks, glass fragments—whatever the mop has picked up from the floor. Use a wringer bucket. (See "Mop Buckets.")

Sandpaper

Abrasive paper is great for smoothing rough surfaces and removing corrosion and blemishes before refinishing or painting, but that's the only way it should be used in cleaning. Some hint and tip artists recommend using fine sandpaper for such things as scrubbing away toilet bowl rings and rust deposits in sinks and lavatories, but that's a mistake. The abrasives used to make sandpaper vary in hardness, but all are aggressive enough to scratch glass, porcelain, china, and metal—the toughest surfaces in your home. When you use sandpaper (even the finest grades), you're *scratching* the surface, making it rough and porous and more susceptible to staining. The only time sandpaper or other harsh abrasives should be used is when you're preparing a surface for refinishing.

Fine sandpaper can be used to blend in cigarette burns and other serious damage to such surfaces as cultured marble, Plexiglas, and Cor-

ian, but recognize that it will dull the surface. You have to use progressively finer grades of abrasive, finishing up with a polishing compound, to restore the shine—it's a lot of work. Aviation supply houses have kits for refinishing Plexiglas airplane windshields that work quite well for this. But don't try sanding surfaces that have a thin finish-layer over a base material or a surface-printed pattern (Formica, fiberglass, etc.), or you'll be sorry. Nor do you want to sand vitreous surfaces such as porcelain or enameled metal—it's too hard to get the shine back afterward.

Sanitize. See "Disinfecting."

Saunas

A sauna, like a bathroom, should be clean and odor-free at all times. Place towels or mats on benches so perspiration doesn't penetrate the wood. Open doors and vents and air out the sauna often when unoccupied. If you enjoy yours daily, it needs to be washed down once a week, following manufacturer's directions, to keep the air fresh and inviting.

In general, use a mild cleaning solution such as liquid dish detergent and water. Avoid strong-smelling cleaners—the smell will be intensified by heat. It's unlikely that mildew will grow in here because of the low humidity, but if your sauna sits for long periods and is located in a damp basement, it could happen. If it does, wash the mildewed area with disinfectant cleaner. Most of the moisture and perspiration in a sauna should go down on the floor, so take out the duck boards over the floor and mop regularly with an odorless disinfectant cleaner.

You don't want to treat the wood in a sauna with any kind of sealant because it can produce toxic fumes, stain the wood, or cause it to warp. In some redwood saunas you can use sandpaper to sand off surface stains. Wipe the heater when it's good and cool to keep it free of dust and lint and prevent fire; this will also get rid of those water spots from splashes pouring water on the rocks. Remove the rocks once a year and rinse them under clear water.

Scissors. See "Knives."

▶ **Scotchgard:** See "Soil Retardants" (unless you know someone in the Scottish military).

Scour

(Ouch! A last resort, please!) The ideal in all cleaning is to use methods and chemicals that dissolve and lift dirt and debris off the surface. When something is lodged (read *glued*) on, however, more aggressive action may be called for. Whenever possible this should be merely *scrubbing*, with a white nylon-backed sponge. *Scouring* means using something (such as steel wool or cleanser or curly metal scrubbers) sharp and strong enough to actually cut or grind away the offending deposit. We scour only when all else fails, and on surfaces that are tough enough to take it. See "Abrasive

Cleaners"; "Steel Wool"; "Cleansers." When you do scour, remember to keep your scouring tool wet. It'll do a lot to prevent scratches—lubricate and protect the surface while helping to dissolve the debris. Rinsing or flushing the area you're scouring several times in the course of your work will wash away harmful filings, speed up the process, and keep you posted on how you're doing.

Scrapers

Scrapers are flat tools with a point at one end (also called *bone scrapers* or *spatulas*) that professional dry cleaners and carpet cleaners use to remove spots and stains. Formerly made of animal bone, now they're often aluminum or plastic. A scraper is used to break up and remove hardened residue, and to work spotting agents into the fabric. Use the rounded edge to rub the spotting chemical into the stain. And when scraping, do so gently, holding the scraper almost flat against the fabric and sliding it back and forth over the stain. Don't gouge the fabric with the sharp edge of the tool, as this can distort and damage the fibers.

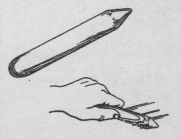

Screens

Windows we at least feel guilty about, but we often forget screens entirely. You'd be surprised what a contribution they can make to darkened, dirty windows. As screens become embedded with bugs, tree sap, dirt, dust, bird droppings, and all kinds of other exterior debris, they not only look bad but even begin to plug up.

First take the screens down, because cleaning them in place is a mess and pressing on them in place to loosen the dirt can bulge or sag them. Find a flat surface, cover it with an old blanket or quilt, and lay the screen down on it flat so that actual screen, not just the frame, is touching it. Then when you wash or scrub the screen it will stay tight on the frame and not stretch or bulge. Mix up a solution of all-purpose cleaner (or even ammonia water if you like the smell), dip a soft brush into it and carefully scrub the screen in four directions, north/south and then east/west. Since the blanket or quilt is wet with the solution, you won't have to turn the screen over— scrubbing the one side will loosen the dirt on both sides. (Do scrub both sides of extra-dirty ones.) Finish by standing the screen up and rinsing it with a hose. Watch with pride as the filth floods off, give it a sharp rap on the side to shake loose the rinse water, and set in the sun to dry. (If it's a real old rusty screen you could give it a light once-over, once it's dry, with a spray can of rust-resistant enamel paint.)

Scrubbing

Even with the great cleaning chemicals of our day, after the solution is applied the surface will often need to be agitated or what is commonly called *scrubbed*. (See "Chemistry of Cleaning.") You may think that the more elbow grease and pressure you apply, the better. Not necessarily so. First, you want to use the right tool: If it's a rough, textured, or indented surface, then a stiff nylon brush will reach in and dig out the dirt. For most other surfaces, in my opinion, nothing beats nylon scrub pads. (See "Scrub Pads, Nylon"; "Scrub Sponges, White Nylon-Backed.")

Nylon pad or scrub brush, don't scrub hard or you run the risk of frizzing fabric and scratching hard surfaces. If you bear down too hard on a brush, the bristles just flatten out and you'll find yourself "scrubbing" with the slick, smooth sides of the bristles! You want to wield a brush in a circular motion, with light pressure that gently massages the surface with the tips of the bristles. A good rule of thumb (and hand too) is to always keep the surface you're scrubbing wet. This will lubricate it and lessen the chance of surface damage. So don't let the scrubbing solution dry on the surface while you're still working on it, and be sure to add more when you need to. And rinse off the surface every so often to remove loosened soil, so you can see whether or not it's really necessary to go on scrubbing.

Scrubbing in a circle or back and forth is not nearly as effective as going in all four directions, north/

south, then east/west. This way you're sure to get the dirt out from all surfaces on all sides.

See also "Scrub Brushes."

Scrubbee Doo, Long-handled Floor Scrubber (also called Doodlebug)

An improved scrubbing tool originally developed by the 3M Company, a Scrubbee Doo is a long wooden handle with a plastic swivel head and a Velcro-like surface to which you can attach nylon scrub pads of different

closeup of attachment hooks on underside of head

nylon scrub pads of different strengths for different cleaning duties

wax applicator head

dust mop head

A long-handled floor scrubber, the tool that made hands and knees a posture of the past.

strengths. You can use it to scrub a floor, wall, or baseboard from a standing position, without ever resorting to hands and knees. Long-handled scrubbers are inexpensive, last forever, and in my opinion are more effective and worth having than a $200 dual-brush home model floor polisher/scrubber. By just changing the head on a long-handled scrubber, you can scrub lightly or heavily. The tougher and meaner pads—black or brown—are for heavy wax removal and scrubbing concrete. Blue is for medium work, white for delicate scratchable surfaces. The pads can easily be replaced if you wear them out or lose them, or the dog gets one. Wax applicator and dust mop heads are available for these handy little tools too.

Scrub Brushes

Brushes don't actually scrub as well or thoroughly as nylon scrub pads (see "Scrub Pads, Nylon"; "Scrub Sponges, White Nylon-Backed"), and they're messier to use because of the solution those springy bristles will always get elsewhere than where you intended. But we do need them for rough surfaces and surfaces with lots of little indentations or depressions, such as tile grout or vinyl flooring with relief designs—whenever we have to reach down deep into something to dig out the dirt.

When you do use a brush, use it carefully to minimize splattering. (See box.) And don't press too hard. Hard brushing will give carpeting an afro, and stiff bristles can actually scratch some surfaces.

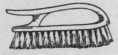

Two types of scrub brush that will keep your knuckles out of the nasties—the larger one is called a utility brush, available at janitorial supply stores.

▶ **Scrub without spattering:** Do you find yourself flicking and splattering the solution all over the place when you're scrubbing with a brush? Here's how to fix it:
1. Use a softer bristle brush, or
2. A sudsier solution. Bubbles will restrict water splashing.
3. Clean in a circular motion with only light pressure.
4. Drape a towel or dropcloth around the target area to help catch splatters.

As for style, you want a brush with a handle—either the kind called *utility brushes* at janitorial supply stores or the ones with a wing grip on top that makes them look like an iron. This will keep your fingers up out of the mire and cleaning chemicals and your knuckles from getting nicked against the walls or corners. Good nylon brushes are almost indestructible. The bristles won't break or flatten as easily as natural bristles, and the bristle bed is crack and chemical resistant and easy to clean. Rinse your brushes well after every use and hang them to dry, so you don't warp the bristles.

Scrub Pads, Nylon

Nylon scrub pads are the scrubbers of the '90s—they're less messy, safer for your household surfaces, and more effective than a brush, for most operations that involve scrubbing.

Nylon scrubbers come both as separate pads and bonded to the back of a sponge (see "Scrub Sponges, White Nylon-Backed"), so you have one side to scrub with and one to absorb, and it's easy to work up a foam or lather if you need one. Because of the open weave of the nylon, odors are not as likely to develop as in other cleaning cloths or pads. But the soil you're cleaning up will cling to the nylon, so you can just shake it off the pad or rinse it away.

As for color, there's a bunch of them out there—white, green, blue, brown. Are they all the same? No way! In general, the darker, the more abrasive the pad. The Scotch-Brite line is color coded: White won't scratch most surfaces, it's safe for dishes, windows, floors, showers and tubs, sinks and faucets, appliances, countertops, walls, and woodwork. Green pads contain abrasives that will mar and scratch such surfaces as plastic, glass, chrome and porcelain. The rule in my cleaning company is "Only use green pads to remove black marks on waxed floors, and use them gently. It doesn't take much to cut through the wax and start digging into the floor itself." Blue pads we use on a long-handled floor scrubber like a Scrubbee Doo to scrub floors. Brown and black are tough abrasive pads with a coarse open weave designed for stripping wax. They can also be used to clean such things as barbecue grills and concrete. Choose the right one for the job!

Scrub Sponges, White Nylon-Backed

Scrub sponges are one of my favorite tools, and you'll hear me refer to them often. They consist of cellulose sponge on one side and a white nylon scrub pad on the other. These scrubbers are safe for most surfaces—they won't scratch. They're handy too, because you can scrub with one side and then just flip them over to wipe or absorb. One good brand is the 3M

Company's Scotch-Brite 63 cleansing sponge. You can find them at variety stores and supermarkets as well as janitorial supply stores.

Sea Grass. See "Cane."

Sealing

Sealing will benefit many home surfaces. Raw wood, brick, stone, concrete, clay tile, and other porous surfaces are prone to staining and hard to clean unless sealed. Sealing fills in the pores and smooths the surface, making it resistant to stain penetration and easier to clean. Even fabrics can be sealed against soiling with soil retardants such as Scotchgard, which coat the fibers with a stain-repellent film. Protective sealers are available for all types of wood and masonry, and they can be chosen to either preserve the natural look or to add a rich, color-deepening gloss. Left unsealed, many surfaces such as concrete and mortar joints are not only hard to clean themselves but con-

SCRUB SPONGES

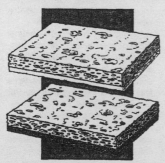

Sponges with a white nylon-backed pad attached are safe for almost any surface

Scrub sponges with a green or blue nylon-backed side can scratch and must be used with caution—read the wrapper!

 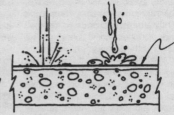

UNSEALED CONCRETE (porous)

Absorbs stains and spills, and gives off gritty dust

SEALED CONCRETE (nonporous)

Has a smooth, easily cleanable surface, and stains and spills can't penetrate.

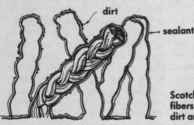

Scotchgard type sealers give carpet fibers a protective coating that keeps dirt and spills from being absorbed.

stantly bleed off bits of sand and concrete dust onto surrounding surfaces.

For sealing suggestions, see individual entries of specific materials.

Set

Setting is the worst thing that can happen to a spot—it becomes a stain before you have a chance to remove it. With proper precautions, you can prevent this. Spots are set by:

1. Letting them sit before treating them. If you can't wash or at least flush it immediately, apply a stain pretreatment stick to the spot as soon as possible, and you can leave it for up to a week before washing.

2. Applying heat to the area before the spot is removed. This can happen from washing the stained item in hot water, drying it in a dryer, ironing the stain, or even leaving a load of dirty clothing lying on top of a running dryer.

3. Using the wrong cleaner or chemical. For example, ammonia will remove blood and protein but will set coffee.

4. Forgetting to pretest. Some chemicals and procedures can cause a permanent color change.

Sewing Machines

Once again, prevention is key. Keep your machine covered when not in use. If you don't have a case, use a plastic bag or stitch up a bonnet for it. Spray a cleaning cloth with all-purpose cleaner and give your cabinet or cover a thorough wipe when it gets dirty and buff dry immediately with a cleaning cloth. On a fine wooden cabinet you might want to use oil soap instead.

Dust, lint, and thread scraps are the culprits that collect on a machine, especially around the bobbin case and behind the faceplate. Remove any accumulated fluff you see on tension discs, thread guides, needle bar, presser bar, or *any* exposed parts—if necessary you can use a pipe cleaner or paintbrush. Or blow the lint away with a few well-aimed squeezes of an empty squeeze bottle. You may be able to perform some other basic maintenance on your machine such as oiling or replacing belts—check your owner's manual. Cleaning beyond this, such as of the motor, should be done at a service center.

Shades and Roll-up Blinds

By the time the dirt on shades and blinds is noticeable enough to merit cleaning, they're so worn as to be hardly worth the chore. Some shades and blinds are made of nonwashable materials. Read the instructions and material content carefully when you buy them. If they're not washable, they can be wiped with a dry sponge (see "Dry Sponges") on both sides. If shades or blinds are washable, they can be cleaned with a neutral cleaner. You can spot-clean shades right on the window, but for overall cleaning, take them down and unroll them on a flat surface. To make sure the moisture doesn't have a chance to soak any dirt into the fabric, wipe them one section at a time with a sponge lightly dampened in the solution, and wipe dry with a clean cloth right behind the sponge. Use as little water as possible. When both sides are clean, hang the shade fully open until it's thoroughly dry; then roll it up all the way and leave it overnight to press out any wrinkles. See also "Blinds."

Woven wood blinds: To keep them looking good longer, be sure to vacuum them regularly (monthly) to control the greasy dust that settles on them. The less water used on woven wood blinds, the better, as it only accelerates their all-too-rapid fading. If they must be cleaned, use a soap recommended for cleaning wood, squeeze your cloth or sponge as dry as you can, and wipe them dry immediately after cleaning.

Shearling/Fleece

Fleece is the wooly hair of a sheep or similar animal, whereas *shearling* is the entire tanned skin plus wool of a sheep that has been recently sheared. It's usually from a young sheep, a byproduct of the leg-of-lamb industry. There is also manmade (synthetic) fleece.

Of all fleece and shearling products, the nonclothing items—rugs, car and bike seat covers, mattress pads, and wall hangings—are most likely to be machine washable, but only if the care label indicates it is safe. Otherwise, washing may take out essential tanning oils, causing your souvenir from Down Under to pull apart like wet cardboard. If there's no label (since shearling is not technically a fabric, it may not have one), stick with dry-cleaning.

To machine-wash, use cold water and mild detergent and the gentle cycle. Do not put any type of wool in the dryer. Let it air-dry on a drying rack and then brush the wool in its natural direction with a metal dog comb or brush. If the wool is over 3 inches deep, just smooth it along the top.

Shearling clothing—jackets, hats, and gloves (which usually have beautifully tanned suede or leather backing)—must be dry-cleaned to retain its shape and protect the leather. You can remove spills from suede or leather, but don't try to do an all-out cleaning job yourself. An oily spot can often be blotted out with dry-cleaning fluid—this works better on light colors than dark ones. You can sometimes remove water spots from suede by rubbing another piece of suede on it. Don't try this on the smooth-leather Napa finish—instead use a damp rag to wipe off any spot. Spots on the wool itself can be removed with a clean towel dampened

with Woolite and cool water, then wiped with a clean damp cloth. Keep solvents of any kind away from the leather backing on shearling.

If a piece is not machine washable, or you are just too faint-hearted to clean it yourself, bring it to a dry cleaner who specializes in leather or will send it out to a specialist. You could attempt to dry clean smaller items, such as hats and gloves, at home with one of the commercial foam products. Don't use dry-cleaning chemicals on your shearling, though, because if you use the wrong one, you'll ruin it.

Rugs and wall hangings can be swabbed on the fur side with a sponge dipped in Woolite solution foam. Let the solution dry on there, then vacuum it away.

For synthetic fleece, dry cleaning is usually safe, but follow the care label. Synthetic fleece is usually washed in warm water with a short cycle, and tumbled dry (not too long!) on low heat.

Sheetrock. See "Wallboard."

Shell/Mother of Pearl/Coral

These are more attractive versions of the hard-water deposits we find on our shower walls—they're composed largely of calcium carbonate (also known as limestone) and will dissolve or melt if you place them in contact with acid. So be sure to avoid bathroom cleaners or any acid-based products when cleaning shell.

Shells, like all inhabitants of mantels and knickknack shelves, are best dusted regularly so dust doesn't have a chance to combine with airborne grease into sticky grime. Use a vacuum dust brush on coral.

Lightly soiled shells and coral can just be washed (or soaked if necessary) in all-purpose cleaner solution, then scrubbed lightly with a soft brush or white nylon-backed sponge. (Shells can be scratched, so go easy here, especially on mother of pearl.)

If you need to go beyond that, you can do what professional collectors do: Clean your shells or coral with a 50:50 water and chlorine bleach solution. (This should not be used on artificially colored or tinted shells or coral.) You can also use a spray bleaching cleaner such as Tilex. Be sure to rinse well after any bleach treatment.

After they're clean and dry, shells and mother of pearl can be shined up by rubbing baby or mineral oil into the surface with a soft cloth. Don't use too much, and blot up any excess. This will give them a nice low luster that doesn't look "varnished."

▶ **Shiny bright:** One of those double adjectives your English teacher was always warning you against. Shininess is a matter of light reflection, not cleanliness—something dirty can shine as long as the light bounces off it.

Shoes, Athletic

When athletic shoes were inexpensive canvas creations, you could just drop them in the washer. Now athletic footwear is highly specialized, and cleaning it isn't so simple.

Although some people routinely launder leather athletic shoes in the washing machine without harming them, all shoe manufacturers warn against this practice. They say the laundry detergents and agitation will damage not only the leather but possibly the adhesives that hold the shoe together. The only shoes safe to wash in the washer are the simple rubber-and-canvas types and the emerging generation of all-synthetic shoes for which machine washing *is* recommended. Most experts advise us to clean all- or part-leather athletic shoes with one of the kits sold by sporting-goods stores. These are effective not only on the leather and nylon uppers and foam midsoles but on liners and inserts as well. Follow directions on the kit.

If you do insist on cleaning without a kit begin by removing laces and inserts and rinsing the shoes with water. Then use a solution of neutral cleaner and a soft brush to scrub the shoes thoroughly, including insoles and liners. Use no bleach, solvents, harsh chemicals, or abrasives. Use a white nylon-backed scrub pad for scuff marks on midsoles and heel counters. But don't get your hopes up when it comes to marks on the polyurethane midsoles used on high-performance sport shoes; this material just doesn't release stains well. After scrubbing, rinse well with water again and drip-dry. Stuff the shoes with absorbent white paper to help them keep their shape as they dry, and don't try to speed the process by using heat or direct sunlight. Many people like to throw laces in with a load of laundry to get them nice and clean while the shoes are drying. Don't wear the shoes or put liners back in until the shoes are completely dry. At that point, an application of white cream shoe polish will help keep white leather parts sharp as well as soft and supple.

Shoes/Boots

Most footwear is pretty tough because it's designed for hard use and exposure to weather, but in general the prettier the less tough.

Leather: First remove any dirt or dried mud with a brush. Then if the leather is delicate, use a cream leather cleaner. Otherwise, using as little water as possible, work up a lather of a mild soap such as saddle soap or baby shampoo and rub it in with a soft cloth. Then wipe remaining foam or moisture off with another clean soft cloth and buff to a glossy finish. Let the shoes air-dry well and then follow with either clear or a matching color shoe polish to protect the leather.

If you get mud on shoes or boots, you want to remove it as soon as you can because the more colorful soils, especially, can permanently stain leather. Sturdy leather work boots and the like can be hosed off quickly before you go in, but mud on shoes and dressier kinds of boots should first be wiped off with a damp cloth. It's not a good idea to soak or saturate them with water. Then let the shoes or boots dry and brush off as much of that remaining Georgia clay as possible. Remove any last traces

with saddle soap and then apply a little leather conditioner, such as Lexol Leather Conditioner.

If manure (horse, cow, or pooch) is the culprit, leave those babies outside. Any home with kids, farmers, ranchers, hunters, horse people, or construction workers should have a mud porch or mud room. It's more trouble (and harder on your shoes) to try to scrape mud off your soles than it is to simply leave muddy footwear in a safe place and change to house shoes or slippers. Besides, with all the traction tread on shoes today, you can never get the last mud clod out, so wiping your feet is never going to prevent track-ins.

Always air-dry leather (heat will shrink it)—and after a major cleaning, you might want to put them on cedar shoe trees to help preserve their shape while drying. Never place leather near heat to speed drying. This dries the leather out and makes it hard.

To remove scuff marks, black marks, grimy spots, and the like: Try a shoe spot remover such as Lexol Spot Remover, available at any shoe repair shop. (A little shoe polish will come off too, but don't sweat it.) Bad scuff marks are generally damaging to the surface and touching them up with a little polish or shoe dye is about their only salvation.

Cowboy boots or hunting boots: Polish or treat with leather conditioner. Most manufacturers of quality hunting boots are now recommending silicone treatment for waterproof boots.

Patent leather or vinyl shoes: Apply patent leather cleaner with a slightly damp, very soft cloth. (Patent leather scratches easily.) Follow directions on the container.

See also "Shoes, Athletic."

Shop Brush. See "Counter Brush or Broom."

Shower and Tub Enclosures

In hard-water areas, tubs and showers can get to be a real mess. Mineral scale builds up on walls and fixtures, soap scum clings to the mineral scale, and before long the whole unit is covered with grungy gray armor plate. To prevent hard-water buildup, consider installing a water conditioner. (See "Water Conditioning.") Quickly wiping down the shower walls with a window squeegee or a towel just before you step out will also do a lot to prevent buildup.

Once the stuff is on there, removal calls for a two-pronged attack. First, use a degreaser to cut the soap scum. Soap scum is an oily/fatty deposit, so a strongly alkaline cleaner is what you need. (See "pH in Cleaning.") Janitorial supply stores also have products specifically designed to remove soap scum, or a handful of automatic dishwasher detergent in a bucket of water will work too. Cover the tub or shower walls completely and leave the solution on there for fifteen or twenty minutes or more to soften the deposits. Keep them wet and let them soak while you do something else. Right after a shower is a good time, as the walls will already be good and wet. Then scrub the walls and floor with a stiff scrub brush or a white nylon-backed scrub sponge. (Don't use colored scrub pads or powdered cleansers—they can scratch. See "Abrasive Cleaners.") Keep soaking and scrubbing until all soap scum is removed, then rinse.

If you have hard water, you'll probably also have to clean with a phosphoric acid cleaner to remove the mineral scale. Put it on, let it soak awhile, and scrub stubborn spots with a stiff brush or white nylon-backed scrub sponge. Be sure to rinse well and let dry. You should have to use the acid cleaner only once in a while, the soap scum remover more frequently. Overuse of strong acid cleaners on ceramic tile showers can deteriorate the grout.

Glass shower doors will need a final spiffing up with glass cleaner (although replacing them with a plain old shower curtain is the low-maintenance way to go). If you decide to keep the glass doors, you'll also have to clean out the metal door tracks by gently scraping with a wet-cloth-wrapped screwdriver. As a final preventive, coat fiberglass tub and shower units with car wax to fill the pores and make them slick and shiny so deposits won't stick so badly next time. (But you'll want to either leave the floor unwaxed or use a nonslip rubber mat.) Silicone sealers work fine on shower walls, but they're too slick for the floor. Ceramic tile can be wiped down with lemon oil after cleaning to make it scum resistant. By the way, Zest soap leaves less soap scum than most bath bars do. See also "Hard-Water Deposits";

"Soap Scum." For shower curtains, see "Vinyl."

▷ The pros stand on an old towel or rag when they do a job like this, to keep grit or dirt on shoes from marking up the tub or shower floor.

Shower Heads

Outside of a quick wipe-down when you clean the shower, shower heads need attention only when they get plugged up. Those small spray holes *can* get plugged with either debris in the water, or with mineral scale. In either case, you have to take the head off the down-spout for cleaning. (It's easy.) Use a layer of heavy cloth or adhesive tape over the chrome of the shower head to protect it from scratches, and gently unscrew it from the spout with a large pipe wrench or adjustable wrench. Working from the side the water comes out of, poke any debris out of the holes with a wooden toothpick, and rinse the entire head well with water. If the holes are encrusted with hard-water scale, soak the head in white vinegar until the scale is dissolved, then rinse and dry. Use plumber's Teflon tape or pipe joint compound on the threads when you screw the head back onto the spout, to provide a good seal and make future removal easier. See "Hard-Water Deposits"; "Water Conditioning."

Sidewalks

If I had many sidewalks to service, I'd be sure I owned a good commercial 24-inch nylon-bristled push broom with a lifetime handle brace. Then dirt, mud, snow, leaves, and gravel kicked up on the sidewalk could be swept away quickly with a few shoulder pushes. Hosing with a nice strong spray is good too in the warmer months, but if the sidewalk is really dirty be sure to sweep first or you'll just be making mud. Then too, many sidewalks have had the ground and grass built up around them, so there's no drainage and any dirt loosened will just puddle in a muddy little lake. A floor squeegee (see "Floor Squeegees") is a neat way to dewater the walk after hosing.

As for sweeping technique, short strokes pushing the dirt off the sides is easiest—assuming, again, the sides aren't so overgrown it has nowhere to go.

Those ugly flattened blobs of chewing gum can be chipped off with a chisel or a hoe, if you wait till it's nice and cool out. Or get a can of Freon "gum freeze" from a janitorial supply store and apply according to directions. Either way, dispose of those little loosened chips and fragments of gum before they resoften and spread the mess. Any last gum residue can be removed with a solvent such as De-Solv-it or dry-cleaning fluid.

Moss or algae can be scrubbed off with warm all-purpose cleaner solution (let it sit there a few minutes first) and a stiff push broom or a long-handled floor scrubber. For oil stains on sidewalks, see "Oil Stains."

Silicone Sealers

Armor All was the original silicone protector designed to preserve and beautify such materials as vinyl, rubber, and plastics. Materials like these get brittle, dry out, and crack with long exposure to ultraviolet radiation from sunlight and ozone and oxygen in the atmosphere. Armor All was developed to protect vinyl tops, tires, seats, and dashboards in cars that sit outside. There are now a number of such products, which claim not only to seal the surface against oxidation and damaging ultraviolet rays but to rejuvenate it as well. They deepen the color, shine up the surface, and actually become a part of what they're applied to, to help protect it.

I know people who swear by silicone sealers and slather them on everything they own. Others claim that using them actually deteriorates the vinyl and causes it to crack sooner. This *can* happen if the sealant in question contains petroleum distillates, so check the label. And remember that the vinyl manufacturers themselves recommend just keeping vinyl clean, not putting any kind of dressing on it, and trying to keep your car out of the sun.

There are times and places where sealing with a silicone protector is unquestionably an advantage. Fiberglass tub and shower walls will resist soap scum and mineral scale buildup when treated with a sealer. (It's too

slick to use on the floor, though.) And a silicone sealer helps protect chrome and other unpainted metals against corrosion and oxidation. It'll put a dirt-shedding sheen on plastic laminate desktops and countertops, and fiberglass boats and campers too.

Just remember it's a sealer, not a cleaner, so be sure to clean the surface in question first (with the right cleaner for that surface) before applying the sealant. Let the sealant penetrate for several hours or overnight; apply additional coats if necessary, and finally wipe away any excess. Some silicone preparations can soften some kinds of plastic (such as the imitation wood-grain veneers used in car interiors), so read the label instructions before you spray. Because silicone is hard to remove from glass and some other surfaces, apply the sealer with a cloth where necessary to prevent overspray. Don't expect miraculous results with surfaces that are already deteriorated. Never use silicone on steering wheels, bicycle seats, or anything painted—it'll make it almost impossible to get future coats of paint to adhere to the surface.

Silver and Silver Plate

Fine silver flatware and decorative pieces should be cleaned with a quality silver polish. This not only removes the tarnish, but the buffing process develops a rich patina that enhances the appearance of the silver and tarnish retardants in the polish help keep the silver bright longer.

Follow directions on the silver polish you select.

Bear in mind that the silver coating on plated silver, especially the cheaper varieties, may wear thin and expose the base metal with repeated polishing. Frequent use and washing will keep such pieces bright and shiny without any polishing. Dip cleaners can be used for utilitarian silver, but they won't develop the rich shine that cream polishes will and they do nothing to retard further tarnishing. Electrolytic cleaning (boiling with aluminum foil and chemicals) is not recommended for fine silver as it tends to dull the finish, damages antique shading, and can loosen hollow handles.

Sulfur causes silver to tarnish quickly and salt corrodes it. Don't leave high-sulfur foods such as eggs, mustard, or mayonnaise, or salt or foods containing a lot of salt sitting for long periods in silver containers. Remove food and wash silver immediately after use. Don't put it on rubber mats to dry or use rubber bands to hold it. (Rubber contains sulfur.) Using silver regularly and washing and drying it by hand will help keep it tarnish-free. If you intend to store it for long periods, polish with a tarnish-retardant polish first, and store it in special tarnish-retardant cloth bags available from jewelers. Sealing silver in plastic bags will also help keep it bright. For care for silver jewelry, see "Jewelry, Fine." See also "Metal Polishes"; "Tarnish, Metal."

Sinks

Kitchen or bathroom, sinks are the most used and noticed fixture in the house. A clean sink's biggest enemies are (1) clutter on and around it that discourage an overall wiping; (2) the use of abrasive cleansers that scratch it and make it ugly and porous and hard to clean.

Sinks are a cinch if cleaned right after use. There's never an excuse not to at least rinse—with water and often a sprayer right at your fingertips and the drain standing ready to spirit it all away. Go light on abrasives in any kind of sink (see "Abrasive Cleaners"; "Cleansers"), and don't use them at all on cultured marble, fiberglass, or plastic.

Keep a white nylon-backed scrub sponge right on or by the sink. Once you've worked it over with this, even plain water will flush away clinging dirt. When sinks get an ickies buildup, I spray them (the whole sink and rim area, including the faucets) with a solution of all-purpose or disinfectant cleaner and let it sit on there for a couple of minutes—this will loosen the dirt and lubricate the process when you lightly scrub it after that. Every couple weeks or so, go after those awful deposits around and under the faucet and faucet handles with a brush or a plastic scraper.

If the sink has a hard-water scale buildup, swab on some phosphoric acid solution. (See "Hard-Water Deposits"; "Phosphoric Acid.") Don't let strong chemical solutions such as ammonia or heavy-duty cleaners soak in your sink for long periods of time—they can etch or discolor it. Don't ever use hydrochloric acid bowl cleaner here—it can damage enameled sinks. To remove rust stains in sinks, use oxalic acid. (See "Oxalic Acid.")

See also "Corian"; "Marble, Cultured"; "Porcelain"; "Stainless Steel."

Sizing. See "Starch."

Skip Cleaning

You've probably already applied this liberating concept in your home. If you haven't, it's time to try it.

When professionals skip clean, they simply forget about cleaning an entire floor of a commercial building every other night. You could skip a different room every time you clean. Or just pass over anything that's already clean or even gives the appearance of clean. For example, if the kitchen appliances or your picture windows just have a couple of smudges on them, just clean the smudges and forget the rest for now. Or every other week you could eliminate dusting anything above eye level. Or just vacuum the traffic areas in a room rather than wall to wall.

Skip cleaning means ignoring some part of the cleaning schedule that doesn't really need to be done—skipping it on purpose, no guilt and no

─────────────

▶ **What to skip?** Therapy for compulsive cleaners: Force yourself to leave a dirty glass in the sink all night.

─────────────

strings. It'll help your agenda crunch, won't hurt a thing, and when you do get back to it you may actually enjoy it more.

Skis

With the exception of wiping off surface dirt and removing old wax with a solvent wax remover from a ski store, there's not much a skier should do to his or her favorite speed sticks these days. If they get muddy or dirty, hose 'em off or wipe them down with all-purpose cleaner solution. Stubborn spots and marks on the plastic tops can be scrubbed off with a white nylon-backed scrub sponge. Any further maintenance should be left to the pros.

The mechanisms of the newer bindings are all sealed, so no cleaning, lubricating, or other maintenance is needed to keep them working right. And the new base materials almost defy home-workbench tinkering. The new plastic bases perform better than the old ones did but require stone grinding that puts a special texture on the base and keeps it absolutely flat. Even the time-honored rite of using a hot iron to melt and smooth the wax on is now forbidden. About the only fine-tuning a person should do at home is to use a honing stone to keep the edges sharp and smooth. All other filing, grinding, and base repair is best left to a trained technician.

Sleeping Bags

Sleeping bags are usually filled with either natural down or a synthetic fiber fill (Hollofil, Quallofil, Polargard, etc.). The down ones, especially, need to be cleaned occasionally not only to keep them inviting to slip into but also to maintain the loft (fluffiness) of the fill material. Don't dry-clean down bags—the solvents can strip the feathers of their natural oils. If the care label on a synthetic-fill bag insists on dry-cleaning, follow the label directions but air the bag out for at least a week before using it again, because the solvents used in dry-cleaning are very toxic. The best treatment for either type of bag is to wash it, either by hand or in a large commercial washing machine. Hand-washing in a bathtub is the safest method for delicate bags, but it's a lot of work and it takes a heap of rinsing to get all the soap out. The best choice for sturdy bags is to use a front-loading washer at the launderette. Top-loading machines agitate bags too hard and can damage the interior baffling.

To machine-wash down bags, use real soap (Ivory Snow, Woolite, etc.), not detergent, which can, again, strip those feather oils. Zip the bag up before washing, and make sure there aren't any pocket knives or old marshmallows lurking anywhere in there. Use warm, not hot, water and the gentle cycle. Add water softener in hard-water areas, and use no bleach or fabric softener. After washing, run the bag through another cycle without soap to get a thorough rinse. Handle the bag very carefully when wet, as the fill material is heavy then and can "avalanche" inside the bag and rip out the baffles if you hold it up by one end. Keeping the bag

wrapped up in a ball and well supported, transfer it to a dryer. Dry with plain air or on very low heat, and throw in a clean rubber-soled tennis shoe or a tennis ball to help break up clumps and fluff the down as it tumbles. If a low heat setting is not available, use no heat. It may take quite a while to dry the bag completely, but it's important to get it thoroughly dry and fluffed up before storing or using it. Damp down will mat together and mildew in storage.

Synthetic-fill bags can be washed in the same manner, but pretreat any stains, use regular laundry detergent, and add fabric softener to the rinse cycle—this reduces static electricity and increases the bag's loft. You can dry a synthetic bag in a clothes dryer on low heat, but it will also dry fine laid out flat outside on a slanted board.

A sleeping bag isn't designed to be washed a lot, so the smart thing is to use a ground cloth and a bag liner to keep it as clean as possible. Sponge off spots or spills and avoid overall washing until it's really needed. If circumstances dictate frequent washing, a Polargard-filled bag holds up better than the other synthetic fills.

Slicers. See "Grinders and Slicers."

Slipcovers

The very nature of slipcovers and their purpose—to protect what's underneath—says cleanable. Many slipcovers are machine-washable and dryable, but be sure to check the care labels, especially if the cover in question is bonded or foam-backed. Wash separately and do not overfill the machine. Zip zippers, remove pins or upholstery screws, stitch up any burst seams, and pretreat spots first. Use any laundry detergent and/or all-fabric bleach in warm water on delicate cycle; dry on regular cycle, remove promptly, and refit on furniture to avoid ironing.

Smoke, Cigarette

Smoke is composed of tiny particles of oils, tars, resins, nicotine, and water vapor floating in the air. But when we talk about cleaning up cigarette smoke, we're usually referring to the yellow film that builds up on surfaces where these particles come to rest. On washable surfaces, smoke film can be wiped up easily with a solution of heavy-duty cleaner or degreaser. A dash of water-soluble deodorizer from a janitorial supply store added to the solution will help neutralize the odor. For smoky windows, add 1 part isopropyl alcohol to 5 parts window cleaner to help cut the oily film.

Smoke on porous surfaces is a tougher proposition. Light smoke film on acoustic ceiling tile can be removed by professional ceiling cleaners, but heavy buildup usually requires painting or replacement of the tile. Upholstered furniture, draperies, and carpeting can be wet- or dry-cleaned as appropriate, after a thorough vacuuming, with water-soluble deodorizer added to the cleaning solution to control residual smoke odor. For instructions on shampooing, see "Furniture, Upholstered"; "Carpet Cleaning—Deep." For deep-down odor that has permeated the interior padding and crevices, professional fogging with specialized smoke-odor counteractants is the only permanent solution.

If you live with a heavy smoker, be sure to change the filters in your air circulation systems often.

▶ **No-smoking buildings:** reduce cleaning, energy use, air-cleaning equipment and filter needs, loitering and could save millions of dollars in labor costs per hour across the country as well as the destruction of furniture, ceilings, and floors. Millions of gallons of deodorizers and odor neutralizers are used each year, for example, to try to remove the smell of cigarette smoke in buildings. No-smoking buildings cut maintenance drastically.

Smoke Alarms

Smoke alarms may save your life someday, so they're worth a few minutes of your time every so often. We all know enough to test the battery of the battery-powered type about once a month, but it's also important to keep the innards of any type of smoke alarm clean, if we want to be sure it will shriek when we need it to.

Pull off the cover and vacuum out the accumulated dust inside at least once a year, using a dusting brush attachment. Vacuum off the perforated sensing chamber, making sure the openings are open and not blocked by lint. Clean any filters per the manufacturer's instructions. (Directions are often printed right inside the cover.) While you have the cover off, you can wash it in soapy water, but don't use water on the alarm box itself.

Smoke and Soot

We have nothing over the cave people around the campfire, except walls, ceilings, drapes, furniture, and windows for smoke to stick on. Woodstoves, fireplaces, central heating, cooking, smoking, and exterior smog sucked into our home all team up against us. Then too, we can get more serious smoke coatings from a cooking, electrical, or other fire or furnace explosion at home. Insurance often covers mishaps like this. (See "Emergency Cleaning.")

Because it can make such a mess, be very careful when cleaning up soot or ashes. Soot, the fine black powder that gives smoke its dark color, is composed mainly of carbon. Small soot particles are often bound together by oils from the combustion process to form large clumps. If you don't think soot can stain, stop to consider that India ink, one of our most permanent dyes, is simply finely ground carbon black (or lamp black) suspended in a solvent.

Your best bet is to vacuum it up. Soot from smoke will stick and hang everywhere, even on the cobwebs, and if it's removed before you do any wet cleaning, you'll save a lot of backbreaking hours. That black pigment will go a long way if you start rubbing it around. For soot-covered walls and ceilings, dust or vacuum first to remove the loose particles, then wipe

down with a dry sponge (see "Dry Sponges") to remove the stuck-on stuff. Professional fire restoration crews use dry sponges to clean smoked walls, ceilings, and other hard surfaces, and they can even pull most of the smoke out of some rough-textured surfaces. Next wash hard surfaces with a warm solution of degreaser. Wipe the area with a sponge and polish dry with a towel. If you have a heavy buildup, it may be necessary to rinse to produce a streak-free surface. To remove soot from carpeting and upholstery: Vacuum well, then clean as usual; send draperies and clothing to the dry cleaner. Launder washables in hot water, using bleach for white and colorfast fabrics.

If you can catch smoke in the act, before it settles on everything, quick and thorough ventilation (from open doors and windows) will work miracles. Let the sun in too; those ultraviolet rays do wonders for smoke odors. Bowls of vanilla or vinegar solution scattered about the house to absorb smoke odors is an old wives' solution; modern odor neutralizing chemicals from a janitorial supply store are a lot faster and more effective.

Sneakers. See "Shoes, Athletic."

Soap

We often use the word *soap* pretty loosely, meaning something you wash with, and when we say "soap and water" we may actually mean detergent and water or something else.

Technically, *soap* still means what it has for hundreds of years—a sodium or potassium salt of animal fat (or a combination of animal fat and vegetable oil). The Pilgrims made soap by boiling tallow with lye leached out of wood ashes. Modern soapmakers use basically the same process, reacting tallow or coconut oil with caustic soda or caustic potash to produce either hard or soft soaps.

Soaps work by reducing the surface tension of water, helping it penetrate, dissolve, and suspend dirt particles, and by breaking down fatty and oily soils. (See "Surfactant"; "Emulsify.") Soap forms an insoluble precipitate (soap curd) in hard water, which makes it a problem in clothes laundering. This irritating characteristic of soap inspired the development of modern detergents, which have largely replaced soap in the laundry room. We see true soap now mostly in bath bars and specialty products, such as Woolite and Ivory Snow.

Soap Powder

Soap powder, such as Ivory Snow, is an old-fashioned or true soap, in granule form. Soap powder is usually a built soap (see "Builder") and may also contain optical brighteners, colorants, and fragrance. Because of soap's tendency to form curds in hard water, it has been almost entirely replaced for everyday laundering by synthetic detergents. (See "Soap"; "Detergent.") Soap powder (and soap flakes, wherever they still exist) is still used for hand- and machine-washing of delicate fabrics, and can be as effective as detergent in soft water. Because washing with soap powder will also produce a soft finish without the use of fabric softener, it's also used to clean the clothing and bedding of babies and other people with sensitive skin. Soap in this form can also be used for general cleaning, although specialized detergent cleaners usually give better results.

When using soap powder for laundry, it's especially important to use the warmest water safe for the fabric, to dissolve the powder in the water before adding clothes, and to add enough of the powder to produce a 1- to 2-inch layer of rich suds on top of the water. This will help prevent the formation of soap curd.

Soap Scum

When soap is used in hard water, an insoluble precipitate called *soap curd* is formed. This is the main ingredient in bathtub ring and the hard grayish film that accumulates on tub and shower surfaces. In laundry, it shows up as white or gray patches or deposits all over your clothes when you take them out of the washer. Even in soft water, soap curd, body oils, and other soils will combine and eventually form a film. Prevention is one answer: Using Zest soap, squeegeeing shower walls before you step out, and wiping tile shower enclosure walls down with lemon oil will all retard the formation of soap scum. When it does build up, see "Shower and Tub Enclosures" for the lowdown on how to get rid of it.

Soil

Whether or not we consider something a soil depends not so much on *what* it is as *where* it is. Mustard is a seasoning as long as it stays on our sandwich, but when it dribbles onto our white shirt it's a soil of the worst sort. Once we decide that something qualifies as dirt, the next question is: How do we get it out? To make it easier to match up dirt with the right cleaning chemical, we classify soils into four broad categories.

Water soluble: Readily dissolved or removed by water or water-based cleaners. The majority of soils fall into this category, which is why most of our cleaners are water-based.

Solvent soluble: Oil, tar, grease, and wax are water resistant and often require the action of an oil-based solvent, such as dry-cleaning fluid, naptha, acetone, and the like. (See "Solvents.") Some heavy-duty water-based cleaners and degreasers include water-soluble solvents in their formulas to aid in emulsifying grease and oil. (See "Butyl Cellosolve.")

Combination: Usually used to refer to stains, such as gravy or creamed coffee, which contain both water-soluble and solvent-soluble soils. Such stains usually have to be treated with a combination of cleaning chemicals.

Protein: Soils and stains of animal origin, such as milk, egg, blood, and so on, which often require the use of an enzyme digester (see "Bacteria/Enzyme Digester") for complete removal.

In addition to these soils, it's often helpful to know the pH of the soil, as acid soils are most easily removed by alkaline cleaners and vice versa. See "pH in Cleaning."

Soil Retardants

Soil retardants is the official term for chemicals used to help textile fibers resist soiling. The older, silicone-based fabric treatments resist water-soluble stains but aren't much good against oil-based soils. More effective are the newer fluorocarbon soil retardants, such as 3M's Scotchgard or Du Pont's Stainmaster products. (See "Fluorocarbons.") These improved soil resisters fend off both water- and oil-based spots and even make dry soil easier to get out. Applied to carpeting, upholstery, and apparel fabrics, fluorocarbon soil retardants actually coat the fibers, leaving a slick finish that dirt and stains can't penetrate. Soil retardants not only make fabrics and fibers easier to clean, they will extend the life of carpet, for example, up to 50 percent. Retardants do come off slowly with wear and repeated cleaning, and you will have to reapply them after you deep-clean anything treated with them.

Solvent Spotters. See "Spot Removers."

Solvents

Any liquid capable of dissolving other liquids or solids is called a *solvent*. Water is the universal solvent. When we refer to solvents in cleaning, though, we almost always mean one of the volatile petroleum or plant distillates used to dissolve oily and greasy soils. The following are some of the more common solvents, where they come from, what they're good for, and what to be careful about.

Petroleum Distillates

Carbon tetrachloride: Long used as a dry-cleaning solvent but highly poisonous; replaced now by safer solvents. (See "Carbon Tet.")

Dry-cleaning fluid: A generic term for the various solvent spot removers sold in supermarkets and variety stores. They're usually a blend of petroleum solvents, designed to clean without leaving residues or rings. These should be your first choice for removing grease and oil stains from fabrics. (See "Dry-Cleaning Fluid.")

Gasoline, benzine: Never use these as cleaners—they're too flammable and too smelly!

Kerosene: The weakest and slowest-drying of the petroleum solvents, kerosene is not suitable for either degreasing or for thinning paints. (See "Kerosene.") It's far better as a fuel.

Lacquer thinner: One of the strongest petroleum solvents available to homemakers, lacquer thinner is designed for thinning lacquer wood and metal finishes. It's also a potent degreaser and paint remover that can be used on glass, metal, ceramics, and similar solvent-resistant finishes. Will damage plastics, rubber, asphalt tile, and painted surfaces. Always test before using to clean something.

Mineral spirits (paint thinner): A mild solvent used to thin oil-base paints and varnishes. Also effective

on many types of oil and grease stains. (See "Mineral Spirits.")

Naptha: Similar to mineral spirits, but a somewhat stronger solvent with a faster drying rate. Generally used to thin and clean up the more exotic oil-base paints and varnishes.

Perchlorethylene (Perc): The solvent used in most dry-cleaning plants. Makes a cheap general-purpose spotter if your dry cleaner will part with some.

Toluol, xylol, MEK: Specialty products used to thin exotic enamels and clear coatings, with solvencies that fall somewhere between turpentine and lacquer thinner. Great degreasers for metal but can be damaging to plastics and paint.

Solvents from Plants and Animals

Acetone: Extracted from alcohol, acetone is one of the most powerful solvents and the fastest drying. Helpful in removing such things as fingernail polish and airplane glue, it's also a dynamite degreaser for bare metal. Be careful, though, this stuff will eat acetate, triacetate, and modacrylic fabrics, most plastics, and painted surfaces, extremely flammable and toxic. Can be diluted with water to reduce its strength.

Alcohol: Distilled from fermented plant matter; mixes with water. Dissolves shellac, grass stains, dye stains, some greasy soils, and some inks and dyes. (See "Alcohol" for additional cleaning uses.)

Glycerine: Derived from natural fats and oils, glycerine is useful for softening a great variety of dried spots and stains, especially on water-sensitive fabrics.

Limonene: An essential oil distilled from citrus peels. An extremely effective solvent, limonene is the basis of the "orange-oil" cleaners and spot removers. (See "Cleaners, Citrus.")

Turpentine: Properly called *gum turpentine*, it's distilled from the resinous sap of pine trees. A high-quality thinner for oil paints but a poor cleaning product, as it leaves a gummy residue. Choose one of the other solvents for degreasing or cleaning.

CAUTION: Most of these solvents are dangerous and must be used with care. Some of them are extremely flammable, and most are toxic. Just breathing the fumes can be dangerous, and some of them are absorbed through the skin. Follow the package directions faithfully for whatever solvent you're using, and take it seriously if it says "Use only with adequate ventilation" or "Keep away from sparks or flame." As a general rule, the more powerful the solvent, the more dangerous it is to use.

Soot. See "Smoke and Soot."

Spas and Hot Tubs

Most hot tubs and spas these days are made of cast acrylic plastic or fiberglass. They're slick and shiny and easy to care for if you're careful not to abuse them. Don't use any harsh acids or alkaline cleaners on them, or strong solvents such as acetone or lacquer thinner. Abrasives too are a no-no because they can scratch and dull the finish, making

future cleaning much harder. Scouring powder, colored nylon scrub pads, steel wool, and the like have no place in spa maintenance, either. If you keep your spa water properly conditioned, you won't need such aggressive cleaning tactics, anyway.

Prevention can do a lot. Cut down the amount of contaminants in the water by requiring spa users to shower first. You'll still have body oils and perspiration to deal with, but getting rid of the suntan oil, cosmetics, and hand lotion before anyone slips into the tub will eliminate a lot of cleaning. Keeping the spa water properly conditioned is key. Your dealer can help you with detailed instructions and supplies to keep the pH, chlorine, and mineral levels where they need to be. If you do this faithfully you shouldn't have problems with scale buildup, algae and bacteria growth, clogged pipes and filters.

Preventive maintenance beyond this is just a few simple weekly procedures such as cleaning the skimmer baskets and pump strainer and doing a little touchup cleaning. Once a month or so, drain the spa and clean it thoroughly with a mild detergent and a white nylon-backed scrub sponge. Rinse and dry the surface and protect it with Spa Fast Gloss or a similar sealer/polish, and you're ready for another month of liquid relaxation.

Spatters

These stray droplets can be hard to clean off because they're thick and often dried on. Curly metal Chore

Boy is one of the best tools for cleaning spatters of any kind (especially the greasy ones behind the range). If you keep the surface wet while you're working on it, those sharp little metal edges cruise safely over the surface until they reach a spatter and then razor it off. Using a good degreaser solution and soaking awhile will help too. Remove any remaining film with a white nylon-backed scrub sponge. Once all the spatters are gone, wipe and polish down the surface with a terry cleaning cloth and rinse out your Chore Boy in hot water so it won't dry plugged up.

Speeding Up Cleaning

Ways to speed up cleaning could rate right up there with "What is the secret of life?" Scores of books and articles have been written on it, and cleaning still takes longer than it should or than we want it to. But the following five principles should speed up any cleaning.

1. *Prevent*: What doesn't get dirty doesn't have to be cleaned. Proper door mats, sealing porous surfaces, non-dirt-inviting design, and keeping things in good repair will cut cleaning time up to 30 percent. See "Mats, Walkoff"; "Sealing"; "Design Dirt Out" in "Before You Start to Clean."

2. *Dejunk*: Almost half of the stuff we're trying to straighten up, clean, and organize is junk and clutter—get rid of it once and for all and you'll get rid of a lot of unnecessary housework.

3. *Use pro tools and chemicals*:

What you clean with determines how fast and how well you clean. Use the right tools and supplies—they're all described in this book.

4. *Get help*: The need for cleaning is seldom ever caused by one person, and it shouldn't be done by one person either. **Anyone old enough to mess up is old enough to clean up**: Educate and delegate accordingly! Professional help is available too, and more and more homemakers are taking advantage of it.

5. *Clean as you go*: If you pick up, put away, close up, and take care of things as you go along, you won't have a lot to do later.

Spills

I can't cover all 10,000 possible spills here (see "Spot and Stain Removal"), but let me give you a few basic principles.

1. Deal with it instantly. Don't hope it will go away or wait for someone with a master's degree in spills to show up. If you leave them, spills will begin to stick, stain, warp, shrink, rust and cause safety hazards. If you can't handle it get help, but don't leave it!

2. Nice absorbent terry cleaning towels are what you want to suck up liquid spills (unless they're nasty stuff such as paint or nail polish, in which case you'll want to go to old rags or paper towels).

3. A wet/dry vac will make quick work of spills resembling minor floods.

4. A squeegee and dustpan will quickly and neatly get up the bulk of gloppy or semisolid spills.
5. Absorbents (such as clean catbox litter) sprinkled on awful goopy messes such as vomit will make them a lot easier to handle.

Sponge (as Used in Stain Removal)

Sponging is a technique frequently called for when applying spotter to stains. To sponge, put down a pad of folded clean white absorbent cloth and lay the stained article on top of it, facedown if possible. Apply the spotting chemical to the back of the stain with another clean cloth. Push the spotting solution through the fabric, working from the outside of the stain toward the center to avoid spreading it.

Keep the damp area as small as possible by using short, light strokes and as little liquid as possible. If either cloth starts to show a color transfer (from either the stain or dye), switch to a fresh cloth immediately to keep from spreading the stain.

Sponge Mops

Sponge mops are quick and convenient for small cleaning tasks, but if you have acres of hard floor, go for a regular string mop. Sponge mops are slow for volume work. A couple of pointers on owning and using a sponge mop:

1. Don't get too big a one; oversize sponges get heavy to carry and

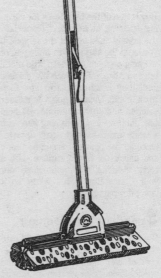

Professional-quality sponge mop, available at janitorial supply stores.

are too wide for the average bucket.
2. The simpler the unit, the easier to use.
3. Experience says buy the kind with replaceable heads.
4. That small sponge surface will soon absorb so much dirt it loses its cleaning effectiveness. Sponge mops need to be squeezed out much more often than most of us do it.
5. Never bleach them or they will soon crumble.
6. Always rinse them well after use and you'll double their life.
7. Never plunge the head into boiling

water or store it wet, resting on the sponge.

8. If the mop's been dry for quite a while and you go to pick up a spill, be sure to wet and soften the sponge first. It'll be much more absorbent and you won't be tearing off chunks.

Sponges

Sponges are charter members of the cleaning tool society! A sponge will hold more solution (without dripping!) and apply or pick it up more efficiently from smooth surfaces than a cloth or any other tool. Cellulose sponges are best for regular cleaning; natural sponges best for glass/windows. If a sponge feels awkward to use, it's probably oversize. Buy a smaller one or cut the sponge to suit you with scissors or a razor blade.

The right way to wet a sponge before you start to use it—hold it as shown and dip it no deeper than a quarter of the way into the water or solution.

There's a right way to wet a sponge before you start to use it. Hold it as shown and dip it no deeper than a quarter or third of the way into the water or solution. Then you'll be able to hold it above your head, even, and the water won't run down your arm.

Sponges will get a little discolored after a while, but as long as you rinse them well after each use (squeeze some clean soapy water through them first if the cleaning job you just finished has gotten them grungy), I wouldn't lie awake at night worrying about it. Squeeze your sponges, never wring them, and they'll last much longer.

▶ Never bleach a sponge to clean it or you'll leave 9,000 little sponges all over whatever you clean next.

Spot and Stain Removal

There are no secrets or shortcuts and no heroes in stain removal. It's all good timing, and good sense, and using the right stuff.

A Short Course in Smart Spot Removal

1. *Do it now.* Remember, a spot is on and a stain is *in*. Any spill, splash, drop, or drip needs a while to work its way into the surface. If you catch it immediately, it can often be flushed away. If it sits on there even a minute or two, it starts to sink in and be absorbed. If it sits an hour or more, or dries on there, the chances of removal are greatly reduced.

2. *Identify the stain*. Ninety percent of stains can be identified if you take a minute to think and ask around; if you don't remember how you did it, someone will usually step forward and 'fess up. Look, feel, and sniff before you decide you don't know what it is. If it's still a mystery, try dry or solvent spotter (see "Spot Removers") first, and if that doesn't work, go to wet spotter. If you're taking something in for professional attention, be sure to tell the cleaner what and where any spots are and what's been done so far to try and get them out.

3. *Pay attention to what it's on*. Is that blob of barbecue sauce on cotton or polyester, a painted wall or nylon carpet, a velour couch or a leather-covered one? Different surfaces and fabrics need to be treated differently, and this has an important bearing on your destaining strategy. (See "Fabrics.")

4. *Read the label*. The little care label that's attached, if there is one. You'll learn things you need to know before you start any stain removal process.

5. *Get rid of the worst of it first*. Never wet when you can just whisk! Why make stain soup out of something if you can just brush or vacuum it away? Even if it's a hardened spot, never apply any kind of chemical or liquid until you've scraped all the stain material you can away first. (See "Scrapers", or just use a dull butter knife.) With liquid spills too, gently blot (See "Blot") up all you can before commencing any kind of chemical attack.

6. *Let your washer do the work whenever you can*. Up to 75 percent of stains can be removed right in the washing machine, if you just observe the following: Wash the stained item NOW, while the spot is still fresh. Remove the worst of it first, as already noted. Pretreat the spot, and be sure to give the pretreat ten or fifteen minutes to work before you start the washer. For extra-stubborn stains, presoak (see "Presoaking") or use chlorine bleach if safe for the fabric. Don't overload the machine, and don't use hot water, unless the specific stain removal instructions that follow say otherwise. LOOK to see if the spot is still there before you dry the item in a dryer, iron it, or apply heat in any form.

7. *Use white cloths*. Pros use white cloths in all stain-removal operations, for two important reasons: (a) You can see if and how much stain is coming out and check your progress; (b) You can tell if the item or surface you're working on is colorfast or not. White will show any bleeding immediately, and you can adjust your method or quit before you ruin anything.

8. *Don't rub or scrub*. Never rub or scrub a stain or spot. Instead, you

want to gently and carefully pull the stain out. Rubbing will spread the stain, and it can fray or abrade the surface, cause pilling. If a spot does seem to require some kind of manual action to help persuade it out, "tampering" (See "Spotting Brushes") is what you want to do.

9. **Work from the outside in** to avoid spreading the stain.

10. **Don't expect miracles.** There's no magic all-in-one stain remover, as TV ads or hint and tip peddlers might try to make you believe. Certain chemicals work on certain classes of stains, and most stains require a combination of chemicals and a several-stage attack for complete removal.

11. **Pretest first.** All stain removal involves some degree of uncertainty, so be sure to do your experimenting where you'll be able to live with any unexpected results. Find an inconspicuous spot somewhere under or in back of, and apply a little of the proposed spotter with a white cloth, to see if the chemical affects it (discolors, melts, etc.).

12. **Don't forget to rinse.** Remember that whatever you use to get a spot or stain out will leave some residue—solvent or detergent—behind. If you remove ballpoint ink, for example, with hairspray, the stuff that makes hair stiff is now where the

ink was, and has to be removed. See the specific stain removal instructions that follow, and also "Rinse"; "Rinsing Agent"; "Residue."

13. **To avoid reappearing spots in carpet**, rinse well when you finish a spot removal operation, then put a thick layer of clean towels over the spot, and weigh them down with a brick or some heavy books. Leave the towels there until the carpet is good and dry, and any traces of stain that may have been left will wick up into them.

14. **If you're left with lingering odors.** Some animal food spills (especially on absorbent materials such as carpet or upholstery, or anywhere they've been left awhile) can smell forever. For this, you need more than a spot remover. You need a bacteria/enzyme digester (see "Bacteria/Enzyme Digester") that removes every bit of the organic material causing the odor.

15. **Go easy on the bleach.** It has its place in stain removal, usually as a last resort. Bleach strips the color out of spots—it doesn't necessarily remove the actual stain. It can also take out a lot more than you intended and weaken and deteriorate

many materials. So bone up on the different types of bleaches (see "Bleach") and go easy, and you'll have fewer of your favorite threads transformed into work clothes.

16. *Stay aware of safety*. In dealing with spots and stains, you're often using genuinely dangerous materials. Keep your stain removal arsenal well up away from little ones and keep the labels on all bottles and containers. Read and *follow* the safety precautions.

17. *Don't hesitate to hand it over to a pro*. It's inexpensive, compared to the cost of replacing a permanently stained or damaged garment or furnishing. Pro dry cleaners are real experts, and they have tools and chemicals at their disposal that we ordinary mortals don't have access to.

Terms and Tools

You'll want to acquaint yourself with the following terms by reading the entry proper:

absorbent	feather
acetone (see	flush
"Solvents")	hydrogen
alcohol	peroxide
ammonia	oxalic acid
amyl acetate	poultice
bacteria/enzyme	presoak
digester	pretreat
bleach	rinse
blot	scraper
citrus cleaners	set
digestant	sponge
dry-cleaning fluid	vinegar
dry spotter (see	wet spotter
"Spot	
Removers")	

How to Remove the Five Basic Types of Stains

1. SUGAR, TANNIN, AND OTHER STAINS that call for an acid spotter: catsup, spaghetti sauce, barbecue sauce, steak sauce, soy sauce, Worcestershire sauce, coffee, tea, soft drinks, beer, liquor, white wine, mustard, syrup, jam, jelly, molasses, honey, candy, perfume.

First: Remove all you can by scraping and blotting. Then sponge with cool water until no more stain is coming out.

Next:

Washables: Apply laundry pretreatment and wash in cool water; air-dry. Use no heat (dryer or iron) until stain is completely gone—heat can set sugar stains. If stain remains, sponge (except cotton, linen and acetate) with a 50:50 solution of vinegar and water; reapply pretreatment and launder again.

Dry-Cleanables: Let water dry, then sponge the spot with dry-cleaning fluid. If stain remains, sponge with a 50:50 solution of vinegar and water; rinse; feather.

If It's Still There: Soak washables in digestant and launder in warm water. Use digestant paste on dry-cleanables (except silk or wool); rinse, feather.

As a Last Resort: Bleach with as strong a bleach as the fabric will tolerate (probably hydrogen peroxide for dry-cleanables). If in doubt, take valuable dry-cleanables in for professional spotting.

2. PROTEIN STAINS THAT CALL FOR AN ALKALINE SPOTTER: blood, egg, ice cream, milk, perspiration stains.

First: Scrape and blot up all you can. Sponge with cool water until no more stain is coming out.

Next:

Washables: Apply laundry pretreatment and wash in cool water; air-dry. Use no heat (dryer or iron) until stain is completely gone. If stain remains, sponge (except silk or wool) with a 50:50 solution of ammonia and water; reapply pretreatment, launder again, and air-dry.

Dry-Cleanables: Let the article dry after you've sponged with water as described above and then sponge

with dry-cleaning fluid. If stain remains, sponge (except silk or wool) with a 50:50 solution of ammonia and water; rinse; feather.

If It's Still There: Soak washables in digestant and launder in warm water. Use digestant paste on dry-cleanables (except silk or wool); rinse; feather.

As a Last Resort: Bleach with as strong a bleach as the fabric will tolerate (probably hydrogen peroxide for dry-cleanables). If in doubt, take dry-cleanables in for professional spotting.

3. GREASY OR OILY STAINS THAT CALL FOR A SOLVENT CLEANING FLUID: grease, oil, tar, greasy food stains such as gravy, butter, margarine, mayonnaise, salad dressing, and the like.

First: Remove all you can by scraping and blotting. Apply an absorbent and leave it on for several hours—give it a chance to absorb as much of the oily material as possible.

Next:

Washables: Sponge with dry-cleaning fluid until no more stain is coming out. (In the case of tar, this may take a while.) Apply laundry pretreatment and wash in warm (not hot!) water; air-dry.

Dry-Cleanables: Sponge with dry-cleaning fluid; feather.

If It's Still There: Soak washables in digestant and launder in warm water. Use digestant paste on dry-cleanables (except silk or wool), rinse; feather.

As a Last Resort: Bleach with as strong a bleach as the fabric will tolerate (probably hydrogen peroxide for dry-cleanables). If in doubt, take valuable dry-cleanables in for professional spotting.

4. LACQUER-TYPE STAINS THAT CALL FOR THE DISSOLVING ACTION OF A STRONG SOLVENT: nail polish, correction fluid (such as Liquid Paper), white shoe polish.

First: Move fast, because these things dry fast and can cause permanent stains. Blot or scrape up all you can.

Next:

Fresh Stains: If the spot is on acetate, triacetate, modacrylic, rayon, silk, or wool, dab glycerin on it and take the article in for professional spotting immediately. On other fabric, try acetone, nonoily nail polish remover, or amyl acetate, in that order. (Be sure to pretest first.) If one

of these products seems safe to use, flush the stain repeatedly with it until no more color is being removed. Tamp if necessary. Flush with dry spotter and air-dry.

Old Stains: Soak with amyl acetate to soften, then treat as above.

If It's Still There: Sponge with alcohol. (Test first.)

As a Last Resort: Bleach with as strong a bleach as the fabric will tolerate. Then try color remover.

5. DYE STAINS: food dyes (food coloring, Easter egg dye, Kool-Aid, Popsicles, etc.), hair coloring, purple dye from meat labels, and so on.

First: If you have a serious red dye stain on anything, or any kind of dye stain on a valuable dry-cleanable, seek professional spotting assistance.

Next:

Washables: Mix up a solution of ½ teaspoon laundery detergent and 2 tablespoons vinegar (or use ammonia if the fabric is cotton or linen) per quart of water and soak the stained article in it for thirty minutes to an hour. Rinse, soak in digestant for the same amount of time, and launder in warm water.

Dry-Cleanables: Sponge with dry spotter until no more dye is coming out, then with dry spotter plus a few drops of vinegar. Rinse with cool water.

If It's Still There: Sponge with a 50:50 mixture of water and alcohol with a few drops of vinegar added. (Leave out the vinegar if it's cotton or linen.) Rinse.

As a Last Resort: Bleach with as strong a bleach as the fabric will tolerate (probably hydrogen peroxide for dry-cleanables).

Stains that Require Special Attention

FRUIT, CLEAR (apple, pear, orange, lemon, grapefruit, etc.)

First: Blot and scrape to remove all you can, then sponge with cool water. If it's an old, dry spot, rub glycerin in to soften it first, then proceed as below. Don't use soap, or heat of any kind, or you may set it.

Next:

Washables: Sponge with a mixture of wet spotter and a few drops of vinegar, then apply laundry pretreatment to the spot and launder.

Dry-Cleanables: Sponge with a mixture of wet spotter and a few drops of vinegar, then rinse with cool water.

If It's Still There:

Washables: Soak in digestant solution for fifteen minutes to an hour, then relaunder.

Dry-Cleanables: Apply a paste of digestant (except to silk or wool), leave it on there and keep it moist for thirty minutes, then rinse.

As a Last Resort: Bleach with as strong a bleach as the fabric can stand.

Fruit, Red (cherry, grape, blueberry, blackberry, raspberry, etc.)

First: Scrape and blot to remove all you can, then sponge with cool water until no more stain is coming out. For tough fabrics that can tolerate boiling water, consider using the boiling water method that follows. It works surprisingly well on fresh red fruit stains.

Boiling Water Method: Lay the stained fabric, facedown, over a large bowl and hold it there with a rubber band. Put the bowl in the bathtub, and pour a quart of boiling water onto the stain from a height of 2 or 3 feet.

Next:

Washables and Dry-Cleanables: Sponge with lemon juice, rinse, blot, and let air-dry.

If It's Still There:

Washables: Sponge with wet spotter plus a few drops of vinegar (dilute the vinegar 1:3 with water for use on cotton or linen), tamp if necessary. Apply laundry pretreatment and launder in warm water.

Dry-Cleanables: Sponge with wet spotter plus a few drops of vinegar (dilute the vinegar 1:3 with water for use on cotton or linen), tamp if necessary. Rinse with cool water.

As a Last Resort:

Washables: Soak in digestant solution for up to an hour and relaunder.

Dry-Cleanables: Apply a digestant paste (except to silk or wool), leave it on there and keep it moist for thirty minutes, then rinse.

GLUE, SYNTHETIC (Super Glue, hot melt, epoxy resin,

plastic model cement, clear household cement, etc.)

First: Get right to work on it before the glue hardens. Carefully scrape off all you can without spreading the spot, then sponge with water.

Next:

Fresh: Soap and water alone will remove some glues if they haven't dried yet. Try soap and water first, then dry spotter. For clear plastic cements, you may need to use acetone, but test first, and never use on acetate, vinyl, or plastic laminate ("Formica"). On acetate, use amyl acetate. Finish up by applying laundry pretreatment to washables and laundering immediately, and take dry-cleanables for dry-cleaning.

Old/Dry: Take valuable dry-cleanables in for professional spotting. You can try soaking other nondelicate fabrics (except cotton and linen) in a 1:10 solution of vinegar and boiling water, then laundering. Some model cements can be removed with water-rinsable paint and varnish remover, or acetone, but test first. Hardened glue can often be gently chipped off hard surfaces with a scraper. On brick, concrete, and other porous surfaces, you may need to use dry spotter, acetone, or amyl acetate, but test first.

GLUE, WATER-SOLUBLE
(casein glues such as Elmer's white glue, mucilage, paste, hide glue)

First: Get right to work on it before the glue hardens. Carefully scrape off all you can without spreading it around, and sponge immediately with water.

Next:

Fresh: Sponge thoroughly with warm water and soap, then if necessary sponge with wet spotter. For animal glues, apply a paste of digestant (except to silk or wool), leave it on there and keep it moist for several hours, then rinse well. Apply laundry pretreatment to washables and launder in warm water.

Old/Dry: Take dry-cleanables in for professional spotting. Soak washables in as hot a water as the fabric will tolerate, and after the glue softens, gently scrape away as much as you can. Then treat as outlined above.

If It's Still There: Take the article in for professional spotting. Or if it isn't cotton or linen and it can take boiling water, boil it in a 1:10 vinegar/water solution for up to half an hour, then rinse.

GRASS

First: Sponge with water.

Next:

Washables: Sponge with alcohol (test first).

Dry-Cleanables: Sponge with alcohol (test first; don't use alcohol on silk or wool and dilute it 1:3 with water for acetate fabrics).

If It's Still There:

Washables: Soak in digestant solution for up to an hour, rinse, and relaunder in warm water with as strong a bleach as is safe for the fabric.

Dry-Cleanables: Sponge with vinegar, then water. If that doesn't do it, apply a paste of digestant (but not to silk or wool), leave it on up to thirty minutes, then sponge-rinse with warm water.

As a Last Resort: Bleach with hydrogen peroxide.

GUM (Chewing Gum)

First: If it's still pliable, gently pull off as much as you can. Freeze the rest with a few squirts from an aerosol can of "gum freeze" from a janitorial supply store. You can also use dry ice or a plain old ice cube to freeze, it, but it won't work as well.

Next:

Fabric or carpeting: As soon as the gum is frozen stiff, strike it with the handle of a butter knife to break it in pieces, and scrape them up with the dull blade (or, if it's a very delicate fabric, your fingernail). You can vacuum the frozen crumbs up too, but be sure to get them all before they resoften.

Hard Surfaces: Use a putty knife to pop off the blob gently when it's cool and hard, or freeze it as above if necessary first.

If It's Still There: Remove any remaining traces with dry spotter, and if the article is washable, apply laundry pretreatment and launder after that.

INK, BALLPOINT PEN

First: Put a bit of ink from the offending pen on a scrap of similar fabric and experiment to see which of the following works best. If the ink is red, treat it as a dye stain.

Next:

Washables: Sponge with water. If this seems to be working, keep going until no more ink is coming out. Let the spot dry and then spray it with hair spray (the inexpensive, no-frills type works best for this). Working from the back side of the fabric, blot the hair spray through the stain into a clean cloth or paper towels until no more ink is coming out. Apply laundry pretreatment and wash in warm water, air-dry. (Magic Wand Stain Removal Stick is especially good for this particular purpose—you may not even need the hair spray.)

Dry-Cleanables: If you really care about the stained article, take it in for professional spotting. Otherwise try the treatment just described for washables, except rinse with warm water as a final step instead of pretreating and laundering in warm water.

If It's Still There: Don't put the stained item in the dryer, iron it, or apply heat of any kind. Try the following in the order listed (test first!) until you find something that works, then sponge the stain with it until no more ink comes out: dry spotter, alcohol, acetone (don't use acetone on acetate), amyl acetate. If you're left with some yellow staining, treat as a rust stain. (See "Rust.") For any other traces left behind use a color remover such as Rit Color Remover or a bleach safe for the fabric.

INK, MARKER

First: Try to determine if it was a permanent or nonpermanent marker. If there's no way of knowing, try the procedure for nonpermanent marker, then the one for permanent. Proceed carefully in all operations to avoid spreading the stain. If the stain is on something dear to your heart, take it in for professional spotting whether it's dry-cleanable or washable.

Next:

Nonpermanent Marker: Dry-cleanables should be taken in for pro spotting if at all possible. Washables and/or expendable dry-cleanables can be treated as follows: Sponge the spot with dry spotter until no more ink is coming out, then apply laundry pretreatment plus a few drops of ammonia to washables and wash in warm water. On water-sensitive fabrics, carpet and upholstery, apply laundry pretreatment and a few drops of ammonia, tamp, then rinse with warm water.

Permanent Marker: Sponge well with Ditto fluid from an office-supply store. Or on surfaces other than spandex, rayon, acetate, plastic, vinyl, or paint, you can (pretest first!) rub in some Cutter's insect repellent, leave it there for a few minutes, then rinse.

If It's Still There: Sponge with alcohol (test first).

As a Last Resort: Bleach with hydrogen peroxide.

LIPSTICK/PASTE SHOE POLISH

First: If the stain is on a valuable article, take it in for professional spotting. If you decide to tackle it yourself, gently scrape up all you can, taking extra care not to spread the stain.

Next:

Fresh: Blot and sponge with dry spotter, and change your blotting cloth and sponging pad often as it absorbs the stain. Work vegetable oil, mineral oil, or shortening into the spot, leave it there for fifteen minutes, then sponge again with dry spotter. Then sponge with wet spotter plus a few drops of ammonia (no ammonia on silk or wool), tamping as needed. Apply laundry pretreatment and wash washables in hot water; rinse dry-cleanables with warm water.

Old/Dry: Apply petroleum jelly for thirty minutes, then proceed as for fresh.

If It's Still There: Sponge with alcohol (test first) and then rinse with water.

As a Last Resort: Use chlorine bleach, if safe for the fabric.

MILDEW

First: Get the mildewed article dried out and into the light. Mildew is a fungus (a tiny plant) that thrives in warm, moist, dark conditions.

Next:

On *hard surfaces* that can take it, use a 1:5 solution of chlorine bleach and water, then rinse and wipe dry. A quaternary disinfectant (see "Disinfectants") solution will also kill mildew. Mildewed *fabrics* should be brushed off (outdoors if possible), then aired out thoroughly in the sun, if possible. Wipe mildewed *leather* with a 50:50 solution of water and denatured or isopropyl alcohol, then dry in the sun or in a current of air. Mildewed *carpeting* needs special attention from a professional carpet cleaner to assure that not only the carpet itself but the backing and pad are dried thoroughly and treated with fungicide.

If It's Still There: Take dry-cleanables in for professional spotting. Wash washables with chlorine bleach, if safe for the fabric. Persistent mildew stains should be pre-soaked in a solution of 4 tablespoons oxygen bleach per quart of water (hot water, if safe for the fabric) for thirty minutes to overnight, then rinsed thoroughly or relaundered.

As a Last Resort: Soak mildewed fabrics (even ones you normally wouldn't, as long as they're colorfast) for fifteen minutes in a solution of 2 tablespoons of chlorine bleach per quart of warm water, then rinse.

PAINT, OIL-BASE

First: Blot up as much as you can with a rag or paper towel.

Next:

Fresh: Flush with the solvent specified on the paint label (test first); tamp if necessary. Sponge with dry spotter and feather.

Old/Dry: Apply water-rinsable paint and varnish remover (test first) to soften the spot, then scrape it, applying more paint remover and tamping as necessary. Rinse with water. If some paint is still there, cover it with glycerin and leave it on for several hours. Then wipe off the glycerin and proceed as for fresh stains. Dried paint drops on carpet can be crushed with a needlenose pliers, then vacuumed up.

If It's Still There:

Washables: Apply laundry pretreatment and wash in warm water, air-dry.

Dry-Cleanables: Apply pretreatment and sponge with cool water—if that doesn't do it, take the article in for professional spotting.

Paint on Hard Surfaces: Dried droplets can be removed from glass,

ceramic tile, and like surfaces with a razor scraper (see "Razor Blades"); from bare metal such as aluminum with lacquer thinner. Don't leave lacquer thinner on vinyl or plastic laminate ("Formica") for long. If a surface won't tolerate either lacquer thinner or razor scraping, wet it with paint thinner (for oil-base paint) or water (for water-base paint) and scrape with a plastic scraper or your fingernail.

PAINT, WATER-BASE

First: Quickly blot up all you can with paper towels, taking care not to spread it or drive it deeper into the surface. Then wet the spot right away with water to keep the paint that's left from drying.

Next:

Fresh: Sponge with warm detergent solution until no more paint is coming out. Then apply laundry pretreatment to washables and wash immediately in warm water. On dry-cleanables or carpeting, sponge with wet spotter, tamping as necessary, then flush with water and air-dry. If you have a serious paint spill on carpeting, flood it with water and then blot the water back out with clean rags or a wet/dry vacuum. Continue until no more paint is coming out, then treat as above.

Old/Dry: Apply water-rinsable paint and varnish remover. (Test first.) Carefully scrape away the paint after it softens, and reapply paint remover if needed. Tamp if needed. If it's not all gone, dab glycerin on it and leave it on there for several hours, then proceed as for fresh stain.

If It's Still There: Sponge with dry spotter and feather.

Paint on Hard Surfaces. See "Paint, Oil-base."

PET STAINS (urine and feces on carpeting and other absorbent materials)

First: Scrape up any solids, being careful not to drive them deeper into the surface. Blot up any liquid by putting towels or absorbent rags over the spot and stepping on them. Start with gentle pressure and keep increasing it (right up to putting your full weight down) and changing to fresh rags or towels, until no more moisture is coming out.

Next:

Fresh: Apply a bacteria/enzyme digester (see "Bacteria/Enzyme Digester") according to directions—it's the only way you can deal effectively not only with the stain but also the odor. Bacteria/enzyme digesters work well but they work slowly, so be sure to leave the solution on as long as it says. Urine or loose stools have probably penetrated down into the carpet and pad, so use enough solution to reach as far down as the stain did. Apply the solution, put plastic over it, and step on the spot several times until the area is well saturated. Then leave the plastic on the whole time the digester is working, to make sure the spot doesn't dry out.

Old/Dry: Aged pet stains are anywhere from hard to impossible to remove, but do try a bacteria/enzyme digester. Just bear in mind that if it's a popular accident site you're treating, the bacteria may produce enough

ammonia in the course of breaking down the stains to create a super-alkaline situation that interferes with their own action. In cases like this you may need to neutralize the spot after the bacteria have been working for about four hours. Mix up a solution of 1 cup vinegar to a gallon of warm water. Rinse the area with this and then apply a fresh batch of bacteria/enzyme solution.

If It's Still There:

Fresh: If any surface staining remains after the bacteria/enzyme treatment, use wet spotter to remove it.

Old/Dry: Call in a professional deodorizing specialist. A complete cure will probably involve cleaning the entire carpet by extraction and replacing the pad underneath, if not replacing the carpet and sealing the subfloor.

RUST. See "Rust."

VOMIT

First: Act fast—scrape, blot, or apply an absorbent for a few minutes to get up all you can. Then flush the spot with water to dilute any remaining gastric juices and keep them from bleaching the fabric. If it's carpeting, sponge on water and then blot it back out.

Next:

Dry-Cleanables: Take water-sensitive fabrics in for professional spotting. On other fabrics, apply wet spotter with a few drops of ammonia added. (Leave out the ammonia on silk or wool.) Tamp if needed, then sponge-rinse with cool water.

Washables: Soak in a solution of 1

teaspoon neutral cleaner and 2 table-spoons ammonia per quart of warm water, tamp if necessary, then rinse with cool water.

Carpeting or Upholstery: Use bacteria/enzyme digester according to directions, then wet spotter to remove any remaining surface spots or water rings.

If It's Still There:

Dry-Cleanables: Apply a digestant paste (but not to silk or wool) for thirty minutes, making sure it stays moist the whole time. Rinse with warm water and feather. If that doesn't do it, try dry spotter.

Washables: Soak in digestant solution for up to an hour, then relaunder in warm water.

As a Last Resort: Bleach with hydrogen peroxide.

WAX (Candle wax, paraffin, crayon)

First: If you have a drip or blob of melted wax, first freeze it with "gum freeze" as described under "gum" so it becomes brittle enough to be shattered and scraped away with a scraper, dull butter knife, or fingernail.

Next:

Washables: If the wax is colorless, you can remove more of it by placing the spot between paper towels or white cotton cloths and running a warm iron over it. Keep using fresh blotters until as much as possible of the wax has been melted out. Then apply laundry pretreatment and wash in hot water if safe for the fabric. If it's colored wax, spray anything that's left after freezing and scraping with WD-40, leave it on there a few min-

utes, then tamp. Finish up by applying laundry pretreatment and washing in hot water if safe for the fabric with a bleach safe for the fabric.

Dry-Cleanables: If the wax is colorless, you can remove more of it by ironing if necessary as just described. After freezing and/or ironing, sponge the area with dry spotter until any remaining wax smudges are gone, and feather the edges.

Hard Surfaces: If you have crayon or the like on wall, floors, or other hard surfaces, spray with WD-40, wait a minute, and you should be able to wipe it away.

If It's Still There:

Dry-Cleanables: Apply WD-40 and leave it on a few minutes, then rinse with dry spotter.

WINE, RED OR ROSÉ

First: Take the article in for professional spotting. If you want to tackle it yourself, then blot up as much as you can and sponge the spot with cool water until no more red is coming out. If it's a fabric that can tolerate boiling water, rub table salt into the stain and then treat with the boiling water method. (See "Fruit, Red.") Otherwise proceed as described below:

Next:

Washables: Sponge with wet spotter mixed with a few drops of vinegar. (Dilute the vinegar 1:3 with water for use on cotton or linen.) When no more wine is coming out, rinse with cool water.

Dry-Cleanables: Sponge with wet spotter mixed with a few drops of vinegar. (Dilute the vinegar 1:3 with water if you're working on cotton or linen.) When no more wine is coming out, rinse with cool water.

If It's Still There:

Washables: Sponge with alcohol (test first), then apply laundry pretreatment and wash in cool water, air-dry. If it's washable, soak it in digestant solution for up to an hour and relaunder in warm water.

Dry-Cleanables: Sponge with alcohol. (Test first, and dilute 50:50 with water if you're working on acetate.) Rinse with water. If it's not gone, apply digestant paste (except on silk or wool), leave it on there and keep it moist for thirty minutes, then rinse and feather.

As a Last Resort: Bleach with as strong a bleach as is safe for the fabric.

▶ **Spotless:** a bleached leopard, an unworn garment, Mrs. America's kitchen, but seldom a normal house.

Spot Removers

General-purpose spot removers for clothing, carpeting, and the like come in two basic types: solvent-based for grease and oil stains and water-based for water-soluble stains and soils. Most all-purpose or "wet" spotters are water-based and are formulated to remove such things as sugar spots (soft drinks, fruit juice, etc.), fresh blood, and food spills. Solvent spotters such as dry-cleaning fluid are most effective against grease, oil, tar, and other solvent-soluble spots. Combination stains such as gravy or creamed coffee, which contain both water-soluble and oily substances, may require treatment with both wet and dry spotters. It's usually safest to start with the dry spotter, then go to the wet one if the stain isn't completely gone. Organic stains such as urine, feces, and vomit usually call for an enzyme digester. Problem spots such as rust, dye, wax, and chewing gum require specialized chemicals and techniques. See "Stain"; "Solvents"; "Bacteria/Enzyme Digester."

Spotting Brushes

Spotting brushes are small, long-handled brushes used for tamping. This means lightly striking stained or spotted areas to help loosen, break up, and work hardened stains, especially, out of fabric, carpeting, or upholstery. A professional spotting brush

The spotting brush—an important part of any serious stain removal kit—and the right way to use it to tamp a stain.

has short, closely set bristles and a scraper at the end of the handle. Make sure all the bristles are of the same length or you will damage the fabric. A spotting brush for carpeting or upholstery will have stiff bristles, while the type used for more delicate fabrics will be softer. You can also use a toothbrush for small areas. For a genuine spotting brush, go to a janitorial supply store.

To tamp, hold the brush at about a 30-degree angle. This way when the bristles contact the fiber they won't snag the weave, injure the pile, or give the area the frizzies (as hard scrubbing generally does). Spotting brushes are inexpensive and an important part of any serious stain removal kit.

Spray Bottles

Spray bottles allow you to apply cleaning solution a lot faster than you can with a cloth and make it easier to reach all the nooks and crannies. They keep your hands out of harsh chemicals too. Best of all, when you buy your cleaners in concentrated form (see "Cleaners, Concentrated") and dilute them into reusable spray bottles, you save money and bottle-lugging and reduce packaging waste.

Buy your spray bottles at a janitorial supply store—they'll last a lot longer than the ones you find at the supermarket or discount store. Pro spray bottles are bigger too—usually a full quart, so you won't run out as often, and the bottle has a good-size base to stand on so it won't tip over easily. Be sure your bottles have Continental or equivalent quality trig-

A professional-quality spray bottle, available at janitorial supply stores.

ger sprayers. If you get see-through bottles, you can color code your cleaners. Not only for safety but because it speeds things up when you can see that the glass cleaner is blue, disinfectant cleaner pink, and all-purpose cleaner green. (Then label the bottles too, for others who may not know your code, with a permanent marker.)

To make the most of your spray cleaning, be sure to adjust the nozzle to the job at hand. A fine spray is great for covering large areas, but you don't want to use too fine a mist in an enclosed area such as the shower, or you'll be inhaling a lot of super-fine cleaning solution. The coarse spray setting puts more solution on the surface faster, and the semimist setting is what you want to spritz on such things as dirty handprints to prevent the cleaner from running down the wall.

When storing spray bottles filled

with chemicals, always turn the nozzle to off and tighten it down to prevent leakage.

Spring Cleaning

Spring cleaning is an old wives' tradition for when to give the deep-cleaning attack to all the places that need it and all the places we clean only once in a while. It made sense in the old days when houses were sealed and boarded up for the winter with grime-generating forms of heat such as coal and wood. Spring was the logical time to open it all up and air it out. Modern construction and ventilation have changed all that. Fall is by far the better time for a big, thorough cleaning campaign. Most dirt invades the house in the warmer months, May to September. When you clean in spring, your home is instantly re-dirtied by all this, and the dirt will stay in the carpet and upholstery for nearly a whole year, depreciating the place. If you clean in fall, say October, you'll get all the summer silt out and your house will be nice and fresh for at least six months, plus company-clean for the holidays. See "Fall Cleaning."

difference in time and results. Luckily they do one of the most dreaded jobs too—windows. Squeegees not only make window cleaning fast and efficient, they make it fun!

Originally invented to remove bath oil and cosmetics from the Roman athlete's body, in the early twentieth century the rubber blade was put to work in glass cleaning. The quality of the rubber and the design of the blade channel has been improved since then, and in my opinion a squeegee is the only way to clean windows. The window wand (see "Window-Washing Wands") applies the cleaning solution and scrubs as necessary, and the squeegee wipes away the loosened dirt and water.

You can find them elsewhere, but the surest way to get a professional-quality squeegee is to get it at a janitorial supply store. Ettore brand brass squeegees will last you a lifetime, and they come in models and sizes to fit any hand or house. A 12-inch squeegee is the best all-around size for the home; for very large panes you might want a 14- or even 16-inch blade. The extension poles and angle-adjusting squeegee handles now available make it possible to

▶ **Spruced up:** An expression that probably originated in the cleaning attack a cowboy would give his cabin using the limb of an evergreen tree.

Squeegees

Squeegees are my favorite cleaning tool, the one that makes the most

A pro quality squeegee such as the Ettore is well worth the investment.

clean high or otherwise out-of-reach windows easily.

Be sure to change the rubber blade on your squeegee as soon as it gets nicked or worn.

▶ **Geepee, geepee, geepee:** The sound a dry squeegee blade makes skipping across dry glass. If you remember to always wipe the blade with a damp rather than a dry cloth between each stroke, it will go *glidee, glidee, glidee,* instead.

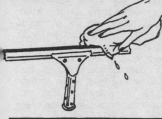

Stains

A stain is anything that doesn't come out with normal cleaning. Often an innocuous spot becomes a problem stain because of the way we handle it. Oil or grease is easily removed when fresh, but let it sit for a few days and it can oxidize and become a permanent stain. Likewise, heat from a clothes dryer or iron will set most sugar and tannin stains (soft drinks, fruit juice, coffee, tea, grass). Ammonia and other alkalies tend to set coffee, tea, and mustard stains. Vinegar and other acids will set bloodstains. Soap will set fruit stains. If you have a stubborn light-brown or yellow stain on something, chances are it's a coffee, sugar, or oil spot that was dried in the dryer or ironed before it was completely removed. Almost any spot or spill, whether on clothing, carpet, or furniture, will benefit from immediate attention, as most spots get worse with age. Simply blotting up a spill and sponging with cool water will increase the chances of removal 200 percent. For spots that have become stains, try the stain removal techniques in "Stain and Spot Removal," or have a professional dry cleaner or carpet/upholstery cleaner perform expert spotting. See "Prespotting"; "Spot Removers."

Stainless Steel

Stainless steel is made from iron alloyed with chromium. This makes it very hard and resistant to rusting and staining, although there are different grades of stainless and the lower grades stain more easily. Stainless may not stain much, but it sure does water spot, and stainless flatware, sinks, countertops, appliances, and cooking utensils should be washed with hot water and dried immediately with a soft cloth to prevent this. Use a white nylon-backed sponge only to scrub stainless if needed. Satin-finish or brushed stainless can be lightly scoured with cleansers and scouring pads, but abrasives will scratch and dull bright mirror finishes. Stainless-steel polish can be used to remove such things as the darkening or mottling caused by certain foods, but why waste time slathering stainless-steel polish all over a stainless-steel sink, trying to get it to match the chrome faucets? Just learn to love the soft gleam of natural stainless.

Stainless-steel flatware, or eating utensils, are usually dishwasher-safe, since they can withstand both very hot water and the strong automatic dishwasher detergents. No matter how you wash it, always hand-dry it to eliminate water spots. Stainless-steel serving dishes will stay new looking indefinitely if you just observe a few precautions. First, never cut or carve on them and don't allow them to come in contact with high heat or flame, as it can cause permanent discolorations. Wash platters and serving dishes like stainless flatware, and hand-dry to prevent water spots. To prevent scratching and marring, don't stack anything on top of stainless serving dishes in storage, and put a layer of tissue or cardboard between them.

The bluish discoloration caused by overheating stainless pots and pans may be removed by scouring (for dull surfaces) or by polishing with silver polish (for bright surfaces). Non–food service surfaces can be rubbed with lemon oil after cleaning to brighten the surface and hide fingerprints. Restaurant cooks rub their stainless down with hot coffee, which leaves a protective oily film. Strong acids should be kept away from stainless, as even their fumes can discolor it, and salt left sitting on stainless can pit it.

Stainless-Steel Wool. See "Steel Wool."

Stairs

Stairs are always neglected. (Because we hate cleaning awkward little areas, or because we're so busy huffing and puffing going up we don't notice the dirt?)

On noncarpeted stairs, I use a broom and clean from the top down. On carpeted stairs, I use an upright vacuum with a beater bar and clean from the bottom up. Bear in mind that 85 percent of the use stairs get is in the center and about seven inches into the tread. So that's where to concentrate with the vacuum to pull out the embedded dirt. As for the no-traffic edges and corners, just sweep them with a broom or wipe with a damp cloth to pick up the dust and loose stuff lying on the surface, and hit 'em occasionally with your canister vac when you do the edges in the rest of the house.

▶ **Standards of cleaning:** Don't compete with someone else's. Some floors don't shine even when they're waxed—set your own standards and be happy with them.

Starch

My uncle Marvin Aslett was the one who (against stiff competition) engineered the process of getting starch out of potatoes. Today spray starch added when ironing is about the whole story, unless you send things out to the laundry. Starch doesn't clean, of course, but will help keep up a fabric's appearance longer and sometimes act as a poor man's soil retardant. (We're always afraid to dirty anything starched.)

Not all the home ironing aids and fabric stiffeners sold today are actually starch. True starch-based products (composed mainly of corn, potato, or wheat starch with water added) are best for cottons. Starch won't adhere to manmade fibers, so restrict your use of pure starch to cotton fabrics, otherwise it will just flake off.

Starch that can be used on either cottons or synthetics is usually called *sizing* or *fabric finish*—it's chemically modified cellulosic polymer that puts a clear, flexible coating on the fabric. This not only gives the fabric more body and reduces pilling by binding loose fibers to the surface, it also helps the iron glide more easily over the fabric. Silicone is often added to prevent the sizing from building up on the soleplate of the iron.

Static

Static isn't just what you get for not making your bed, it refers to the electrostatic charge generated by friction between two surfaces. Static builds up, for instance, from the friction between your shoe soles and the carpet as you walk across a room, then discharges in a spark as soon as you touch something metal. Static electricity causes charged surfaces to be attracted to each other, which is what causes static cling in clothing and dust, dirt, and lint particles to cling so desperately to certain sur-

faces. Effects of static can range from annoying, as when your trousers stick to your socks or your slip rides up, to devastating, as when you erase the year's payroll records from your computer by touching it when you're charged up. To lessen cling in laundered clothing, use a fabric softener. Antistatic sprays are available to take the shock out of carpeting, but some of them attract soil. Antistat sprays and wipes help decharge such static dust attractors as Plexiglas and CRT screens, and antistat mats help keep you grounded when working at a computer. Static is much more pronounced in dry air, so just adding a little humidity to a room will often eliminate the problem.

Steel

Because it rusts so readily, most steel (except stainless) has to be coated or protected in some way. Most structural steel is painted; steel trim on automobiles and appliances is chrome-plated (see "Chrome"); some steel parts are coated with epoxy, vinyl, or rubberized substances. Steel appliance cabinets are protected with a porcelain or baked enamel finish. (See "Enameled Metals.") As far as cleaning goes, we treat steel according to what's covering it. If vinyl-coated, follow the instructions for vinyl; if painted, treat as a painted surface; and so on. The main caution with steel is to make sure the protective coating is in good shape and is keeping water from reaching the metal underneath. If the finish is cracked, chipped, or pitted and rust spots are showing, the coating needs to be repaired to keep the steel from deteriorating. When cleaning steel, it's important to dry it immediately to keep rust from forming. Stainless-steel knives stay bright and shiny, but carbon steel utensils take on a dark color with use. This is nothing to worry about, but if you start seeing reddish-brown spots, you know they're staying wet too long. See also "Wrought Iron."

Steel Wool

Steel wool pads, either plain or soap-filled, have long been our allies in the really tough cleaning jobs, but in this age of plastic and other soft home finishes, they must be used with ever more caution. Steel is a very hard metal and will scratch not only other metals (including brass, bronze, aluminum, copper, silver, gold, pewter, and tin) but also plastic, wood, paint, fiberglass, and most other home finishes as well. (See "Abrasive Cleaners.") Use steel wool only as a last resort in cleaning, and then choose the finest grade that will get the job done and apply only very gentle pressure. For scouring cookware and removing heavy greasy soil, the curly Chore Boy–type scrubbers are safer than steel wool. Use the stainless-steel or copper variety for scrubbing metal pots and pans and the plastic type for nonstick and softer surfaces. To scrub paint, plastic, fiberglass, and other soft household surfaces, use a white nylon-backed scrub sponge, which is safe for these surfaces. (See "Scrub Pads, Nylon.")

Steel wool is still a useful cleaning and maintenance tool, however, as long as you're careful how you use it. It's available in grades from 0000 (super fine) to 4 (extra coarse). 0000 and 000 are usually used for rubbing varnished and lacquered surfaces smooth, either between coats or to give a satin finish. 00 is used for delicate cleaning jobs, such as rubbing rust spots off polished metal, and for cleaning softer metals, such as copper and brass. Grade 0 is used for cleaning whitewall tires, scouring aluminum and stainless steel cookware, and other heavy-duty cleaning chores. The coarser grades are used for removing stuck-on hair and lint between coats of paint, and progressively from coarser to finer, for buffing wood floor finishes, removing old wax and varnish, and sanding and smoothing wood. Steel wool is especially good for sanding, smoothing, and removing paint, varnish, wax, and even dirt on irregular surfaces, because the flexible pad can follow contours and reach into dips and hollows.

When using steel wool, be sure to get up all the tiny metal bits it sheds (with a vacuum or tack cloth, available at paint stores) before applying a fresh coat of paint, varnish, or wax, or you'll end up with a metal-studded surface. And don't leave wet steel wool lying around on anything—it can leave nasty rust stains. Stainless-steel wool is available in many grades for use where rust is a problem.

Steps, Outdoor

Best for outdoor steps is the broom and the hose. When it comes to steps or stoops or any type of porch area, when and if you can, after sweeping, hose them down, as long as you don't have to worry about water freezing there. It's fast and will really dedust the surface.

If the sides of the steps are against the house, sweep everything to the outside. If the stairway is enclosed, whisk the corners out with an angle broom and sweep both sides to the middle and then down. Then pick it all up with a counter brush and dustpan. You can also use a leaf or shop vac blower to corral all the debris to one area and then pick it up with a dustpan.

Stains on stairs can be removed the same way as stains on the driveways. (See "Oil Stains"; "Concrete.")

Much of the problem with outdoor steps and porch areas is the heavy use they get, which means worn and raw surfaces that really absorb the mud and stains. To save lots of cleaning effort, give the heavy-use areas several coats of good-quality deck enamel, or cover them with runners of outdoor carpeting.

Sterilize. See "Disinfecting."

Stickers. See "Label, Sticker, and Decal Removal."

Stone

Natural stone is used in both homes and commercial buildings, inside and out, for floors, walls, countertops, tables, fireplaces, and other surfaces. There are many different types of stone, but they all fall into four basic groups.

Granite: The king of building stones, granite is hard and extremely durable. It can be left rough textured, honed to a smooth, dull surface, or polished to a high shine. It holds up well to weathering and abrasion and is unaffected by most chemicals. Together, marble and granite account for over 90 percent of all natural stone used in building.

Just about any cleaner can be safely used on granite—solvents, acids, and strong heavy-duty cleaners. Smooth interior granite surfaces can be washed like ordinary walls, using the two-bucket method. (See "Walls.") Rough-hewn or any granite outdoors can be cleaned with a pressure washer, and if a stain appears on granite like this, it can be removed with a poultice. (See "Poultice.")

Marble: This term is used to refer to not only true marble (metamorphosed limestone) but also decorative limestone, dolomite, and travertine. These stones are composed mainly of calcium carbonate and are relatively soft and prone to attack by acids and strong chemicals. They are not a good choice for areas exposed to heavy foot traffic or acids (fruit juice, vinegar, urine, etc.). For care of this type of stone, see "Marble." If polished marble is protected with floor finish, the finish must be buffed or burnished and periodically replaced to keep the surface protected and looking good.

Sandstone: Not usually used for flooring because it's rather soft and very absorbent, sandstone is most often used for walls but is sometimes found as a flagstone.

Slate: Because of its tendency to

split into flat, uniform sheets, slate (a rock formed from compressed shale or clay) has long been used for flooring and roof shingles. Usually a light to deep gray color, it is of medium hardness and quite resistant to chemicals. Follow general stone care instructions below. Some people like to put floor wax or finish on slate floors, but it usually doesn't bond to the stone well. Maintaining slate with a stone soap and buffing will eventually build up a nice patina that calls for much less care than waxing.

The care of all types of stone is essentially the same. All stone will absorb water to a degree, so it must be sealed to prevent staining. This can be done with a stone impregnator that penetrates the surface and forms a below-surface seal or with a sealer that forms a clear protective coating on top of the stone surface. Impregnators usually last the longest and require the least maintenance, while seals give the best stain protection but require more upkeep and wear off with time. Routine care of either type of sealed stone should include regular sweeping or dust-mopping to keep damaging grit off and damp-mopping with a neutral cleaner solution. Stone care specialists sell a Stone Care Soap, which leaves a light protective film on the surface of the stone that can be buffed to a handsome low luster. To restore scratched or damaged polished stone floors, consult a professional marble contractor—this isn't a job for a home handyman. For specialized stone care products, contact a stone care specialist such as HMK Stone Care Products, 2585

Third Street, San Francisco, CA 94107.

See also "Sealing"; "Fireplace, Facing."

Stoneware. See "Clayware."

Storage of Cleaning Equipment

Having the right cleaning equipment is the number-one priority; having it stored safely and conveniently is number two.

This doesn't mean under the sink—those jumbled heaps and piles down there are an invitation for accidents as well as total confusion when you're looking for something to clean with.

Make yourself a home janitor closet

Some Principles of Smart Storage

1. *Up high.* Out of reach of children

and pets, on a sturdy shelf or a secure cupboard.

2. *Lids tight and on everything.* Spills and child or fire hazards can be avoided with secure lids. If it doesn't have a lid, use it up now or get rid of it.

3. *Label.* Don't keep any cleaning chemical if you don't know exactly what it is. We too often switch bottles to gain a good plastic jug or whatever and pour the contents into a fruit jar or pop bottle, and leave it. It's useless then because others won't know and we generally forget what it is. If you don't know what it is, dispose of it *now.* Keep all cleaning chemicals and solutions (and that includes those in spray bottles) clearly identified. A black permanent marker will do the job well.

4. *Decentralize.* Some undersink storage is okay if you don't have small children and what you have there is stored in a handy leakproof unit such as a cleaning caddy or maid basket. (See "Caddy, Cleaning"), filled with the materials needed to clean that room or area regularly. It makes sense to have several of these little customized cleaning kits throughout the house in strategic locations.

5. *Unplug it.* Just moving the switch to off isn't enough protection. Never store or leave any electrical cleaning machine or device plugged in.

6. *Hang it.* There's always more room on the walls of a closet than on the floor, and there are all kinds of hangers now available

from Rubbermaid, Bassick, and other manufacturers that can easily be mounted on a closet or other wall. Hanging cleaning tools not only makes them easy to find and use, but assures enough ventilation to dry them. It'll also keep them in shape, rather than warped or contorted from standing or lying in a corner or in a heap.

7. *Don't put tools away wet or dirty.* This just gives them a chance to mildew or sour, contaminate the next batch of cleaning water, or scratch or dirty the surface you'll be trying to clean.

8. *Keep them neat and organized for the obvious reasons.* (If you just fling your tools down, a whole room won't be enough to store them.)

▶ Limit (another way to say this is *simplify*) your cleaning supplies. All you really need are a few basics: all-purpose cleaner, disinfectant cleaner, glass cleaner, heavy-duty cleaner or degreaser, a mild phosphoric acid cleaner to keep hard-water scale in check, and perhaps some dry spotter and wet spotter. You could almost store all these in a shoe box. The whole secret of effective cleaning is regular cleaning with the right supplies. A whole cabinetful of powerful and specialized chemicals is no replacement for timely, intelligent cleaning.

Straightening Up

When we're young straightening up usually means our back or our act.

Now it has more to do with that stuff strung out all over. Straightening up is the short form of housecleaning, and it takes no special skill or machinery. It's simply getting things neater or more squared away, slowing down long enough to put everything back where it belongs or in order. What's open is shut, what's crooked is straightened, what's out is put away, and what's rolling around is replaced. The average home needs to be straightened far more often than it needs to be cleaned, so this is a talent well worth cultivating in every member of the family.

A lot of us find it helpful to always do our straightening at the same time of the day, such as first thing in the morning, or right after the kids go to bed.

Straightening up (the pros call it policing) starts with eyeballing it. Walk into the room and make a quick inventory. What's out of place? Then start on the right side of the room and move to your left, quickly replacing things. Carry a small bag or bucket with you for trash. Place furniture back where it belongs, straighten drapes, pillows, and magazines, and set everything right. Haul off any shoes, clothes, or toys and put them in a bin for the owners to claim and put away. In minutes the entire place will look cleaner, and it'll be safer too!

Watch out though—once you get committed to straightening things up, you won't be able to stop.

Straw

Whether hats or wall hangings, you have to be careful with straw, as prolonged contact with moisture (rain or cleaning solution!) will not merely discolor or soften straw items, causing them to lose their shape but can mildew or even rot them. Prevention is the best approach. Keep your straw stuff vacuumed or dusted and under protective wrapper or cover when not in use. If you must clean it, wipe with a cloth dampened with neutral cleaner solution and then with plain water. Blot well and dry right away with a thick terry towel. If a straw item is really dirty, its chance of survival is less because you have to use more solution and maybe scrub lightly with a soft brush, then rinse and dry. Always air-dry straw, but not in the sun or it may shrink. Stained and damaged straw can't be healed with positive thinking, but I have resorted to a can of spray paint occasionally.

For straw hats, see "Hats and Caps."

Streaks

Streaks are embarrassing evidence that we didn't get it clean—they're dirt or soap left on the surface, and they really stand out because they reflect light differently from the clean, well-rinsed rest of it. Streaks can also result from too heavy a coat in some spots or missed areas when waxing, and even from letting part of the nap of carpet or upholstery dry at the wrong angle.

I've avoided streaks ever since I learned the following: (1) Clean thoroughly and rinse thoroughly; (2) Overlap strokes when wiping, waxing, painting, and the like to make sure you don't leave any missed areas; (3) All reflective surfaces (including shiny enamel paints) should be dried with a cloth, not left to air-dry; (4) Stand or brush the nap of pile fabrics all in one direction before it dries.

Stripping Floors. See "Floors, Stripping for Waxing."

Stripping Wood Floors. See "Wood Floors."

Stuff Sacks. See "Backpacks."

Stuffed Animals/Toys

To rephrase a famous potato chip commercial, when it comes to stuffed animals, "No one can own just one." And when they finally need cleaning, the fun's over. The wide variety of fabrics and stuffings they're made of, and all the doo-dads stuck to the little critters makes cleaning them a real zoo.

One word of advice: Don't throw a stuffed animal into the washer unless: (1) You've been wanting an excuse to finally throw it away; or (2) You enjoy scooping from your washer blobs of unidentifiable fabric, paper, foam rubber, and even nutshells often used as filling; or (3) A care label clearly states that machine washing is safe. Usually animals with acrylic fur and 100 percent polyester stuffing, such as those made for infants, are washer safe.

To machine wash: Pretreat spots, check for split seams, place the pet inside a mesh bag, and add a couple of towels or other soft washables to balance the load. Set the machine on gentle or delicate, and if it's a light-colored pet that's yellowed badly, add an enzyme bleach such as Biz or Axion to the washer along with the detergent. To dry, use the stationary drying rack if your dryer has one, or set the toy somewhere in the sun to air-dry.

Surface clean: Treat the rest of your menagerie as follows: First, get out your canister vac or one of the handy little hand-helds and vacuum the fur thoroughly to remove all the embedded dust. In a bucket, work up a lather of carpet and upholstery cleaner; Woolite and water; or Tide and water mixed with a few drops of ammonia.

Use as little solution and rinse water as possible. If you wet your pet too much, the biggest share of the dirt will just be wicked down inside and into the roots of its fur. Sponge a light amount of *suds only* on the soiled areas, rub it in gently, and then wipe it off with a clean towel. Use another sponge or cloth dampened in plain water to rinse, so the animal won't dry all sticky and soapy.

After washing, dry immediately with a clean towel, wiping with the nap. A wet/dry vac could also be used to suck the moisture out. Then let the animal sit in a place with good air circulation for a day or two so that it dries completely. Finally, run a brush or comb over it to fluff it back up.

Suds

We all tend to think of suds—a frothy head on the tub or bucket—as an index of cleaning power, a sign that the cleaning solution we just mixed up is really going to do it. The cleaning chemicals we add to water are usually necessary for forming suds, because water by itself is fairly resistant to forming lasting bubbles. The surfactants in most cleaning preparations break the surface tension of water so it will mix easily with air (as when we run the faucet onto a blob of detergent to create a sudsy sinkful of dishwater).

When we cleaned mainly with soap, the amount of sudsing was an important indicator of whether there was enough cleaner in our cleaning brew. Even now when we use a soap product such as Ivory Snow, it's important to be sure we add enough of it to create a couple of inches of foam on top of the water in the washer. But suds don't mean much otherwise because modern laundry detergents are carefully designed to create different levels of suds—including low suds and no suds. Some even have suds suppressors added to assure that so many suds aren't created in that powerful agitation as to jam the washer or dishwasher. Even in hand-cleaning too much suds will not only waste chemical but make a lot of extra rinsing necessary. (If you end up with too many suds in the washer, adding a half cup of vinegar should get things back under control.)

On the other hand, suds themselves are sometimes useful in cleaning—which is why some products such as oven cleaner and laundry pretreatments are designed to be dispensed as foam. Suds or foam like this is a light, airy mixture of water and the cleaning chemicals, and it will cling to the surface we want to clean and keep the moisture and chemical on there for quite a while to do their work, without evaporating or running down. And when foam alone is used to clean, as in upholstery shampooing and saddle soap used properly, it wets the surface and applies the cleaning chemical to it without getting it too wet.

▶ Suds' value is often psychological—they serve mainly to put a head on our imagination!

Sulfuric Acid

Sulfuric acid is a strong corrosive acid used in drain cleaners and some toilet bowl cleaners. Sulfuric acid is used in drain cleaners because it has the ability to dissolve a wide range of organic matter yet is not as damaging to pipes as other strong acids. But the pipes can sometimes get so hot from the chemical reaction between the acid and the drain-blocking material that they break. Caustic (lye) drain cleaners, while not as fast-acting, are safer to use than sulfuric acid. (See "Drain Cleaners.") If you find it necessary to use a sulfuric drain opener, use extreme caution, as this acid can cause severe skin burns and inhaling the fumes is hard on your lungs. The chemical action of sulfuric acid on drainpipe contaminants produces noxious gases too, so provide plenty of ventilation. Be sure to keep sulfuric acid stored safely—the ingestion of even small amounts of it is guaranteed to do some damage and can even be lethal.

▶ **Supermom:** A woman setting the breakfast table at midnight.

Surfactant

Surfactant is a shortened form of the term *surface active agent,* the main

ADDING SURFACTANT (in this case, liquid detergent)

Stain, grease, etc., on clothing fiber

(water)

Detergent makes the water wetter to help it dissolve the stain

Stain broken up and ready to rinse away

active ingredient in soaps and detergents. By decreasing the surface tension of the water, surfactants make the water wetter, enhancing its ability to penetrate dry soils and enabling it to break up and emulsify oils. Spray some soap or detergent and water and some plain water side by side on a piece of cardboard, and see which is absorbed sooner—you'll immediately understand the value of a surfactant. Soap and detergent formulas are based on surfactants, to which are added various emulsifiers, wetting agents, and builders to meet specific cleaning needs. See also "Detergent;" "Soap"; "Emulsify"; "Chemistry of Cleaning"; "Builder."

Sweeping

For sweeping small floor areas, use one of the flagged-tip nylon-bristle angle brooms. (See "Brooms.") They're much easier to use and hold up better and longer than the old corn straw brooms. The professional-strength ones sold in janitorial supply stores are larger than the supermarket variety, and cover more ground in less time. Just remember to keep the broom hung up when not in use—standing it on the bristles will put a permanent curl in them.

Good sweeping technique calls for holding the broom handle at a slight angle and dragging the dirt particles along. Holding a broom straight upright and flicking the dirt along stirs up too much dust. Sweep corners and edges first and work toward the middle, moving the dirt with you as you go. Finish up by sweeping your pile of accumulated stuff into a dustpan.

For large expanses of smooth floor, a treated dust mop is the fastest way to go. Get a good commercial dust mop and use a dust treatment such as Velva-Sheen so the mop will pick up and hold fine dust. (See "Dust Mop"; "Dust-Mopping"; Dust Treatments.") Vacuuming hard floors with a floor brush attachment is also an effective way to sweep hard floors, especially if you have dust allergies. It's slow and noisy, but it'll do the most thorough job in all the corners and crevices when getting up every last split pea and stray Cheerio is important.

For large areas of rough flooring, such as concrete garage floors, driveways, and sidewalks, use a 24-inch nylon push broom. The kind with coarse bristles inside and an outside row of finer bristles for picking up fine dust is best. With a big broom like this, push the dirt ahead of you in a straight path and drop your sweepings at the end of each swath. This leaves you with a row of dirt at each end of the area, which can be swept up into two piles and picked up with a dustpan.

▶ **Switchplates:** What husbands and children do with their dishes when one gets dirty, and a spot you never want to miss when you spot clean.

T

Thou shalt dust before you vacuum.

Tablecloths

Spray a new tablecloth with soil retardant (such as Scotchgard) so that spills will bead up and wipe away.

Your best defense otherwise is to read care labels when available, clean tablecloths as soon as possible after use, and never allow spots and stains to sit for long periods of time. Pretreat spots before laundering, and don't use hot water or dry with heat, till you've checked the instructions under the specific stain in this book. (For lace tablecloths, see "Lace.")

Tablecloths are in a hopeless position—bound to get spilled and dripped on—so try to pick fabrics, colors, and patterns that will show less and clean easier. Or go to washable place mats, plastic or disposable tablecloths, or no tablecloth, just a good-looking, well-sealed wood or laminate tabletop.

Tamp. See "Spotting Brushes."

Tank Brushes. See "Scrub Brushes."

Tape Players/Recorders

Those fingerprints all over the outside of your cassette player won't do anything for your image, but it's dirt *inside* that can cause real problems. It'll affect your player's sound quality and can even cause it to start "eating" your valuable tapes. Whether your tape player is a tiny headphone portable, an automotive unit, or a large reel-to-reel job, the inner workings are basically the same. A magnetic coating (iron oxide) on the tape stores information that the heads pick up and interpret as music. As the tape slides over the transport system and the pickup heads, minute particles of the oxide are scraped off the tape and onto the parts of the player. As the dirt and oxide builds up, not only do your tapes start sounding bad but transport components become sticky and start catching the tape instead of letting it roll through. This is what damages tapes.

To clean up inside, moisten a cotton swab with commercial tape head cleaner or denatured alcohol, and swab the heads and transport system thoroughly. (See your owner's manual for details.) Specialized head cleaners are better for your machine, as plain alcohol tends to dry out the rubber pinch roller. Don't splash fluid

all over the inside of the unit, but do use enough to dissolve all the gunk. Clean the heads, the capstan (the rotating metal shaft that moves the tape past the heads), the pinch roller (the rubber roller that "pinches" the tape against the capstan), and any tape guides. If you can't reach the components to clean them by hand, use one of the special cleaning cassettes sold by music stores. Be sure to get the nonabrasive kind that requires the application of a cleaning solution—the dry types just grind the oxide off, and they can slowly grind away the heads and other components too.

An invisible kind of contamination builds up inside tape players too: excess magnetism. While you're in there, use a head demagnetizer (also available at your local audio shop) to remove it, otherwise you'll get a hissing sound when you play your tapes. The cabinets and ventilation grilles of home tape decks should be vacuumed periodically to remove accumulated dust too. Plastic and metal cases and cabinets for all types of recorders can be cleaned by damp-wiping (with all-purpose cleaner if necessary)—but be careful not to get moisture inside the case.

Tapes, Cassette (Audio and Video)

Audio- and videocassette tapes both work the same way, they're just different shapes and sizes. A plastic tape coated with magnetic material runs from one reel to another past an opening where it is read by the recording and playback heads. Normally the cassettes shouldn't require any cleaning, but the tape itself and the tape transport system are sensitive to dust, dirt, heat, smoke, and magnetic fields. Keep tapes in their protective cases when not in use, and away from sources of heat or magnetism such as magnetic screwdrivers and other magnetic tools, electric motors, and speakers. Don't leave cassettes lying around naked where they can get full of dust, and don't store them on the dashboard or in the back window of your car.

If a cassette has been lying out and is dusty, the best first aid is to carefully vacuum it clean—but keep the tape tight while you do or you'll be retrieving 70 miles of tape from inside the vacuum. If you find it necessary to wipe soil or fingerprints off the surface of a cassette, be careful not to get any moisture in the openings. The part of your audio or video system that requires regular cleaning is the *player*. Dirty heads and tape drive mechanism on the player not only interfere with sound and picture quality, but can cause the unit to start eating tapes. See "Tape Players/Recorders"; "Videocassette Recorders and Camcorders."

Tapestries

With tapestries, as with Oriental rugs, great care must be taken. Regular gentle vacuuming will help prevent the soiling that will eventually call for cleaning.

If a tapestry is at all valuable, don't try to clean it yourself. It may seem easy enough to do—just soak it in a tub, clean with a mild soap or detergent, and then hang to dry—but you can easily injure a tapestry unless you know what you're doing. You could cause the dyes to run or damage the fabric. Many a tapestry is unable to hold its weight when wet and may tear in two if hung to dry!

Even an ordinary tapestry is better brought to a dry cleaner. A more costly one should be taken to a professional textile conservator. This is not the same type of person who will reweave a cigarette burn in your sofa. Professional conservators have a giant soaking tank in which they can lay out a tapestry and soak it for a couple of days, if necessary. Then they hang it properly (distributing the weight evenly). If a piece can't be hung to dry, they have the equipment to dry it out flat.

Look in the Yellow Pages under "Art Conservation and Restoration." Almost every major city has textile-related guilds, and you could also contact one of these to get a recommendation.

Tarnish, Metal

Some metals react with salts, acids, and oxygen in the air to form metal oxides, sulfides, and other substances that build a film called *tarnish* on the surface of the metal. We've all seen metal oxidation in the form of rust (iron oxide) on iron and steel. The black tarnish on silver is silver sulfide, formed from sulfur in the atmosphere, rubber that the silver comes in contact with, and so on. Brass, copper, and bronze also tarnish readily. Ordinary table salt or sodium chloride will corrode aluminum, so wherever there's salt in the air, you'll see the telltale white powdery oxide on storm doors, awnings, and other outdoor aluminum.

Most tarnishes tend to coat the metal and retard further oxidation, but for the sake of appearance, we take the protective coating off and expose the metal to further attack. Luckily for our polishing arm, for some things (such as bronze sculptures and antique pewter) it's considered chic to leave the dark patina intact. See also "Aluminum"; "Brass"; "Bronze"; "Copper"; "Silver"; and "Metal Polishes."

Taxidermy

First, a few preventative measures to help keep your mounted creatures clean.

1. Locate them well away from greasy kitchen vapors, cigarette smoke, fireplaces, or any other source of heat, including direct sunlight, which will eventually turn your black bear to a bleached blond.
2. Place them out of reach of pets, kids, and guests, preferably in a glass case. (For birds and white animals, it's essential.) Animal rugs should be mounted on the wall, because soil from shoes will ruin them. Never put them in the washer. (They can be dry-cleaned, but the backing must be removed first.)
3. Avoid touching the fur with your bare hands—the oils from your

hands will leave fingerprints that attract dust.

General Care

You can wipe horns, noses, teeth, and the like with a lightly dampened cloth, but keep moisture in any form off skin or fur—it'll stretch it! Likewise, don't use any type of solvent on any part of your trophies, especially fish, which are painted with lacquer.

Dust your specimens regularly with a feather duster, carefully flicking in the natural direction of the fur—never against. Or you can blow the dust off with a blow drier on a cool setting or your vacuum on a low blower setting—never suction. A large animal can be wiped with a soft cloth, again, in the direction of the fur. Occasionally realign the hairs as needed with a soft brush or a fine wire dog-grooming brush. Don't brush or wipe birds with anything, or you'll distort or destroy the feather patterns.

Glass eyes can be cleaned with glass cleaner spritzed onto a cloth. Horn and tusks can be brightened up with a bit of baby oil applied with a small soft cloth.

Every ten or fifteen years, have the animal cleaned by the taxidermist who mounted the piece. Since taxidermists know what processes were used to prepare it, they can clean it safely.

Tea Kettles

Clean the outside of a tea kettle according to its finish: copper, stainless steel, enamel, glass. A tea kettle kept on the stovetop is likely to accumulate a coating of airborne grease and spatters and need regular cleaning.

Dip-It coffeepot cleaner will work inside your tea kettle to remove hardwater deposits and oils. Or you can bring a quart of water and a cup of vinegar to a boil in the kettle and let it stand overnight; rinse thoroughly. Then boil a kettle full of water and dump it to remove any lingering taste or smell.

▶ **Teenage mess:** Make up a sign that says "Enter at your own risk." And forget it. (The advice of a parent who had eight teens home at once.)

Telephones

Reach out and touch your telephone with a cleaning cloth occasionally. Spray a soft cloth with all-purpose cleaner (or if you prefer, disinfectant cleaner) solution. Then wipe the entire phone, paying particular attention to the mouthpiece and earpiece. Always spray the cloth, not the phone—spritzing cleaner directly on the button area or into the transmitter holes, especially, could put you on hold for quite a while. To dust between the buttons use a Masslinn cloth (see "Dustcloths") or if necessary you can always detail with a damp cotton swab. If you talk into a cartoon character's rump or a specialty or vintage phone, be extra careful and use only a damp cloth to clean it and then polish dry with a soft cloth. Go easy too around all the gizmos and attachments—arms, legs, or answering machines—that make up many a home phone system. Never use harsh cleaners or abrasives on a phone because phone plastic, like all plastic, can't take it. And aggressive cleaning may remove eyes, colors, or even the wood finish of some of today's endless array of telephones. See also "Cords," especially if you have one of the extra-long ones.

Televisions

TVs are the most used appliance in many a modern home but rarely see any cleaning action. The screen collects dust by static attraction and should be dusted at least weekly, not with an oil rag, but with a Masslinn or electrostatic dustcloth. (See "Dustcloths.") Unplug the set first before this or any cleaning operation. Keep liquid and aerosol cleaners and solvents of any kind away from a television, and never poke anything into the ventilation slots at the back of the set. If fingerprints and smudges cloud your screen, go after them with glass cleaner. Just don't spray the screen itself—spray the cleaner into a soft cloth and then wipe the screen and polish dry. You might want to do the knobs and buttons too. The rest of the exterior can be dusted or wiped lightly with a cloth dampened with neutral cleaner (see "Cleaners, Neutral"); wooden parts can be polished with furniture polish. (Again, spray only the cloth.)

Tents

Most tents are made of canvas or nylon, with either polyethylene or coated nylon floors. Whatever it's made of, a tent's worst enemy is mildew. Most tent fabrics are treated to retard mildew growth, but no fabric is mildew-proof if not cared for properly. Don't just roll a tent up and put it away after using it—even if the rest seems dry, the floor is probably damp. Get a tent up off the ground and spread it out to dry before storing it away. Don't store tents on concrete floors or against basement walls where they can wick up moisture from the concrete.

If a tent needs washing, pitch it in your yard and spray it with a garden hose. Using a sponge or a soft brush, gently scrub soiled parts with all-purpose cleaner solution, holding a pad of toweling on the opposite side of the fabric to avoid stretching or tearing. Go ahead and wash the inside too, if it needs it. Rinse well and leave it to dry—sponge puddles off waterproof floors so the inside will dry quickly. Then hang the whole thing up so the underside of the floor can dry before you put it away. Don't wash tents in an automatic washer. Don't use solvents or abrasive cleaners, which can damage the fabric's water repellency. Protect coated nylon and polyethylene floors from abrasion and punctures by setting them up with a ground cloth underneath, and you can put a rug or cloth down inside as well. If you use chairs or tables in a floored cabin tent, put pieces of wood or cardboard under the legs to prevent punctures.

Terrazzo

Terrazzo flooring is made by embedding marble chips in a Portland cement matrix, which is then ground smooth. Some terrazzo is formed in tiles separated by metal strips and some is seamless, and in either type many different colors of chips and matrix are available. Terrazzo is a very handsome and durable floor when properly maintained, but careless cleaning can ruin it.

Since raw terrazzo is porous, easily stained, and susceptible to chemical damage, it should always be sealed. For an attractive low sheen, it can be treated with a penetrating sealer that seals the pores but doesn't build up a shiny coating on top of the stone. For the high-gloss look, seal with an acrylic terrazzo sealer and then apply several coats of self-polishing floor finish.

Regular maintenance of terrazzo includes sweeping with a broom (ideally horsehair bristle) or a treated dust mop and regular damp mopping. If your terrazzo is unsealed, the cement matrix will absorb oil easily, so a nonoily dust mop treatment is what you want. If a floor finish is used, it can be machine-buffed or burnished. Mopping should be done with a neutral cleaner only. (See "Cleaners, Neutral.") Strongly alkaline or acid cleaners and solvent stain removers will attack terrazzo, detergents containing phosphates can form crystals that weaken the floor, and soaps will leave a dulling film. (See "Soap"; "Detergent"; "Phosphates.") Built detergents (see "Builder") can also combine with minerals in the water to form a hard discoloring coating known as *metal plate*. This can be removed only by grinding or with special stone cleaners. For stain removal, consult a stone care specialty company, such as HMK Stone Care Products, 2585 Third Street, San Francisco, CA 94107.

Textured Ceilings. See "Textured Walls and Ceilings."

Textured Walls and Ceilings

Textured walls and ceilings are good-looking and hide a multitude of structural sins, but they can drive a well-meaning cleaner insane. The sharp points prick fingers and catch and chew up sponges and clothes. Texture is a water-soluble "mud" (plaster and latex mixture) sprayed, stamped, rolled, or troweled onto a wall or ceiling—it can be applied heavily (½ inch thick) or lightly (1/32 of an inch skim) and in a great variety of designs, some barely protruding from the surface and some with giant needle-sharp stalactites. Unless it has a couple of good coats of paint on it, texture will dissolve when you try to wash it. And cheap flat paint (such as in many tract homes and apartments) will often allow the brown color of the underlying mud to stain through if you attempt to wash it.

If you're dealing with deep, extreme texturing, I'd get a 4-foot board and drag it over the surface to knock off the needle tips. (It won't hurt the looks.) You could also work the surface over with coarse sandpa-

per. Then roll one or two coats of a good low-sheen enamel on it. The paint will fill the pores and make the surface a lot smoother. The texture will be easier to wash then with a sponge or brush, depending on how deep it is, and a solution of all-purpose cleaner (1 ounce per gallon of water) plus a ¼ cup of ammonia per bucket. Then wipe and blot with a towel afterward to remove the loosened, suspended dirt.

Thermos Bottles. See "Vacuum Bottles."

Ties. See "Neckties."

Tile, Acoustical. See "Acoustical Tile."

Tile, Asphalt. See "Asphalt Tile."

Tile, Ceramic. See "Ceramic Tile."

Tile, Clay

While technically *clay tile* refers to any such tile fired in a kiln, it is used here to mean unglazed clay tiles such as the popular red quarry tile or unglazed Mexican-style tile used for flooring and fireplace surrounds. For glazed ceramic tile, see "Ceramic Tile." Quarry and other unglazed tiles are used extensively in high-traffic areas such as restaurant kitchens, where they are traditionally left unfinished for slip-resistance and ease of maintenance. In a home setting, these tiles can likewise be left unfinished for a low-luster natural look, or they can be sealed and waxed to provide better stain resistance and a glossy appearance. For the glossy look, first thoroughly clean the floor, then apply an acrylic terrazzo sealer according to instructions, followed by one or more coats of polymer floor finish. Dust-mop and damp-mop regularly to remove abrasive grit, and recoat with floor finish as needed to maintain the shine. Unsealed tile just needs regular sweeping and mopping. It will eventually self-seal and require less maintenance as time goes on. Even if you don't seal the tile, the grout should be sealed with a grout waterproofer to prevent staining.

Tile, Vinyl. See "Vinyl Tile."

Tile, Vinyl Asbestos. See "Vinyl Asbestos Tile."

Tile Cleaners

The term *tile cleaner* can mean different things to different people. If you go to a masonry supplier and ask for tile or brick cleaner, you'll get a strong solution of muriatic acid used to clean mortar drops off newly laid brick and tile. It's intended to be used one time only, to clean up freshly laid masonry. Some people mistakenly think this powerful solution is okay to use to clean smoke off fireplaces and for regular cleaning of tiled floors. Not so. Muriatic acid is not an all-purpose cleaner, and repeated use will eat away at the mortar or grout and eventually damage it to the point of needing repair.

Another type of tile cleaner is the phosophoric acid tub and tile cleaners sold by janitorial supply stores to clean hard-water scale and soap scum off tiled tub and shower walls. Even this type of product can be damaging to tile grout over time, and shouldn't be used any more than is strictly necessary. *Preventing* mineral scale and soap scum buildup makes more sense than constantly removing it. See "Shower and Tub Enclosures"; "Soap Scum"; "Hard-Water Deposits."

Tin

When it's new, tin is a bright, shiny, silvery metal, but it darkens with age. The fact that it's often been used as a rust-proof coating over steel cooking utensils has given rise to such names as pie tin, cake tin, and cookie tin. Though not manufactured in the United States anymore, tinware is still being imported from Mexico, France, and other places, and there are a lot of old pieces still in use.

Don't lose any sleep trying to keep kitchen tinware bright and shiny; it absorbs heat better after it gets dark, and too much scrubbing will wear away the thin plating of tin and expose the steel underneath to rust. Don't wash tinware in a dishwasher, and don't store food in it. Acid foods can eat right through the plating. Never use abrasives on tinware. Instead, let it soak in hot water to loosen baked-on food and then, if still necessary, scrub with a plastic scrubber. Dry thoroughly immediately after washing to prevent rust spots. If rust develops, rub it out with fine steel wool moistened with vegetable oil. Purely decorative tinware can be coated with paste wax or lacquer to protect the finish.

Toaster Ovens

Toaster ovens are handy-dandies we love to use until they get coated with baked-on crud, then we have the urge to slip them in the garage sale bin. You can't use oven cleaner here— toaster ovens have too many parts it could corrode—so the trick is to wipe up spills, spatters, and crumbs after each use. Unplug and wait till it's cool, then remove food bits with a damp paper towel. Wipe (or scrub gently with a white nylon-backed sponge, as necessary) the inside with water or all-purpose cleaner solution. Many toaster ovens have removable doors, racks, drip pans, or crumb trays that can be washed or soaked in hot sudsy water. Some parts are dishwasher safe. Follow manufacturer's directions carefully because many of the newer models have continuous cleaning interiors that are damaged by any cleaning agent other than plain water, and left-behind paper towel lint or sponge shreds can interfere with the self-cleaning function on some models. Avoid dripping any water or cleaner inside, or poking around with utensils; they can damage the element or heat sensor.

As for the exterior, spray a cleaning cloth with all-purpose cleaner solution or glass cleaner and wipe, then polish dry. If you come upon a sticky spot or dried spill, soak it with a damp cloth until it's soft enough to wipe away. Abrasives will mar the finish

and steel wool pads used anywhere in a toaster oven can leave behind metal particles that will touch electrical parts and give you a shock.

You can't use oven cleaner on the door either—it will inevitably get on the aluminum trim or paint and ruin it. Spray the door with degreaser solution and leave it on a couple of minutes. If it's become impossible to keep an eye on the minipizzas, you could take a razor scraper (see "Razor Blades") to the glass.

Toasters

Unplug your toaster and let it cool, then empty the crumb tray over the sink and brush any malingerers off with a pastry brush. If your toaster doesn't have a crumb tray, use the time-honored technique of upending it over the garbage can or sink and shaking it. Wipe the exterior with a cloth dampened with a Windex-type glass cleaner and polish dry. Place a paper towel soaked with a heavy-duty cleaner such as Formula 409 over stubborn spots for several minutes, then clean as above. Never poke anything into a toaster or let cleaning solution drip into it.

Toilet Bowl Brush

A toilet bowl brush is a bristle brush often with an oval-shaped head used to brush the inside of a toilet bowl. Not to be confused with the toilet swab, which is the right way to apply bowl cleaner (see "Toilet Bowl Swab"), this brush is basically a toilet toothbrush. A bowl brush won't really do anything for hard-water deposits, but the ordinary scum and residue that collects on the walls of the bowl every few days can be dislodged swiftly with a brush and then flushed away. The curved neck of the brush allows it to reach easily under the lip and down the throat of the toilet. You can be enthusiastic with the brush—it won't hurt the toilet. A good stiff nylon-bristle brush with a plastic handle won't rust and will hold up longer than natural bristle, which tends to flatten after a while.

Toilet Bowl Caddy

A toilet bowl caddy is a plastic-pitcher–like container available at jan-itorial supply stores that holds a bottle of bowl cleaner and a toilet bowl swab or Johnny Mop. It makes your toilet cleaning kit easy to carry, a little more presentable, a snap to store, and, best of all, it gives you a place to set the cleaner and the swab so they won't drip or leave acid burn rings on the floor of the tub or on the counter where you happened to set them while cleaning. And in a caddy you can safely set the bowl cleaner up high to keep it out of the reach of little hands, because you don't have to worry about *what* you set it on. The pistol-grip handle of a caddy makes it a snap to pick up and move from place to place. Caddies are inexpensive, and once you have one you'll like it so well you'll take it to church with you! See also "Toilet Bowl Swab."

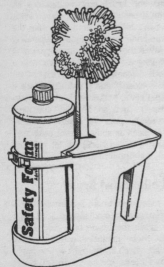

A bowl caddy is the safe, easy way to store and carry your bowl cleaning kit.

▶ **Caddy:** Something we use to carry golf clubs around on Sunday, and bowl cleaners and toilet bowl swabs around on Saturday.

Toilet Bowl Cleaners

There are a number of in-tank or automatic toilet bowl cleaners that help freshen and sanitize the bowl with each flush. Generally speaking, these put a little chlorine and maybe some detergent (and maybe a little blue dye) in the water as it sits in the flush tank. These products help bleach out stains and aid in bowl cleaning, but don't take the place of periodic swabbing with a good bowl cleaner.

What is a true bowl cleaner? Something that not only kills germs but can get tough with hard-water deposits such as bowl ring. Most bowl cleaners contain (in addition to possibly a quaternary disinfectant) either hydrochloric or phosphoric acid. There are nonacid cleaners, safer to use, but less effective on hard-water scale. The phosphorics are the safest of the acid cleaners, for both you and your bathroom surfaces, but slower acting. Formulations containing hydrochloric acid will get rid of hard-water deposits faster but must be handled with GREAT CARE, as they can damage skin, fabrics, carpeting, and metals. Never use bowl cleaners anywhere except the inside of the toilet bowl, and always use rubber gloves and eye protection when you apply them. Nine percent hydrochloric is reasonably safe to use—bowl cleaners with over 20 percent HC1 should be left to the pros. See also "Toilet Bowl Ring" under "Toilets."

▶ Greater regularity (of toilet cleaning) will keep rings away entirely.

Toilet Bowl Swab

A toilet bowl swab, or Johnny Mop, is a little bunny taillike ball of rayon, acrylic, or cotton on the end of a 12-inch plastic handle. Swabs are designed to clean a toilet without scratching it, and if that round head is thrust vigorously into the throat of the toilet several times it will drive the water down and out of the bowl

so it is empty and easy to clean. You then use a swab for everyday cleaning of the bowl, using my speed bathroom cleaning system and to deep-clean a bowl with bowl cleaner (see "Toilets"). Don't forget up under the rim where the orifices (little water inlets) often get clogged with mineral scale.

After use, swabs should be rinsed, shaken dry, and stored in a bowl caddy.

Toilets

No, the "magic" bowl cleaners that sit in your toilet tank don't end toilet cleaning forever. They help sanitize the bowl, control stains, and stretch out the time between cleanings, but they don't take the place of a good periodic scrubbing with toilet bowl cleaner. (See "Toilet Bowl Cleaners.")

Here's the quick and easy professional approach to toilet cleaning:

1. Don't pour bowl cleaner directly into the bowl—all that water in there will dilute the chemical's effectiveness. Push a bowl swab down hard into the throat of the toilet several times to force the water out of the bowl. Then wring out the swab.
2. Apply full-strength bowl cleaner to the swab and mop all around the

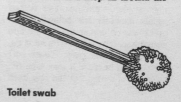

Toilet swab

inside of the bowl. (Take extra care to swab easily missed places, such as under the rim and down the throat of the toilet.) Let the chemical sit for a few minutes to do its work.

3. Flush the toilet, rinsing the swab in fresh water as it flushes.

4. Spray the entire outside of the fixture with disinfectant cleaner. This means the top *and* the bottom of the lid, the underside of the seat, all around the rim of the bowl (especially in the *front*), around the hinges where the seat attaches to the bowl, the very back of and behind the bowl, and the entire base where the bowl is anchored to the floor. Urine has a way of accumulating down there and causing odors. After the cleaner has been on there a couple of minutes, buff it off with a terry cleaning cloth.

You always sanitize the seat and rim *after* the acid cleaner used inside the bowl is rinsed away, or before you use the acid cleaner. NEVER mix the two products.

Toilet Bowl Ring

If you live in a hard-water area, you've undoubtedly noticed that your toilet, all by itself, will form a hard raised ring on the inside of the bowl, right at the waterline. The ring is simply minerals left behind at the point where water meets air and evaporates. The longer you let it go, the heavier it will grow. Bleach isn't the solution because it may take the color out of a ring, but the ring itself

remains and keeps on building up and staining. When a ring is young and tender, an enthusiastic brushing with acid bowl cleaner will generally remove it. If the chemical action of the bowl cleaner doesn't entirely dissolve the mineral buildup, you can scrub it with an abrasive (green) nylon-backed scrub pad while the acid is working. An old ring is a real encrustation that calls for mightier measures. Forget about sandpaper, razor blades, and other remedies that can result in damage to you as well as the bowl surface. Take a pumice stone (see "Pumice"), wet it in the toilet water, and rub it on the ring, being sure to keep it wet the whole time you're scrubbing. Don't use pumice bars on colored, enameled, or plastic fixtures—only on vitreous china toilets and urinals.

Once a ring has been removed with a pumice bar, weekly use of bowl cleaner thereafter should keep it from reforming. In extreme hard-water areas, installing a water conditioner will help control bowl ring and other mineral scale buildup. See also "Water Conditioning"; "Toilet Bowl Cleaners."

See also "Toilet Bowl Brush"; "Toilet Bowl Swab"; "Toilet Bowl Caddy."

Toothbrushes, Old. See
"Grout Brushes."

▶ **Tops of things, cleaning:**
Should be delegated to any tall, critical people in the household.

Toys

Whew! Toys are an enormous topic and most don't come with cleaning instructions, but there are some commonsense safeguards most moms already know about.

• When buying stuffed toys for infants, pay extra and get only machine-washable ones.

• Hand-me-down toddler toys and any shareables should be washed to discourage the spread of germs. Water-safe toys can be run through the sink like dishes and drip-dried in the drainer. Others can be wiped with a cloth wrung nearly dry in soapy water. (Avoid potentially poisonous cleaners and *always* rinse.) Pay special attention to handles, knobs, and heads. Tub toys and other toys—especially many of the ones made for kids under two years old—are safe in the top rack of the dishwasher—a great way to disinfect rattles, pacifiers, and teething toys.

• Most plastic and rubber surfaces can be safely wet-washed. Strong and harsh cleansers and scrub pads will remove paint, eyes, and the like, so be careful. Most battery-operated toys will be ruined if immersed, so just wipe them clean. For electronic toys and gizmos, lightly spray the cleaning cloth—not the toy—with mild detergent solution and carefully wipe the surface clean. Board games and pieces can usually tolerate a quick wipe-down, and so can wooden toys. The marching band horns and kazoos deserve special attention since they're among the most likely to pass on the latest virus. The nearly indestructible fast food chain giveaways will hold up to just about any cleaning you're willing to dish out. And if you can manage to spirit Fuzzy Wuzzy away while snookums is asleep, see "Stuffed Animals/Toys"; "Dolls."

If it's not cleanable, don't give it to a kid.

▶ **Toy cleaning tools:** I like what I see on the toy aisles lately, scaled-down child-size hand vacs, toy vacuums, mops, irons and ironing boards. These aren't just for little girls—let's start early to encourage the idea that *we all clean.*

Tracks of Sliding Doors

Tracks are a natural settling place for things—the insect casualty contributions blend together with dust, hair, dead leaves, and all kinds of other fallout and the moisture that always condenses on glass or mirrors. Then you have a sticky stubborn track. If you let it get to the point where the thing won't push shut or slide easily, someone will spring it or force it askew. To reverse the situation, use a spray bottle of all-purpose cleaner solution. Spray the track generously and let it attack the track buildup. Lots will loosen, so first just wipe the bulk of it out with a paper towel and toss it. If your fingers won't fit down in those little grooves, drape a terry cleaning cloth over a screwdriver blade and run it up and down a few times until the buildup is gone. Then spray again and let the solution work again (much more effectively this time); repeat until the track is gleaming. Run the door back and forth vigorously a few times at the end to clean the wheels or glides, then wipe dry. Then aim a couple of shots of WD-40 at them.

Trash Cans. See "Garbage Cans."

Trash Compactors

With its ability to reduce household trash to one-fifth of its original volume, a compactor is a handy appliance to have. Most of the problems with these are the result of procrastination and improper use. First of all, limit the amount of wet garbage you compact; put wet garbage down the disposer in your sink, if you have one. If not, consider bagging such things as meat and fish scraps and extremely wet things and disposing of them separately. Also, don't put disposable diapers, personal hygiene items, and other odor-prone materials in the compactor. Because a compactor compresses trash so effectively, filling it often takes a while and smelly stuff can get pretty ripe before the bin is ready to empty.

The easiest compactors to use and clean are those where the compaction bucket lifts right out, such as the GE Compactall. This type will accept generic bags, or you can use no bag at all, saving on expensive special compactor bags. Whatever type you have, you need to open it up once in a while and clean out the inside. Before working on your unit, be sure to lock

it in the OFF/LOCK position, according to your instruction manual. Remove the compactor bucket or drawer, and wipe down the inside of the cabinet with disinfectant cleaner. (See "Cleaners, Disinfectant.") Wear rubber gloves and be careful, because the interior of the compactor can hide glass fragments from broken bottles. The instructions that come with your compactor will tell how to get the ram down so you can clean the top of the ram pad. While you're inside there, replace any depleted odor-control filters or deodorant canisters. In good weather, the easiest way to clean the compaction drawer or bucket is outside, the same way you clean a garbage can. (See "Garbage Cans.") Finish up by wiping down the outside of the cabinet and polishing it with a dry cloth. Appliance wax can be used too, to keep it shiny and protected.

Trashing

Trashing sounds like a honky-tonk adventure or a junk food diet, but it's just the professional term for removing the contents of garbage cans and wastebaskets. Trash-handling is a big part of cleaning, and there are ways to streamline it and make it less obnoxious:

1. When you clean the whole house, or when trash pickup day is upon you, use the approach we use in commercial buildings. Leave the receptacles where they are and go from one to another with a large box or can and empty them all into it. This method is much better than ten trips back and forth with ten trash cans.

You can also empty the largest trash can first (the tall Rubbermaid kitchen can in our house) and use it as your collector. (That's much easier than trying to empty things into a loose plastic bag.) This way you only have to make one trashing trip. Never set the large container in a central location and bring all the little ones to it. Carry the larger one right to each smaller one, dump, and move on to the next. Most of those little cans and baskets contain light things such as paper and cloth scraps, so your big container shouldn't get too heavy to handle.

2. Tip, don't lift. Some of the larger plastic bags full of garbage can weigh 30 pounds or more and are often lodged tightly in the can or barrel. Lifting them up and out is a back and neck strainer for sure. I learned something at twenty-five from a seventy-year-old janitor who emptied the trash faster than I (and the trash cans janitors have to deal with can be *50 pounds* or more): He'd tilt the can over—this releases the vacuum that often holds the bag in—and drag the bag out, never lifting a thing!

3. Use good, sturdy plastic containers and don't bother with plastic liners. I know those little baggies are convenient, but they aren't really necessary in most wastebaskets. You may need to use them in places such as the kitchen or in the alley for final pickup, but wherever you can, just use plain plastic cans and wash them a couple of times a month. This will cut costs and send fewer plastic bags to the landfills. Use liners only when you're up against wet or dirty trash.

For environmental considerations, use paper liners whenever possible.

4. Cut your garbage and you cut the handling. Every time I haul trash out of a house or commercial building, I can't help thinking how unnecessary much of it is. The next time the neighbor's dog hits your garbage, take a look at what's strung out all over the lawn.

TSP (Trisodium Phosphate)

One of the complex phosphates used as builders (see "Builder") in detergent formulation, TSP has largely been replaced by sodium tripolyphosphate because tripoly is a more effective water softener. Window cleaners used to favor TSP for cleaning exterior windows, until they learned it was streaking and etching the aluminum spandrels on modern skyscrapers. Though you still see TSP recommended in hint and tip columns for everything from mopping floors to soaking laundry, it's really a cleaning dinosaur. It was superseded long ago for most purposes by safer and more effective products. It is still used to provide alkalinity in powdered cleansers, however, and to clean and degloss old oil-based gloss enamel paint before repainting. See also "Phosphates"; "Detergent."

Tub Enclosures. See "Shower and Tub Enclosures."

Tub and Tile Cleaners. See "Hard-Water Deposits."

Tung Oil

An oil extracted from the fruit of the tung tree, tung oil is used not only as an ingredient in paints and varnishes but as a sealer and protective coating for fine wood surfaces and sometimes metal surfaces such as brass as well. Tung is a natural product that dries to a satin patina with many of the characteristics of varnish, though it's less durable. It's particularly effective when rubbed into a wood surface by hand. The excess is then removed by wiping with a dry cloth.

Turntables, Record

Turntables have a way of collecting dust, which is bad news, because dust and dirt can easily drift from the turntable to the records and the stylus themselves and wear them out before their time, besides worsening sound quality.

This is why most turntables come equipped with a dust cover, which should be IN PLACE not only when the machine is not being used but even while records are playing.

Because dust covers never manage to keep all the dust away, you should dust your turntable (and the dust cover, inside and out) at least weekly. A clean soft lint-free cloth with no chemical treatment or polishes on it is best for this. You can also use an ammonia-free glass cleaner such as Sparkle, being sure to unplug the machine first and spray the cloth, not the turntable. Never use solvents of any kind on the turntable face or base; they could dissolve the finish. Put the tone arm into the locked po-

sition while you wipe around on there, so you don't risk jarring its delicate balance out of alignment. Don't dust the cover during play, or you'll create static electricity that can pull the tone arm right up off the record!

The rubber or vinyl circle the record rests on (the platter—often removable) can be cleaned with a cloth lightly dampened in neutral cleaner solution (see "Cleaners, Neutral") or with alcohol. Beneath the platter (depending on the type of turntable you have—gear or belt driven) are gears or a belt that should be cleaned according to manufacturer's instructions with alcohol or Freon cleaner from an audio store. Never put oil or oily cleaning products on the gears or belt or *anywhere* on a turntable.

Turpentine

A volatile solvent distilled from the resins of pine trees, turpentine is used widely as a paint thinner. Perpetuators of old wives' tales love to recommend turpentine as a spot remover, an ingredient in home-brewed cleaners, and even as a medicine. Because of turpentine's aroma, flammability, and tendency to leave gummy deposits, however, another solvent would be a far better choice for removing oil and grease stains. (See "Solvents.") As a liniment, who knows? Check with your horse doctor.

Typewriters

The dust cover—remember the dust cover that came with your typewriter? (That thing you stuffed in the desk drawer and forgot?) Well, that's the key to maintenance here. If you don't cover your typewriter it will quietly fill up with dust, hair, and oily deposits from the air that will eventually cause key skips, stuck keys, and other little irritations. Electronic models are nearly maintenance-free if you keep a lid on them. Wipe the keys as needed (weekly if you're a prolific writer) with a cloth dampened with all-purpose cleaner or alcohol. Your owner's manual may tell you how to remove the platen (paper roller) and wipe it with alcohol. This is a good time to brush or blow out dust, hair, and erasure debris too. A can of compressed air is good for this purpose. Older models need to have the type cleaned with a gum-type cleaner available at stationery stores.

A long-neglected typewriter should be taken in to a professional repair shop for reconditioning. It'll be disassembled and chemically cleaned even in the impossible-to-reach spots, lubricated, tightened and realigned as necessary, and checked out for overlooked injuries and impending repairs.

U

"Urinal Colonel," one of my nicknames

▶ **Uglied out:** The condition carpet reaches when it's worn and dirt saturated to the point of no return. It won't clean up properly and it's so far gone it isn't worth trying. Replacing it is the only real solution.

Ultrasonic Cleaning

Ultrasonic cleaning is a process in which ultrasonic sound waves (those above the frequencies audible to the human ear) are passed through a cleaning solution to provide a gentle, invisible scrubbing action. The object to be cleaned is immersed in a tank of cleaning solution that is vibrated by ultrasound. The agitation created by the sound waves cleans more effectively than the solution's chemical action alone ever could. Ultrasonic cleaning is used most often for delicate items or ornate objects with recesses it would be difficult to reach with a scrub brush. Today it's used for cleaning everything from jewelry, dentures, and contact lenses, to machine parts and window blinds. You can take your ritzy rubies to a jeweler for ultrasonic cleaning, or buy one of the small units available for home use. And a phone call will bring an ultrasonic blind cleaning truck right to your door.

Umbrellas

To keep your umbrellas good-looking and in good working order, the best advice from Mary Poppins and me is to avoid getting or letting them stay

▶ **Unblemished:** Unused or unlived in.

wet on the *inside,* where the joints might rust. Always leave an umbrella open to dry after use. Mud can just be hosed off when you get home, then shake and dry the umbrella before storing. If it's dirtier than that, water-based cleaning products won't hurt an umbrella, but solvents can dissolve the glue and the acrylic (waterproofing!) coating on it. Sponge on a solution of all-purpose cleaner or hand dishwashing detergent, let it sit on there a minute or two to dissolve the dirt, then rinse and dry.

For grease and other stains on umbrellas, see "Spot and Stain Removal."

Under Cleaning

Under—the realm of dead spiders, frayed moths, and ants cemented in the syrup we spilled six months ago. No wonder we usually confine our "under" cleaning to about the first two inches.

You weren't always this anti-under cleaning, till you tried it. Remember when you tied a soapy rag or wet towel around a yardstick and attempted to make a pass or two? The yardstick came out bare on the second whisk . . . and that towel, now stiffer than a starched sock, is still under there somewhere.

Don't just wait till you move to clean under (the washer, dryer, dresser, or refrigerator). The only moral thing to do is about once or twice a year (and that's enough), get some help for an hour or so and go through the house and move and clean under everything.

First, pick up any nuts, bolts, marbles, pens, or petrified pet food that might damage your vacuum. Use your vacuum to remove the dustballs, dryer lint, dead bugs, mouse manure, and less threatening loose stuff. Then attack the stuck-on soil and dried puddles of heaven-knows-what. Apply a liberal quantity of all-purpose cleaner (a little disinfectant or deo-dorizer added is a nice touch too) and let it soak. After a few minutes, wipe it up and hit any remaining stubborn soil with a white nylon-backed scrub sponge, mop, sponge, or squeegee up the cleaning water and rinse.

Don't do any other cleaning when you do this, just the under stuff, and you'll be done before you know it. See also "Cushions, Underneath."

Utility Brushes. See "Scrub Brushes."

V

Varsity, my cleaning company that started as a college crew

Vacuum Bags

First of all, don't let vacuum bags get more than half full! The function of a vacuum bag is to let air pass through while trapping dust and dirt. As a bag fills, there's less surface area available for air passage. The pores of a bag also fill up with dirt particles over time, impeding the flow of air. It's that air movement that creates a vacuum's suction, so when it's cut off or reduced, the cleaning power of a vacuum drops dramatically.

Not long ago, all vacuum bags were cloth. The disposable paper bag was developed to overcome some of the drawbacks of cloth bags, so now you can choose the type of bag that best meets your needs.

Paper bags have smaller pores that don't load up with dirt as quickly as those in a cloth bag. And since we dispose of the bag when it's full (which as just noted means *half* full) and install a new one, there's no gradual reduction of air flow and cleaning power as time goes on. Your old vacuum cleaner can breathe like new again each time you change the bag.

Disposable paper bags are also better at filtering out very small dust particles than their cloth cousins. And the whole bag-emptying operation is quicker and neater. But this added efficiency and convenience costs: almost a dollar every time you replace a disposable bag, whereas a cloth bag costs nothing to empty. And you do have to store the replacement bags and find them when you need them. (Some upright models, including Eureka, have extra bag holders right on the machine.)

Cloth bags are long-lasting and reusable, but because they're so susceptible to dirt clogging, they tend to reduce suction after a while, even when maintained meticulously (which most of us don't do). If you decide to go for a cloth bag, here's how to get maximum performance from it: Empty it when it's no more than one-third full—before it gets seriously asthmatic. After you empty it, take it outside or in the garage and give it a good shaking—this knocks impacted dirt out of the pores. Hold the mouth of the bag down on a piece of newspaper with your feet and shake the daylights out of the rest of it. If the bag closure unhooks from your vacuum so you can leave it on the bag until you're through shaking, this makes it easier to keep dust from escaping and flying around. Don't ever attempt to wash a cloth bag, but once in a while, turn it inside out and vacuum the inside carefully with a canister vac to get it really clean. Inspect the bag periodically for leaks or holes, and replace as needed. When you put the bag back on, make sure all seals and openings are snapped tight and shut, to prevent air (and dust!) leakage. Cared for in this manner, a cloth bag can be *almost* as good as a disposable, and a whole lot cheaper. That's why I personally still use them.

Vacuum Bottles

We seem to like to age vacuum bottles awhile in the backseat or trunk of the car, or somewhere in our desk at work before we actually clean them, but the right way to go about it, in case you've ever wondered, is as follows:

Glass-lined bottles may be easy to break, but they're also easy to clean. Just wash them out with hot dish detergent solution, rinse, and set them upside-down to dry. Be sure to leave them open until they dry, otherwise the same vacuum that keeps the chicken broth and the cocoa hot will create a wonderful warm little breeding chamber for bacteria. Never put anything—brush, cloth, or finger—down into a glass vacuum bottle and scrub around with it or shake it around—not even ice—or you risk hearing that familiar old clinking sound inside.

Steel bottles are lined with stainless steel, which makes them safe from breakage—you can wield your bottle brush at will—but there is a little line inside where the steel of the bottle is welded together and it is vulnerable. Never use any chlorinated cleaner such as chlorine bleach or bleaching cleanser in a steel bottle or it will attack the weld and destroy the vacuum. Again, just use dish detergent, hot water, rinse well, and up-end to dry.

Proceed carefully with all-plastic bottles (the kind that keep Junior's soup barely warm until noon). Check the packaging it came in, or the bottle itself—many are not dishwasher-safe. Clean with soapy water and bottle brush, rinse well, and upend to dry.

You don't want to immerse any kind of vacuum bottle, because there is always the chance of water seeping down between the bottle and the lining. You can fill them with soapy water and soak the inside, though, if you have a tough puddle of hardened tomato soup in there. Keep abrasive cleansers and scrub pads off plastic and steel exteriors alike; on the former you risk marring the surface or removing any decoration on there, and on the latter, scratching or dulling the paint.

About the only stains that afflict vacuum bottles are hard-water and coffee stains. On both glass and steel interior bottles, these can be removed with Dip-It, the coffeepot cleaner. To freshen the inside of musty, odd-smelling or tasting bottles, fill with baking soda-and-water solution and soak. A soak of strong tea should banish a metallic undertaste. (If you store your vacuum bottles with the stopper off, you're much less likely to have odors to remove.)

Vacuum Care

Here's how to keep your vacuum running long and strong:

- Keep the bag emptied—even a half-full bag will sap cleaning power up to 40 percent.
- Don't run over the cord or let it be pinched in doorways. Interrupt your vacuuming frenzy and move the plug *before* you hit the end of the cord and bend the plug prongs.
- Don't use extension cords on a vacuum—they can overheat the motor.
- Replace worn or stretched belts.
- Don't vacuum up marbles, thumbtacks, coins, paper clips, forks, and other hard objects—they can damage the interior of your machine and cut down suction.
- Check impeller blades or fans once a year or so. If they're chipped, replace them to keep air flow and suction strong.

The impeller fan of a vacuum, the part that creates the suction

- Replace beater bar or brush roll brush strips as needed—worn, stubby brushes can't reach down to pull out deeply imbedded dirt.
- Check the beater bar for cracks or

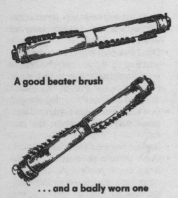

A good beater brush

... and a badly worn one

jagged edges that can snag carpet pile, and clean any accumulated string and hair off the beater bar bearings and pulleys.

- Keep bags, filters, seals, and gaskets in good repair to prevent fine dust from being blown back into the air as you vacuum.
- Don't let the kids ride on it or your spouse take it in to work.
- Always buy genuine original-manufacturer parts from a dealer or manufacturer. Most warranties are invalidated if you ruin a vacuum by using a renegade filter or bag.

Vacuuming

Nothing will extend the life of carpets (and for that matter, other furnishings) more than faithful vacuuming. Regular vacuuming removes the dirt and grit that grind and wear away at carpet fibers as we walk over the floor. An effective carpet vacuum must have two things: a beater bar or brush or brush roll to vibrate embedded dirt up out of the carpet, and a strong enough air flow to pick up the loosened dirt and whisk it into the bag. (See "Vacuum Care" for how to keep your vacuum running strong.) Be sure to adjust the height on the pile adjustment so the beater brushes just lightly whisk the top of the carpet—if the motor slows down noticeably when you lower it onto the carpet, the beater is adjusted too low.

Don't use a beater bar on wood or hard-surface floors, especially wood. It does no good and also can catch something like a piece of gravel, and throw it into the surface of the floor and dent or scar it. Use a plain brush floor tool to vacuum hard-surface floors.

Always police (pick up) the area before you vacuum. No matter how expensive and powerful your vacuum, if you vacuum up coins, apple cores, and small toys, they will tear the turbulator off the fan inside, and you'll eventually be left with no suction. Always reach down and pick the big stuff up and put it in your pocket.

Vacuum into the room. Almost all of us head for the far corner of the room and start to vacuum our way out, backward, backing over and into furniture and fighting the cord all the way. We do this so we won't footprint our freshly vacuumed carpet. Everyone else will be tromping all over it in a few minutes anyway, so what will your single steps matter? Next time (and from now on) vacuum into a room, it's much faster and your cord will last longer.

Don't feel obliged to vacuum every square inch of carpeting every time—the edges and out-of-the way areas don't get walked on, so even if a little soil accumulates there it won't hurt them. A good vacuuming program will include the traffic areas every day (okay, two or three times a week if that's the best you can do) and edges and corners maybe once a week. In your daily vacuuming pay special attention to heavy-use areas, such as entrances and hallways. Vacuum slowly and carefully here, and overlap your strokes, to get out all of the tracked-in grit and dirt. When you're vacuuming anywhere, going over the carpet once slowly does more good than zipping over it three times quickly. Take your time and let the vacuum work for you. The beater bar needs time to loosen the dirt and the air flow needs time to suck it up.

As for stairs, they aren't so bad anymore because there are lots of

ways these days to get them: a canister vac with attachments; hand-held vacs such as Eureka's Step-Saver with a beater bar, or your upright. I like wielding my upright on the riser—I can actually hear the dirt rattle out of the carpet—but this is too cumbersome for some. The center edge of the stair is where most of the dirt ends up, so concentrate your efforts there. In between vacuumings I swipe a damp cloth in the corners and along the back to pick up any lint, grass seed, what have you.

Vacuums

Uprights: For vacuuming carpet day in and day out, notice what the professional maids in hotels and hospitals use—a professional-quality upright. A machine like this will not only do an

VACUUMS

hand-held with power head

hand-held cordless

canister

wet/dry vacuum

self-propelled upright

professional-quality upright

▶ **Fast pickup!** If you attach a VacuMag magnet strip (manufactured by Korsen Industries, Boise, Idaho) to the bottom edge of the front bumper of your vac, it'll pick up all those nails, bolts, staples, paper clips, and other metal pieces that usually clunk-click up your vacuum. No more bending and retrieving, and the fan in your vac won't have to be replaced as often!

excellent job, it's so maneuverable it can be handled easily with one hand. It has a good strong beater brush or bar in the head that thumps and vibrates the carpet, to move all that stuff down deep in the pile up to the top so the air flow can suck it away. A professional-quality or commercial upright not only has stronger suction, it has a heavier motor and bearings and is more durable overall. You can even get one with a 50-foot cord. You can find commercial uprights at janitorial supply stores; for home use you want one with a 12-inch-wide head.

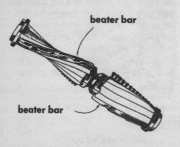

beater bar

beater bar

The beater bar of an upright vacuum

Canister vacs: A good strong canister vac with a power head or brush roll is okay too, but more cumbersome to assemble and use. Where a canister unit comes in handy is for upholstery, stairs, corners, edges, and underneath things. Canister vacs are at their best in noncarpet vacuuming and in jobs that call for attachments, such as dust brushes and crevice tools.

Vacuum Attachments

Here is a generic guide to attachments that will end, once and for all, that embarrassing quandary: "But which attachment do I use?" Attachments are available for canister, upright, and wet/dry vacuums, but uprights tend to become awkward and tip over when you clamp on the converter needed to connect the attachments to the machine. Although they vary slightly from manufacturer to manufacturer, each species of attachment does have distinct characteristics that will aid you in identification:

1. *Crevice tool:* A long, narrow tube with a flattened tip to reach into those hard-to-get-at places such as corners and the crevices at the sides of appliances.
2. *Dusting brush:* A small, usually circular brush for blinds, windowsills, baseboards, and shelves—anything that might get nicked if those little brushes weren't there to cushion things.
3. *Floor tool:* A wide (approximately 12-inch) head with brushes for vacuuming hard-surface floors;

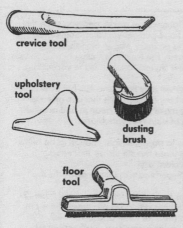

crevice tool

upholstery tool

dusting brush

floor tool

Vacuum attachments

there is also a version without brushes for carpeting, called a rug tool.

4. *Upholstery tool:* A small wedge-shaped nozzle—usually without brushes—used for cleaning upholstery, stairs, and car interiors.

5. *Power head* (for canister vacuums only): A motorized head with beater brushes that really work that carpet over. If your vacuum has one, it will not only pick it all up—fast—but give you a sense of power and make the rug look well-groomed as well as litter-free.

6. *For wet/drys:* Squeegee-head attachments for pushing water into a pool that can be vacuumed up much more easily.

Cordless vacs: The hand-held type is great for quick pickups and spot vacuuming in home, car, and RV, and

the cordless uprights offer the same kind of convenience. These are part of the resurgence of the electric broom type of vac such as the Superbroom. Handy? Yes. Easy to empty? Sure. Convenient? You bet. Good for deep cleaning? Nope. These little wonders are for any small area cleanup that doesn't call for a beater bar—kitchen, dining room, patio, bathroom, and so on.

Wet/dry vacs: For versatility, nothing beats wet/dry vacs, which can be used for a shop vac, cleaning out the car, picking up wet spills, and disposing of water. They can pick up large, dry debris as well as liquid and can be fitted with a wand attachment for water or flood pickup. They can also be a big help in stripping hard floors, cleaning out fireplaces, construction cleanup, emptying the fish tank, and other imaginative applications.

A type of vacuum we'll be seeing more of in the future is the *central vac*. This is a powerful unit mounted in the basement, attic, or garage, with piping that leads to an outlet in every area of the house you vacuum. All you carry around is a lightweight vacuuming hose and head. All the noise, bag-emptying, and mess are confined to the remote central unit. Central vacs can be installed in existing homes as well as new ones, and beater-brush heads are available for them.

Specialized, high-efficiency vacuums are also available for those with dust allergies. These include the Rainbow water-collection vacs and those with HEPA filters.

▶ **Vacstravaganza:** We've come a long way in carpet cleaning since the rug beater and the old (preelectricity) hand-pumper vacuums. Some of us haven't come very far past the plain old ordinary plug-in models, though. They do a good job so we stick with them. The twenty-first century is upon us, so do be aware that we have some new choices to aid us in the vacuuming process.

1. *Handhelds* were almost a novelty when they first came out, but now have much better bags and even beater bars or brush rolls that can effectively remove pet hair, and the like. They make it easy to clean in and around things and adjust for all the angles of stairs and upholstery.
2. *Micro-vacs* (See "Computers.")
3. *Full-size cordless vacs.* They're easy to store and light enough to be really easy to use, and they can be put in those remote places that need vacuuming but may not even have electricity!
4. *Better electric brooms* such as the Superbroom are more powerful than some of the old full-sizers.
5. *Wide-track vacs.* Standard vacuums for standard houses usually have 12-inch-wide heads. But now, for big homes with acres of carpet, there are 16-inch machines that cover the carpet a lot faster and just as well.
6. *Self-propelled vacs* do more to make life easier than a self-propelled mower. Don't make light of the idea until you've tried one.

Vaporizers

After every use, drain the water from the vaporizer tank—be careful if it's hot. Then rinse the tank with warm water and dry. To get those last elusive little puddles of water, you can stuff a cleaning cloth or hand towel inside. To sanitize, add ½ cup chlorine bleach to a half-filled tank, rotate so the solution comes in contact with the entire tank, rinse well and dry. The outside of the tank—and the whole unit—can be cleaned with a cloth dampened with all-purpose cleaner.

In hard-water areas, mineral deposits can build up quickly inside a vaporizer and clog the heating element, causing excess steaming or even overheating. The operating instructions that came with your vaporizer will tell you how to disassemble it and remove mineral scale from the critical parts, especially the steam outlet holes and safety vents and electrodes. Using distilled water or rainwater instead of tap water, or the special cleaning tablets provided by some manufacturers will at least slow down mineral buildup.

For cool-mist vaporizers, see "Humidifiers."

Varnished Surfaces

As used here, *varnish* means any finish that forms a clear protective coating over wood, such as shellac, lacquer, varnish, or urethane. It's often hard to tell exactly what kind of clear finish a particular piece of furniture or wall paneling may have, but they can all be cleaned pretty much the same. Even though the wood is protected by the finish, it's a good idea to limit the amount of water used and to keep the time the water is on there to a minimum. Some of these finishes will develop white spots and cracks if wetted for too long, and water seeping into cracks and crevices can swell and deteriorate the wood itself. Wood furniture and paneling is best maintained by regular dusting, spot-cleaning to remove spots and spills, and polishing with a furniture polish as needed. (See "Furniture Polishes.")

When wet cleaning is necessary, as for greasy kitchen cabinets, wash with a mild detergent solution (or a stronger solution if necessary—see "Cabinets, Kitchen") and polish dry with a soft cloth. The oil soaps formulated especially for wood do a good job because they leave a slight oily residue on the surface that can be buffed up to a nice shine. A white nylon-backed scrub pad is okay for removing stubborn spots, but don't use heavy-duty cleaners, abrasives, steel wool, or colored scrub pads unless absolutely necessary, as they can scratch and dull the finish. Avoid the use of strong solvents such as lacquer thinner or alcohol too, as they can soften and mar the finish. If the finish looks dull and hazy after washing, you can apply furniture polish to restore the shine and bring out the color of the underlying wood. Remember that polishes containing wax will build up and eventually need to be

removed. For wood floor care, see "Wood Floors."

Vases. See "Bottles/Vases."

Velcro

There's nothing handier than Velcro for closing things or keeping babies entertained (how many little ones do you know who can resist playing with the Velcro fasteners on their shoes or diapers?). But before long we have fuzzed-up Velcro (always the rough or "hook" side). If it gets bad enough, it can prevent those little fastener strips from performing their very important function—catching or closing securely. To remedy, take a clean piece of Velcro (again, the "hook" side) and run it through the contaminated piece—this acts as a comb to remove any fibers and threads caught in the hooks.

To keep your Velcro inviolate, always close all such fasteners before laundering. Then the lint and other debris in the water won't be able to catch on the hooks (and the hooks won't be able to catch and injure sheer or delicate fabrics).

If you stain or otherwise soil a Velcro fastener, it's made of nylon, and can be spotted and cleaned like any other nylon fabric.

Velour

Though *velour* is sometimes applied to lighter-weight velvet-type fabrics used in jackets and other apparel, the heavyweight velvet pile fabrics used for upholstery and draperies are what is usually referred to as *velour*. Velour upholstery should be regularly vacuumed or brushed to remove dust and lint. Spot-clean as needed to remove spills and stains. (See "Stains"; "Spot and Stain Removal.") For thorough cleaning, follow the directions under "Furniture, Upholstered." For crushed or flattened pile, steam the area with a steam iron, then brush the nap upright with a stiff brush. Velour draperies require professional dry cleaning. If in doubt, send it out!

Velvet

Once mainly silk or wool, rich-looking velvet fabrics are now more likely to be manmade fibers. A few velvets (such as jersey velvet) are washable, but the rayon and acetate/rayon velvets used in evening wear and other garments should be dry-cleaned. If in doubt, take it in for professional cleaning—this is not a fabric to gamble with. *Velveteen* is the name often given to cotton or cotton blend velvets, and most often these are washable—check the care label. If you do wash velvet, turn it inside out to reduce linting, wash in warm water on the delicate cycle, and tumble dry.

Between cleanings, velvet should be brushed to remove lint and dust and hung on padded hangers. Never fold it for storage or hang it with pins, clamps, or clips, or cram it into a crowded closet. Crushed pile can be brought back to life by hanging it over a steaming bathtub and gently brushing. Never iron velvet—steam it. For velvetlike upholstery fabrics, see "Velour."

Velvet shadows are caused by velvet drying at an angle that reflects the light. After cleaning velvet (especially furniture), it pays to brush or smooth the pile all in one direction.

Vicuña

Luxurious yarns and garments are made from the soft, silky hair of the vicuña, a wild llama-like animal of the Andes Mountains. Vicuñas can't be domesticated and no shearer is nimble-footed enough to clip a wild one, so the fiber is rare and expensive. Vicuña coats are in the same price category as fur. Because of their cost, vicuña garments should be cared for by a professional dry cleaner familiar with the handling of furs and fine fabrics.

Videocassette Recorders and Camcorders

You may not be high-techy enough to record on the thing, but you better take a minute and learn how to clean it. Especially when you add up how much you've got tied up in video tapes, camcorder, and VCR—not to mention the home entertainment center to display it all in.

The video heads are the heart of a VCR, and to get the sharpest picture and brightest color from the tapes, they have to be clean. Over time tapes shed oxide particles onto the heads, and the usual airborne pollutants—smoke, dust, pet hair, and dirt—also build up on them. Rental videos make it worse by transferring gunk from someone else's machine to yours. All this accumulates not only on the heads but on the VCR drive system and eventually causes a distorted picture and sound—and will even start damaging your tapes!

Replacing the heads costs as much as the whole machine, and cleaning at the service center is also expensive. You can avoid all this by using a cleaning cassette regularly. There are wet and dry tapes; I prefer the former. You put a couple drops of the special solution provided on the ribbon of the cleaning cartridge and pop it in the machine. As it goes around, the wet part of the ribbon dissolves gunk on the head and the drive system (capstan and pinch roller), the dry part wipes it away. Godzilla never looked so good!

Vinegar

Vinegar is forever being recommended as a cleaner, for everything from windows and floors to false teeth. It may squeak, but it isn't really very good at what we might call basic wet cleaning—removing soil and breaking down grease. Because most soils are acid, an alkaline cleaner is much more effective at cutting them. (See "Chemistry of Cleaning.") Vinegar doesn't have the emulsifying ability of a soap or detergent either. (See "Emulsify.") Vinegar does have value as a rinsing agent, though. Custodians have long used a vinegar rinse (½ cup vinegar per gallon of water) to neutralize the alkaline residue left by wax strippers and floor cleaners and leave surfaces bright and streak-free. Likewise, added to the rinse water it will remove detergent

residue and assure you shinier, less spotted glassware and brighter colored laundry. Undiluted, vinegar is also a fair lime scale remover. It works slower than a phosphoric acid descaler, but it's better, tastewise, for such things as coffeemakers and coffee- and teapots. Vinegar's acid personality also makes it good for brightening stained aluminum and (mixed into a paste with salt) for removing tarnish on brass and copper. Vinegar is used in many stain-removal procedures, especially on silk and wool, which don't tolerate ammonia well. It functions as an acid spotter, a neutralizing agent, and a mild bleach. You don't want to use it on cotton, linen, or acetate, however. Vinegar (as in bowls of vinegar water set around the affected area) does have some deodorizing ability, but odor neutralizers (see "Odors") do a better job.

When you do use vinegar for any of the above, make sure it's plain white distilled vinegar.

Vinyl

The vinyl plastics, all made of vinyl chloride, are a diverse family of materials found in everything from plumbing pipe and floor covering, to shower curtains and beach balls. As vinyl flooring is covered separately (under "Vinyl Sheet Floors"; "No-Wax Floors"), the following refers to the vinyl fabrics and imitation leather used for upholstered furniture and automobile interiors, wall coverings, and the like. For everyday cleaning, simply damp-wipe vinyl with all-purpose cleaner solution and buff dry with a towel. Textured vinyl can be scrubbed with a brush. For tough soil and occasional deep cleaning, use one of the specialty vinyl cleaner/conditioners. In addition to effective yet safe cleaners, these products contain plasticizers that rejuvenate the vinyl to help keep it soft and supple. Plasticizers are what keep vinyl pliable, but they tend to leach out over time, especially in the presence of sunlight and ozone. If not treated with a conditioner from time to time, vinyl will eventually get hard and brittle and crack. Using strong or harsh cleaners on vinyl will only hasten the process.

Don't attempt to oil vinyl as you would leather—some oils (even body oil) will cause vinyl to harden. For this reason, it's a good idea to clean the headrest and armrest areas of vinyl-covered furniture regularly.

Don't use abrasive cleaners on vinyl; they will dull the shine and may eventually scrub away any pattern printed on the fabric. Some insect sprays will soften vinyl, and heat (such as from a lighted cigarette) will scorch or melt it. And solvents such as acetone, lacquer thinner, dry-cleaning fluid, and nail polish remover will damage if not dissolve it. Alcohol can be used to remove inkstains, but be sure to rinse it off afterward. Plastic products can be disinfected safely with chlorine bleach, but be careful not to combine it with dish detergent. This creates a chemical combination that could harm the surfaces being cleaned. First wash the vinyl article as usual, then rinse. Then rinse again with a solution of 1 tablespoon chlorine bleach to 1 gallon of water and air-dry. Do not rinse the bleach solution off; allow it to disinfect the surface. At this concentration bleach is not harmful to plastics.

As for vinyl car tops, if you have a light-colored top—tempting as it may be—don't bleach it! After a thorough scrub and rinse with vinyl top cleaner (plain soap and water will have a tough time removing vinyl top grime and oxidation) and a *plastic* bristle brush, allow the vinyl to dry. Then apply a vinyl conditioner such as McGuire's 40, available at industrial paint and hardware supply stores. Vinyl conditioners contain special ultraviolet protectors and should be used as often as one washes the car to prolong the life of the vinyl. And don't park that car in the sun!

Vinyl shower curtains and tablecloths can be washed in the washing machine in a short gentle cycle and warm water (with maybe a couple towels for cushioning), and then a warm rinse and a short spin cycle. Or you can take them out of the washer just before the last spin cycle, shake out all the water you can, and hang them up nice and straight to dry. If you put a vinyl curtain in the dryer, make sure it's low or no heat or put it in only for a few minutes, then take it out and hang it while it's still warm. You can add chlorine bleach to the washwater if you need to kill mildew.

Vinyl Asbestos Tile

Before it was discovered that certain types of asbestos fibers are carcinogenic, a lot of vinyl composition tile (VCT) was made with asbestos.

Safer mineral fillers are now being used to make VCT, but much vinyl asbestos tile is still in use, and care in maintaining it is advisable. Studies have shown that even some ordinary maintenance procedures can release asbestos in dangerous amounts. Tile of this type should be kept well covered with a protective layer of floor finish and stripped as infrequently as possible. Only wet-stripping and wet-scrubbing should ever be done on it, using the least abrasive pad and slowest machine speed possible. Dry-scrubbing, dry-buffing, dry-burnishing, or dry-stripping—or for that matter foot traffic on unwaxed tile—can release hazardous amounts of asbestos into the air.

Removing old asbestos tile is a job best left to asbestos removal specialists, who can do the job without endangering health.

Vinyl Sheet Floors

All sheet flooring sold nowadays is vinyl, either inlaid or what is called *rotovinyl*. Inlaid vinyls are the top of the line in price and quality. They're thick and resilient and the pattern goes all the way through the sheet. Rotovinyls (short for *rotogravure*) have a thin, photographically reproduced or printed pattern layer, overlaid with a clear wear layer of vinyl or polyurethane. Most no-wax flooring (see "No-Wax Floors") is this type. Rotovinyls vary in price and quality—in general, the thicker the wear layer, the more durable and expensive the flooring. Many vinyls also have a cushioning layer to muffle noise and

provide comfort underfoot. Most sheet goods sold today for residential use are no-wax, but there's still a lot of needs-wax vinyl in older homes and commercial buildings where the heavy traffic demands the renewable protection of wax.

To maintain waxable vinyl, first remove any dressing or temporary finish that may have been applied at the factory, and apply several coats of emulsion floor finish. (See "Floors, Stripping for Waxing"; "Waxing Floors.") Sweep and mop regularly to remove damaging grit and keep appearance bright. Scrub and recoat traffic areas with floor finish as needed to maintain uniform gloss and protection. (See "Waxing Floors.") When the finish gets discolored and dirty-looking, strip off the old finish and rewax. Finish can be maintained with a floor polishing machine if desired. (See "Buff"; "Burnish.") For maintenance of no-wax floors, see "No-Wax Floors." For black marks on vinyl, see "Black Marks."

Vinyl Tile

Vinyl tile can be solid vinyl, VCT (vinyl composition tile) in which various mineral fillers are bound in with the vinyl, or no-wax vinyl. Solid vinyl tiles are the best and the most expensive—they're softer underfoot, more flexible, and they won't chip. VCT is a durable flooring used widely in commercial buildings and, along with asphalt tile, was also popular in homes for a long time. In the past, vinyl composition tile was often made with asbestos fiber, and even though the asbestos has since been replaced by safer mineral fillers, there's still a lot of this type of flooring in use. (See "Vinyl Asbestos Tile.") No-wax or rotovinyl tile (see "No-Wax Floors") is the type most commonly available for do-it-yourself installation.

Maintenance of vinyl tile is the same as for sheet vinyl flooring (see "Vinyl Sheet Floors"), except that extra care must be taken not to let water stand on the floor. Flooding can loosen the adhesives that glue the tile to the floor, causing it to curl up at the seams.

W

Wonderful things happen when you come clean.

Waffle Irons

Waffle irons are easier to clean than they used to be. Manufacturer's directions will tell you how to season the grids with cooking oil and give you any special instructions for clean-ing the particular finish on yours—metal, Teflon, and so on. Doing so will give you a nonstick surface that doesn't take much maintenance. In general, let your iron cool, unplug it, and wipe off any splashes on the out-side while they're still soft with a soapy sponge or all-purpose cleaner. Then wipe-rinse and polish dry. Brush crumbs from the grids and wipe with a water-dampened cloth. If you do have stubborn burned-on batter on there, don't scrape or scour. Dip a paper towel in ammonia or just plain old clean dishwater and leave it on the spot for several hours or overnight. On anything but nonstick finishes, any last traces can then be removed with a soapy steel wool pad. Removable grids can be washed in hot soapy water. Rinse and dry well and reseason after washing.

Wallboard

You shouldn't be cleaning any unfinished wallboard! Raw wallboard and other gypsum wallboards will soak up water like a sponge, and the water will make it swell and crumble. Unfinished wallboard should have the joints taped and then be primed and painted to protect it from water damage. For good cleanability, you want to put on one coat of PVA drywall sealer followed by one or more coats of latex semigloss or satin (or even gloss) enamel. Wallboard finished in this manner can then be cleaned according to the directions given under "Painted Surfaces."

Wall Coverings

Wall coverings come in four basic types: the old-fashioned, nonwashable printed wallpaper; modern (plastic-coated) washable papers; vinyl wall coverings; and fabric wall coverings. Each type has distinct cleaning requirements.

Nonwashable paper: Fortunately, there's less and less of this around. If you're not sure what kind of paper you have, test by wetting with a mild detergent solution in an inconspicuous place. If the paper absorbs the water, darkens, or the colors run, it's nonwashable. Wipe this kind down with a rubber dry sponge (see "Dry Sponges"), an art gum eraser, or one of the dough-type wallpaper cleaners. Grease spots can be removed with K2r. Crayon marks can sometimes be lifted by placing a piece of blotting paper on the stain and ironing with a warm iron. Ink and dye stains are generally not removable. Never scrub it and just remember—it's *paper*!

Washable paper: Coated with plastic to resist water, this can be gently wiped with a damp cloth or sponge. Use a neutral cleaner and go easy on the water, especially on seams and edges. Don't flood the surface, and don't leave it wet for more than a minute. They may say "washable," but most plastic-coated papers won't tolerate harsh detergents, hard scrubbing, abrasive cleaners, or prolonged exposure to water. Mild solvents such as dry-cleaning fluid and alcohol can be used to remove ink or greasy stains.

Vinyl wall coverings: Usually called "scrubbable" by the manufacturers. These can be solid vinyl or have fabric or paper backing, but the vinyl surface is completely washable and can even withstand scrubbing with a brush or a white nylon-backed scrub pad. Just take care not to overwet the seams. Mild solvents such as alcohol and dry-cleaning fluid can be used for ink, wax, and similar stains, but don't use acetone, lacquer thinner, or harsh abrasives unless you're tired of the design. (See "Vinyl.")

Fabrics: Available in everything from silk brocade and linen to burlap and jute, even string cloth and grasscloth. Most fabric wall coverings are not cleanable with water. They should be vacuumed periodically to remove dust and dry soil. Marks and smudges can often be removed with an art gum eraser. Gentle blotting with dry-cleaning fluid may help with some spots, but most stains on this type of wall covering are not very removable. Loose strings can be glued back in place with Elmer's Glue-All.

Wall Coverings, Woven

It may look like burlap, but chances are it's a clever imitation. While natural grasscloth and woven wall coverings are still being made, the vast majority of these handsome textured backdrops are now made of vinyl. This durable and easy-care material can be made to look so much like burlap and other natural fibers, it's hard to tell unless you run your hand over them or get up real close. Considering the susceptibility of natural fibers to stains, moisture damage, and mildew, it had to happen. For care of vinyl wall coverings, see "Wall Coverings."

If you do have true burlap or other woven wall coverings, the best thing to do is to vacuum periodically with a dusting brush attachment to keep dirt from accumulating. Oily stains can be treated sparingly with dry cleaning solvent or K2r, but don't use water at all. Some spots and stains will respond to gently wiping with an art gum eraser or a dry sponge. See "Dry Sponges."

Wallpaper. See "Wall Coverings."

Walls

Here's how to wash painted walls and ceilings like a pro. After vacuuming or dry sponging (see "Dry Sponges") the wall if it's really dirty, find yourself a sponge and fill one bucket three-quarters full with a warm solution of neutral cleaner or hand dishwashing detergent. If the latter, squirt in about the same amount you'd squirt into a sinkful of dishes. Have another, empty bucket for wringing out your sponge. Dip the flat face of the sponge into the cleaning solution only about half an inch—this will keep water from dribbling down your arm as you work. Start at the top of the wall and spread the solution over as large an area as you can easily reach—the detergent will immediately begin to dissolve the soil. Now squeeze (don't twist) your sponge out into the empty bucket and go back over the wetted-down area a second time. On this second pass, the wrung-out sponge will absorb the dirt-laden water and leave the wall almost entirely clean. With the other hand, polish the sponged area dry with a terry cleaning cloth. (See

"Cloth, Cleaning.") Squeeze the dirty sponge into the empty bucket again, then dip it into the cleaning solution and repeat on the next section of the wall. When you finish, the catch bucket will be full of dirty water, and your cleaning solution will have stayed crystal clear and full-strength the whole time. See also "Textured Walls and Ceilings."

► When cleaning walls in the kitchen, you might want to use degreaser solution behind the range and in other grease-catching areas.

Washing Machines

Take a good look around the top of the washer before you drop in the next load—at the control panel, under the lid, in those charming little dispenser pockets, around the rim of the washer drum and even on top of the agitator. (Dust! Dirt! Fingermarks and spills! Pocket residue and petrified detergent!) Pick up any loose debris with a damp cloth and use a soggy sponge to wet down any hardened residue for a while to soften it for easy removal.

The control panel, front, and sides of the washer can be spritzed with glass cleaner and wiped dry with a soft cloth.

Icky dispensers can be scrubbed out with all-purpose cleaner and a small brush. Dispenser pockets with a mineral scale buildup can be cleaned with phosphoric acid cleaner.

To get under the washer top to clean: Unplug the machine and re-

lease the spring clips/tabs under the front corners of your washer top. Wipe away any crusty stuff with a damp sponge, presoaking for a while if necessary to soften. Dry.

Clean the lint trap: If it isn't self-emptying, remove the lint trap after each use; check your manual for the exact location—it's often in the rim of the washer basket or in the top of the agitator. Rinse clean, scrubbing if necessary with an old toothbrush or small scrub brush. The lint filter is easiest to clean when the lint is wet: Remove it and knock it hard against a wastebasket. If any lint remains, rinse the filter under warm water and clean with a brush if needed.

Washer tub: Use a soft, dry cloth to wipe the inside dry after use. Leave the lid up until the basket is dry. To sanitize the washer, select a rinse cycle and fill the washer for the smallest load size. Before agitation starts, add 1½ cups of liquid chlorine bleach to the water, and close the lid.

Some Don'ts for Interiors

Don't soak anything in chlorine bleach, vinegar, or acid solutions in the washer; don't use the washer to soak things indefinitely or store wet laundry, especially urine-soaked clothes.

Exterior

- Don't do any pretreating on or near the washer or dryer. These products can damage the finishes and dials.
- To prevent dulling or damaging of the finish, wipe up spills right away with a damp soft cloth.

- Don't place sharp or heavy objects on or in a washer/dryer. Check pockets for nuts, bolts, or tools. Remove pins, buckles, and the like.

Washing Soda

Washing soda is a strong alkaline salt (sodium carbonate) that occurs in nature as soda ash. It is used in most laundry detergents and other powdered cleaners to boost alkalinity and help soften hard water. (See "pH in Cleaning"; "Detergent "; "Builder.") Washing soda is recommended as an all-purpose cleaner in all the old USDA bulletins, but it can't compete in cleaning effectiveness with modern detergents.

Watches

From expensive jeweled movement beauties to disposables, watches are hydrophobic. Even the ones labeled water-resistant are meant to endure only accidental contact with moisture, and their resistance can easily be weakened by wear and damage. So don't just keep cleaning solutions or any liquid well away from your watch: Remove it when you wash your hands or when you're working with water and only wipe it with a dry cloth. Don't even use water on the band—it's too likely to end up on the watch itself. The band may tolerate a damp cloth, but keep the watch itself dry. Leather bands can be cleaned with saddle soap and metal bands with a tiny bit of ammonia on a soft cloth, but remove the band from the watch first (by removing the spring-action pins at either side of the case that hold it on). Dry a watch immediately if it does happen to get wet, and if it takes a bath (a lot of watches are drowned in the kitchen sink), take it to a qualified repairperson as soon as possible.

Fine watches are designed to give the wearer a lifetime of use, but that doesn't mean you should just use them until they quit, without a thought to maintenance, as we do. The oil that lubricates the inner workings thickens and congeals over time, and dust can accumulate and increase the friction on the moving parts. You can't clean the insides, that's a jeweler's job. Watches should be professionally serviced at least every three to five years to prevent undue wear if not untimely demise. The smaller a watch, the harder it works and the more often it needs cleaning.

Replace a scratched or broken crystal immediately, before it has a chance to let in dust or moisture. And try to replace the battery in electronic watches before it runs down, to head off damaging corrosion from dead and leaking batteries. Watch batteries last six months to two years, depending on how many functions besides mere time-telling the watch is performing.

Hand creams, perfumes, aftershaves, and the like are hard on watches and can discolor the crystal or turn it milky as well as corrode the case plating. The more creams and powders you use, the more often your watch should be cleaned. Wiping with a soft cloth after each wearing is the best remedy. Silver polishes and jeweler's cloth contain abrasives, and many of even the best watches are plated, so after several such cleanings the precious metal will be wearing thin.

Water

This precious substance covers three-quarters of the earth's surface, is necessary to sustain every form of life we know, and we sure couldn't do without it in cleaning.

1. It is a universal solvent—it can dissolve a wide range of soils, unaided by any chemicals.
2. We can easily add chemicals to it that have the ability to penetrate and dissolve additional soils.
3. It holds dissolved soil—in "suspension" during the cleaning process, until we can flush or wipe it away.
4. Whether in an automatic clothes washer, a high-pressure spray, or a simple hosing, its gentle currents or powerful stream can provide mechanical action that further aids cleaning.

Water's amazing ability to penetrate, dissolve, and suspend soils is further enhanced by the surfactants, emulsifiers, and other active ingredients in today's cleaning formulations. See also "Chemistry of Cleaning"; "Surfactant"; "Detergent"; "Soap"; "Emulsify"; "Soap Scum."

The type of water you use, however, will make a big difference. Hard water diminishes the power of soaps and detergents and may form dingy gray soap curds in laundry and bathtubs. It also forms hard-water scale on plumbing fixtures, which increases cleaning time and effort. (See "Hard-Water Deposits"; "Water Condition-

ing.") Hot water is much more effective for cleaning than cold water, especially if it can be kept hot. For floor mopping, wall washing, and the like, where a small amount of water is spread over a large surface, the cleaning solution quickly becomes room temperature anyway so hot water doesn't make much difference. Cold water will cut down your cleaning power even in such situations, though, and may make it hard to dissolve some types of cleaning compounds.

▶ **Water alone:** Won't clean dirt well, especially old dirt. You need a chemical—soap, detergent, or solvent—to penetrate, lift, and loosen the dirt. So don't try to clean without a cleaning solution. Hosing off the walk or driveway is about the limit!

Waterbeds

Never fear, you won't have to empty the waterbed in order to clean it. You do want to keep a conditioner in the water at all times, though, to prevent the growth of bacteria. Blue Magic Water Conditioner is a good one, used according to the manufacturer's instructions. Cleaners specially formulated for waterbeds are generally available where you purchased the bed.

For the vinyl bag ("mattress" or "bladder" portion of the bed), use a vinyl cleaner and conditioner. It removes hair and body oils, perspiration, and body ash. It also refreshes the plasticizers in the vinyl. There are many brands on the market; the best is Blue Magic Vinyl Conditioner and Cleaner. You may notice that the vinyl appears to be dusty when you're changing the linens. It isn't actually dust, but rather a bleeding-off from the vinyl itself. This is a definite sign that a vinyl conditioner is needed. Follow label directions for frequency.

Water Conditioning

Water conditioning can mean any treatment of water to improve its purity, clarity, taste, or smell. The conditioning we're most concerned with when it comes to cleaning is water "softening," or the removal of minerals that interfere with the action of soaps and detergents, form hard-water scale, and stain fabrics and fixtures. Hard-water scale also clogs pipes and water heaters, complicates the cleaning of plumbing fixtures, and makes clothes and linens wear out faster. (See "Hard-Water Deposits.")

The main culprits in the creation of scale are calcium and magnesium, and the minerals that most often cause stains are iron and manganese. Eighty-five percent of the United States and a large part of Canada has water hard enough to benefit from water conditioning. There are two ways to accomplish this:

1. *Chemical water conditioners.* These are usually powders that can be added to water to counteract hardness minerals. Most laundry detergents contain water-softening ingredients, and mild hardness can often be overcome just by using more detergent. For extremely hard water, a powdered water softener added to wash water may give better results.

However, this takes care of the problem wash water only, it doesn't do anything for rinse water or scale buildup in pipes and on plumbing fixtures.

2. *Mechanical water conditioners.* These are appliances that remove hardness minerals through a process known as *ion exchange.* A water conditioner is tied into your home plumbing and will condition all the water used throughout the house. People on low-sodium diets often leave the kitchen cold water hard for drinking and cooking, as the ion exchange process does add sodium to conditioned water.

Installing a water conditioner will make cleaning chores go faster and easier and can save a family of four up to $50 a month by decreasing plumbing repairs and the amount of soap and detergents used, by lengthening the life of laundered clothing, and by increasing the efficiency of hot water heaters and other water appliances. In addition to softeners, water treatment dealers have filters and other devices to improve the quality of drinking water. See also "Water"; "Soap"; "Detergent"; "Soap Scum."

Water Softening. See "Water Conditioning."

Wax. See "Floor Finish"; "Waxes."

Wax Applicators

We're generally so relieved to finally have the floor stripped and clean we'll use any old rag or cloth available to apply the wax. True, anything that

A wax applicator attachment to a long-handled floor scrubber

will spread wax in a thin, even coat will work (mop, cloth, sponge). The important thing is to have the applicator folded or formed into the shape of a pad so that it holds the wax and distributes it evenly, and doesn't cause it to bubble, foam, or streak. The ideal applicator for home use is a lambswool pad on a long-handled tool (see "Scrubbee Doo") so you can wax from a standing position. You can see better and wax faster and your back won't hurt later.

You can use a supermarket grade sponge mop when laying a supermarket wax because a lower-grade finish

like this has fewer solids. A commercial-grade finish (see "Floor Finishes") will hold up much longer, but will bubble more if applied with a sponge mop, and sometimes the bubbles may not completely level out.

If you're using a sponge, dampen it to soften it before you start. But it isn't necessary to wet a lambswool applicator before you use it. This time-honored custom is meant to prevent the applicator from soaking up so much wax, but the wax will eventually wick up and replace the water anyway.

Pour a 4-foot-long "rope" of wax out on the floor, stick your applicator in the middle, and spread the wax as evenly as possible. Then pour additional "ropes" of wax out as you need them, as you go, and spread them. Don't pour out a big puddle or you'll end up working too large an area at once.

Don't go over and over the floor when you're applying wax, or it will foam and bubble. Covering the surface a couple or at most three times should be enough to catch any skips. If you do see a few small streaks or tiny bubbles as the wax is drying, don't worry—most waxes today have what is called a leveling agent in them, so little things like this should smooth themselves out as the floor dries. If you go back over and over the surface before it dries you'll have a big mess!

Wax Buildup

The term *wax buildup* refers to the accumulation of wax or floor finish in low-traffic areas, such as corners,

▶ **Shine on!** If the surface you just cleaned doesn't shine like it used to, check these possibilities: (1) It wasn't rinsed and soap scum or detergent residue was left on there; (2) you didn't use the right type of cleaner to dissolve the kind of dirt on there, so the dirt's still there; (3) you used too strong a cleaner and cut or clouded the surface of the wax or floor finish. Decide which is your problem and change your ways!

along edges, and underneath furniture. Manufacturers have made giant strides in developing nonyellowing floor finishes, but most of them still take on a dirty, hazy appearance over time. This is because of dirt incorporated into the wax layers and the natural darkening of the finish with age. After six or eight coats of finish have been applied to a floor over a year or so, the whole floor, and especially the corners and edges, will start to look dark and dirty. This is because foot traffic never wears the wax off in these areas, and it just sits there and gets old and ugly. The only cure is to strip off the discolored wax and start over. To minimize buildup, smart waxers wax the corners and edges only twice. Then they recoat only the traffic areas after that, when they get dull. See also "Waxes"; "Floor Finishes"; "Waxing Floors"; "Floors, Stripping for Waxing."

Wax Strippers

Cleaning hints and tips and old wives' tales would have us stripping wax with everything from ammonia to Spic and Span, but a professional wax stripper will do the job faster and better. Go to a janitorial supply store and ask what they would recommend for the specific type of flooring and floor finish you have. If your floor is a modern vinyl (no-wax, vinyl tile, or vinyl composition tile) and you've been using a water-based floor finish, the best bet will probably be a rinseless stripper. These products soften old wax quickly and don't require as much scrubbing and rinsing as traditional strippers. The labels on some of these will say that you don't have to scrub or rinse at all, but you'll find that a certain amount of both will be necessary.

For asphalt tile and linoleum, you'll have to be careful what stripper you use. Ammoniated and harshly alkaline products, as well as some of the rinseless strippers, can damage and discolor these older floors. Wood floors that have been waxed with solvent-based waxes need a solvent stripper.

Waxes

Though we often use the term *wax* to mean any type of floor finish or polish, a true wax is a naturally occurring substance of animal, vegetable, or mineral origin. Beeswax, for example, is an animal wax; carnauba (from palm trees) is a vegetable wax; and paraffin is a mineral (petroleum) wax. Waxes have been used for centuries to protect and shine things. Today various waxes are blended to make finishes for flooring and wood paneling and for polishing furniture. Synthetic polymer (plastic) floor finishes have largely replaced the true waxes in floor care, with the exception of wood and cork floors, which are still maintained with solvent-based waxes. (See "Floor Finishes"; "Wood Floors.") Waxes are softer than polymer floor finishes and usually must be buffed to produce a shine. They are fairly water resistant but very easily dissolved by solvents, and tend to be slippery. Carnauba is still widely used to maintain wood furniture and paneling, but care must be taken not to overuse paste wax as it will build up over time. (See "Furniture Polishes.") Car waxes used to be just that, but today they're complicated mixtures of natural waxes, silicones, and polymers designed to offer optimum protection to your car's paint.

Waxing Floors

Waxing is the term we use for applying a floor finish, whether it's a true wax or a synthetic polymer finish. (See "Waxes"; "Floor Finish.") Most floor finishes today are polymers (liquid plastic); the true waxes are reserved for wood, cork, and other water-sensitive floors. *The following instructions are for the polymer finishes;* for waxing wood floors see "Wood Floors"; for waxing cork floors see "Floors, Cork."

Before waxing, always make sure the floor is clean and free of detergent residues. (See "Floors, Stripping for Waxing"; "Floors, Scrubbing and Waxing.") Sealing very rough or porous floors with an acrylic sealer before you ever put on any wax will give a smoother, glossier surface. Wax with a clean string mop or a

lambswool wax applicator used exclusively for this purpose. Waxing with the same mop you apply detergent with will contaminate the wax and cause it to break down and wear off quickly.

To wax an average, home-size or small floor, use a lambswool applicator. It isn't necessary to wet the lambswool before use, just pour a 4-foot-long "rope" of finish on the floor and spread it out with the applicator.

For a large area, use a string mop. Wet the mop with water first, and wring it out as dry as possible before putting it in the wax. Put the wax in a wringer bucket and spread with the mop.

Spread the finish in a smooth, even film—if it puddles or bubbles, it's too thick; if you have streaks and skipped places, it's probably too thin. When waxing with a mop, use smooth, overlapping, side-to-side strokes—push/pull strokes cause bubbling.

Be sure that each coat is completely dry (it usually takes thirty to forty-five minutes) before putting on another coat. On a freshly stripped floor, apply the first two coats wall to wall, After that, to maintain, just recoat the traffic areas when they get dull. Constantly recoating corners and edges and under furniture where wax never wears off just invites wax buildup and sets you up for more frequent stripping. Two to four thin coats should be applied on a freshly stripped floor, to provide uniform gloss and good protection. Several thin coats are better than a big thick one that will not dry evenly.

Wet/Dry Vacs. See "Vacuums."

Wet Spotters. See "Spot Removers."

Wetting Agents

Wetting agents are chemicals that enhance the ability of a liquid to wet a surface. The surfactants in soap and detergent are wetting agents. Among other things, they lower the surface tension of the water, allowing it to sheet out over the surface and penetrate soil. Without wetting agents added, water tends to bead up, especially on oily soil. The rinsing agents used to achieve streak-free drying in dishwashers and car washes are also wetting agents. See "Surfactant"; "Rinsing Agent."

Whisk Brooms

Whisk brooms are still used in the major leagues to dust off home plate. These miniature brooms may not even have a handle, just straw laced together tightly with twine. These can come in handy in tight spots where a big broom won't or can't work, or where there isn't space to store one. They're great to aid in dustpan pickup, to quickly whisk out the car, and to clean off incredibly dusty, grimy ledges and countertops in awful places like the cellar, garage, and shed. Many things a whisk broom can do, a counter or shop brush (see "Counter Brush or Broom") or handheld vac can do better.

Wicker

Wicker is a term used loosely to refer to furniture made from woven reed, rush, cane, willow, and other plant fibers. Note that word *woven*—don't confuse wicker with furniture made entirely from solid stalks of rattan or bamboo. (See "Rattan and Bamboo.") You may hear that it's good to hose down wicker furniture or even put it in the shower occasionally, but don't believe it! Treatment like that may be okay for unfinished rattan, cane, and bamboo (experts spend their spare time arguing about this), but it's definitely not good for woven rush or reed. Most experts recommend that you don't put water on unfinished wicker at all. Overwetting raw rush or reed items will only shorten their life. And if the wicker is finished with a clear sealer or paint (which most of it is), soaking with water will swell the fibers and make the finish crack and peel. Don't put any furniture polishes, waxes, or oils on wicker either—they just leave a sticky film that attracts dirt.

Regular dusting with a vacuum

brush attachment is what the wicker doctor prescribes. Occasional damp-wiping won't hurt sealed wicker and may even help keep it from drying out, but don't get it too wet. An old toothbrush can be used to reach all those little knots and loops and crevices.

Wicker holds up fairly well in humid areas but soon gets brittle and fragile in arid climates. For hard use or families with young children or cats, it's not a very good choice. For proper care of rattan or bamboo furniture, see "Rattan and Bamboo." For woven cane, sea grass, or fiber rush seats, see "Cane."

Willow. See "Baskets"; "Wicker."

Window Cleaners. See "Glass Cleaners."

Windows

The only way to clean windows, or any large expanse of glass, is with a squeegee. It does a faster and better job, and it's more fun. So stop trying to do it with supermarket sprays and homemade brews, paper towels, rags, and newspapers.

You need a professional-quality squeegee, a window wand, and an extension pole if you'll be doing high windows. See "Squeegees"; "Window-Washing Wands"; "Extension Poles." The basic process is simple—apply the cleaning solution with the window wand, then pull all the dirt and water off with the squeegee.

Now the details:

1. Put a capful of ammonia or 5 drops of liquid dish detergent in 2 gallons of water. Resist the urge to use too much detergent; that is what causes streaks.

2. Dip your window scrubbing wand or a sponge ¾ of an inch into the solution, picking up just enough water to wet the window without flooding it. Wet the entire window, then go back over it once to loosen any stubborn soil. Last, go all around the window against the frame with the scrubber to pick up any dirt you've pushed against the frame.

3. Dampen the squeegee blade before you start, and wipe it with a damp cloth between strokes. A dry blade will skip and jump on the window instead of gliding smoothly.

4. Tilt the squeegee at an angle so that only about an inch of the rubber blade presses lightly against the top of the window glass. Then pull the squeegee across the window horizontally. This will leave a 1-inch dry strip across the top of the window. By squeegeeing across the top first, you eliminate drips running down.

5. Place the squeegee close to the frame in the dry area near the top, and pull down to about 3 inches from the bottom of the glass. Continue this way all across the window, overlapping into the clean, dry area with each stroke, and wiping the blade with a damp cloth after each stroke.

6. Finish with a horizontal stroke across the bottom, and wipe any water off the sill with a damp cloth.

On some windows, it's easier to cut the water off the frame side as well as the top, and then squeegee the entire pane using horizontal strokes.

Large (picture) windows should be wet and squeegeed half at a time, the top half first.

Window-Washing Wands

Use a window-washing wand to apply the cleaning solution before you squeegee a window and it will indeed be like a magic wand. Pros developed these wands for speed of application and minimum drip. They also have just the right degree of scrub for the amount and type of dirt and debris on the average window. Window wands can be used for shower walls and car washing, and the like as well, and they'll fit on the end of an extension handle (see "Extension Poles") for higher reach. There are even angle-head wands available that enable you to do a lot of windows without changing position.

Window wands consist of a sheep-skinlike or soft nylon mesh cover that slips over a T-shaped head. Some models have a nylon scrub strip set on one side of a lambswool head, and all can easily be replaced when they have scrubbed one window too many. You can get wands at hardware and janitorial supply stores. For home use, the 10- or 12-inch size is best.

To use a window wand, dip it about three-fourths of an inch into window cleaning solution (a rectangular or diamond-shape bucket comes in handy here—see "Buckets"), just enough to wet the glass, then use it like a

Window-washing wand

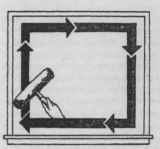

When using a window wand, wet the whole surface of the window and go over it again quickly to dislodge any stubborn dirt. Then go all around the edge of the window to pick up any dirt you may have pushed against the frame.

giant paintbrush to swab the window. Go over the surface once to wet it and then again quickly to dislodge the bug bodies and bird droppings. Last, go all around the edge of the window to pick up any dirt you may have pushed against the frame. Then squeegee the window dry. Give the wand a good bath in warm soapy water when you're through, then rinse it well and let it dry before putting it away.

Wood

Architects love to design raw cedar and redwood planking into homes because of the rustic look and rich aroma. But professional cleaners know that leaving raw wood exposed anywhere is just asking for trouble. Wood is very porous, and unless sealed it will absorb every stain and be extremely hard to clean. (See "Sealing.") If you're in love with the natural look, use a penetrating sealer that doesn't alter the appearance of the wood. For maximum cleanability, choose a satin or semigloss urethane or varnish that covers the wood with a clear protective coating and gives it a slight gloss that enhances the natural color. Oiled wood is better than no finish at all, but it's not anywhere near as cleanable as something like urethane. Once a finish like urethane is on, you're not really cleaning wood, you're cleaning the urethane or paint or whatever—just follow the directions for those surfaces.

If you do have raw, unfinished wood that needs cleaning, try a rubber dry sponge first. (See "Dry Sponges.") Anything the dry sponge won't take off will probably have to be sanded out. A damp cloth may remove some stains from hard, close-grained woods, but water will usually just spread stains and drive them farther into soft and open-grained woods. Using more than just a touch of dampness can cause many unfinished woods to swell, warp, and buckle. Wood with a good waterproof finish (paint, varnish, urethane, lacquer) can be washed like any other wall or ceiling, but limit the amount of water being used and keep the time wetted to a minimum. See also "Painted Surfaces"; "Plywood"; "Particle Board";

"Varnished Surfaces"; "Wood Floors."

Wood Floors

Wood floors are back in style. People everywhere are ripping up carpets and restoring the hardwood floors they couldn't wait to cover up with shag rugs 20 years ago. As wood floors get a new lease on life, we're also changing the way we care for them. The traditional method has been to apply a penetrating sealer and then wax the floor with a buffable paste wax. This is a laborious process and was probably the reason folks couldn't wait to convert to carpet originally. There are a variety of new finishes available today, from factory-finished seals to hard, quick-dying catalyst seals, and if you have a relatively new floor you will want to contact the manufacturer for specific care recommendations. On an older floor the smart move is to convert it to a no-wax floor by giving it two to three coats of polyurethane or other finish designed for wood floors. (See "Varnished Surfaces.") This forms a tough, protective film over the wood, which then only requires care similar to a no-wax floor. NOTE: Just like the no-wax floors, different wood finishes will eventually become dull from traffic and require some kind of waxing or refinishing to maintain the desired gloss.

New Wood Floors and Factory-finished Wood Floors

Many newer wood floors are factory finished, because of the ease of installation. Most parquet floors in homes, for example, are factory finished with either hot wax or polyurethane. If your wood floor has V-shaped grooves between the planks, it's probably factory finished, and you'll need information from the manufacturer on what kind of finish has been applied and whether it needs waxing.

If you aren't sure what kind of floor you have, the safest approach is to call a professional wood floor dealer who will come out to your home (usually for a modest fee) and render an opinion. For an existing floor that has been waxed, the best bet is to keep on waxing—at least until it is time to refinish the floor.

Waxing

Most older wood floors have been waxed or are safe to wax. For waxed floors, use either a liquid or paste wax (solvent base) formulated specifically for wood floors. Liquid is easier to apply, but paste lasts longer. The one-step clean-and-polish products are easiest of all, but they don't stay on the floor long enough to make the effort worthwhile. Use a water-based floor wax only if the floor has a sealed finish in good condition. Wax buildup and the eventual wet-stripping it calls for can damage floors without a sound seal. To apply solvent-base paste wax, you'll want to rent or own a commercial-grade single disc floor polisher—15 inches is a good size for home floors. Use a steel wool pad on the polisher to clean the floor and apply new wax, then a buffing brush

or pad to bring up the shine. Solvent-based liquid wax can be applied with a lambswool applicator (see "Wax Applicators") on a Scrubbee Doo, but many still need to be buffed to get a good shine. Always follow the manufacturer's directions for whatever wax you're using.

Stripping Off the Wax

Because of their sensitivity to moisture, wood floors should generally be screened (see "Refinishing") rather than stripped to remove old wax. You might, however, want to strip before screening if there is a heavy buildup. Screening off a thick coat of wax takes time and clogs the sanding screens. When stripping a wood floor buy a good commercial stripper. Wood floors that have been waxed with solvent-based waxes will need a solvent stripper. Mix up the solution and do a small area at a time; get a friend to help you if possible so you can move fast. Mop the solution on and give it a quick scrub (see "Floors, Stripping for Waxing"), then wet/dry vacuum the solution back up. The main thing is to get the solution on and off the floor swiftly.

Refinishing

In the past, sanding was the usual way to remove the old finish from floors when refinishing. The problem is that floor manufacturers have engineered the thickness of wood floors very precisely for maximum life and minimum cost and weight. Every time you sand a floor, you remove ¹⁄₁₆ to

⅛ inch of the wood. Too much sanding will weaken the structure and strength of a floor, causing cupping and cracking. Sanders are also hard to control and can leave unremovable gouges in the floor if not used properly. Screen sanding is much easier on you and your floor. A sanding screen looks much like a window screen. It attaches to a professional buffing pad and comes in different grits, like sandpaper. It takes very little wood off the floor but cuts through the finish. A professional buffer with a sanding screen is fairly easy to operate, and the chances of permanent damage to the floor are almost zero. After screening, the floor can be resealed with two coats of polyurethane or other sealer designed for wood.

Regular Maintenance

Whether the floor is waxed or urethaned, regular care is the same. Dirt grinding under people's feet is a wood floor's number-one enemy, so the first step is to dust-mop, sweep, or vacuum daily to keep the floor free of grit and dust. (See "Sweeping"; "Dust-Mopping"; "Dust and Dust Control"; "Mats, Walkoff.") Mat all entrances with good commercial walkoff mats and wipe up spills immediately. You can damp-mop urethaned floors with a light neutral cleaner solution occasionally to keep them clean and shiny. Always rinse the floor with clean water. Because water is damaging to wood, it is a good idea to limit its use even on urethane-finished floors. Use just a damp mop, not a dripping wet one,

and don't flood the floor with water or let moisture remain on the floor for more than a minute or two. For waxed floors, periodic buffing and rewaxing will be necessary.

Wood Cabinets. See "Cabinets, Kitchen."

Wooden Bowls/Utensils

Season unvarnished wooden bowls and utensils with mineral oil before using; this seals the wood to keep food and liquids from penetrating it and will ensure that the grain stays smooth. Especially if the bowl or utensil in question is used for food service, mineral oil is the only oil you want to use, because it's nonpoisonous and won't go rancid. Pretreat with oil at least once a year, applying it generously all over, inside and out, and then let it sit on there for several hours or overnight.

Never put anything made from wood in a dishwasher. Instead, clean your woodenware with a damp cloth and mild soap or detergent solution. If necessary, immerse it quickly in warm soapy water, rinse, and dry it immediately. *Never* soak woodenware in water, or it will swell and crack or split. And don't store it in very hot or humid places.

Woodwork

Woodwork (painted, stained, or varnished) might be easy to forget, but it's also one of the easiest things in the house to clean. All we have to do is dust (with a lambswool duster) or vacuum (with a dust brush) it. When it needs more than that, simply wipe it with a sponge dipped in all-purpose cleaner solution and gently scrub as necessary. Then polish it dry with a clean terry towel. Most woodwork (casings on doors, around windows, etc.) is well sealed or varnished so water can be used on it. Baseboard woodwork is more of a hassle because it collects lots of marks and scuffs as well as lint, hair, and other debris that seems to delight in gathering and sticking there. If you just wash it, the fur and dead flies will get on your sponge and in your solution and all over everything. So the first thing to do after you vacuum or sweep the floor is to take a damp paper towel and wipe your way over all the baseboard. This will pick up all the loose junk off the board and even the edge of the carpet. From there it'll be a cinch to wash and clean.

Black marks on baseboards should be removed not with steel wool or powdered cleanser—which will leave a dull patch more obvious than the original mark—but with all-purpose cleaner, a white nylon-backed scrub sponge, and a little patience. See also "Baseboards."

Woven Wood Blinds. See "Shades and Roll-up Blinds."

Wrought Iron

In decorative railings, fences, gates, security bars, outdoor furniture, and the other places we usually see it, wrought iron rusts easily and must always be protected from moisture. This is generally accomplished with a coating of rust-inhibiting primer and paint. The maintenance of exterior wrought iron usually consists not so much of cleaning as it does keeping the protective coating intact to prevent rust. As the paint weathers and begins to chip and crack, it must be reapplied to keep the metal protected. Preparation should involve removing all rust down to bare metal by wire brushing, sanding, or sandblasting. The bare spots should then be primed with rust-inhibiting metal primer and repainted with an oil-based industrial enamel or rust-resistant metal paint. Painting over rust or using water-based paints may provide temporary relief, but the problem will soon be back to haunt you. Important as it is to cover the surface thoroughly when you paint, don't put it on too thick, or those graceful lines will start looking gobby (and a chip will look like a miniature Grand Canyon). If/when you do have to clean exterior wrought iron (it's a target that bird bombs rarely miss), just hit it with all-purpose cleaner solution and a scrub brush, then hose to rinse.

Interior wrought iron isn't such a rust problem, and can be kept looking good with just regular dusting and occasional damp wiping. Just make sure you dry it immediately and don't leave water puddled on it.

X-rated cleaning!

▶ **X:** What to make in the bottom of the bowl if the men keep missing the toilet.

Y

You heard right. There's nothing wrong with making a mess, it's *leaving* it. . . .

Yellowing

Fabrics: Over time, light-colored and white fabrics can take on a dingy, yellow cast. This can be caused by storing them in the dark for long periods but is usually the result of in-

complete removal of body oils, especially in polyesters. To prevent: Use as hot a wash as the fabric will tolerate, and don't skimp on detergent. A hot-water wash with extra detergent and extra agitation time will usually remove built-up oils. The use of a bleach safe for the fabric or fabric whitener/brightener may also be called for. Hanging yellowed clothing or linens in bright sunlight will also help bleach and whiten them.

Bleach-sensitive fabrics such as spandex, silk, wool, and even nylon can be yellowed (often permanently) by washing them with chlorine bleach. (Read the care label!) If the care label says "dry out of direct sunlight," it means the fabric contains fabric brighteners that will be irreversibly yellowed by exposure to sun.

Hard surfaces: If you take down a picture that has hung in one spot for a long time, the wall may be yellowed behind it. This is because many paint pigments tend to yellow over time, but the bleaching effect of ultraviolet light keeps them white. When you cover the surface so the light can't get at it, yellowing occurs. Many plastics, such as the resins in floor finish, vinyl flooring, and vinyl upholstery, will yellow similarly with age. Once a surface is yellowed, there isn't much you can do to reverse it, although continued exposure to light may bleach and lighten it over time. A fresh coat of paint or stripping off the old wax or varnish and redoing it is the only instant cure.

▶ **Where to get pro cleaning supplies by mail:** Send for a free *Clean Report*, P.O. Box 39-E, Pocatello, ID 83204.

Z

ZZZZZZ—What you can do when you finish cleaning the easy, professional way I've outlined in these pages.

INDEX

A

Abrasive cleaners, 13
Absorbent compound cleaning, carpet, 60
Absorbents, 13–14
Acetate, 136
Acetic acid, 14, 71
Acetone, 299
Acid cleaners, 71–72
Acoustical tile, 14–16
Acrylic fabric, 136
Acrylic sheet, 253
Aerosol cleaners, 72
Afghans, 16
Agitation, 67
Airborne grease and soil, 16–19
Air cleaners, electrostatic, 17
Air conditioners, 18
Alcohol, 19, 299
Alkaline cleaners, 72–73
Allergies, dust, 120–121
All-purpose cleaners, 73
All-purpose spotters, 316
Alpaca, 19–20
Aluminum, 20
    cookware, 20, 89
    luggage, 217
Ammonia, 21, 40
Ammoniated cleaners, 73–74
Amyl acetate, 21
Angora, 21–22
Anodized (colored) aluminum, 20
Antiques, 22
Antiredeposition agent. See Detergent
Antiseptics, 109
Appliances, 22–23
    drain pans, 115
    filters, 143–144
Aprons, cleaning, 23
Aquariums, 23–25
Area rugs, 217
Artificial flowers and plant, 152–153

Art objects, 25–26
Ash, 145
Ashtrays, 26
Asphalt, 87
Asphalt tile, 26–27
Athletic shoes, 287–288
Attics, 27–28
Attitude, 28
Automatic dishwashers, 108
Automatic dryers, 119, 208
Automatic ice makers, 187–188

B

Baby clothes, 29–30
Backpacks, 30–31
Bacteria/enzyme digester, 31
Baking soda, 31
Bamboo, 265
Barbecue grills, 171–173
Baseball caps, 179–180
Baseball gloves, 32
Baseboards, 32
Basements, 32–33
Baskets, 33
Bathrooms, 33–34
Bathroom sinks, 292
Bathtub rings, 35
Bathtubs, 34–35, 289
Beams, exposed, 35
Beds, 36
Bedspreads, 37–38
Behind things, 38
Benzene, 299
Biodegradable, 38
Black marks, 38–39
Blankets, 39–40
Bleach, 15, 40, 109, 205–206, 208
Blenders, 40–41
Blinds, 41–42, 285
Blocking, 38, 42, 111
Blotting, 43

Bluing, 43
Bone, 43
Bone scrapers, 279
Bonnet system of carpet cleaning, 61–62
Books, 43–44
Boots, 288
Borax, 44–45, 104
Bottles, 45
Bowl caddy, 340
Brass, 45–46, 55–56
Breast milk stains, 30
Brick, 46–47
Brocade, 47
Bronze, 47
Brooms, 47–49, 95–96, 113, 375
Brushes
    cleaning, 48
    counter, 95–96
    grout, 174
    paint, 241–242
    scrub, 281–282
    spotting, 316–317
    toilet bowl, 339–340
Buckets, 49–50, 112, 225–226
Buffing, 50
Builder (in soaps and detergents), 50
Built-in furniture, 7
Burlap wall coverings, 367
Burnish, 50–51
Butcher blocks, 69
Butyl cellosolve, 51, 74

C

Cabinets, kitchen, 52–53
Caddy, cleaning, 53–54
Calcium carbonate, 54
Calphalon cookware, 89–90
Camcorders, 360–361
Camel hair, 54
Cameras, 54–55
Candlesticks, 55–56
Cane, in woven furniture, 56–57
Canister vacuums, 356
Can openers, 55
Canvas, 57, 217, 287
Caps, 179–180
Carbon tetrachloride, 57–58, 299
Carpets, 58–59
    care basics, 59
    deep cleaning, 60–61
    surface cleaning, 61–62

Carpet sweepers, 62–63
Cart, cleaning, 63
Cassette tapes, 332–333
Cast iron, 63–64, 90
Caustic, 64
CDs, 84–85
Ceiling fans, 141
Ceilings, 64–65, 337
Central vacuums, 357
Ceramic cooktops, 88
Ceramic cookware, 90
Ceramics, 56, 70
Ceramic tile, 65
Chamois, 66
Chandeliers, 66–67
Chemical water conditioners, 371
Chewing gum stains, 311
Chimneys, 67–68
China, fine, 68–69
Chlorhexidine, 109
Chlorine bleach, 40, 109, 206, 208
Chopping boards or blocks, 69
Chrome, 69–70
Cigarette smoke, 235, 295
Citric acid, 70, 71
Citrus cleaners, 74
Clay flowerpots, 152
Clay tile, 337–338
Clayware, 70
Cleaners
    abrasive, 13
    acid, 71–72
    aerosol, 72
    alkaline, 72–73
    all-purpose, 73
    ammoniated, 73–74
    citrus, 74
    concentrated, 8, 74–75, 176
    disinfectant, 76
    drain, 115, 117
    glass, 166
    heavy-duty, 73, 76
    homemade, 176, 183
    laundry, 205–207
    neutral, 73, 76–77
    oven, 73, 237
    pine oil, 77, 109
    tile, 338
    toilet bowl, 340–341
Cleaning
    aprons, 23
    attitude, 28

caddy, 53–54
cart, 63
chemistry of, 67
cloth, 79–81
compliments for, 84
deep, 77, 160, 161
design and, 6–8
emergency, 128
energy saving, 130–131
excuses for not, 132
fall, 141
frequency of, 155–156
inventions, 188
kamikaze, 198
order of, 236–237
pH in, 247
prevention of, 6
professional help, 61, 259, 260, 301
reasons for, 3–4
responsibility for, 4–5
safety in, 3, 274–278
simplifying, 8–9, 325
skip, 293
solution, 77–78
speeding up, 301
spring, 318
standards of, 320
storage of equipment, 324–325
ten favorite tools, 58
ultrasonic, 349
under, 349–350
under-the-cushion, 99–100
Cleansers, 78
Clocks, 78–79
Closets, 79
Cloth, cleaning, 79–81
Cloth-covered blinds, 42
Clotheslines, 81
Clothespins, wooden, 81
Cloth vacuum bags, 352
Clutter, 193–195
Coats, 81–83
Cobwebs, 83
Coffee grinders, 173
Coffee makers, 83
Collections, 83
Color remover, 40
Combs, 84
Comforters, 261–262
Compact disc players, 84
Compact discs, 84–85
Compound, polishing, 254–255

Computers, 85
Concentrated cleaners, 8, 74–75, 176
Concrete, 86
Concrete block, 86–88
Cooktops, ceramic, 88
Cookware, 89–92
Coolers and jugs, picnic, 92–93
Cooling filters, 144–145
Copper, 90, 92
Copy machines, 93
Coral, 286–287
Cordless vacuums, 357
Cords, 93–94
Corduroy, 137
Corian, 94
Cork, 94
Cork floors, 149–150
Corners, 94–95
Cosmetic cases, 95
Costume jewelry, 191–192
Cotton, 99, 136–138
Counter brush or broom, 95–96
Counters, kitchen, 96–97
Cow trails, 52
Cross stitch, 231
Crumbs, 97
Crystal, 56, 166–167
Cuisinarts, 154
Cultured marble, 220
Curlers, 98
Curtains, 98–99
Cushions, underneath, 99–100
Cut glass, 165–166
Cutlery, 199

D

Decal removal, 200
Decoupage, 101–102
Deep cleaning, 77, 160, 161
Defrosting freezer, 267
Degreasers, 17, 73, 102
Dehumidifiers, 102
Dejunking, 27, 32, 79, 164, 194–195, 301
Delimer (descaler), 102
Design, 6–8
Detergent, 102–103
   dishwashing, 103–104
   laundry, 205–208
Diamonds, 104
Diaper pails, 104
Diapers, 104

Diatomaceous earth, 104
Digestant, 31, 104–105
Dishcloths or towels, 105
Dish drainers, 105
Dishes, hand-washing, 73, 106–107
Dish mops, 107
Dishpans, 107
Dishrags, 107–108
Dish towel, 105
Dishwasher detergent, 103
Dishwashers, automatic, 108
Dishwashing detergent, 73, 76, 103–104, 171
Disinfectants and disinfecting, 76, 109–110
Disposable filters, 144
Doilies, 110–111
Doll houses, 224–225
Dolls, 111–112
Doodlebug, 281
Doorknobs, 190
Doormats, 52
Doors, 113–114
Dough, 114
Down, 82–83
Drain pans, appliance, 115
Drains
  blockages, 114
  cleaners, 115, 117
  hair in, 177
  preventing clogs, 115–116
  smelly, 116
Drapes, 98–99
Drawers, 117–118
Dried flowers, 153
Dried paint stains, 88
Driveways, 118
Dry cleaning, 118, 119, 231–232
Dry-cleaning fluid, 118–119, 299
Dryers, automatic, 119, 208
Dry sponges, 15, 119–120
Dry spotters, 316
Dust allergies, 120–121
Dust and dust control, 121
Dust bunnies (dust balls), 121–122
Dustcloths, 122
Dusters
  feather, 122
  lambswool, 122–123
Dusting, 123–124
Dust-mopping, 124–125
Dust mops, 113, 124
Dustpans, 125

Dust ruffles, 125
Dust treatments, 125–126
Dye stains, 308–309

E

Earthenware, 70
Edges (floor, carpet), 127
Efflorescence, 87
Electric cords, 93–94
Electric frypans, 156–157
Electric knives, 199
Electric mixers, 225
Electric shock, 275
Electric space heaters, 180–181
Electrolytic cleaning, 292
Electronic filters, 145
Electrostatic air cleaners, 17
Emerald, 193
Emergency cleaning, 128
Emulsify, 129
Enamel, 130
Enameled metals, 129–130, 255
Energy saving, 130–131
Etched glass, 165
Etching, 131–132
Excuses for not cleaning, 132
Exhaust fans, 18, 132
Exposed beams, 35
Extension poles, 132–133
Eyeglasses, 133–134

F

Fabric bags, 178
Fabric care symbols, international, 58, 204
Fabric finish, 321
Fabrics, 135–141, 169
Fabric softener, 206–208
Fabric wall coverings, 367
Fabric yellowing, 383–384
Fall cleaning, 141
Fans
  ceiling, 141
  exhaust, 18, 132
  portable, 141
Faucets, 141–142
Feather dusters, 122
Feathering, 142–143
Feather pillows, 251
Fiberglass, 34, 143
Fiber rush, 57

Filters
  appliance, 143–144
  heating and cooling, 144–145
Filth, 144
Fine china, 68–69
Fine jewelry, 104, 192–193
Fireplace ash, 145
Fireplace facing, 146
Fishing reels, 146–147
Fishing rods, 147
Fleece, 285–286
Flock and foil wall coverings, 147
Floor finish, 147–148
Floor polishers, 148–149
Floors
  cork, 149–150
  no-wax, 232–233
  refinishing, 379–380
  resilient, 150
  rubber, 269–270
  scrubbing, 150–151
  stripping for waxing, 151–152
  vinyl sheet, 363
  waxing, 151, 374, 379
  wood, 378–380
Floor squeegees, 149
Floppy disks, 152
Flowerpots (clay), 152
Flowers and plants
  artificial, 152–153
  dried, 153
Fluorescent whitening agent, 236
Fluorocarbons, 153
Flush, 153–154
Foam rubber, 154
Foil wall coverings, 147
Food graters, 170
Food processors, 154
Formula stains, 30
Foxtail brush, 96
Freezers, 266–267
Frequency of cleaning, 155–156
Fruit and fruit juice stains, 30, 309, 319
Frypans, electric, 156–157
Fuller's earth, 14, 157
Fur, 82
  genuine, 157–158
  imitation, 158
Furnaces, 158–159
Furniture
  built-in, 7
  hard-surface, 160

  plush, 160–161
  polishes, 162
  upholstered, 161–162
  woven, 56–57

G

Garages, 164
Garbage cans, 164
Garbage compactors, 344
Garbage disposers, 165
Gas grills, 172–173
Gasoline, 299
Gas ovens, 238–239
Genuine fur, 157
Glass, 56, 165–166
Glass cleaners, 166
Glass cookware, 90
Glass-lined vacuum bottles, 352
Glassware, 166–167
Gloves, 167–168
Glue stains, 309–310
Glycerine, 299–300
Gold and gold plate, 168
Golf clubs, 168–169
Gore-Tex, 169
Graffiti, 87, 169–170
Granite, 323
Grass cloth, 367
Grass stains, 310–311
Graters, food, 170
Graying of laundry, 170
Grease removal, 170–171
Grease stains, 307–308, 319
Griddles, 171
Grills, barbecue, 171–173
Grinders, 173–174
Grout, 174
Grout brushes, 174
Guest mess, 163
Guitars, 228
Guns, 175

H

Hairbrushes, 177–178
Hair cleanup, 176–177
Hair rollers, 98
Handbags, 178
Handles, 178
Hand-washing dishes, 73, 106–107
Hard-surface furniture, 160

Hard-surface yellowing, 384
Hard-water deposits, 54, 179
Hats, 179–180
Heaters, space, 180–181
Heating filters, 144–145
Heat pumps, 17–18
Heat types and cleaning, 181–182
Heat vents/grates/registers, 182
Heavy-duty cleaners, 73, 76
High chairs, 183
Homemade cleaner, 176, 183
Hoods, range, 183–184
Hot tubs, 300
Hot water extraction, 60
Houseplants, 184
Humidifiers, 185
Hydrochloric acid, 71, 185
Hydrofluoric acid, 72, 185–186, 271
Hydrogen peroxide, 40, 186

I

Ice makers, automatic, 187–188
Ideas, 188
Imitation fur, 158
Ink stains, 311–312
Instruments, musical. See Musical instruments
International fabric care symbols, 58, 204
Inventions, cleaning, 188
Ion exchange, 371
Ironing, 208–209
Irons, steam, 188–189
Ivory, 43

J

Jackets, 81–83
Janitorial supply store, 190–191
Janitors, 190
Jewelry
  costume, 191–192
  fine, 104, 192–193
Jugs, picnic, 92–93
Junk, 164, 193–195
Jute browning, 195

K

Kamikaze cleaning, 198
Kerosene, 196, 299
Kerosene space heaters, 181

Kettle grills, 172
Kettles, 334–335
Kitchens, 17, 196–198
  cabinets, 52–53
  counters, 96–97
  sinks, 292
Knickknacks, 198–199
Knives, 199
KP, 197, 199

L

Label removal, 200
Lace, 99, 200–201
Lacquer thinner, 299
Lacquer-type stains, 308
Ladders, 274
Lambswool duster, 122–123
Lamps, 201–202
Lampshades, 202
Lattice-type things, 202–203
Laundry
  cleaners and aids, 205–207
  drying clothes, 208
  graying of, 170
  international fabric care symbols, 204
  ironing, 208–209
  loading washer, 207–208
  preparing clothes, 205, 256–257
  setting controls, 207
  sorting, 203, 205, 212–213
Leather, 82, 167, 178, 210, 217, 273, 274, 287–288
Ledges, 210
Lemon oil, 211
Lexan, 253
Lick and promise, 211
Lifting, 275
Light fixtures, 211
Limonene, 300
Linen fabric, 137
Linoleum, 212
Linseed oil, 212
Lint, 212–214
Lipstick stains, 30, 312
Litter, 214
Litter boxes, 214–215
Living rooms, 215–216
Long-handled floor scrubber, 281
Louvered doors, 216
Lucite, 253
Luggage, 217–218

Lunchboxes, 218
Lye, 64, 218, 237

M

Macrame, 219
Marble, 220, 323
Masslinn cloth, 122
Mats, walkoff, 220–221
Mattresses, 36
Meat grinders, 173–174
Meat slicers, 174
Mechanical water conditioners, 371
Medallion mess, 222
MEK, 299
Melamine, 253
Metal plate, 337
Metal polishes, 221–222
Metal tarnish, 333–334
Microwave cookware, 90
Microwave ovens, 222–223
Mildew, 87–88, 223–224, 312–313
Mineral spirits, 224, 299
Miniatures, 224–225
Mini blinds, 42
Mirrors, 225
Mixers, electric, 225
Modacrylic, 137
Mohair, 21–22
Mop buckets, 225–226
Mopping, 226–227
Mops, 112, 113, 124, 227
Mother of pearl, 286–287
Muriatic acid, 71, 185
Musical instruments, 227–229

N

Naptha, 299
Neatnik, 230
Neat's-foot oil, 230
Neckties, 230–231
Needlework, 231–232
Neutral cleaners, 73, 76–77
Nonstick cookware, 90–91
Nonstop chores, 232
Nook and cranny, 233
No-smoking buildings, 295
No-wax floors, 232–233
Nylon carpet, 58–59
Nylon fabric, 38, 79, 137–138, 217
Nylon scrub pads, 282–283

O

Odors, 234–235
Oil paintings, 26
Oil soaps, 33, 235
Oil stains, 235–236
Old wives' tales, 234
Olefin, 138
Optical brightener, 236
Order of cleaning, 236–237
Organs, 229
Outdoor steps, 322–323
Oven cleaners, 73, 237
Ovens, 237–238
    gas, 238–239
    microwave, 222–223
    self-cleaning, 239–240
Overkill, 240
Oxalic acid, 72, 240, 271
Oxygen bleach, 40, 206

P

Pack Rat, 241
Paintbrushes, 241–242
Painted surfaces, 242–243
Paint stains, 313–314
Paint thinner, 224, 299
Paneling, 243–244
Paper towels, 244–245
Paper vacuum bags, 351–352
Particle board, 245
Patent leather, 288–289
Patios, 245
Pearls, 192–193
Perchlorethylene, 299
Permanent filters, 144–145
Pests, 245–246
Pet hair, 161, 177
Pet stains, 314
Pewter, 56, 246–247
Phenolics, 109
pH in cleaning, 247
Phonograph records, 247–248
Phonograph stylus (needle), 248
Phosphates, 248–249
Phosphoric acid, 71, 179, 249
Photographs, 249–250
Pianos, 228–229
Pilling, 250
Pillows, 250–251
Pine oil cleaners, 77, 109

Place mats, 251
Plants, 184
Plaster, 251
Plastic flowers, 152–153
Plastic laminates, 52–53, 96, 252
Plastics, 252–253
Plastic tile, 252
Plexiglas, 253–254
Plush furniture, 160–161
Plywood, 254
Polishes
  furniture, 162
  metal, 221–222
Polishing compound, 254–255
Polyester, 38, 79, 99, 138
Porcelain, 63, 129, 130, 255
Pot scrubber, 91
Potty stains, 30
Poultice, 256
Premeasured cleaners. See Cleaners, concentrated
Presoaking, 256
Prespotting, 256–257
Pressboard, 254
Pressure cookers, 257–258
Pressure washers, 257–258
Pretreating, 205, 258
Professional help, 61, 259, 260, 301
Protein soil, 298
Protein stains, 307
Pumice, 259–260
Purses, 178

Q

Q-tips, 261
Quarry tiles, 261
Quaternaries, 109
Quilts, 261–262

R

Radiant heating systems, 182
Radiators, 263–264
Rags, 264
Ramie, 139
Range hoods, 183–184
Ranges, 264–265
Rattan, 265
Rawhide, 210
Rayon, 38, 79, 139
Razor blades, 266

Record turntables, 346
Recycling, 9, 164
Redd up, 266
Refinishing floors, 379–380
Refrigerators, 179, 266–267
Residue, 267
Resilient flooring, 150
Rinse, 268
Rinsing agents, 268–269
Rollers
  hair, 98
  paint, 241–242
Rotovinyl, 363
Rottenstone, 269
Rubber, 269
Rubber floors, 269–270
Rubber gloves, 270–271
Ruffled curtains, 99
Rugs, area, 271
Rump print, 263
Rust, 271–272

S

Saddle soap, 272–274
Safety in cleaning, 3, 274–278
Sandpaper, 278
Sandstone, 323
Sanitize. See Disinfectants and disinfecting
Satin, 38
Saunas, 278–279
Scissors, 199
Scotchgard, 298
Scouring, 279
Scrapers, 279
Screens, 280
Scrubbee Doo, 281
Scrubbing, 279, 280–281
Scrub brushes, 281–282
Scrub pads, nylon, 282–283
Scrub sponges, white nylon-backed, 283
Sea grass, 57
Sealing, 47, 283–284
Self-cleaning ovens, 239–240
Setting, 284–285
Sewing machines, 285
Shades, 285
Shampooing carpets, 60
Shearling, 274, 285–286
Sheetrock, 366
Sheets, 36–37
Shell, 286–287

Shoes, 288–289
  athletic, 287–288
Shop brush, 96
Shower enclosures, 289
Shower heads, 290
Shutters, 216
Sidewalks, 290–291
Silicone sealers, 291
Silk, 38, 139
Silk flowers, 152
Silver and silver plate, 55, 291–292
Simplifying cleaning, 8–9, 325
Sinks, 292–293
Sizing, 321
Skip cleaning, 293
Skis, 293
Slate, 323–324
Sleeping bags, 293–294
Slicers, 174
Sliding door tracks, 343–344
Slipcovers, 294–295
Smelly drains, 116
Smoke, 296
  cigarette, 235, 295
Smoke alarms, 295–296
Sneakers, 287–288
Soap, 296–297
Soap powder, 297
Soap scum, 289, 297
Soil, 298
Soil retardants, 298
Solvents, 74, 298–300
Solvent soluble soil, 298
Solvent spotters, 316
Soot, 296
Sorting laundry, 203, 205, 212–213
Space heaters, 180–181
Spandex, 139–140
Spas, 300
Spatters, 300–301
Spatulas, 279
Speeding up cleaning, 301
Spills, 301–302
Sponge mops, 302–303
Sponges, 112–113, 303
  dry, 15, 119–120
Sponging, 302
Spot and stain removal, 303–316
Spot removers, 316
Spotting brushes, 316–317
Spray bottles, 317–318
Spray buffing, 50

Spring cleaning, 318
Spruced up, 318
Squeegees, 318–319
Stain, 319
Stained glass, 165–166
Stainless steel, 319–320
Stainless steel cookware, 91
Stainless-steel wool, 322
Stain removal. See Spot and stain removal
Stairs, 320
Standards of cleaning, 320
Starch, 320–321
Static, 321
Steam irons, 188–189
Steel, 321–322
Steel cookware, 91
Steel vacuum bottles, 352
Steel wool, 322
Steps, outdoor, 322–323
Sterilize. See Disinfectants and disinfecting
Sticker removal, 200
Stone, 323–324
Stoneware, 70
Storage of cleaning equipment, 324–325
Straightening up, 325–326
Straw, 326
Straw bags, 178
Streaks, 326–327
Stripping floors, 151–152, 379
Stuffed animals, 327–328
Stuff sacks, 30–31
Suds, 328
Suede, 167, 178, 210, 274
Sugar stains, 306, 319
Sulfuric acid, 71, 328–329
Superfatted soap, 273
Supermom, 329
Surfactant, 329–330
Suspended furniture, 7
Sweeping, 330
Switchplates, 330

T

Tablecloths, 331–332
Tamping, 316–317
Tannin stains, 306, 319
Tape players/recorders, 332
Tapes, cassette, 332–333
Tapestries, 333
Tarnish, metal, 333–334
Taxidermy, 334

Tea kettles, 334–335
Teenage mess, 335
Telephones, 335
Televisions, 335
Tents, 57, 336
Terra cotta, 70
Terrazzo, 336–337
Textured glass, 165
Textured walls and ceilings, 337
Thermos bottles, 352–353
Throw pillows, 251
Ties, 230–231
Tile
  acoustical, 14–16
  asphalt, 26–27
  ceramic, 65
  clay, 337–338
  cleaners, 338
  plastic, 252
  quarry, 261
  vinyl, 363–364
  vinyl asbestos, 362–363
Tin, 56, 338–339
Tinted glass, 165
Toaster ovens, 339
Toasters, 339
Toilet bowl
  brush, 339–340
  caddy, 340
  cleaners, 340–341
  swab, 341
Tolul, 299
Tools, 58, 272
Toothbrushes, 174
Toys, 327–328, 343
Tracks of sliding doors, 343–344
Trash cans, 164
Trash compactors, 344
Trashing, 344–345
Triacetate, 140
TSP (trisodium phosphate), 345
Tub and tile cleaners. See Hard-water deposits
Tub enclosures, 289
Tung oil, 45–46, 346
Turntables, phonograph, 346
Turpentine, 300, 346
Typewriters, 346–347

U

Ultrasonic cleaning, 192, 349

Umbrellas, 349
Under cleaning, 349–350
Under-the-cushion cleaning, 99–100
Upholstered furniture, 161–162
Upright vacuums, 355–356
Utility brushes, 282

V

Vacuum attachments, 356–357
Vacuum bags, 351–352
Vacuum bottles, 352–353
Vacuum care, 353–354
Vacuuming, 59, 99, 122, 354–355
Vacuums, 355–356, 358
Vaporizers, 358
Varnished surfaces, 358–359
Vases, 45
Velcro, 359
Velour, 38, 359–360
Velvet, 38, 360
Velveteen, 360
Vertical blinds, 42
Vicuña, 360
Videocassette recorders, 360–361
Vinegar, 40, 361
Vinyl, 83, 178, 217, 361–362
Vinyl asbestos tile, 362–363
Vinyl sheet floors, 363
Vinyl tile, 363–364
Vinyl wall coverings, 366–367
Vitreous china, 255
Vomit stains, 30, 314–315

W

Waffle irons, 365–366
Walkoff mats, 220–221
Wallboard, 366
Wall coverings, 366–367
  flock and foil, 147
  woven, 367
Wallpaper. See Wall coverings
Walls, 367–368
Washing machines, 368–369
Washing soda, 369
Watches, 369–370
Water, 370
Waterbeds, 370–371
Water conditioning, 371
Water soluble soil, 298
Wax. See Floor finish; Waxes

Wax applicators, 371–372
Wax buildup, 372–373
Waxes, 373–374
Waxing floors, 151, 374, 379
Wax stains, 315
Wax strippers, 73, 373
Wet/dry vacuums, 113, 357
Wet spotters, 316
Wetting agents, 375
Wheat grinders, 173
Whisk brooms, 375
Wicker, 33, 375–376
Willow, 33, 375
Window cleaners, 166
Windows, 376–377
Window-washing wands, 377
Wine stains, 315–316

Wood, 55, 377–378
Wood cabinets, 52, 53
Wooden bowls/utensils, 380
Wood floors, 378–380
Woodwork, 380–381
Wool, 38, 54, 63, 82, 140–141
Woven furniture, 56–57
Woven wood blinds, 285
Wrought iron, 381

X

Xylol, 299

Y

Yellowing, 383–384

ABOUT THE AUTHOR

Don A. Aslett, "America's No. 1 Cleaning Expert," is the man the world calls on when cleanup action is called for. Founder and chairman of the board of one of the nation's premier cleaning contractors, he earned his expertise the hard way in over 35 years of hands-on work in the professional cleaning industry. He has made thousands of media appearances, authored more than a dozen books, and designed and taught college courses and seminars, all dedicated to helping us achieve our goal of clean—clean homes, clean offices and workplaces, and a clean environment. A speaker and professional consultant on cleaning, Don has a world-famous cleaning museum and a cleaning reference library that the media and fellow professionals alike benefit from. Mr. Aslett is fifty-seven and the father of six children and has thirteen grandchildren.

"My first thrust toward dealing dirt a death blow was a book called *Is There Life After Housework?* wherein I first shared with homemakers all the methods and tools of the professional cleaners. Then I answered 200 of the biggest questions about cleaning in *How Do I Clean the Moosehead?* and *Do I Dust or Vacuum First?* I cornered the culprit that causes at least 40 percent of housework—junk and clutter—in two best sellers, *Clutter's Last Stand* and *Not for Packrats Only.* A nice volume of spot solvers also shows up on the shelf as *Don Aslett's Stainbuster's Bible,* and I went after the inequality in cleaning in *Who Says It's a Woman's Job to Clean?* to help get men and kids to do their share (any!). I helped our four-legged friends by making cleaning up after them much less of a hassle in *Pet Clean-Up Made Easy,* and I've even done a revolutionary volume—a book on how to design cleaning out of our lives: *Make Your House Do the Housework.* For those who want pro secrets in a quick reference guide, I put together *Clean in a Minute: 72 Pages of the Best of Don Aslett.*"